The BIG BOOK *of*

SLOW COOKER RECIPES

2

The BIG BOOK of
SLOW COOKER RECIPES

More Than 700 Slow Cooker Recipes for Breakfast, Lunch, Dinner and Dessert

Rachel Rappaport, author of *The Everything® Healthy Slow Cooker Cookbook*

Aadamsmedia

Avon, Massachusetts

Published by Adams Media, a division of F+W Media, Inc.
57 Littlefield Street, Avon, MA 02322. U.S.A.
www.adamsmedia.com

ISBN 10: 1-4405-6069-2
ISBN 13: 978-1-4405-6069-9
eISBN 10: 1-4405-6070-6
eISBN 13: 978-1-4405-6070-5

Printed in the United States of America.

10 9 8 7 6 5 4 3 2 1

Contains material adapted and abridged from:
The Everything® Freezer Meals Cookbook by Candace Anderson with Nicole Cormier, RD, copyright © 2010 by F+W Media, Inc., ISBN 10: 1-4405-0612-4, ISBN 13: 978-1-4405-0612-3; *The Everything® Gluten-Free Slow Cooker Cookbook* by Carrie S. Forbes, copyright © 2012 by F+W Media, Inc., ISBN 10: 1-4405-3366-0, ISBN 13: 978-1-4405-3366-2; *The Everything® Healthy Slow Cooker Cookbook* by Rachel Rappaport with B. E. Horton, MS, RD, copyright © 2010 by F+W Media, Inc., ISBN 10: 1-4405-0231-5, ISBN 13: 978-1-4405-0231-6; *The Everything® Indian Slow Cooker Cookbook* by Prerna Singh, copyright © 2012 by F+W Media, Inc., ISBN 10: 1-4405-4168-X, ISBN 13: 978-1-4405-4168-1; *The Everything® Kosher Slow Cooker Cookbook* by Dena G. Price, copyright © 2013 by F+W Media, Inc., ISBN 10: 1-4405-4350-X, ISBN 13: 978-1-4405-4350-0; *The Everything® Low-Salt Cookbook* by Pamela Rice Hahn, copyright © 2004 by F+W Media, Inc., ISBN 10: 1-59337-044-X, ISBN 13: 978-1-59337-044-2; *The Everything® No-Trans-Fat Cookbook* by Linda Larsen, copyright © 2007 by F+W Media, Inc., ISBN 10: 1-59869-533-9, ISBN 13: 978-1-59869-533-5; *The Everything® Potluck Cookbook* by Linda Larsen, copyright © 2009 by F+W Media, Inc., ISBN 10: 1-59869-990-3, ISBN 13: 978-1-59869-990-6; *The Everything® Slow Cooker Cookbook, 2nd Edition* by Pamela Rice Hahn, copyright © 2009 by F+W Media, Inc., ISBN 10: 1-59869-977-6, ISBN 13: 978-1-59869-977-7; *The Everything® Slow Cooking for a Crowd Cookbook*, by Katie Thompson, copyright © 2005 by F+W Media, Inc., ISBN-10: 1-59337-391-0, ISBN-13: 978-1-59337-391-7; *The Everything® Soups, Stews, and Chilis Cookbook*, by Belina Hulin, copyright © 2009 by F+W Media, Inc., ISBN-10: 1-60550-044-5, ISBN-13: 978-1-60550-044-7; *The Everything® Vegan Slow Cooker Cookbook* by Amy Snyder and Justin Snyder, copyright © 2013 by F+W Media, Inc., ISBN 10: 1-4405-4407-7, ISBN 13: 978-1-4405-4407-1; and *The Everything® Vegetarian Slow Cooker Cookbook* by Amy Snyder and Justin Snyder, copyright © 2012 by F+W Media, Inc., ISBN 10: 1-4405-2858-6, ISBN 13: 978-1-4405-2858-3.

Always follow safety and commonsense cooking protocol while using kitchen utensils, operating ovens and stoves, and handling uncooked food. If children are assisting in the preparation of any recipe, they should always be supervised by an adult.

This book is available at quantity discounts for bulk purchases. For information, please call 1-800-289-0963.

CONTENTS

PART I: To Start

PART II: Entrées

8 Turkey and Lamb 191

9 Beef 215

10 Pork 243

20 Stews 463

21 Chilis 487

22 Casseroles 507

PART III: Sides

PART IV: Something Sweet

INTRODUCTION

Slow cookers are lifesavers for busy people leading hectic lives. Simply assemble the ingredients, toss them in the pot, turn it on, and come back hours later to a delicious meal that's been filling your home with yummy smells—a savory onion soup, a hearty beef stew, or macaroni and cheese.

Slow cookers aren't just for piping-hot soups and stews on wintry evenings, however. They're perfect for serving appetizers to a crowd, cooking with fresh vegetables from your garden, and trying out some more exotic flavors from around the world. In this vast cookbook, you'll find recipes for all sorts of mouthwatering dishes, from beverages to breads and dips to desserts:

- Salted Caramel Mocha Lattes
- Party Seasoned Nuts
- Shrimp and Artichoke Dip
- Smoky Barbecue Sauce
- Slow-Cooked Oatmeal with Dried and Fresh Fruit
- Curried Chicken in Coconut Milk
- Poached Swordfish with Lemon-Parsley Sauce
- Simple Brisket
- Pumpkin Wild Rice Chowder
- Chorizo and Potato Casserole
- Fresh Apple Bread
- Rosemary-Garlic Mashed Potatoes
- Pineapple Upside-Down Cake
- Not Your Grandma's Chocolate Cake

You'll also find slow-cooker classics, such as:

- Hot Mulled Cider
- Classic Sloppy Joes
- Yankee Pot Roast
- Pulled Pork
- Chicken Noodle Soup
- Tex-Mex Chili
- Cuban Black Beans
- Classic Italian Risotto
- Hot Fudge Fondue

Is someone in your household on a vegetarian, vegan, or gluten-free diet? You'll find meals the whole family will love:

- Meatless Moussaka
- Vegetarian Lasagna
- Tofu Ranchero
- Gluten-Free Blueberry French Toast Casserole
- Gluten-Free Shortcut Chicken Parmesan

With more than 700 recipes, you're sure to find a dish for every mood and meal from healthy, hearty breakfasts to indulgent desserts. There are also recipes for every size family, with meals serving 1 to 2 people using small slow cookers, and recipes serving a dozen using the largest-sized slow cooker.

The slow cooker lifestyle helps ensure you can enjoy a fresh, delicious meal even if you're not home to make it! Since a slow cooker uses low, indirect heat there is usually no need to stir the food or monitor it at all while it cooks. Even better, there is almost zero risk of burning food in the slow cooker—so even if that work meeting or kids' soccer practice runs late, your food will still be tasty when you finally make it home for dinner.

With the hundreds of delectable recipes packed into this cookbook, you'll be inspired to use your slow cooker more often and in new ways!

SLOW COOKING 101

The Benefits of Slow Cooking

Slow cookers can be used to make main dishes, one-pot meals, side dishes, even desserts. Most recipes call for a few minutes of prep time and zero hands-on time during the actual cooking. For a small amount of effort in the morning, you can come home to a hot meal after a full workday. The recipes with shorter cooking times are perfect for those instances when space and time are limited when you're running errands, throwing a party, or trying to fit in a meal during the holidays.

The long cooking times associated with most slow cooker recipes mean that cheaper, leaner cuts of meat come out just as tender as a $30 well-marbled steak. You can turn affordable root vegetables into mouthwatering soups, stews, and side dishes with minimal effort. You can also make pantry staples such as homemade stocks, barbecue sauce, pasta sauces, and even granola for mere pennies in the slow cooker.

While slow cookers are closely associated with wintertime stews, soups, and roasts, they are wonderful to use year-round. Since they do not heat the house the way oven or stovetop cooking does, slow cookers are perfect for warm weather, too. In-season fruits and vegetables at the peak of their flavor and nutritional value make excellent additions to slow cooker dishes.

Healthy Choices

It is quite easy to make healthy food in the slow cooker. Very little oil or fat is needed because keeping ingredients from sticking to the cooker is not an issue. Since liquids do not evaporate in the slow cooker, very lean meats will not dry out or overcook the way they might on the stovetop or grill, leaving them amazingly tender. Additionally, using lean meats ensures that your chili, soup, or roast won't be unappetizingly greasy.

Whole grains like oatmeal, wheat berries, barley, rice, and corn are all well suited to use in the slow cooker. A variety of dishes incorporate nuts and seeds, a wonderful way to introduce healthy fats and fiber into your diet. High-fiber fruits, vegetables, and legumes are at the center of most slow cooker meals.

Types and Sizes of Slow Cookers

Slow cookers have come a long way from their avocado-green, one-size-fits-all days. Now they're available in several sizes and with many modern features. The small 1½- to 2-quart slow cooker is perfect for smaller families and couples. The 4-quart cooker, the most popular size, is capable of making meals that serve four to six people. The largest models are 6–7 quarts and can feed a crowd of eight or more. Hamilton Beach manufactures a three-in-one slow cooker that comes with a set of 2-, 4-, and 6-quart ceramic inserts that can be used one at a time in the same base, eliminating the need to own multiple slow cookers.

Settling on Settings

Look for slow cookers that have at least a low and high setting. This is standard for the mid- to large-size models, but many 2-quart models only have an on/off option. Temperature control is essential if you make full meals in a small slow cooker. Slow cookers equipped solely with an on/off switch are suitable only for keeping fondues, dips, or beverages warm.

Lifestyle Choices

It is important to choose a slow cooker with features that fit your lifestyle. Many slow cookers have a warm setting that will keep your food warm at approximately 160°F. This setting may be manual, but if the slow cooker is digital, it will automatically turn on after the programmed cooking time has finished. The automatic switch to warm is especially helpful for people who are not sure when they will have dinner. If you enjoy cooking large cuts of meat, look for a model that comes with a probe thermometer that takes an exact temperature of the food inside. Once the meat reaches the desired temperature, the slow cooker will switch to warm to avoid overcooking. If you plan to take your slow cooker to parties or potlucks, there are several models that have secure latches to hold the lid on while in transit. Some models made for travel come with built-in serving spoon holders and rests. There are also models that have an insulated case for the stoneware insert. If cutting down on the number of dirty dishes is important, look for a slow cooker that has an insert that can be placed on top of the stove. Those inserts can brown meats and vegetables and can be put back in the base to finish cooking.

Shape Matters

For most recipes, you can use either an oval or a round slow cooker. However, for roasts, meatloaf, or lasagna, or for slow-cooking large pieces of fish, an oval cooker is preferable because it allows the food to lie flat.

The Perfect Ingredients

Nearly any food works well in the slow cooker, but certain ingredients are especially well suited to slow cooking.

Canned Goods

Evaporated milk is shelf-stable canned milk, which is made by removing 60 percent of the water from regular milk. When mixed with an equal amount of water, evaporated milk becomes the equivalent of fresh milk. Rehydration is often unnecessary in slow cooking. Using the evaporated milk straight from the can is a great way to add a creamy, dairy flavor without the fat. Unlike fresh milk, evaporated milk is safe to use in recipes with long cooking times without fear of curdling.

Canned beans are precooked and recipe-ready unlike dried beans, which still need to be soaked and fully cooked before being added to the slow cooker. Beans are a wonderful source of protein and fiber and are virtually fat free. Be sure to drain and rinse canned beans prior to use. You can substitute cooked, rehydrated dried beans equally for canned.

Canned tomatoes are better tasting than out-of-season fresh tomatoes. Unless otherwise noted, add the juice to the slow cooker along with the tomatoes. It can add much-needed moisture to a dish without having to add water or broth.

Produce

Onions are essential to many slow cooking recipes. Due to their high moisture content, onions give off a lot of liquid as they cook. Instead of adding water or broth to a recipe, which can dilute the flavor of the dish, try onions to provide both moisture and flavor. Onions are especially useful when cooking large cuts of meat or other dishes where you want a drier final product.

Root vegetables such as carrots, parsnips, beets, celeriac, rutabaga, turnips, and potatoes are exceptionally suited to the slow cooker because they retain their shape and texture even after being cooked for hours. Peel carrots, beets, rutabaga, turnips, and parsnips before using them. Potatoes can be used peeled or unpeeled.

Corn, broccoli, cabbage, snow peas, green beans, apples, pears, mangoes, figs, cranberries, strawberries, raspberries, blackberries, blueberries, and tomatoes are all suitable for slow cooking and are high in dietary fiber, which is essential to digestive tract health.

Vegetables can lose valuable nutrients during long cooking times. Blanching the vegetables by cooking them briefly in boiling water helps them retain vitamins. Sautéing vegetables prior to adding them to the slow cooker also optimizes nutrient retention.

Stock Tips

Stock—whether beef, chicken, turkey, vegetable, or seafood—can be used instead of water in almost any dish made in the slow cooker. Recipes made with stock are more flavorful than those made with water.

Cooking with Meat

Lean cuts of meat are perfect for the slow cooker. The long cooking time tenderizes the meat, leaving it fork tender. Additionally, using lean meat in dishes like chili is necessary because it's not possible to skim off the fat after cooking. When cooking with beef, look for the least marbled cuts; choose lean cuts such as tri-tip, top or bottom round roast, top sirloin, or flat half-brisket, all of which meet the governmental standards for very lean or lean meats. When shopping for pork, look for pork tenderloin, boneless pork loin chop, and boneless pork top loin, all of which contain less than 5 percent fat per serving. Boneless, skinless chicken breasts and thighs are also great sources of lean protein. Most grocery stores carry 94 percent lean ground chicken, turkey, pork, and beef.

Dairy Dos and Don'ts

Dairy products, like sour cream, cream cheese, or milk, do not hold up well over long cooking times. To avoid curdling, add them during the last half hour of cooking. If you are making a hot dip, do not heat it for more than an hour unless otherwise instructed. If milk is a major ingredient, for example, in a creamy sauce or soup, substitute an equal amount of evaporated milk. Evaporated milk can be used directly from the can, and since it has been heat-processed, it can withstand long cooking times. Due to the relatively short, low-heat cooking time of the last half hour, low-fat sour cream, cream cheese, or milk can be used with great success in the slow cooker despite having a tendency to separate while cooked using traditional methods.

Slow-Cooking Tips

The first time you use a slow cooker, it is helpful to be home to check in on the dish to see how it is cooking. Some slow cookers may run hotter or cooler than others, and it is important to know whether the cooking time needs to be adjusted. Additionally, you don't want to come home to a cold, raw meal because the slow cooker did not turn on or work properly.

Slow cookers work best when they are at least one-half to two-thirds full. Less food will cook more quickly and less evenly. Choose a slow cooker that is the proper size for the recipe for best results.

Pay attention to layering instructions. Place slower-cooking ingredients like root vegetables near the bottom of the slow cooker unless otherwise noted.

Remove any visible fat from meat before adding it to the slow cooker. Also be sure to drain off any rendered fat before putting browned meat in the slow cooker.

Safety First

Heating an empty ceramic insert may cause it to crack. Be sure the insert is at room temperature when placed in the slow cooker base. Sudden changes in temperature can also cause cracks in the ceramic insert.

Defrost all frozen meats in the refrigerator before placing them in the slow cooker. The food in the slow cooker must reach the safe temperature of 140°F as soon as possible. Using frozen meat may lower the temperature of the dish into the danger zone for an extended period. Small frozen vegetables like peas or corn will not lower the temperature enough to be dangerous but add them toward the end of the cooking time for best texture and flavor.

To keep the temperature constant in the slow cooker, avoid removing the lid during the cooking time. Removing the lid can reduce the temperature in the cooker, adding to the overall cooking time. Additionally, do not repeatedly add new items to the slow cooker during the cooking process. It can cause the internal temperature to dip below what is considered safe. If additional ingredients need to be added, they should be added all at once toward the end of the cooking time.

The outside of some slow cookers can become quite hot. Do not place flammable items or items that may melt near the slow cooker while it is in use. All modern slow cookers have short cords to reduce the risk of tipping over, but it is still important to keep them away from small children and pets. Contents in the slow cooker can be near boiling temperatures and the hot exteriors can cause burns or skin irritation.

PART I
TO START

CHAPTER 1

BEVERAGES

RECIPE LIST

SPICED CHERRY PUNCH

An ounce of tart cherry juice concentrate is added to 7 ounces of water to make a cup of cherry juice. The apple and orange juices in Spiced Cherry Punch add natural sweetness, but you can also stir in some sugar to taste if you prefer a sweeter punch.

Serves 14

INGREDIENTS:

8 cups (2 quarts) apple cider or apple juice

½ cup tart cherry juice concentrate

3 cups water

2 cups orange juice

1½ teaspoons whole allspice berries

1½ teaspoons whole cloves

2 (3-inch) cinnamon sticks

Optional: 1 tablespoon aromatic bitters

Optional: Cinnamon sticks for garnish

Optional: Dark rum or other adult beverage

1. Add the apple cider or apple juice, tart cherry juice concentrate, water, and orange juice to a 4-quart slow cooker.

2. Add the allspice berries and whole cloves to a muslin spice bag or a piece of cheesecloth that has been rinsed and wrung dry; secure with a piece of kitchen twine and add to the juices in the cooker.

3. Add the cinnamon sticks. Stir in the aromatic bitters if using. Cover and cook until very hot but not boiling, or 2 hours on high or 4 hours on low.

4. Remove the spices in the muslin bag or cheesecloth and cinnamon sticks from the cooker. The punch can be kept at serving temperature by setting the slow cooker on low, keeping in mind that the flavors will become more concentrated the longer the punch is uncovered and on the heat. Serve in punch glasses or mugs garnished with cinnamon sticks if desired. Have dark rum or another adult beverage available for those who wish to add it to the punch.

Tart Cherry Juice Concentrate

Tart cherry juice concentrate is available at most natural food stores or online through Michigan producers like Brownwood Acres Foods, Inc. (*www.brownwoodacres.com*) and King Orchards (*www.mi-cherries.com*).

WASSAIL

To make a nonalcoholic version of this recipe, substitute additional apple juice for the sherry and ale.

Serves 20

INGREDIENTS:

6 cups apple juice

2 cups cranberry juice or lemonade

6 cups orange juice

¼ cup brown sugar

1 cup water

2 cups semisweet sherry

2 (12-ounce) bottles of ale

4 (3-inch) cinnamon sticks

1 orange

1 teaspoon whole cloves

1 lemon

12 whole allspice berries

1 tablespoon chopped candied ginger

Optional: 1 tablespoon aromatic bitters

1. Add the apple juice, cranberry juice or lemonade, orange juice, brown sugar, water, sherry, ale, and cinnamon sticks to a 4-quart slow cooker.

2. Stud the orange with the whole cloves, cut the orange and lemon into quarters and remove any seeds, and add to the slow cooker.

3. Add the allspice berries and candied ginger to a muslin spice bag or a piece of cheesecloth that has been rinsed and wrung dry; secure with a piece of kitchen twine and add to the juices in the cooker. Stir in the bitters if using.

4. Cover and cook on low for 4 hours. Remove cinnamon sticks, spice bag, and orange and lemon wedges before serving.

Slow-Cooking Alcoholic Beverages

If you're in a hurry and want to bring an alcoholic punch to temperature quicker, you can begin the slow-cooking process on high; however, be sure to watch the punch carefully and be sure that you switch the cooker to low *before* the liquids come to a boil.

RICH AND INDULGENT HOT CHOCOLATE

If you prefer to indulge in a darker chocolate beverage, substitute 12 ounces of chopped bittersweet chocolate for the chocolate chips. You can let the milk mixture come to temperature for up to 6 hours on low before you add the chocolate and serve this drink.

Serves 8

INGREDIENTS:

2 cups heavy cream

6 cups whole milk

Optional: 2 (3-inch) cinnamon sticks

1 (12-ounce) package semisweet chocolate chips

1 tablespoon vanilla

Optional: Marshmallows

1. Add the cream and whole milk to the slow cooker; stir to combine. Add the cinnamon sticks if using. Cover and cook long enough to bring the milk mixture to temperature: approximately 3 hours on low or 1½ hours on high.

2. If a "skin" has developed on the milk, skim it off and discard. Whisk in the chocolate until melted. Stir in the vanilla. Ladle into mugs and serve immediately. Top each mug with marshmallows if desired.

LOW-FAT HOT CHOCOLATE

For a richer drink, unwrap 24 York peppermint patties (a 12-ounce package) and add them 2 hours into the cooking time; stir until they're melted into the drink. Cover and continue to cook until ready to serve.

Serves 12

INGREDIENTS:

12 cups water

5 cups nonfat dry milk

¾ cup cocoa

1 cup sugar

Optional: 2 teaspoons mint or almond extract

1. Add the water to the slow cooker; cover and cook on low while you mix together the dry milk, cocoa, and sugar in a bowl. Whisk the dry ingredients into the water. Add extract if using. Cover and cook on low for 3–4 hours.

GERMAN MULLED WINE

To add a touch more sweetness to this drink, sprinkle a few pieces of cinnamon red-hot candies into each serving.

Serves 12

INGREDIENTS:

5 cups apple cider

5 cups burgundy wine

½ cup honey

1 teaspoon whole cloves

12 whole allspice berries

Zest of 1 lemon

2 (3-inch) pieces stick cinnamon

1. Add the cider, wine, and honey to a slow cooker.

2. Put the cloves, allspice berries, and lemon zest in a muslin spice bag or a piece of cheesecloth that has been rinsed, wrung dry, and secured with a piece of kitchen twine; add to the slow cooker along with the cinnamon sticks.

3. Cover and cook on low for 3–4 hours.

According to Your Personal Sweet Tooth

While honey adds an extra flavor dimension to the German Mulled Wine drink, you can omit adding it during the slow-cooking portion of this recipe. You can then sweeten the finished drink using honey, sugar, brown sugar, or sugar substitute according to your personal taste and preference.

HOT MOMMAS

Serves 8

INGREDIENTS:

5 cups tomato juice or vegetable juice cocktail

3 cups Beef Broth (Chapter 19)

Hot pepper sauce, to taste

2 teaspoons celery seeds

1 tablespoon prepared horseradish

1 tablespoon Worcestershire sauce

1 cup vodka

1 tablespoon fresh lime juice

Optional: Celery sticks

Optional: Lime wedges

For a cocktail with a kick, add ½ teaspoon or more of the hot pepper sauce and double the amount of horseradish that you stir into this drink. It can be served as a satisfying start to a winter morning brunch or along with the appetizers at a buffet or dinner party.

1. Add the tomato juice or vegetable juice cocktail, broth, pepper sauce, and celery seeds to a slow cooker. Stir to combine. Cover and cook on low for 4 hours or until very hot.

2. Just before serving, stir in the horseradish, Worcestershire sauce, vodka, and lime juice. Taste for seasoning and add additional horseradish, Worcestershire sauce, and hot pepper sauce if desired. Ladle into large mugs and garnish with celery sticks and lime wedges if desired.

Cup of Soup

Omit the vodka from the Hot Mommas recipe and you end up with warm mugs of spicy soup that you can serve alongside toasted cheese or roast beef sandwiches.

HOT CRANBERRY-PINEAPPLE PUNCH

If you prefer, you can omit the brown sugar and water and sweeten it with 2 cups of apple juice instead.

Yield: About 18–22 cups

INGREDIENTS:

8 cups cranberry juice

8 cups unsweetened pineapple juice

2 cups brown sugar, packed

2 cups water

2 (3-inch) cinnamon sticks

2 teaspoons whole cloves

Optional: 3–4 cups vodka

1. Add the cranberry juice, pineapple juice, brown sugar, and water to the slow cooker.

2. Break the cinnamon sticks into smaller pieces and add them along with the whole cloves to a muslin spice bag or wrap them in cheesecloth tied shut with cotton string or kitchen twine. Add to the slow cooker. Cover and cook on low for 1 hour.

3. Uncover and stir until the brown sugar is dissolved into the juice. Cover and cook for another 7–8 hours.

4. Uncover the cooker and remove the spice bag or cheesecloth; holding over the slow cooker, squeeze to extract the seasoned juice. To serve, ladle into heatproof mugs and add vodka to taste to each serving.

Chilled Cranberry-Pineapple Punch

After slow cooking, allow the punch to cool to room temperature and then chill until needed. Add 3–4 cups lemon-lime soda or Mountain Dew. Serve in punch cups or in tall glasses over ice, garnished with a maraschino cherry.

HOT BUTTERED RUM

Time the cooking of this drink so that you can stir in the rum and let it "mull" for 20 minutes before serving.

Serves 12

INGREDIENTS:

1 stick (½ cup) unsalted butter

8 cups water

2 cups firmly packed light brown sugar

Pinch salt

½ teaspoon freshly ground nutmeg

⅛ teaspoon ground cloves

⅛ teaspoon ground cinnamon

1 cup dark rum

1. Add the butter and 2 cups of the water to the slow cooker. Cover and cook on high for ½ hour or until the butter is melted.

2. Stir in the brown sugar, and then add the remaining water, salt, nutmeg, cloves, and cinnamon. Cover and cook on low for 2–4 hours.

3. Twenty minutes before serving, stir in the rum; cover and cook for 20 minutes. To serve, ladle into small heatproof mugs.

IRISH COFFEE

The coffee, which is best made using medium-roast beans, can be made ahead and added to the slow cooker two hours before you plan to serve dessert.

Serves 24

INGREDIENTS:

16 cups coffee

½ cup sugar

Irish whiskey

Whipped cream

1. Add the chilled coffee to the slow cooker. Cover and cook on low for 1 hour. If you're using fresh-brewed coffee, you can skip this step.

2. Stir in the sugar until it's dissolved; cover and cook on low for 1 hour. To serve, ladle into heatproof mugs. Add whiskey to taste and garnish with a dollop of whipped cream.

MEXICAN HOT CHOCOLATE

This drink is rich enough that you can use half whole milk and half water or all low-fat milk. You can serve this drink with a complete Southwestern-style breakfast. A simpler, yet delicious alternative is to dunk buttered slices of toast made from homemade bread into the drink.

Serves 16

INGREDIENTS:

1 gallon milk

1⅓ cups dark brown sugar

1 cup masa harina (corn flour)

7 tablespoons cornstarch

4 ounces bittersweet chocolate, chopped

2 (3-inch) cinnamon sticks

3 tablespoons vanilla

Optional: Ground cinnamon

1. Add 3 cups of the milk to the slow cooker. Add the brown sugar, masa harina, and cornstarch to a bowl and mix well, and then whisk into the milk in the slow cooker. Whisk in the remaining milk. Cover and cook on high for 30 minutes to bring to a simmer.

2. Add the chocolate and whisk until it's melted and combined with the milk mixture. Add the cinnamon sticks. Cover and cook on low for approximately 2 hours, stirring occasionally; the drink is done when it is thickened and lightly coats the back of a spoon. Just before serving, stir in the vanilla. Ladle into mugs and garnish with ground cinnamon if desired.

Chocolate Chips Instead

You can substitute semisweet chocolate chips for the chopped bittersweet chocolate. If you do, reduce the amount of brown sugar to ¾ cup. Taste the drink for sweetness midway through the cooking time and add more sugar if desired.

CHAI TEA

Store any leftover tea in a covered container in the refrigerator. It can be reheated, but leftover tea is best served over ice.

Serves 12

INGREDIENTS:

5 cups water

6 slices fresh ginger

1 teaspoon whole cloves

2 (3-inch) pieces stick cinnamon

1½ teaspoons freshly ground nutmeg

½ teaspoon ground cardamom

1 cup sugar

12 tea bags

6 cups milk

1. Add the water to the slow cooker. Put the ginger and cloves in a muslin spice bag or a piece of cheesecloth that has been rinsed, wrung dry, and secured with a piece of kitchen twine; add to the cooker along with the cinnamon, nutmeg, and cardamom. Cover and cook on low for 4–6 hours or on high for 2–3 hours.

2. Stir in the sugar until it's dissolved into the water. Add the tea bags and milk; cover and cook on low for ½ hour. Remove and discard the spices in the muslin bag or cheesecloth, cinnamon sticks, and tea bags. Ladle into tea cups or mugs to serve.

Sweet Tip

If you prefer, you can omit adding the sugar during the cooking process and allow each drinker to add sugar or sugar substitute to his or her serving according to taste.

CAPPUCCINO

Simmering the cinnamon in milk adds a more subtle, yet distinctive flavor to this drink than what's achieved by just sprinkling cinnamon on top of the frothed milk.

Serves 10

INGREDIENTS:

2 cups milk

2 (3-inch) sticks cinnamon

8 cups hot coffee or espresso

1. Add the milk and cinnamon sticks to the slow cooker. Cover and cook on low for 2 hours; keep the milk on the warm setting until ready to serve.

2. Remove the cinnamon sticks. Add the coffee to the slow cooker. Use an immersion blender to add froth to the drink. Ladle into mugs. Repeat using the immersion blender, if necessary, to create more froth between ladling out the servings.

Frothy Milk

If you prefer, you can skip adding the coffee or espresso to the slow cooker. Instead, use an immersion blender to froth the milk in the slow cooker, repeating as necessary as you top individual servings of the coffee or espresso with frothed milk ladled into the drinks according to taste. This method works better if you or another guest's preference is to sweeten the drink; stir in the sugar or sweetener to taste, and then top with the froth.

MOCHA

If you prefer lower-fat mocha, replace the cream with milk.

Serves 12

INGREDIENTS:

10 cups coffee

2 cups heavy cream

1 (12-ounce) bag semisweet chocolate chips

1. Add the coffee and cream to a slow cooker. Stir to combine. Cover and cook on low for 3–6 hours. If a "skin" has developed on top from the cream, skim it off and discard. Whisk in the chocolate chips until melted. Ladle into mugs and serve immediately.

Chocolate Chips Substitute

In the mocha recipe, you can use ½ cup cocoa and 1 cup sugar or the all-natural sugar substitute Whey Low (*www.wheylow.com*) instead of the chocolate chips. Mix the cocoa and sugar or Whey Low together in a bowl, and then whisk it into the hot coffee and cream mixture. You can serve it immediately or let the coffee, cream, cocoa, and sugar or Whey Low cook covered on low for an additional hour or two.

HOT MULLED CIDER

This classic is a must for the fall and winter holidays. Serve it to guests with dessert on a snowy evening.

Yields about 8 cups

INGREDIENTS:

2 quarts apple cider

½ cup brown sugar

¼ teaspoon salt

1 teaspoon whole allspice

1 teaspoon whole cloves

1 3-inch stick cinnamon bark

20 whole cloves

1 orange

1. Combine the cider, brown sugar, and salt in the slow cooker.

2. Tie the allspice, 1 teaspoon cloves, and cinnamon in a small piece of cheesecloth; add to the cider.

3. Cover and heat on a low setting for 2–3 hours.

4. Press 20 cloves in circles around the orange. Slice the orange between the clove rings. Half an hour before serving, add the clove-studded orange slices to the slow cooker. Remove spice bundle before serving.

Watch Your Wiring

Before or after cooking, don't put your slow cooker in the refrigerator unless the crockery is removable and can go in alone. Otherwise the electrical components may rust and leave you needing a whole new appliance.

GINGER PUNCH

This punch is not only delicious, but it's also good for you. Fresh ginger has healthful effects.

Yields about 10 cups

INGREDIENTS:

1 inch fresh gingerroot

1 cup sugar

8 cups water

6 cloves

1 stick cinnamon bark

½ cup lemon juice

1½ cups orange juice

1 sprig mint

1. Peel and mince the gingerroot.

2. Put the ginger, sugar, water, cloves, and cinnamon in the slow cooker.

3. Cover and heat on a low setting for 2–3 hours.

4. An hour before serving, add the fruit juices and the mint.

Be Prepared

Make a few dishes ahead of time and keep them in plastic containers in the freezer. On the morning of party day, line up the slow cookers, pop in your frozen delicacies, turn the heat on low, and when you get back from work you'll be ready to go.

FAMILY PARTY PUNCH

This nonalcoholic punch is great for the whole family. You can also chill the leftover punch and drink it with ice.

Yields about 9 cups

INGREDIENTS:

½ large lemon

1 12-ounce can frozen orange juice concentrate

1 12-ounce can frozen raspberry juice concentrate

4 cups water

3 cups lemon-lime soda

1 stick cinnamon bark

3 oranges

1. Thinly slice the lemon. Put the lemon, juice concentrates, water, soda, and cinnamon in the slow cooker.

2. Cover and heat on a low setting for 2–3 hours.

3. Thinly slice the oranges. Before serving, replace the lemon slices with the orange slices.

MAPLE PUMPKIN SPICE LATTES

This warm latte is reminiscent of a drink you would pay big bucks for at a local coffee chain. By making your own you're not only saving money, but you'll have enough for a whole week's worth of breakfasts or after-dinner coffees. Try it with a whipped cream topping.

Serves 8

INGREDIENTS:

2 cups very strong coffee or espresso

4 cups whole milk

¾ cup plain pumpkin purée

⅓ cup maple syrup

1 tablespoon vanilla

2 teaspoons of pumpkin pie spice

1. In a 4-quart slow cooker whisk together all ingredients. Cover and cook on high for 1½ hours or on low for 3 hours. When serving, turn slow cooker to the warm setting for up to 2 hours. Serve warm.

Make Your Own Pumpkin Pie Spice
If you don't have pumpkin pie spice, mix together 3 tablespoons ground cinnamon, 2 tablespoons ground ginger, 2 teaspoons ground nutmeg, 1½ teaspoons ground allspice, and 1½ teaspoons ground cloves. Store in an airtight container.

WARM SPICED TURMERIC TEA

A soothing tea with a peppery kick made purely from spices, this tea is delicious served with several tablespoons of coconut milk or half-and-half stirred in right before drinking.

Serves 4

INGREDIENTS:

4 cups water

⅓ cup honey

2 tablespoons ground cinnamon

1½ tablespoons ground turmeric

1 tablespoon ginger

2 teaspoons nutmeg

1 teaspoon cloves

1. Add water, honey, and all spices to a 2.5-quart slow cooker. Whisk together thoroughly to combine spices into the water.

2. Cover and cook on high for 2–3 hours or on low for 5–6 hours. Occasionally remove the lid and whisk tea. Serve warm.

A Note on Turmeric

Turmeric has been used for centuries in Chinese and Indian medicine because of its natural anti-inflammatory properties. It's a deep yellow-orange in color and is often used in Indian curries. Turmeric is also a good source of manganese, iron, vitamin B_6, and potassium.

SALTED CARAMEL MOCHA LATTES

The slight hint of salt in this warm, creamy drink balances out the sweetness of the caramel. When serving this sweet drink offer whipped cream, additional caramel sauce, chocolate syrup, or sea salt for toppings.

Serves 6

INGREDIENTS:

3 cups whole milk

3 cups strongly brewed coffee

2 tablespoons unsweetened cocoa

⅓ cup sugar

¼ teaspoon salt

1 teaspoon vanilla extract

⅓ cup caramel sauce

1. Place all ingredients in a 4-quart slow cooker. Use a whisk to combine ingredients thoroughly.

2. Cover slow cooker and cook on high for 1–2 hours or on low for 2–3 hours, until mixture is hot and simmering.

Strongly Brewed Coffee

To get a very strong coffee flavor in this drink use about 3–4 tablespoons of ground coffee per cup of water. The coffee will be diluted when combined with the milk in this recipe and will be creamy and delicious.

PEPPERMINT MOCHA LATTES

A refreshing coffee drink made right in your slow cooker. You could also make a chilled peppermint mocha latte by refrigerating the leftovers and serving the drink over ice the next day!

Serves 6

INGREDIENTS:

3 cups whole milk

3 cups strongly brewed coffee

¼ cup unsweetened cocoa

⅓ cup sugar

½ teaspoon peppermint extract

⅛ teaspoon salt

2 cups whipped heavy cream

1. Add milk, coffee, cocoa, sugar, peppermint extract, and salt to a 4-quart slow cooker. Use a whisk to combine ingredients thoroughly.

2. Cover slow cooker and cook on high for 1–2 hours or on low for 2–3 hours, until mixture is hot and simmering.

3. Serve in large mugs or coffee cups with whipped cream.

How Much Peppermint?

Peppermint extract is made from the essential oils of the peppermint plant. It is a *very* strongly flavored extract and a little goes a long way. Start with using ½ teaspoon in this batch of peppermint lattes and if you prefer more add ⅛ a teaspoon at a time until it's as minty as you like! For more peppermint flavor, crush 2 candy canes or a few peppermint hard candies to sprinkle on top.

VANILLA BEAN WHITE HOT CHOCOLATE

Children love this creamy, rich, warm vanilla-y drink made with white chocolate baking pieces.

Serves 8

INGREDIENTS:

8 cups whole milk

1 (12-ounce) package white chocolate chips

2 tablespoons vanilla extract

⅛ teaspoon salt

1 vanilla bean

2 cups whipped heavy cream

1. Add milk, white chocolate chips, vanilla, and salt to a 4-quart slow cooker. Use a whisk to combine ingredients thoroughly.

2. Using a sharp knife, cut the vanilla bean in half and scrape out the tiny seeds and add them to the milk mixture.

3. Cover slow cooker and cook on high for 1–2 hours or on low for 2–3 hours, until mixture is hot and simmering.

4. Serve in large mugs or coffee cups with whipped cream on top.

ORANGE MOCHA

Serve this rich drink with a twist of orange peel as a garnish. Flame the orange peel briefly to bring out the scent.

Yields about 9 cups

INGREDIENTS:

8 cups brewed coffee

¼ cup cocoa powder

¾ cup sugar

½ cup orange liqueur

½ cup coffee liqueur

1 cup heavy cream

1. Combine the coffee, cocoa, and sugar in the slow cooker.

2. Cover and heat on a low setting for 2–3 hours.

3. Half an hour before serving, stir in the liqueurs.

4. Whip the cream and provide as a garnish for individual servings.

STEAMY MINT MALT

This is a great way to use leftover Halloween candy. Turn it into a yummy hot drink.

Yields about 5 cups

INGREDIENTS:

6 chocolate-covered mint patties

6 chocolate Hershey's Kisses

5 cups milk

½ cup malted milk powder

1 teaspoon vanilla

1 cup heavy cream

1. Combine the candies, milk, malt powder, and vanilla in the slow cooker.

2. Cover and heat on a low setting for 2–3 hours.

3. Before serving, beat with a rotary mixer until frothy.

4. Whip the cream and provide as a garnish for individual servings.

BEACH TEA

This delicious drink is great for soothing a cold. You can also add some rum to this, for an extra warming effect.

Yields about 9 cups

INGREDIENTS:

1 orange

6 cups water

⅓ cup sugar

2 tablespoons honey

1½ cups orange juice

1½ cups pineapple juice

6 tea bags

1. Thinly slice the orange.

2. Combine the orange, water, sugar, honey, and juices in the slow cooker.

3. Cover and heat on a low setting for 2–3 hours.

4. Half an hour before serving, add the tea bags for 10 minutes; then remove and discard the tea bags.

Be Cool, But Not Too Cool

Don't add icy cold ingredients to a preheated slow cooker. Sudden temperature changes can crack the crockery pot. That's a surprise you definitely don't want on the day of your party.

BELGIAN COFFEE

This is excellent after dinner, or after ice cream, and looks beautiful with an additional garnish of fresh raspberry and a mint sprig.

Yields about 9 cups

INGREDIENTS:

8 squares dark chocolate

8 cups coffee

1 cup mint liqueur

1 cup heavy cream

8 chocolate mint sticks

1. Grate or chop the dark chocolate.

2. Combine the coffee, liqueur, and dark chocolate in the slow cooker.

3. Cover and heat on a low setting for 2–3 hours.

4. Whip the cream. Provide the whipped cream and chocolate mint sticks as a garnish for individual servings.

HOMEMADE COFFEE LIQUEUR

You can also serve this chilled, over ice. Or drizzle it over your favorite chocolate cake and let it seep in overnight.

Yields about 7 cups

INGREDIENTS:

4 cups dark coffee

3 cups sugar

5 teaspoons vanilla extract

3 cups vodka

1. Combine the coffee, sugar, and half the vanilla in the slow cooker.

2. Cover and heat on a low setting for 2–3 hours. Stir twice to blend in the sugar as it dissolves.

3. An hour before serving, add the remaining vanilla and the vodka.

Get with the Program

Update your slow cooker collection with a newer model that has a removable crockery pot. It simplifies preparing ahead, storage, and cleanup, plus you can pop the crockery pot in an insulated carrying case and do your entertaining on the road.

CAFE VIENNA

This rich drink is even better if you use the best coffee available. You can also substitute brown sugar or turbinado sugar.

Yields about 8 cups

INGREDIENTS:

4 squares dark chocolate

8 cups coffee

½ cup sugar

½ cup heavy cream

¼ teaspoon ground nutmeg

8 sticks cinnamon bark

1. Grate or chop the chocolate.

2. Combine the chocolate, coffee, sugar, cream, and nutmeg in the slow cooker.

3. Cover and heat on a low setting for 2–3 hours.

4. Provide the cinnamon sticks as garnish for individual servings.

CAFE VALLARTA

Use a potato peeler to shave thin orange peel twists from a fresh orange. Avoid crushing the shavings, which releases their oils too early.

Serves 6–8

INGREDIENTS:

8 cups coffee

8 ounces orange liqueur

8 ounces coffee liqueur

½ cup sugar

8 sticks cinnamon bark

8 orange peel twists

1. Combine the coffee, liqueurs, and sugar in the slow cooker.

2. Cover and heat on a low setting for 2–3 hours.

3. Provide the cinnamon and orange peels as garnish for individual servings.

Peeling Oranges

To make peeling oranges easier, pour boiling water over the oranges and let them sit for five minutes. The white part will come off with the peel. Don't do this when the peel is needed for your recipe; it strips away some of the flavor.

ROSY RED CHEEKS

This drink is excellent for a cold winter evening. Add a few drops of red food coloring for extra holiday color.

Yields about 6 cups

INGREDIENTS:

2 cups cranberry juice cocktail

1 6-ounce can frozen orange juice concentrate

1 tablespoon sugar

¼ teaspoon ground allspice

1 bottle dry red wine

1 orange

10 whole cloves

1. Combine the cranberry juice, orange juice concentrate, sugar, allspice, and wine in the slow cooker.

2. Cover and heat on a low setting for 2–3 hours.

3. Slice the orange and stud the orange slices with the cloves. Half an hour before serving, put the orange slices in the slow cooker.

SUGAR ON FIRE

This recipe will grab all your guests' attention. Serve it when there's a lull in your party to get everyone energized again.

Yields about 8 cups

INGREDIENTS:

2 bottles dry red wine

1½ cups granulated sugar

6 whole cloves

1 cup orange juice

½ cup lemon juice

6 1-inch strips orange peel

4 1-inch strips lemon peel

1 orange

½ cup rum

½ cup sugar cubes

1. Combine the wine with the granulated sugar (not the cubes), cloves, fruit juices, and peels in the slow cooker.

2. Cover and heat on a low setting for 2–3 hours.

3. Slice the orange; set aside.

4. Heat the rum in a saucepan over low heat until the rum steams. Soak the sugar cubes in the rum. Place the cubes in a metal strainer or metal slotted spoon just over the punch.

5. Ignite the sugar cubes. As they flame, gradually pour the rest of the heated rum over the cubes. When the sugar has all melted into the punch, add a few orange slices.

A Slick Trick

Before measuring sticky liquids like honey and molasses, grease your measuring cup and then rinse it with hot water. The molasses will still flow slowly like . . . well, molasses, but you won't lose half of your measurement on the sides of the measuring cup.

MEDICINAL BLACKBERRY CORDIAL

This drink should be served in small glasses. It's also excellent over vanilla ice cream or soaked into white cake.

Yields about 8 cups

INGREDIENTS:

3 pounds blackberries

1 cup sugar

1 teaspoon cinnamon

1 teaspoon mace

1 teaspoon ground cloves

½ cup water

2 cups brandy

1. Combine the blackberries, sugar, and spices in the slow cooker. Mash them together with a potato masher.

2. Add the water. Cover and heat on a low setting for 2–3 hours.

3. An hour before serving, add the brandy.

CAFE AROMATICA

This nonalcoholic brew is ideal for a gray winter afternoon, or for the end of the evening, before your guests head out into a storm.

Yields about 6 cups

INGREDIENTS:

2 oranges

6 cups double-strength coffee

¼ cup sugar

2 teaspoons aromatic bitters

1 cup heavy cream

1. Peel and slice the oranges, and cut ½ cup of the peel into very thin strips.

2. Combine the coffee, orange slices, ½ cup peel strips, sugar, and bitters in the slow cooker.

3. Cover and heat on a low setting for 2–3 hours.

4. Whip the cream and provide as a garnish for individual servings.

SPICED GRAPE TEA

This is a good drink to be sipping indoors with friends on a rainy day. Try using white grape juice in this recipe.

Yields about 10 cups

INGREDIENTS:

3 sticks cinnamon bark

¼ cup loose tea

10 cloves

3 cups grape juice

½ cup sugar

7 cups water

1. Put the cinnamon, tea, and cloves in loose cloth bag.

2. Combine the spice bag with the grape juice, sugar, and water in the slow cooker.

3. Cover and heat on a low setting for 2–3 hours.

4. Before serving, remove the cloth bag.

SPICED GRAPE JUICE

This hot drink is better if made the day before, left overnight in a cool place, then reheated and served.

Yields about 12 cups

INGREDIENTS:

12 1-inch sticks cinnamon bark

12 whole cloves

12 cups grape juice

½ cup sugar

⅛ teaspoon salt

¼ cup lemon juice

1. Tie the cinnamon and cloves in a cloth bag.

2. Combine the spice bag with the grape juice, sugar, and salt in the slow cooker.

3. Cover and heat on a low setting for 2–3 hours.

4. Before serving, remove the cloth bag and add the lemon juice.

Maturation

Slow cooking allows flavors to mature, meaning they actually go through chemical changes that simply take time. This happens in other slow systems that use time as an asset, such as the aging of wine and cheese.

SPICY SUNDAY TEA

This aromatic tea will not only give your home a lovely scent while you cook it, but it will also warm you up on the inside.

Yields about 9 cups

INGREDIENTS:

¼ teaspoon cinnamon

¼ teaspoon whole cloves

6 teaspoons tea

8 cups water

1 cup sugar

1 lemon

2 oranges

1. Tie the cinnamon, cloves, and tea in a loose cloth bag. Place the bag in the slow cooker.

2. Boil 2 cups of the water. Pour it over the spice bag in the slow cooker and let this steep 5 minutes.

3. Add the remaining water and sugar to the slow cooker. Cover and heat on a low setting for 2–3 hours.

4. Extract the juice from the lemon and oranges. Half an hour before serving, remove the spice bag and add the juices.

COCONUT MILK

The milk and "used" coconut solids can be frozen for later use in curries, sauces, puddings, and cakes.

Yields about 3 cups

INGREDIENTS:

2 cups coconut pieces

2 cups water

1. Remove any remaining coconut shell or brown lining from the coconut meat. Put the coconut meat and water in the blender. Blend until smooth.

2. Transfer to the slow cooker.

3. Cover and heat on a low setting for 2–3 hours. Strain.

HOT APRICOT SOOTHER

Apricots have a sweet-tart flavor and beautiful, deep orange-yellow color in this pretty and warming drink.

Serves 10

INGREDIENTS:

8 cups apricot nectar

2 cups water

2 tablespoons honey

4 whole cloves

2 canned apricot halves

1 cinnamon stick

2 tablespoons lemon juice

1. In 3-quart slow cooker, combine nectar, water, and honey. Stick cloves into the apricot halves and add to slow cooker along with cinnamon stick.

2. Cover and cook on low for 4–5 hours or until mixture is blended and hot. Stir in lemon juice and serve immediately.

Party Fun

You can serve this mixture or any hot punch with cinnamon-stick stirrers. Just add a cinnamon stick to each cup or mug. This will release more cinnamon flavor into the drink, and it looks pretty too. Or you can sprinkle the top of the soother with ground cinnamon just before serving.

COCONUT EGGNOG

Eggnog can be served hot or cold; after cooking, this mixture can be chilled for 4–5 hours; beat well again before serving.

Serves 12

INGREDIENTS:

1 (14-ounce) can cream of coconut

2 (14-ounce) cans coconut milk

1 (14-ounce) can sweetened condensed milk

2 cups whole milk

Pinch salt

¾ cup white rum

¼ cup bourbon

1 teaspoon vanilla

1 teaspoon cinnamon

1. Combine all ingredients except rum, bourbon, vanilla, and cinnamon in 3½-quart slow cooker. Beat well with eggbeater. Cover and cook on low for 4–5 hours until hot.

2. Beat again, then add rum, bourbon, vanilla, and cinnamon. Stir well and serve. You can chill the nog at this point and serve cold.

Make It Healthy

Coconut oil, which makes coconuts taste rich, is actually good for you. It has saturated fat, but those fats are medium length, which the body digests easily, so it isn't stored in the liver. You could use low-fat sweetened condensed milk in this recipe to reduce calories a bit.

CHAPTER 2

APPETIZERS, PARTY FARE, AND SNACKS

SASSY AND SWEET CHICKEN WINGS

For larger servings or to increase the number of servings, substitute 4 pounds of chicken drumettes (the meatiest pieces of the chicken wings) for the whole chicken wings.

Serves 12

INGREDIENTS:

4 pounds chicken wings

2 cups Brooks Rich & Tangy Ketchup

1 (12-ounce) can Coca-Cola

1. Add the chicken wings and ketchup to the slow cooker in alternating layers. Pour the cola over the chicken and ketchup. Cover and cook on low for 6–8 hours. Uncover and continue to cook on low until sauce is thickened. To serve, reduce the heat setting of the slow cooker to warm.

Tangy Substitutions

An alternative to using Brooks Rich & Tangy Ketchup is to substitute 1 cup of regular ketchup and 1 cup of chili sauce.

STICKY HONEY WINGS

Making wings in the slow cooker is not only easy, it is a great way to keep wings warm throughout an entire party or game. Just switch the setting to warm after cooking and the wings will stay hot and sticky.

Serves 10

INGREDIENTS:

3 pounds chicken wings, tips removed

¼ cup honey

¼ cup low-sodium soy sauce

½ teaspoon freshly ground pepper

2 tablespoons chili sauce

½ teaspoon garlic powder

1. Place the wings into an oval 4-quart slow cooker.

2. In a small bowl, whisk the honey, soy sauce, pepper, chili sauce, and garlic powder. Pour over the wings. Toss to coat with sauce.

3. Cook for 6–7 hours on low. Stir before serving.

FABULOUS FONDUE

For six servings, cut the recipe in half and prepare in a small (1½-quart) slow cooker. To make it easier for your guests to access the fondue and to ensure that it is maintained at the proper temperature to prevent the cheese from separating, transfer the prepared fondue to an electric fondue pot.

Serves 12

INGREDIENTS:

2 cloves of garlic, peeled and cut in half

2 cups evaporated milk

1 cup dry white wine or sparkling white grape juice

1 teaspoon hot pepper sauce, or to taste

¼ cup all-purpose flour

1 teaspoon dry mustard

4 cups Swiss cheese, cubed

4 cups fontina cheese, cubed

Optional: Salt and freshly ground black pepper

1. Rub the inside of the slow cooker crock with the cut cloves of garlic. (For a stronger garlic flavor, leave the garlic in the cooker and use a slotted spoon to remove them just before serving.) Add the milk, wine or sparkling grape juice, and hot pepper sauce to the slow cooker.

2. Add the flour and dry mustard to a large zip-closure bag. Seal and shake to mix well. Add the cheese cubes to the bag; seal the bag and shake well to coat the cheese cubes in the flour. Pour the contents of the bag into the slow cooker and stir to combine. Cover and cook on low for 4 hours or until heated through and the cheese has melted.

3. Whisk the fondue to incorporate the melted cheese fully into the liquid. Taste for seasoning and add more hot sauce and/ or salt and freshly ground pepper if desired.

Fabulous Fondue Serving Suggestions

Cheese fondue is traditionally served with bread cubes that are each pierced with a fondue fork and dipped into the fondue. Steamed or roasted asparagus spears and raw or cooked baby carrots, broccoli florets, cauliflower florets, cucumber or pickle slices, radishes, snow peas, and sweet bell pepper strips are also delicious dipped in a savory fondue sauce.

PARTY-PLEASING CHICKEN LIVERS

The resulting sauce will be a bit sweeter, but if you prefer not to use white wine you can substitute an equal amount of red currant or apple jelly or apple juice.

Serves 18

INGREDIENTS:

6 slices bacon, diced

6 green onions with tops, chopped

2 pounds chicken livers

1 cup all-purpose flour

1 teaspoon salt

¼ teaspoon freshly ground black pepper

2 cups Chicken Broth (Chapter 19)

1 (10½-ounce) can condensed cream of mushroom soup

1 (10½-ounce) can condensed cream of chicken or celery soup

2 (4-ounce) cans sliced mushrooms, drained

½ cup dry white wine

1. Add the diced bacon and onion to the slow cooker. Cover and cook on high for ½ hour or until fat begins to be rendered and the onions are transparent.

2. Cut the chicken livers into bite-sized pieces. Add the flour, salt, and pepper to a large zip-closure bag. Seal and shake to mix. Add the chicken livers to the bag and toss to coat them with the seasoned flour.

3. Add the broth, soups, mushrooms, and wine to the slow cooker. Stir to combine. Add the chicken livers and fold them into the soup mixture. Cover and cook on low for 6–8 hours. Serve on buttered toast points.

RETRO MEATBALLS

This recipe is an adaptation of an appetizer recipe popular in the 1960s. You can ladle the meatballs directly from the slow cooker and then provide toothpicks to make them easier for your guests to eat.

Serves 8

INGREDIENTS:

2 tablespoons extra-virgin olive oil or vegetable oil

2 pounds frozen precooked meatballs

1 (12-ounce) jar chili sauce

1 cup grape jelly

1. Add the oil to the bag of frozen meatballs; close and toss to coat the meatballs in the oil. Add to the slow cooker. Cover and cook on high for 4 hours. (To prevent the meatballs on the bottom of the cooker from burning, carefully stir the meatballs every hour to rearrange them in the cooker.)

2. In a measuring cup or bowl, mix the chili sauce together with the grape jelly. Pour over the meatballs in the slow cooker. Cover and cook on low for 2 hours or until the sauce is heated through and thickened. To serve, reduce the heat setting of the slow cooker to warm.

In a Hurry Retro Meatballs

Preheat the oven to 425°F. Arrange the oil-coated frozen meatballs on a baking sheet; bake for 30 minutes, use tongs to turn the meatballs, and continue to bake for 15–30 minutes or until warmed through. Add the meatballs to the slow cooker and continue with Step 2 of the Retro Meatballs recipe.

ROYAL MEATBALLS

These flavorful meatballs are prepared with Regal Caper Sauce (Chapter 4). Serve them either skewered, as an appetizer, or with slices of mini pumpernickel.

Serves 6

INGREDIENTS:

1 onion

6 shallots

3 tablespoons butter

½ pound lamb

½ pound veal

½ pound bacon

1 small bunch parsley

12 anchovies

¼ cup chives

1 clove garlic

½ teaspoon salt

¼ teaspoon pepper

¼ teaspoon nutmeg

⅛ teaspoon cayenne pepper

½ cup water

2 eggs

3 cups Regal Caper Sauce (Chapter 4)

1. Mince the onion and shallots, then sauté in the butter in a pan over medium heat until soft. Transfer the onion and shallots to a mixing bowl and set aside the pan with remaining butter.

2. Coarsely grind or mince the meat. Finely chop the parsley, anchovies, and chives. Crush the garlic and then mince it.

3. Combine all ingredients except Regal Caper Sauce with the onion mixture in the mixing bowl and mix well. Form into ¾-inch balls; heat the meatballs in the pan over medium heat until browned, then drain.

4. Arrange the meatballs in the slow cooker and cover with Regal Caper Sauce.

5. Cover and heat on a low setting for 3–4 hours.

PAPRIKA MEATBALLS

These can be served with skewers as a finger food or over pasta as a main dish. They are excellent with fresh angel hair pasta.

Serves 8

INGREDIENTS:

1 pound veal

1 pound pork

1 clove garlic

¼ pound Mozzarella cheese

3 eggs

1 tablespoon paprika

1 teaspoon salt

1 cup bread crumbs

½ cup milk

2 tablespoons vegetable oil

2 tomatoes

1 cup tomato sauce

1. Coarsely grind the meat. Crush and mince the garlic; grate or finely dice the cheese.

2. Combine the meat, garlic, and cheese in a mixing bowl with the eggs, paprika, salt, crumbs, and milk; mix well.

3. Form into ¾-inch balls and sauté in oil in a pan over medium heat until browned. Drain and arrange the meatballs in the slow cooker.

4. Dice the tomatoes. Pour the tomatoes and tomato sauce over the meatballs.

5. Cover and heat on a low setting for 3–4 hours.

Pasta and Slow Cooking

Pasta is a great addition to slow-cooked meals, but it should not be made in your slow cooker. To serve pasta with a dish, cook the pasta separately, then serve on the side, or add it to the slow cooker just before serving. If the pasta is coated with a little butter or oil, it can be kept warm by itself in a slow cooker.

ITALIAN TURKEY MEATBALLS

Frozen Italian meatballs make this appetizer a snap to make. Look for them near the meat products in your grocer's freezer.

Serves 6

INGREDIENTS:

12 frozen Italian-style turkey meatballs

1 teaspoon canola oil

3 cloves garlic, minced

1 small onion, diced

1 carrot, diced

28 ounces canned crushed tomatoes

2 tablespoons tomato paste

⅛ teaspoon salt

½ teaspoon freshly ground black pepper

1 tablespoon minced basil

1. Defrost the meatballs according to package instructions. Place them into a 2- or 4-quart slow cooker.

2. Heat the oil in a nonstick pan. Sauté the garlic, onion, and carrot until the carrots and onions start to soften. Add the crushed tomatoes, tomato paste, salt, pepper, and basil. Stir. Simmer until most of the liquid has evaporated.

3. Pour the sauce over the meatballs, and stir to coat them. Cook on low up to 6 hours.

Using Tomato Paste

Tomato paste is a thick paste made from skinned, seeded tomatoes. Its concentrated taste is perfect for slow cooking because it adds a lot of flavor without adding extra liquid. When combined with canned tomatoes, the result is a richer-tasting sauce.

TIPSY MEATBALLS

Beer adds rich and smooth flavor to this updated appetizer recipe.

Serves 8–10

INGREDIENTS:

2 onions, chopped

1 (16-ounce) package frozen meatballs

1 (12-ounce) can beer

1 cup ketchup

½ cup chili sauce

2 tablespoons mustard

¼ cup pickle relish

1. Place onions in 4-quart slow cooker. Add meatballs. In medium bowl, combine remaining ingredients and pour into slow cooker.

2. Cover and cook on low for 5–7 hours until meatballs are hot and tender. Serve with toothpicks.

Keep It Healthy

The alcohol in the beer will not cook out of the sauce, even after hours of cooking. You can use nonalcoholic beer, but even that contains a tiny amount of alcohol. A nonalcoholic substitute would be 1½ cups Beef Broth (Chapter 19). Be sure to tell your guests there is beer in this recipe.

SPICY APRICOT FRANKS

Apricot preserves, tomato sauce, and some spices make a delicious sauce for mini frankfurters in this easy slow cooker recipe.

Serves 8

INGREDIENTS:

⅔ cup apricot preserves

⅓ cup tomato sauce

2 tablespoons apple cider vinegar

1 onion, finely chopped

3 cloves garlic, minced

⅓ cup Chicken Broth (Chapter 19)

2 tablespoons soy sauce

½ teaspoon ground ginger

⅛ teaspoon white pepper

2 pounds mini cocktail franks

1. In 3- to 4-quart slow cooker, combine all ingredients except franks and mix well. Stir in franks.

2. Cover and cook on low for 7–8 hours, or on high for 3–4 hours, until sauce bubbles and franks are hot.

WELSH RAREBIT

Welsh Rarebit can be served as a party dip or spooned over toast points and then dusted with paprika. It's also good served as part of a breakfast buffet to be spooned over scrambled eggs or egg-topped English muffins.

Serves 8

INGREDIENTS:

2½ cups beer

2 tablespoons butter

Hot sauce, to taste

Worcestershire sauce, to taste

2 pounds (4 cups) medium or sharp
   Cheddar cheese, grated

2 tablespoons all-purpose flour

2 teaspoons dry mustard

2 large eggs

Optional: Paprika

1. Pour 2 cups of the beer and the butter, hot sauce, and Worcestershire sauce into the slow cooker. Cook uncovered on high for ½ hour.

2. Put half of the grated cheese and the flour in a zip-closure bag. Shake well to coat the cheese with flour, adding as much of the cheese to the bag as will fit and still allow room to mix it with the flour. Add all of the cheese-flour mixture and remaining cheese to the slow cooker. Cover and cook on low for 1 hour or until cheese is melted.

3. Add the dry mustard and the eggs to a bowl or measuring cup; whisk to combine. Whisk the remaining ½ cup of beer into the egg mixture and then slowly stir the egg mixture into the slow cooker. Cover and cook on low for ½ hour. To serve, reduce the heat setting of the slow cooker to warm. Dust servings with paprika if desired.

Leftover Welsh Rarebit

Refrigerate leftover Welsh Rarebit in a covered container for up to a week. Reheat slowly (so the cheese doesn't separate) and serve over steamed vegetables or as a baked potato topper.

SLOW COOKER SNACK MIX

Making a snack mix with whole-grain cereal is a breeze in the slow cooker. Unlike the oven method, there is virtually no risk of burning and little attention or hands-on time is needed.

Serves 20

INGREDIENTS:

2 tablespoons melted butter

1 teaspoon garlic powder

1 teaspoon onion powder

1 teaspoon paprika

1 teaspoon dried thyme

1 teaspoon dill weed

1 teaspoon chili powder

1 teaspoon Worcestershire sauce

1½ cups crispy corn cereal squares

1½ cups crispy wheat cereal squares

1½ cups crispy rice cereal squares

1 cup pretzel wheels

1 cup roasted peanuts or almonds

1. Pour the butter, spices, and Worcestershire sauce into the bottom of a 6-quart slow cooker. Stir. Add the cereal, pretzels, and nuts. Cook uncovered on low for 2–3 hours, stirring every 30 minutes.

2. Pour onto a baking sheet and allow to cool. Store in an airtight container.

Snack Mix Variations

Mexican: Substitute 1 teaspoon each cayenne pepper, ground chipotle, hot New Mexico chili powder, and oregano for the thyme, dill weed, and Worcestershire sauce. Japanese: substitute wasabi peas for the peanuts, and 1 teaspoon each sesame seeds, soy sauce, ground ginger, and white pepper for the paprika, thyme, dill weed, and Worcestershire sauce.

LOW-CARB SNACK MIX

For this recipe, use raw almonds, cashews, pecans, shelled pumpkin seeds, shelled sunflower seeds, walnuts, and raw or dry-roasted peanuts. The amounts you use of each kind of nut is up to you, although because of their size, ideally the recipe shouldn't have more than 1 cup of sunflower seeds.

Yield: 24 (⅓-cup) servings

INGREDIENTS:

4 tablespoons butter, melted

3 tablespoons Worcestershire sauce

1½ teaspoons garlic powder

2 teaspoons onion powder

Optional: Seasoned salt or sea salt, to taste

8 cups raw nuts

1. Add all ingredients to the slow cooker. Stir to coat the nuts evenly. Cover and cook on low for 6 hours, stirring occasionally.

2. Uncover and continue to cook on low for another hour to dry the nuts and seeds, stirring occasionally, and then evenly spread them on a lined baking sheet until completely cooled. Store in a covered container.

Pepitas

Raw pumpkin seeds are also known as "pepitas" when sold in Latino food markets.

ROASTED PISTACHIOS

Raw pistachios are available at Trader Joe's (www.traderjoes.com) or health food stores. Roasting your own lets you control the amount of salt on the nuts, which makes them a snack that perfectly matches your tastes.

Yield: 16 (1-ounce) servings

INGREDIENTS:

1 pound raw pistachios

2 tablespoons extra-virgin olive oil or melted butter

Optional: 1 teaspoon sea salt, or to taste

1. Add the nuts, oil or butter, and salt, if using, to the slow cooker. Stir to combine. Cover and cook on low for 1 hour. Stir the mixture and, if using salt, taste for seasoning; add more salt and stir into the nuts if desired. Cover and cook for 2 more hours, stirring the mixture again after 1 hour. Store in an airtight container.

Putting Roasted Pistachios to Work

You can make 8 servings of a delicious coleslaw alternative by mixing together 3 very thinly sliced heads of fennel; ½ cup roasted, chopped pistachios; 3 tablespoons extra-virgin olive oil; 2 table-spoons freshly squeezed lemon juice; and 1 teaspoon finely grated lemon zest. Taste for seasoning and add sea salt, freshly ground black pepper, and additional lemon juice if desired. Serve immediately or cover and refrigerate up to 1 day.

SPICED PECANS

If spicy-hot Cajun seasoning isn't to your liking, you can use sweet-hot barbecue seasoning blend, savory Italian seasoning blend, or another seasoning mix instead.

Yield: 16 (1-ounce) servings

INGREDIENTS:

3 pounds pecan halves

2 tablespoons extra-virgin olive oil or melted butter

2 tablespoons Cajun seasoning blend

1. Add the pecans, oil or butter, and Cajun seasoning blend to the slow cooker. Stir to combine. Cover and cook on low for 1 hour. Taste for seasoning, and add more Cajun spices if desired. Stir the mixture.

2. Cover and cook for 2 more hours, stirring the mixture again after 1 hour. Store in an airtight container.

SUGARED WALNUTS

Sugared walnuts are a snack that will satisfy any sweet tooth. Cooled sugared walnuts can be stored at room temperature in a covered container for up to 3 days.

Yield: 16 (1-ounce) servings

INGREDIENTS:

1 pound walnut halves

1 stick (½ cup) butter, melted

⅔ cup pure cane or powdered sugar

1. Add the walnuts, butter, and sugar to the slow cooker. (If using powdered sugar, sift it to remove any lumps.) Stir to combine. Cover and cook on high for 15 minutes.

2. Reduce heat to low and cook uncovered for 2 hours, stirring occasionally. At the end of the cooking time, evenly spread the walnuts on a lined baking sheet until completely cooled.

CINNAMON AND SUGAR NUTS

Not only a good snack, chopped Cinnamon and Sugar Nuts are good sprinkled over French toast.

Serves 24

INGREDIENTS:

3 cups raw almonds, pecan halves, or walnut halves

3 tablespoons butter, melted

2 teaspoons vanilla

½ cup sugar

1 teaspoon cinnamon

Salt, to taste

1. Add all ingredients to the slow cooker. Stir to coat the nuts evenly. Cover and cook on low for 6 hours, stirring occasionally.

2. Uncover and continue to cook on low for another hour, stirring occasionally, to dry the nuts. Next evenly spread the nuts on a lined baking sheet until completely cooled. Store in a covered container.

BUTTERSCOTCH CARAMEL–GLAZED NUTS

These nuts taste even better when tossed together with some popcorn.

Serves 32

INGREDIENTS:

4 cups raw almonds, pecan halves, or walnut halves

½ cup Butterscotch Caramel Sauce (Chapter 28)

Optional: 1½ teaspoons cinnamon

1. Add all ingredients to the slow cooker. Stir to coat the nuts. Cover and cook on low for 3 hours, stirring at least once an hour.

2. Uncover and, stirring the mixture every 20 minutes, cook on low for 1 more hour or until the nuts are almost dry. Next evenly spread the nuts on a lined baking sheet until completely cooled. Store in a covered container.

PARTY SEASONED NUTS

Whether or not you add salt to this recipe will depend on whether or not the nuts you use are already salted. Store leftovers in a covered container for up to a week or freeze them.

Serves 16

INGREDIENTS:

4 tablespoons butter, melted

3 tablespoons curry or chili powder, or taco seasoning

Salt, to taste

8 cups mixed nuts

1. Add the butter and choice of seasoning to the slow cooker. Stir to combine. Add the nuts and stir to coat them with the seasoning. Cover and cook on high for ½ hour. Stir well. Cover and cook on high for an additional 30 minutes. Stir again.

2. Cover, reduce the heat to low, and continue to cook (and occasionally stir) for an addition 1–2 hours or until heated through.

SOY ALMONDS

These slightly spicy almonds are a wonderful alternative to plain or sweetened almonds. Try them in a salad.

Serves 15

INGREDIENTS:

2 cups whole almonds

2 tablespoons low-sodium soy sauce or tamari

½ teaspoon sesame oil

1 teaspoon Chinese five-spice powder

1. Place all ingredients into a 4-quart oval slow cooker. Stir.

2. Cook for 15 minutes on high, uncovered. Reduce heat to low and continue to cook, uncovered, for 1 hour, stirring occasionally, or until the almonds are dry.

HOT CINNAMON CHILI PEANUTS

These seasoned peanuts are a surprising hit with chili powder and cinnamon and just a hint of sweetness with honey and brown sugar.

Yields 1½ cups

INGREDIENTS:

1½ cups peanuts

¼ cup brown sugar

2 teaspoons cinnamon

1½ teaspoons chili powder

¼ teaspoon salt

2 teaspoons honey

2 teaspoons oil

1. Combine all ingredients and place in a greased 2.5-quart slow cooker.

2. Cover slow cooker and vent lid with a chopstick or the handle of a wooden spoon. Cook on high for 2 hours or on low for 4 hours. If using a larger slow cooker, you will probably need to reduce the cooking time to only 1 hour on high or 2 hours on low.

3. Pour peanut mixture out onto a baking sheet lined with parchment paper. Allow to cool and dry and then transfer to a container with an airtight lid. Store in the pantry for up to 2 weeks.

BALSAMIC ALMONDS

These sweet and sour almonds are a great addition to a cheese platter or appetizer plate.

Serves 15

INGREDIENTS:

2 cups whole almonds

½ cup dark brown sugar

½ cup balsamic vinegar

½ teaspoon kosher salt

1. Place all ingredients into a 4-quart slow cooker. Cook uncovered on high for 4 hours, stirring every 15 minutes or until all the liquid has evaporated. The almonds will have a syrupy coating.

2. Line 2 cookie sheets with parchment paper. Pour the almonds in a single layer on the baking sheets to cool completely. Store in an airtight container in the pantry for up to 2 weeks.

Healthy Almonds

Botanically speaking, almonds are a seed, not a nut. They are an excellent source of vitamin E and have high levels of monounsaturated fat, one of the two "good" fats responsible for lowering LDL cholesterol.

CHAPTER 3

DIPS AND SPREADS

CHILI-CHEESE DIP

You can substitute 3¾ cups homemade chili for the canned chili. For a thicker dip to serve with tortilla chips or celery sticks, stir in a pound of cooked and drained ground beef. This dip also makes a delicious topper for baked potatoes.

Serves 12

INGREDIENTS:

1 (15-ounce) can chili

1 pound Velveeta cheese, cut into cubes

1. Add the chili and cheese to a slow cooker. Cover and, stirring the mixture every half hour, cook on low for 2–3 hours or until the cheese is melted. To serve, reduce the heat setting of the slow cooker to warm.

MEXICAN DIP

This recipe makes enough dip to feed a hungry crowd, which makes it popular for a snack following a youth group meeting or at a Super Bowl party. Warm up leftover Mexican Dip and use it as the dressing for a taco salad or as a baked potato topper.

Serves 24

INGREDIENTS:

3 pounds lean ground beef, cooked and drained

1 large sweet onion, peeled and diced

1 (15-ounce) can refried beans

1 (10½-ounce) can condensed tomato soup

1 package taco seasoning

1 cup salsa

2 pounds Velveeta cheese, cut into cubes

1. Add all ingredients to the slow cooker. Stir to combine. Cover and cook on low for 4–6 hours, stirring every 30 minutes until cheese is melted. Once cheese is melted, taste for seasoning and add more salsa if desired. To serve, reduce the heat setting of the slow cooker to warm.

Processed Cheese

Processed cheeses like Velveeta and American cheese will stand up to long periods of heat without separating.

PARMESAN ARTICHOKE DIP

For a more savory dip, reduce the amount of mayonnaise to 2 cups and then stir in 2 cups of room temperature sour cream immediately before serving. For fewer servings, cut the recipe in half and reduce the cooking time.

Serves 24

INGREDIENTS:

2 (13½-ounce) jars of marinated artichoke hearts

4 cups mayonnaise

2 (8-ounce) packages of cream cheese, cubed

12 ounces (3 cups) freshly grated Parmesan-Reggiano cheese

4 cloves of garlic, peeled and minced

1 teaspoon dried dill

Freshly ground black pepper or white pepper to taste

1. Drain and chop the artichoke hearts. Add to the slow cooker along with the mayonnaise, cream cheese, Parmesan-Reggiano cheese, garlic, dill, and pepper. Stir to combine. Cover and cook on low for 2 hours; uncover and stir well.

2. Re-cover and cook on low for an additional 2 hours or until the cheese is melted completely and the dip is heated through. To serve, reduce the heat setting of the slow cooker to warm. Serve with crackers, toast points, pita crisps, or crusty rye or country whole grain bread.

CARAMELIZED ONION DIP

Caramelized onions give this dip an amazing depth of flavor.

Yields 1 quart

INGREDIENTS:

⅔ cup Caramelized Onions (Chapter 26)

8 ounces reduced-fat cream cheese

8 ounces reduced-fat or fat-free sour cream

1 tablespoon Worcestershire Sauce

¼ teaspoon white pepper

⅛ teaspoon flour

1. Place all ingredients into a 1½- to 2-quart slow cooker.

2. Heat on low for 2 hours. Whisk before serving.

PINEAPPLE-MANGO CHUTNEY

Try this as a sandwich spread or as a dip.

Serves 6

INGREDIENTS:

3 cups fresh pineapple, cubed

1½ cups fresh mango, cubed

1 tablespoon ginger, freshly grated

2 tablespoons onion, minced

¼ cup balsamic vinegar

2 cloves garlic, minced

3 tablespoons lime juice

⅓ cup dark brown sugar

1 jalapeño, minced

1. Put all ingredients into a 2- to 4-quart slow cooker. Stir. Turn to high and cook 3 hours until soft.

2. Uncover and continue to cook on high for 1 hour.

BLACK AND WHITE BEAN DIP

Cannellini beans make this dip incredibly creamy.

Serves 25

INGREDIENTS:

1 teaspoon canola oil

1 habanero pepper, seeded and minced

1 small onion, diced

3 cloves garlic, minced

½ teaspoon hot paprika

¼ teaspoon cumin

¼ cup reduced-fat sour cream

2 tablespoons lime juice

15 ounces canned black beans, drained and rinsed

15 ounces canned cannellini beans, drained and rinsed

1. Heat the oil in a nonstick skillet. Sauté the habanero, onion, and garlic until soft and fragrant, about 2–3 minutes. Pour into a medium-sized bowl. Add the spices, sour cream, lime juice, and beans. Mash the mixture with a potato masher until the dip looks creamy but with some black and white beans still distinct.

2. Scrape into a 1½- to 2-quart slow cooker. Cook on low for 2 hours. Stir before serving.

Paprika

Hungarian paprika comes in two aptly named varieties: sweet and hot. The spice is used to flavor and, in some cases, color dishes. Spanish paprika is also known as smoked paprika and adds a smoky, spicy note to food.

BLACK BEAN AND CORN DIP

Try this dip with whole-grain tortilla chips or pita crisps.

Serves 16

INGREDIENTS:

1 teaspoon canola oil

1 jalapeño, seeded and minced

1 small onion, diced

2 cloves garlic, minced

½ teaspoon ground cayenne pepper

¼ teaspoon cumin

2 tablespoons lime juice

¼ teaspoon green hot sauce

¼ cup reduced-fat sour cream

15 ounces canned black beans, drained and rinsed

½ cup fresh or defrosted frozen corn kernels

1. Heat the oil in a nonstick skillet. Sauté the jalapeño, onion, and garlic until soft and fragrant, about 2–3 minutes. Pour into a medium-sized bowl. Add the spices, lime juice, green hot sauce, sour cream, and beans. Mash with a potato masher until most of the beans are mashed. Stir in the corn.

2. Scrape into a 1½- to 2-quart slow cooker. Cook on low for 2 hours. Stir before serving.

Black Bean Facts

Black beans are also known as turtle beans. They are an excellent source of cholesterol-lowering fiber. They are also virtually fat free, making them a great addition to dips, chili, and side dishes.

PIZZA DIP

Serve this low-fat dip with pita chips, crackers, a sliced baguette, soft pretzels, or garlic bread.

Serves 16

INGREDIENTS:

½ teaspoon canola oil

¼ cup diced onion

2 cloves garlic, minced

¼ cup quartered turkey pepperoni

½ teaspoon minced basil

2¼ ounces canned sliced black olives, drained

28 ounces canned crushed or coarsely ground tomatoes

1. Heat the oil in a nonstick skillet. Add the onions and garlic and sauté until the onions are soft.

2. Put the onions, garlic, pepperoni, basil, olives, and tomatoes into a 1½- to 2-quart slow cooker. Stir to distribute the ingredients evenly. Cook on low for 2 hours or on high for 1 hour.

Cooking with Smaller Slow Cookers

Small (1½- to 2-quart) slow cookers are great for making meals for two, side dishes, and dips. A cooker with variable settings rather than a dip-only model, where the only settings are on or off, will allow you to cook full meals for two.

BROCCOLI DIP

Serve this vegetable-rich creamy dip with crisp raw vegetables and pumpernickel pretzels.

Serves 15

INGREDIENTS:

4 cups steamed broccoli florets

1 cup fresh baby spinach

1 shallot

1 jalapeño, stem and seeds removed

1 tablespoon Worcestershire sauce

½ tablespoon nonpareil capers

1 cup nonfat plain yogurt

¼ teaspoon freshly ground black pepper

2 tablespoons lemon juice

1. Place the broccoli, spinach, shallot, jalapeño, Worcestershire sauce, and capers in a food processor. Pulse until the mixture is mostly smooth. Add the yogurt, pepper, and lemon juice. Pulse until smooth.

2. Pour into a 1½- to 2-quart slow cooker. Cover and cook on low for 1 hour.

How to Steam Vegetables

Bring about 1" of water to boil in a heavy-bottomed pot. Add the vegetables and cook until fork-tender but not soft. Drain and season.

CREAMY, LOW-FAT SPINACH-ARTICHOKE DIP

Try this lighter version of the classic dip at your next party. It is great with raw vegetables and pita chips.

Serves 15

INGREDIENTS:

½ teaspoon canola oil

½ cup diced onion

8 ounces frozen artichoke hearts, defrosted

3 ounces baby spinach

¼ cup diced red onion

6 ounces reduced-fat sour cream

1 tablespoon Worcestershire sauce

¼ teaspoon salt

½ teaspoon freshly ground black pepper

⅓ cup reduced-fat Italian-blend cheese

1. Heat the oil in a nonstick skillet. Sauté the onions, spinach, and red onions until the onions are translucent and the spinach wilts. Drain any extra liquid.

2. Place into a 2-quart slow cooker. Stir in sour cream, Worcestershire sauce, salt, pepper, and cheese.

3. Cover and cook for 1 hour on low. Stir before serving.

Cooking with Artichoke Hearts

Frozen artichoke hearts are an affordable way to use artichokes. They are fat free and ready to use. If the hearts are very large, cut them in half for easier eating.

BABA GANOUSH

Serve this with pita and fresh vegetables.

Serves 12

INGREDIENTS:

1 1-pound eggplant

2 tablespoons tahini

2 tablespoons lemon juice

2 cloves garlic

1. Pierce the eggplant with a fork. Cook on high in a 4-quart slow cooker for 2 hours.

2. Allow to cool. Peel off the skin. Slice it in half and remove the seeds. Discard the skin and seeds.

3. Place the pulp in a food processor and add the remaining ingredients. Pulse until smooth.

Tahini Tips

Tahini is a paste made from ground sesame seeds. The most common tahini uses seeds that have been toasted before they are ground, but "raw" tahini is also available. The two can be used interchangeably in most recipes, but occasionally a recipe will specify one or the other. Look for tahini near the peanut butter, in the health food section, or with the specialty foods in most grocery stores.

SLOW-COOKED SALSA

This may be the easiest salsa recipe ever, but it tastes so much fresher than jarred salsa.

Serves 10

INGREDIENTS:

4 cups grape tomatoes, halved

1 small onion, thinly sliced

2 jalapeños, diced

⅛ teaspoon salt

1. Place all ingredients into a 2-quart slow cooker. Stir. Cook on low for 5 hours.

2. Stir and lightly smash the tomatoes before serving, if desired.

SHRIMP AND ARTICHOKE DIP

This unusual dip is delicious with sesame pretzels or pita chips.

Serves 20

INGREDIENTS:

8 ounces reduced-fat cream cheese

½ cup reduced-fat sour cream

½ cup diced green onion

1 tablespoon Worcestershire sauce

1½ teaspoons Chesapeake Bay seasoning

12 ounces frozen artichoke hearts, defrosted

8 ounces peeled salad shrimp

1. Place the cream cheese, sour cream, green onion, Worcestershire sauce, and Chesapeake Bay seasoning in a food processor. Pulse until smooth and well blended. Add the artichoke hearts and pulse twice.

2. Scrape into a medium bowl. Add the shrimp and stir to evenly distribute.

3. Scrape into a 2-quart slow cooker. Cook on low 40 minutes. Stir before serving.

Cooking with Cream Cheese

While reduced-fat cream cheese can be successfully cooked, fat-free cream cheese separates when heated. Do not use fat-free cream cheese unless it is specifically called for. In addition, always use brick cream cheese. Whipped or spreadable cream cheese has additives to make it spread easily that separate during cooking.

BALTIMORE CRAB DIP

This dip is on the table at practically every party held in Baltimore, Maryland, where blue crab is king.

Serves 22

INGREDIENTS:

1½ tablespoons Chesapeake Bay seasoning

1 teaspoon dry mustard

½ teaspoon garlic powder

8 ounces reduced-fat cream cheese, at room temperature

⅓ cup reduced-fat sour cream

1 teaspoon lemon juice

1 shallot, grated

16 ounces blue crab claw meat

1½ teaspoons Worcestershire sauce

1½ tablespoons canola oil mayonnaise

⅓ cup grated reduced-fat sharp Cheddar

1. In a medium bowl, thoroughly mix together the spices, cream cheese, sour cream, lemon juice, shallot, crab, Worcestershire sauce, and mayonnaise. Scrape into a 2-quart slow cooker.

2. Smooth the top of the dip and sprinkle with an even layer of cheese. Cover and cook on low for 45–60 minutes before serving.

Homemade Chesapeake Bay Seasoning

In a small bowl, whisk together 1 tablespoon ground bay leaves, 2 teaspoons celery seed, 1¼ teaspoons dry mustard, 1 teaspoon freshly ground black pepper, ½ teaspoon garlic powder, ½ teaspoon ground nutmeg, ¼ teaspoon ground cloves, ¼ teaspoon ground ginger, ½ teaspoon paprika, ½ teaspoon ground cayenne pepper, ⅛ teaspoon ground mace, and ⅛ teaspoon ground cardamom. Store in an airtight container up to one year.

BLACKBERRY COMPOTE

Try this on toast or an English muffin.

Serves 6

INGREDIENTS:

2 cups blackberries

¼ cup sugar

¼ cup water

1. Place all ingredients into a 2-quart slow cooker. Cook on low for 3 hours, remove the lid, and cook on high for 4 hours.

PEAR BUTTER

Try this creamy spread on English muffins, oatmeal, or even as an ingredient in barbecue sauce.

Yields 3 quarts

INGREDIENTS:

9 Bartlett pears, sliced

1 cup water or pear cider

¼ cup brown sugar

¼ cup sugar

¼ teaspoon ginger

¼ teaspoon cinnamon

¼ teaspoon mace

1. Place all ingredients in a 4-quart slow cooker. Cook on low for 10–12 hours.

2. Uncover and cook on low for an additional 10–12 hours or until thick and most of the liquid has evaporated.

3. Allow to cool completely; then pour into the food processor and purée. Pour into clean glass jars. Refrigerate.

HUMMUS

Serve this Middle Eastern spread with pita, vegetables, or falafel.

Serves 20

INGREDIENTS:

1 pound dried chickpeas

Water, as needed

3 tablespoons tahini

3 tablespoons lemon juice

3 cloves garlic

¼ teaspoon salt

1. Place the chickpeas in a 4-quart slow cooker and cover with water. Soak overnight. The next day, cook on low for 8 hours.

2. Drain, reserving the liquid. Place the chickpeas, tahini, lemon juice, garlic, and salt in a food processor. Pulse until smooth, adding the reserved liquid as needed to achieve the desired texture.

Easy Snacking

Keeping hummus and fresh vegetables around makes healthy snacking easy. Cut carrots, celery, and radishes into snack-friendly sizes. Place them in a bowl with a tightly fitting lid. Fill the bowl two-thirds with water. They will keep crisp in the refrigerator up to 1 week.

MIXED VEGGIE DIP

Try this vegetable-rich dip with pita chips or baked potato chips.

Serves 20

INGREDIENTS:

8 ounces low-fat cream cheese, at room temperature

½ cup reduced-fat sour cream

1 teaspoon low-fat mayonnaise

½ teaspoon white pepper

½ teaspoon garlic powder

½ teaspoon onion powder

½ teaspoon Worcestershire sauce

1 carrot, minced

1 stalk celery, minced

3 tablespoons minced fresh spinach

¼ cup minced broccoli

1. Thoroughly mix all ingredients in a 2-quart slow cooker. Cook on low for 2 hours. Stir before serving.

SUMMER FRUIT DIP

Kiwi, strawberries, star fruit, banana, and citrus are all excellent dipping choices for this fruity dip, which is also delicious served cold.

Serves 20

INGREDIENTS:

½ cup raspberry purée

8 ounces reduced-fat cream cheese, at room temperature

1 tablespoon sugar

¾ cup reduced-fat sour cream

1 teaspoon vanilla

1. In a small bowl, whisk together all ingredients. Pour into a 2-quart slow cooker. Cook on low for 1 hour. Stir before serving.

SUN-DRIED TOMATO AND PESTO DIP

Tart, rich sun-dried tomatoes are the perfect partner for a fresh-tasting pesto in this creamy dip.

Serves 20

INGREDIENTS:

2 cloves garlic

1 tablespoon reduced-fat mayonnaise

¾ ounce fresh basil

1 teaspoon toasted pine nuts

¼ teaspoon white pepper

¼ cup julienne-cut dry (not oil-packed) sun-dried tomatoes

8 ounces reduced-fat cream cheese or Neufchâtel, at room temperature

1. Place the garlic, mayonnaise, basil, pine nuts, and pepper in a food processor. Pulse until a fairly smooth paste forms. Add the sun-dried tomatoes and pulse 4–5 times. Add the cream cheese and pulse until smooth.

2. Scrape into a 2-quart slow cooker. Cook on low for 1 hour. Stir before serving.

How to Toast Pine Nuts

Preheat the oven to 350°F. Place the pine nuts on a cookie sheet or cake pan. Roast for 5–8 minutes in the oven. Pine nuts will be slightly browned and fragrant when fully toasted. Cool before using.

MIXED SEAFOOD DIP

Many stores carry frozen mixes of cooked seafood like shrimp, scallops, squid, and clams. Defrost overnight in the refrigerator before using.

Serves 12

INGREDIENTS:

8 ounces reduced-fat cream cheese

½ cup reduced-fat sour cream

½ cup diced green onion

⅔ cup minced cooked mixed seafood

1 tablespoon tarragon vinegar

1 tablespoon minced parsley

1 teaspoon dried chopped onion

⅛ teaspoon celery seed

1. In a medium bowl, stir together all ingredients. Scrape into a 2-quart slow cooker. Cook on low for 1 hour or until heated through.

2. Stir before serving.

Little Dipper

Slice a baguette into ⅛"-thick slices. Brush lightly with olive oil and sprinkle with dried tarragon and rosemary. Bake at 350°F for 10 minutes or until crisp.

FIG AND GINGER SPREAD

This rich-tasting spread is great swirled into Greek yogurt or spread on whole-wheat English muffins.

Serves 25

INGREDIENTS:

2 pounds fresh figs

2 tablespoons minced fresh ginger

2 tablespoons lime juice

½ cup water

¾ cup sugar

1. Place all ingredients in a 2-quart slow cooker. Stir. Cook on low for 2–3 hours. Remove the lid and cook an additional 2–3 hours until the mixture is thickened.

2. Pour into airtight containers and refrigerate up to 6 weeks.

APPLE AND PEAR SPREAD

Make the most of in-season apples and pears in this easy alternative to apple or pear butter.

Yields 3 quarts

INGREDIENTS:

4 Winesap apples, cored and sliced

4 Bartlett pears, cored and sliced

1 cup water or pear cider

¼ cup brown sugar

¼ cup sugar

¼ teaspoon ginger

¼ teaspoon cinnamon

¼ teaspoon nutmeg

¼ teaspoon allspice

1. Place all ingredients into a 4-quart slow cooker. Cook on low for 10–12 hours.

2. Uncover and cook on low for an additional 10–12 hours or until thick and most of the liquid has evaporated.

3. Allow to cool completely then pour into the food processor and purée. Pour into clean glass jars. Refrigerate up to 6 weeks.

Do-It-Yourself Brown Sugar

Brown sugar is simply white sugar that has been mixed with molasses. Make brown sugar by combining 1 cup granulated sugar with ¼ cup molasses. Store in an airtight container.

CREAMY PECAN BEEF DIP

Try this with thin slices of French baguettes to make tiny sandwiches. Provide plenty of bread—these will go quickly!

Serves 6

INGREDIENTS:

3 ounces sliced smoked beef

2 tablespoons finely chopped onion

½ cup finely chopped pecans

2 tablespoons minced green pepper

8 ounces cream cheese

½ cup sour cream

2 tablespoons milk

⅛ teaspoon white pepper

1. Finely shred the smoked beef.

2. Combine all ingredients in the slow cooker.

3. Cover and heat on a low setting for 2–3 hours or until dip bubbles at edges. Do not overheat.

TANGY CRAB DIP

For a little extra kick, add more horseradish than this recipe calls for. If you're really adventurous, try doubling the horseradish measurement.

Serves 6

INGREDIENTS:

6 ounces crabmeat

8 ounces cream cheese

1 tablespoon milk

½ teaspoon horseradish

¼ teaspoon salt

¼ teaspoon pepper

¼ cup toasted almonds

1. Shred the crabmeat. Cut the cream cheese into cubes. Combine all ingredients except almonds in the slow cooker.

2. Cover and heat on a low setting for 2–3 hours.

3. Before serving, sprinkle the dip with the almonds as a garnish.

Leftovers to Go

Spread the wealth. Set out "to go" containers for your guests and they'll help take care of those pesky leftovers. And take notice of which foods they bring home—these are the dishes they *really* enjoyed.

PEPPY CHEDDAR DIP

Try this with other cheeses or different dried meats such as prosciutto. Provide halved or whole red cherry tomatoes as a garnish.

Serves 16

INGREDIENTS:

1 pound mozzarella cheese

1 pound Cheddar cheese

¼ cup green chilies

½ pound pepperoni

½ cup black olives

2 cups mayonnaise

1. Dice or shred the cheese, and finely mince the chilies.

2. Slice the pepperoni, then cut it into strips. Pit and dice the olives.

3. Combine all the ingredients in the slow cooker.

4. Cover and heat on a low setting for 2–3 hours, or until all the cheese is melted and the mixture is bubbling.

CREAMED CHEESE BEEF DIP

Use real Parmesan cheese, chipped from a block, for this dish. It's the little things that make the difference your guests will sense!

Serves 8

INGREDIENTS:

1 onion

1 clove garlic

1 pound ground beef

1 cup tomato sauce

¼ cup ketchup

1 teaspoon oregano

1 teaspoon sugar

½ pound cream cheese

¼ pound Parmesan cheese

1. Chop the onion and finely mince the garlic.

2. Sauté the beef with onion and garlic in a pan over medium heat until the meat is browned.

3. Add the tomato sauce and ketchup to the meat mixture. Simmer 5 minutes, then collect surface fat with a spoon and discard.

4. Combine the meat mixture with oregano, sugar, and cheeses in the slow cooker.

5. Cover and heat on a low setting for 2–3 hours.

CHAPTER 4

SAUCES AND CONDIMENTS

VODKA CREAM SAUCE

If you prefer not to use vodka in this recipe, you can skip Step 1 and use ½ cup tomato sauce instead.

Yield: About 3½ cups

INGREDIENTS:

1 cup vodka

2 tablespoons olive oil

2 medium shallots, peeled and minced

3 cloves of garlic, peeled and minced

2 (28-ounce) cans crushed tomatoes in purée

1 teaspoon dried oregano

1 teaspoon sugar

Salt and freshly ground pepper, to taste

2 cups heavy cream

1. Add the vodka to the slow cooker. Cook uncovered on high for 1 hour or until reduced by half.

2. Add the olive oil and minced shallots to a microwave-safe bowl. Cover and microwave on high for 1 minute. Uncover and stir in the garlic. Cover and microwave on high for 30 seconds. Add to the slow cooker along with the tomatoes, oregano, sugar, salt, and pepper. Stir to combine. Cover and cook on low for 10–12 hours.

3. Shortly before serving, stir the cream into the sauce. Cook uncovered on low until heated through. Taste for seasoning and, if necessary, add additional oregano, sugar, salt, and pepper if needed.

4. Any leftover sauce can be refrigerated in a covered container or frozen.

Serving Suggestion for Vodka Cream Sauce

Serve Vodka Cream Sauce over cooked penne pasta or fried eggplant. Top with freshly grated cheese if desired.

HOT PICKLED VEGETABLES

You can adjust the vegetables that you use according to your tastes. Chop the vegetables and add some to give some kick to meatloaf or crab cakes. Dress with extra-virgin olive oil and serve antipasto-style or serve as a condiment for Mexican or Italian sandwiches.

Yield: About 4 quarts

INGREDIENTS:

4 cups baby carrots

1 (7-ounce) jar of whole jalapeño peppers, undrained

1 large sweet onion, peeled and sliced

1 tablespoon vegetable oil

½ cup white wine vinegar

Salt and freshly ground black pepper, to taste

2 cups frozen green beans, thawed

1 cup frozen corn, thawed

1 cup frozen baby peas, thawed

1. Cut the baby carrots in half and add to the slow cooker along with the jar of jalapeño peppers, onion, oil, vinegar, and salt and pepper. Cook on low for 2 hours or until the carrots are crisp-tender.

2. Uncover and stir in the green beans, corn, and baby peas. Transfer to glass jars and allow to come to room temperature before storing in the refrigerator. Chill before serving.

Mild Pickled Vegetables

Substitute a jar of roasted red peppers for the jalapeño peppers. Chop the red peppers into bite-sized pieces and add them along with the juice from the jar to the slow cooker.

SWEET PICKLED VEGETABLES

You can substitute 2 cups of (white) cane sugar or 1½ cups of cane sugar and ½ cup light brown sugar for the Sucanat. Chopped sweet pickled vegetables are a delicious addition to salmon patties or chicken salad.

Yield: About 3 quarts

INGREDIENTS:

2 teaspoons sea salt

2 cups Sucanat or raw pure cane sugar

1½ teaspoons cracked or freshly ground black pepper

½ teaspoon celery seed

1½ cups organic cider vinegar

1 (1-pound) bag of baby carrots

1 large sweet onion, peeled and diced

1 green bell pepper, cleaned and diced

1 yellow bell pepper, cleaned and diced

1 red bell pepper, cleaned and diced

2 stalks celery, finely diced

1 cup frozen corn, thawed

1 cup frozen green beans, thawed

1. Add the salt, Sucanat or sugar, pepper, celery seed, and cider vinegar to the slow cooker. Cover and, stirring every 15 minutes, cook on high for an hour or until the sugar is dissolved.

2. Cut the baby carrots into four pieces each and add to the slow cooker. Cover, reduce the heat to low, and cook for 1 hour or until the carrots are crisp-tender.

3. Add the onion; green, yellow, and red peppers; celery; corn; and green beans to the slow cooker. Stir to combine with the carrots.

4. Transfer to glass jars and allow to come to room temperature before storing in the refrigerator. Chill before serving. Can be stored in the refrigerator for several weeks if the vegetables are completely submerged in the sweet vinegar.

Sweet Pickled Beets and Vegetables

Substitute 1 or 2 (11- to 16-ounce) cans of drained sliced beets for an equal amount of the diced peppers, corn, or green beans called for in the Sweet Pickled Vegetables recipe.

PLUM SAUCE

Plum sauce is often served with egg rolls. It's also delicious if you brush it on chicken or pork ribs; doing so near the end of the grilling time will add a succulent glaze to the grilled meat.

Yield: 4 cups

INGREDIENTS:

8 cups (about 3 pounds) plums, pitted and cut in half

1 small sweet onion, peeled and diced

1 cup water

1 teaspoon fresh ginger, peeled and minced

1 clove of garlic, peeled and minced

¾ cup granulated sugar

½ cup rice vinegar or cider vinegar

1 teaspoon ground coriander

½ teaspoon salt

½ teaspoon cinnamon

¼ teaspoon cayenne pepper

¼ teaspoon ground cloves

1. Add the plums, onion, water, ginger, and garlic to the slow cooker; cover and, stirring occasionally, cook on low for 4 hours or until plums and onions are tender.

2. Use an immersion blender to pulverize the contents of the slow cooker before straining it or press the cooked plum mixture through a sieve.

3. Return the liquefied and strained plum mixture to the slow cooker and stir in sugar, vinegar, coriander, salt, cinnamon, cayenne pepper, and cloves. Cover and, stirring occasionally, cook on low for 2 hours or until the sauce reaches the consistency of applesauce.

PEACH MARMALADE

As you'd expect, you can spread this on toast. It can also be used to turn an ordinary cracker into a delicious snack.

Yield: About 8 cups

INGREDIENTS:

2 pounds peaches, peeled and chopped

½ cup (about 6 ounces) dried apricots, chopped

1 (20-ounce) can pineapple tidbits, in unsweetened juice

2 medium oranges

1 small lemon

2½ cups granulated cane sugar

2 (3-inch) sticks cinnamon

1. Peel, pit, and chop the peaches and add to a food processor along with the apricots and can of pineapple tidbits and juice.

2. Remove the zest from the oranges and lemon; add to food processor or blender. Peel the oranges and lemon. Cut into quarters and remove any seeds; add to the food processor or blender. Pulse until entire fruit mixture is pulverized. Pour into the slow cooker.

3. Add the sugar to the slow cooker and stir to combine with the fruit mixture. Add the cinnamon sticks. Cover and, stirring occasionally, cook on low for 4 hours or until the mixture reaches the consistency of applesauce.

4. Unless you process and seal the marmalade in sterilized jars, store in covered glass jars in the refrigerator.

Innovative Peach Marmalade Uses

By keeping this marmalade the consistency of applesauce you have the added versatility of using it as a condiment to top cooked chicken breasts, easily mix it together with barbecue or chili sauce to create a sweet and spicy dipping sauce, or use it to replace applesauce in many recipes.

CRANBERRY SAUCE

Serve this warm cranberry sauce directly from the slow cooker at your next holiday buffet. You can make it several days in advance, store it in the refrigerator, and then bring it back to temperature in the slow cooker. Or pour it into a mold and refrigerate until ready to remove it from the mold and serve it chilled.

Serves 10

INGREDIENTS:

2 (12-ounce) bags fresh cranberries

2 cups sugar

2 tablespoons frozen orange juice concentrate

Pinch salt

Optional: Cinnamon and ground cloves, to taste

1. Rinse and drain the cranberries. Remove and discard any stems or blemished cranberries.

2. Add the cranberries to the slow cooker along with the sugar, orange juice concentrate, and salt. Stir to combine, adding the cinnamon and cloves if using. Cover and cook on low for 4 hours.

3. Remove the cover. Stir well, breaking the cranberries apart with a spoon or mashing them slightly with a potato masher. Taste for seasoning and adjust if necessary.

4. Cover and cook on low for another hour or until the cranberries are cooked through and soft and the sugar is completely dissolved.

5. If storing the cranberry sauce in a mold, allow it to cool to room temperature before pouring it into the mold and refrigerating.

In the Spirits Cranberry Sauce

For additional flavor, stir in a couple of tablespoons of orange liqueur, bourbon, or brandy if desired.

HOMEMADE KETCHUP

If you like zesty ketchup, you can add crushed red peppers, Mrs. Dash Extra Spicy Seasoning Blend, or salt-free chili powder along with, or instead of, the cinnamon and other seasonings. Another alternative is to use hot paprika rather than sweet paprika.

Serves 32

INGREDIENTS:

1 (15-ounce) can no-salt-added tomato sauce

2 teaspoons water

½ teaspoon onion powder

½ cup sugar

⅓ cup cider vinegar

¼ teaspoon sea salt

¼ teaspoon ground cinnamon

⅛ teaspoon ground cloves

Pinch ground allspice

Pinch nutmeg

Pinch freshly ground pepper

⅔ teaspoon sweet paprika

1. Add all ingredients to the slow cooker. Cover and, stirring occasionally, cook for 2–4 hours or until ketchup reaches desired consistency.

2. Turn off the slow cooker or remove the crock from the slow cooker and stir in the paprika. Allow mixture to cool, then put in a covered container (such as a recycled ketchup bottle). Store in the refrigerator until needed.

EASY APPLESAUCE

Homemade applesauce is easy to make and tastes so much better than what you can get in the store. Choose the apples according to your preference. Combine varieties if you want. It freezes well, too, so you can make extra when apples are in season.

Yield: About 4 cups

INGREDIENTS:

10 medium apples

2 tablespoons fresh lemon juice

2 tablespoons water

Optional: 6-inch cinnamon stick

Optional: Sugar, to taste

1. Peel, core, and slice the apples. Add to the slow cooker along with the lemon juice, water, and cinnamon stick if using; stir to mix.

2. Cover and cook on low for 5 hours or until the apples are soft and tender. For chunky applesauce, mash the apples with a potato masher. For smooth applesauce, purée in a food processor or blender, use an immersion blender, or press through a food mill or large mesh strainer. While applesauce is still warm, add sugar to taste if desired. Store covered in the refrigerator for up to 2 weeks or freeze.

TRADITIONAL APPLE BUTTER

To ensure that the peels haven't been waxed, buy your apples directly from an orchard or at a farmers' market. (The natural pectin in the peels helps thicken the butter.) Don't forget to pick up some freshly pressed cider while you're there.

Yield: About 3 cups

INGREDIENTS:

4 pounds (Jonathan, MacIntosh, or Rome) apples

1 lemon

1⅓ cups light brown sugar, packed

1 cup apple cider

Optional: 6-inch cinnamon stick

1. Core and quarter the apples. Add to the slow cooker. Stir in the zest and juice from the lemon, brown sugar, and cider. Add the cinnamon stick if using. Cover and cook on low for 10 hours or until the apples are soft and tender.

2. Uncover and, stirring occasionally, cook on high for an additional 8–10 hours or until the mixture has reduced to about 3 cups.

3. If used, remove and discard the cinnamon stick. Use a spatula to press the apple butter through a large mesh strainer to remove the peel. Ladle the warm apple butter into hot sterilized jars. Screw two-piece lids onto the jars. Allow to stand at room temperature for 8 hours; refrigerate for up to 6 months.

TRADITIONAL BARBECUE SAUCE

Use this sauce as you'd use any barbecue sauce, as a serving sauce served on the side, or as a dipping sauce. Most barbecue seasoning mixes contain salt, so salt isn't added to this recipe.

Yield: About 2½ cups

INGREDIENTS:

2 cups ketchup

¼ cup apple cider vinegar

¼ cup Worcestershire sauce

¼ cup light brown sugar, firmly packed

2 tablespoons molasses

2 tablespoons prepared mustard

1 tablespoon barbecue seasoning

½ teaspoon freshly ground black pepper

Optional: 2 teaspoons liquid smoke

Optional: 1 tablespoon hot sauce, or to taste

1. Add all ingredients to the slow cooker. Stir to mix. Cover and, stirring every 15 minutes, cook on high for 1 hour or until the mixture reaches a simmer. Reduce the heat to low and, continuing to stir every 15 minutes, cook uncovered 1 hour or until the sauce has reached desired thickness. Ladle into glass jars; cover and store in the refrigerator for up to 3 months.

Customizing Barbecue Sauce

You can change up the flavor of Traditional Barbecue Sauce by using a mix of prepared (yellow) mustard and Dijon or stone-ground mustard, adding red pepper flakes or some Mrs. Dash (Extra Spicy or Southwest Chipotle) seasoning, or substituting lemon juice for the vinegar.

BLACKBERRY BARBECUE SAUCE

A red wine with distinct berry aroma like Pinot Noir works best in this recipe. The sauce complements chicken, duck, or game hen.

Yield: About 2 cups

INGREDIENTS:

1 tablespoon vegetable oil

1 small sweet onion, peeled and diced

2 cloves of garlic, peeled and minced

¼ cup red wine

¼ cup apple cider vinegar

2½ pounds blackberries

¼ cup light brown sugar, packed

1 tablespoon Worcestershire sauce

1 lemon

Pinch salt

Pinch red pepper flakes

1. Add the oil and onion to a microwave-safe bowl. Cover and microwave on high for 1 minute or until the onion is transparent.

2. Stir in the garlic; cover and microwave on high for 30 seconds.

3. Add the onion-garlic mixture to the slow cooker along with the wine, vinegar, blackberries, brown sugar, Worcestershire sauce, grated zest from the lemon, salt, and red pepper flakes. Stir to combine. Cover and cook on low for 8 hours or until thickened.

4. Stir in the lemon juice. Strain through a mesh strainer if desired. Can be refrigerated in covered containers for up to 2 weeks.

Change Things Up

Make a meatloaf using ground chicken or turkey, and instead of adding and glazing the meatloaf with ketchup, use Blackberry Barbecue Sauce instead.

WINE VINEGAR–BASED BARBECUE SAUCE

This sauce is thinner and more like a mop sauce than a traditional thick barbecue sauce. You can use it as a basting sauce for grilled tender cuts of meat. It's even good mixed into a glass of tomato juice or tomato soup.

Yield: About 3 quarts

INGREDIENTS:

½ cup brown sugar

½ cup Worcestershire sauce

½ cup Dijon mustard

1⅓ cup ketchup

⅛ cup freshly ground black pepper

1 tablespoon red pepper flakes, or to taste

1 quart (4 cups) red wine vinegar

2⅔ cups water

1⅓ cups white wine

Salt, to taste

1. Add all of the ingredients to the slow cooker. Stir to mix. Cover and, stirring every 15 minutes, cook on high for 1 hour or until the mixture has come to a simmer. Reduce heat to low and cook covered for an additional hour. Ladle cooled sauce into glass jars, cover, and store in the refrigerator. Keeps for 6 months or longer.

Pulled Venison

Wine Vinegar–Based Barbecue Sauce is perfect for wild game. To remove any gamy taste, add a 4-pound venison roast to the slow cooker. Add enough water to cover the roast and ⅓ to 1 cup of cider vinegar; cook on low overnight. The next morning, pour off and discard that water and replace it with Wine Vinegar–Based Barbecue Sauce. Cover and cook on low for 4 hours or until the meat is tender and pulls apart.

RED COUNTY BARBECUE SAUCE

This sauce stores well, so take advantage. Make some extra and refrigerate or freeze it, to reheat later as needed.

Yields about 4 cups

INGREDIENTS:

2 yellow onions

¼ cup oil

6 tomatoes

1 cup ketchup

1 teaspoon salt

1 teaspoon celery seed

¼ cup brown sugar

¼ cup Worcestershire sauce

½ cup vinegar

1. Coarsely chop the onions. Sauté the onion in oil in a pan over medium heat until browned.

2. Cube the tomatoes. Combine the tomatoes and onion with the other ingredients in the slow cooker.

3. Cover and heat on a low setting for 3–4 hours.

Serving Sizes

A good party strategy is to keep the bowls and plates small. This will give guests more reason to move around the party and mingle with different people, while having the chance to try all of your different foods a little at a time.

SMOKY BARBECUE SAUCE

Marjoram and liquid smoke can be found in the spice sections of most grocery stores. Marjoram is also available fresh in some stores, in the produce section.

Yields about 2½ cups

INGREDIENTS:

2 cloves garlic

2 onions

¼ cup oil

½ cup tomato paste

½ teaspoon salt

¼ teaspoon dry mustard

¼ teaspoon ginger

¼ teaspoon marjoram

¼ teaspoon seasoning salt

½ teaspoon rosemary

½ teaspoon oregano

1 tablespoon Worcestershire sauce

¼ teaspoon soy sauce

½ teaspoon A.1. sauce

¼ teaspoon Tabasco sauce

¼ teaspoon liquid smoke

½ cup vinegar

1 cup red wine

½ cup water

1. Crush and slice the garlic; finely chop the onions. Sauté the garlic and onions in oil in a pan over low heat until soft.

2. Add the garlic and onion, tomato paste, salt, spices, sauces, liquid smoke, vinegar, wine, and water to the slow cooker.

3. Cover and heat on a low setting for 2–3 hours.

MARINARA SAUCE

You can serve Marinara Sauce separately or toss it with the pasta before bringing it to the table. Serve pasta along with a tossed salad, garlic bread, cooked meatballs, or Italian sausage, and have lots of freshly ground Parmesan-Reggiano cheese and a pepper grinder available.

Yield: Sauce for 2 pounds of pasta

INGREDIENTS:

2 tablespoons extra-virgin olive oil

2 medium onions, peeled and diced

4 cloves garlic, peeled and minced

1½ teaspoons dried oregano

⅛ teaspoon red pepper flakes

1 (6-ounce) can tomato paste

1 cup dry red wine

4 (28-ounce) cans crushed tomatoes with basil

½ cup (1 ounce) freshly grated Parmesan-Reggiano cheese

Optional: ¼ cup fresh basil, minced

Sea salt, to taste

1½ teaspoons sugar

1. Add the oil and onions to the slow cooker. Cover and, stirring occasionally, cook on high for 30–45 minutes or until onions are golden brown. Stir in the garlic, oregano, red pepper flakes, and tomato paste. Cover and cook on high for 15 minutes.

2. Stir in the wine and undrained tomatoes. Cover and cook on low for 4 hours or until sauce is no longer watery. Stir in the cheese, additional basil if using, salt, and sugar. Taste for seasoning and adjust if necessary.

CREAMY PARMESAN FONDUE

Use this either as a sauce or a fondue. You can spoon it over pasta, vegetables, or meats, or use it for dipping.

Yields about 5 cups

INGREDIENTS:

1 pound cream cheese

2 cups milk

2 cloves garlic

¼ onion

½ pound Parmesan cheese

½ teaspoon salt

½ teaspoon pepper

1. Cut the cream cheese into cubes and place in the slow cooker.

2. Cover and heat on a low setting for 1 hour or until the cream cheese is melted. Stir in the milk until blended.

3. Mince the garlic. Finely slice the onion. Grate the Parmesan cheese. Add the garlic, onion, Parmesan, salt, and pepper to slow cooker.

4. Cover and heat on a low setting for 2–3 hours.

REGAL CAPER SAUCE

This savory sauce is excellent on rabbit, fish, or other delicately flavored meats. Use the stock that corresponds with the meat you choose.

Yields about 3 cups

INGREDIENTS:

2 tablespoons butter

2 tablespoons flour

3 cups stock

½ teaspoon salt

½ teaspoon black peppercorns

1 egg yolk

1 tablespoon butter

6 tablespoons capers

1. Melt the butter in a saucepan over medium heat and mix in the flour, stirring until the flour is well mixed and slightly browned. Add one cup of the stock and mix well, then transfer to the slow cooker.

2. Add salt and peppercorns. Cover and heat on a low setting for 1–2 hours.

3. Half an hour before serving, skim with a strainer. Stir in the yolk and butter, then add the capers.

BOLOGNAISE SAUCE

Also called Bolognese or ragù alla Bolognese, this sauce combines vegetables and meat to create the perfect sauce for pouring over spaghetti.

Serves 6

INGREDIENTS:

2 teaspoons olive oil

½ pound 94% lean ground beef

½ pound ground pork

1 onion, minced

1 carrot, minced

1 stalk celery, minced

3 ounces tomato paste

28 ounces canned diced tomato

½ cup fat-free evaporated milk

¼ teaspoon ground black pepper

¼ teaspoon salt

⅛ teaspoon nutmeg

1. Heat the oil in a nonstick pan. Brown the ground beef and pork. Drain off any excess fat.

2. Add the meats and remaining ingredients to a 4-quart slow cooker. Cook on low for 8–10 hours. Stir before serving.

JALAPEÑO-TOMATILLO SAUCE

Serve this sauce over rice or in burritos or tacos.

Serves 4

INGREDIENTS:

1 teaspoon canola oil

2 cloves garlic, minced

1 onion, sliced

7 tomatillos, large dice

2 jalapeños, minced

½ cup water

1. Heat the oil in a nonstick pan. Sauté the garlic, onion, tomatillos, and jalapeños until softened.

2. Place the mixture into a 4-quart slow cooker. Add the water and stir. Cook on low for 8 hours.

LEMON DILL SAUCE

Serve this sauce over salmon, asparagus, potatoes, or chicken.

Serves 4

INGREDIENTS:

2 cups Chicken Broth (Chapter 19)

½ cup lemon juice

½ cup chopped fresh dill

¼ teaspoon white pepper

1. Place all ingredients into a 2- or 4-quart slow cooker. Cook on high, uncovered, for 3 hours or until the sauce reduces by one-third.

A Peek at Peppercorns

Black peppercorns are the mature fruit of the black pepper plant, which grows in tropical areas. Green peppercorns are the immature fruit of the pepper plant. White peppercorns are mature black peppercorns with the black husks removed. Pink peppercorns are the dried berries of the Brazilian pepper.

PART II
ENTRÉES

CHAPTER 5

BREAKFAST AND BRUNCH

RECIPE LIST

CRUSTLESS QUICHE LORRAINE

Ham is often already salty, so take that into consideration when deciding how much salt you add to the egg mixture.

Serves 4

INGREDIENTS:

Nonstick spray

4 slices toast

4 teaspoons butter

2 cups Swiss cheese, grated

½ pound cooked ham, cut into cubes

6 large eggs

1 tablespoon mayonnaise

½ teaspoon Dijon mustard

1 cup heavy cream

Optional: Salt and freshly ground pepper to taste

Optional: Dash of cayenne pepper

1. Spray the crock of the slow cooker with nonstick spray. If desired, remove the crusts from the toast. Butter each slice with 1 teaspoon of butter, tear the toast into pieces, and arrange the toast pieces butter side down in the slow cooker.

2. Spread half of the cheese over the toast pieces, and then spread the ham over the cheese, and top the ham layer with the remaining cheese.

3. In a bowl, beat the eggs together with the mayonnaise, mustard, and cream, and salt, pepper, and cayenne pepper if using. Pour the egg mixture into the slow cooker. Cover and cook on high for 2 hours or until the eggs are set.

Or, Try a Biscuit Crust Instead

Rather than using toast to create the crust for this quiche, instead melt the butter and toss it together with 4 small, crumbled buttermilk biscuits. Arrange the buttered buttermilk biscuit crumbs over the bottom of the slow cooker and then complete the recipe as described in Steps 2 and 3.

BRUNCH CASSEROLE

You can substitute Worcestershire sauce for the steak sauce if you prefer. Because of the usually high sodium content in canned soup, this recipe doesn't call for added salt. Country hash browns are blended with onion and red and green bell peppers.

Serves 8

INGREDIENTS:

2 (7-ounce) packages brown-and-serve sausage links

Nonstick spray

1 (10¾-ounce) can condensed cream of potato soup

⅔ cup milk

2 teaspoons steak sauce

¼ teaspoon freshly ground black pepper

1 (28-ounce) package frozen country hash browns, thawed

1 (9½-ounce) package frozen vegetables in cheese sauce, thawed

2 ounces (½ cup) Cheddar cheese, grated

1. Brown the sausage links according to package directions. Cut into ½-inch pieces.

2. Treat the crock of the slow cooker with nonstick spray. Add the sausage, soup, milk, steak sauce, pepper, hash browns, and vegetables; stir to combine. Cover and cook for 6 hours on low.

3. Turn the cooker to warm. About 45 minutes before you'll be serving the casserole, sprinkle the Cheddar cheese over the cooked mixture in the slow cooker. After 30 minutes, uncover the casserole and let stand for 15 minutes before serving.

Vegetables in Cheese Sauce

Choose the frozen vegetables you use in the Brunch Casserole according to your tastes. A broccoli and cauliflower blend is good, as is the California Blend from Birds Eye that includes carrots.

EGGS FLORENTINE

Freshly ground black pepper goes well in this dish. You can use up to a teaspoon in the recipe. If you prefer to go lighter on the seasoning to accommodate individual tastes, be sure to have a pepper grinder at the table for those who want to add more.

Serves 4

INGREDIENTS:

Nonstick spray

9 ounces (2 cups) Cheddar cheese, grated

1 (10-ounce) package frozen spinach, thawed

1 (8-ounce) can sliced mushrooms, drained

1 small onion, peeled and diced

6 large eggs

1 cup heavy cream

½ teaspoon Italian seasoning

½ teaspoon garlic powder

Freshly ground black pepper, to taste

1. Treat the crock of the slow cooker with nonstick spray. Spread 1 cup of the grated Cheddar over the bottom of the slow cooker. Drain the spinach and squeeze out any excess moisture; add in a layer on top of the cheese. Next add the drained mushrooms in a layer and then top them with the onion.

2. Beat together the eggs, cream, Italian seasoning, garlic powder, and pepper in a bowl or measuring cup. Pour over the layers in the slow cooker. Top with the remaining cup of Cheddar cheese.

3. Cover and cook on high for 2 hours or until eggs are set.

BREAKFAST WELSH RAREBIT

Think of this as a German-style Eggs Benedict. If you're serving it for brunch, when you make the Welsh Rarebit you can substitute beer for the milk.

Serves 4

INGREDIENTS:

1 tablespoon butter, melted

Pinch cayenne pepper or hot sauce to taste

1 teaspoon Worcestershire sauce

1 cup whole milk

2 teaspoons cornstarch

1 teaspoon dry mustard

1 pound (4 cups) medium or sharp Cheddar cheese, grated

4 (thick) slices bread or English muffins, toasted

4 tomato slices

8 strips bacon, cooked and drained

4 poached or fried eggs

1. Add the butter to the slow cooker and stir in the cayenne pepper or hot sauce and Worcestershire sauce. Cover and cook on high for 15 minutes. Uncover, stir in the milk, and when the milk begins to bubble around the edges of the crock (reaches a simmer), lower the heat setting to low. (You must melt the cheese over a low temperature to prevent the cheese from separating into a greasy mess.)

2. Sift the cornstarch and dry mustard to remove any lumps; toss together with the grated cheese. Add the cornstarch- and mustard-coated cheese to the milk mixture. Cook uncovered, stirring occasionally, for 1 hour or until the cheese is melted.

3. Place the toast on individual plates; evenly ladle Breakfast Welsh Rarebit over the top of each slice.

4. Top each slice of toast with a tomato slice, criss-crossed bacon slices, and an egg. Top with more Breakfast Welsh Rarebit.

Luncheon Welsh Rarebit

Sauté a chopped, small onion and 8 ounces mushroom slices in butter, and stir into the Welsh Rarebit along with a 10½-ounce can of condensed cream of tomato soup; bring to temperature. To serve, arrange slices of hard-boiled egg over toast slices and top with a generous helping of the Luncheon Welsh Rarebit.

BACON AND BROCCOLI CRUSTLESS QUICHE

This recipe requires a heatproof 1½- to 2-quart casserole dish that can rest on the cooking rack in your slow cooker.

Serves 6

INGREDIENTS:

Nonstick spray

2 cups frozen broccoli cuts, thawed

8 ounces (2 cups) Colby cheese, grated

6 slices bacon, cooked

4 large eggs

2 cups whole milk

Salt and freshly ground black pepper, to taste

½ teaspoon Dijon mustard

1 tablespoon mayonnaise

Water

1. Treat the casserole dish with nonstick spray. Arrange the broccoli cuts over the bottom of the dish, and top them with the grated cheese. Cut the bacon into pieces and sprinkle them evenly over the top of the cheese.

2. Add the eggs to a bowl or large measuring cup. Lightly beat the eggs and then stir in the milk, salt, pepper, mustard, and mayonnaise. Pour over the broccoli mixture in the casserole dish.

3. Place the casserole dish onto the cooking rack in the slow cooker. Pour water into the slow cooker so that it comes up and over the cooking rack and about an inch up the sides of the casserole dish. Cover and cook on low for 4 hours.

4. Turn off the slow cooker. Uncover and allow to cool enough to allow you to lift the casserole dish out of the cooker. Cut the crustless quiche into six wedges. Serve warm or at room temperature.

COTTAGE CHEESE CASSEROLE

This recipe is good made with Birds Eye Steamfresh asparagus, gold and white corn, and baby carrots vegetable blend. If you use a vegetable mixture without corn, omit the masa harina or cornmeal and use another ¼ cup of flour instead.

Serves 4

INGREDIENTS:

Nonstick spray

4 large eggs

1 cup cottage cheese

⅛ cup unbleached all-purpose flour

⅛ cup masa harina or fine cornmeal

Salt and freshly ground black pepper, to taste

¼ teaspoon baking powder

⅛ cup (2 tablespoons) melted butter

8 ounces (2 cups) Cheddar cheese, grated

1 cup frozen vegetable mix, thawed

Optional: Chopped red onion, shallots, or scallions to taste

Optional: 4 brown-and-serve sausage links, cut into pieces

1. Treat a heatproof 1½- to 2-quart casserole dish that can rest on the cooking rack in your slow cooker with nonstick spray.

2. Add the eggs and whisk until fluffy. Stir in the cottage cheese. Add the flour, masa harina or cornmeal, salt, baking powder, and butter, and mix well. Fold the cheese and the vegetables into the egg–cottage cheese mixture. Stir in the onion, shallots, or scallions, and sausage pieces if using.

3. Place the casserole dish onto the cooking rack in the slow cooker. Pour water into the slow cooker so that it comes up and over the cooking rack and about an inch up the sides of the casserole dish. Cover and cook on low for 4 hours.

4. Turn off the slow cooker. Uncover and allow to cool enough to allow you to lift the casserole dish out of the cooker. Cut the casserole into four pieces. Serve warm or at room temperature.

BANANA WALNUT FRITTATA

You can add another flavor dimension to this dish by sprinkling some cinnamon to taste over the banana layers. Another option is to serve it with blueberry or strawberry syrup.

Serves 6

INGREDIENTS:

1 tablespoon butter

1 (1-pound) loaf bread, cut into cubes

1 (8-ounce) package cream cheese

2 ripe bananas

1 cup walnuts, coarsely chopped

12 large eggs

¼ cup maple syrup

1 cup milk or heavy cream

¼ teaspoon salt

Optional: Additional maple syrup at serving

1. At least 12 hours before you plan to begin cooking the frittata, ready the crock in the slow cooker by coating the bottom and sides with the butter. Place ⅓ of the bread cubes (about 4 cups) in the bottom of the crock. Cut the cream cheese into very small cubes and evenly spread half of them over the bread cubes. Slice one of the bananas, arrange the slices over the cream cheese layer, and sprinkle half of the walnut pieces over the banana. Add another 4 cups of bread cubes and create another cream cheese, banana, and walnut layer over the top of the bread. Add the remaining 4 cups of bread cubes to the cooker. Press the mixture down slightly into the crock.

2. Add the eggs to a bowl; whisk until frothy. Whisk in the syrup, milk or cream, and salt. Pour over the bread in the crock. Cover and refrigerate for 12 hours.

3. Remove the crock from the refrigerator and place in the slow cooker. Cover and cook on low for 6 hours. Serve with warm maple syrup if desired.

Try Berries

You can substitute 1 cup of blueberries, raspberries, or blackberries for the bananas and use toasted pecans instead of walnuts, or omit the nuts entirely.

MAPLE SYRUP–INFUSED SLOW-COOKED OATMEAL

Feel free to substitute other dried fruit according to your tastes such as a tropical mix of coconut, papaya, pineapple, and mango or strawberries, and blueberries. It's even a way you can sneak some prunes into your diet.

Serves 8–10

INGREDIENTS:

2 cups steel-cut Irish oats

5 cups water

1 cup apple juice

½ cup dried apples

¼ cup golden raisins

¼ cup maple syrup

1 teaspoon ground cinnamon

½ teaspoon salt

Optional: Brown sugar or maple syrup

Optional: Chopped toasted walnuts or pecans

Optional: Milk, half and half, or heavy cream

1. Add the oats, water, apple juice, apples (cut with kitchen shears into small pieces), raisins, maple syrup, cinnamon, and salt to the slow cooker and stir to mix.

2. Cover and cook on the low-heat setting for 6–7 hours.

3. Serve the oatmeal warm topped with brown sugar or additional maple syrup; chopped nuts; and milk, half and half, or heavy cream.

Cooking Ahead

Once the oatmeal has cooled, divide any leftovers into single-serving containers and freeze. Later, transfer the frozen oatmeal to a microwave-safe container (or better yet: freeze it in a microwave-safe container and save yourself a step!) and put it in the microwave to defrost while you get ready to start your day. Cover the bowl with a piece of paper towel (to catch any splatters), then microwave on high for 1–2 minutes and enjoy!

SAUSAGE AND CHEESE CASSEROLE

Serve this casserole with toasted whole-grain bread spread with some honey-butter and you have a comfort-food breakfast feast.

Serves 8

INGREDIENTS:

1 tablespoon extra-virgin olive oil or vegetable oil

1 large onion, peeled and diced

1 green pepper, seeded and diced

1 pound ground sausage

4 cups frozen hash brown potatoes, thawed

Nonstick spray

8 large eggs

¼ cup water or heavy cream

Optional: A few drops hot sauce

Salt and freshly ground pepper, to taste

½ pound Cheddar cheese, grated

1. Preheat a deep 3½-quart nonstick sauté pan over medium-high heat and add the oil. Once the oil is heated, add the onion and pepper and sauté until the onion is transparent, or about 5 minutes. Add the sausage, browning (and crumbling) and cook for 5 minutes. Remove any excess fat, if necessary, by carefully dabbing the pan with a paper towel. Stir the hash browns into the sausage mixture, and then transfer the mixture to the slow cooker treated with nonstick spray.

2. Whisk together the eggs, water or heavy cream, hot sauce if using, and salt and pepper. Pour over the sausage–hash browns mixture in the slow cooker. Cover and cook on low for 4 hours.

3. Turn the cooker to warm. About 45 minutes before you'll be serving the casserole, sprinkle the Cheddar cheese over the cooked mixture in the slow cooker. After 30 minutes, uncover the casserole and let stand for 15 minutes before serving.

Feeding a Crowd

You can stretch this recipe to even more servings by increasing the amount of chopped peppers you sauté with the onion. In fact, a mixture of red, green, and yellow peppers makes for a delicious combo.

BACON AND EGG CASSEROLE

You can substitute 2 large peeled and diced potatoes for the hash browns if you prefer.

Serves 8

INGREDIENTS:

Nonstick spray

1 (1-pound) loaf bread

12 large eggs

1 cup milk or heavy cream

¼ teaspoon salt

1 pound bacon

1 medium onion, peeled and diced

2 cups frozen hash brown potatoes, thawed

Optional: ½ cup Cheddar cheese, grated

1. Ready the crock in the slow cooker by coating the bottom and sides with nonstick spray. Remove the crusts from the bread and cut the bread into cubes. Place ⅓ of the bread cubes (about 3 cups) in the bottom of the crock. Add the eggs to a bowl; whisk until frothy. Whisk in the milk or cream and salt. Pour ⅓ of the egg mixture over the bread in the crock.

2. Preheat a deep 3½-quart nonstick sauté pan over medium-high heat. Cut the bacon into pieces and add to the skillet. Once the bacon begins to render its fat, add the onion; sauté until the onion is transparent and the bacon is cooked through. Remove any excess fat, if necessary, by carefully dabbing the pan with a paper towel. Stir the hash browns into the sausage mixture.

3. Evenly spread half of the bacon mixture over the top of the bread cubes in the slow cooker. Pour half of the remaining egg mixture over the bacon mixture, add another 3 cups of bread cubes, and pour the remaining bacon mixture over the top of the bread. Add the remaining 3 cups of bread cubes to the cooker. Press the mixture down slightly into the crock. Pour the rest of the egg mixture over the top. Cover and cook on low for 6 hours.

4. If adding the cheese, turn the cooker to warm. About 45 minutes before you'll be serving the casserole, sprinkle the Cheddar cheese over the cooked mixture in the slow cooker. After 30 minutes, uncover the casserole and let stand for 15 minutes before serving.

BREAKFAST BUFFET TOMATO TOPPER

You can substitute Teleme goat cheese for the mozzarella. Zinfandel is a good choice for the wine.

Serves 12

INGREDIENTS:

2 tablespoons extra-virgin olive oil

2 large shallots, peeled and diced

1 (28-ounce) can crushed tomatoes with basil, undrained

¾ cup robust red wine

1 tablespoon orange zest, finely grated

1 tablespoon fresh Italian parsley, minced

1 tablespoon fresh basil, chopped

Salt and freshly ground black pepper, to taste

8 ounces fresh whole-milk mozzarella cheese

1. Add the oil and shallots to a microwave-safe bowl; cover and microwave on high for 1 minute; stir and repeat in 30-second increments until the shallots are soft and transparent. (You do not want them to brown.) Add to the slow cooker along with the tomatoes and wine. Cover and cook on high for 1 hour or until the mixture begins to bubble around the edges. If your slow cooker has a simmer setting, use that at this point. Otherwise, continue to cook uncovered, stirring occasionally, until the sauce is thickened.

2. Stir in the orange zest, parsley, basil, salt, and pepper. Reduce heat to low. Cut the cheese into small cubes and add it to the slow cooker, making sure it's completely covered with the tomato mixture. Cover and cook on low for 1 hour or until the cheese is melted. Stir well.

3. If serving as a sauce, have a ladle available alongside the slow cooker. If serving as a fondue, provide fondue forks and appropriately sized pieces of crusty baguettes.

Serving Breakfast Buffet Tomato Topper

For open-face brunch BLTs, top toast slices with grated lettuce and bacon; ladle the tomato topper over the top. Or you can ladle the sauce over toasted English muffin halves topped with scrambled, fried, or poached eggs. Serve crisp bacon slices, ham, Canadian bacon, or sausage links on the side or under the egg on top of the muffin.

SOUTHERN-STYLE GRITS

Serve with eggs and bacon for a classic Southern breakfast. Refrigerate leftovers in meal-sized portions and reheat them throughout the week.

Serves 12

INGREDIENTS:

1½ cups stone-ground grits

4¼ cups Chicken Broth (Chapter 19) or water

½ teaspoon ground black pepper

¼ teaspoon salt

¼ cup shredded reduced-fat sharp Cheddar

1. Add the grits, stock, pepper, and salt to a 4-quart slow cooker. Stir. Cook on low for 8 hours. Stir the cheese into the grits before serving.

SPINACH AND CANADIAN BACON BREAKFAST CASSEROLE

This casserole is more of a soufflé; the eggs puff up and the whole dish is delightfully light and fluffy. No one would guess how easy it is to make!

Serves 6

INGREDIENTS:

1 cup defrosted frozen spinach

1 teaspoon paprika

6 eggs

1½ cups fat-free evaporated milk

¼ cup diced green onion

1 cup shredded low-fat sharp Cheddar

4 ounces sliced Canadian bacon, diced

3 slices sandwich bread, cubed

1 cup sliced button or crimini mushrooms

1. Thoroughly squeeze out all water from the spinach. Spray a round 4-quart slow cooker with nonstick cooking spray. In a small bowl, whisk the paprika, eggs, evaporated milk, and green onion.

2. Sprinkle the bottom of the slow cooker with half of the cheese. Top with an even layer of spinach. Top that with a layer of half of the Canadian bacon. Add all of the bread cubes in one layer. Top with a layer of mushrooms, and then the remaining Canadian bacon. Sprinkle with the remaining cheese. Pour the egg mixture over the top and cover. Cook for 2 hours on high.

Canadian Bacon versus American Bacon

American bacon is made from smoked and cured pork belly. It is high in fat and is known in other countries as "streaky bacon." Canadian bacon, as used in the United States, refers to bacon made from the pork loin. It is much lower in fat than American-style bacon.

WHEAT BERRY BREAKFAST

Serve this as-is or with a sprinkling of brown sugar on top.

Serves 6

INGREDIENTS:

1 cup wheat berries

2½ cups water

¼ cup sweetened, dried cranberries

1. Add the wheat berries, water, and cranberries to a 2- or 4-quart slow cooker. Stir. Cook for 8–10 hours.

2. Stir before serving to distribute the cranberries evenly.

What Are Wheat Berries?

Wheat berries are the entire kernel of wheat. Often ground into flour to be used in baking, wheat berries can also be eaten whole. They have a nutty flavor and a slightly chewy texture.

HEARTY MULTIGRAIN CEREAL

Wake up to this high-fiber, satisfying breakfast!

Serves 6

INGREDIENTS:

¼ cup wheat berries

¼ cup long-grain rice

1 cup rolled or Irish-style oats

3½ cups water

1. Add the wheat berries, rice, oats, and water to a 2- or 4-quart slow cooker. Stir. Cook for 8–10 hours.

2. Stir before serving.

Sweet or Savory Breakfast

Oatmeal and other hot breakfast cereals can be served two ways. The most popular is sweetened with a bit of sugar or fruit. An equally tasty way to eat your morning grains is to serve them savory; top the cereal with a small pat of butter and a small sprinkle of salt.

SPINACH QUICHE

This is an easy but festive dish that would be a perfect addition to brunch.

Serves 6

INGREDIENTS:

1 teaspoon ground cayenne pepper

4 eggs

½ cup shredded low-fat sharp Cheddar

6 ounces baby spinach

1½ cups fat-free evaporated milk

¼ cup diced green onion

2 slices sandwich bread, cubed

1. Spray a round 4-quart slow cooker with nonstick cooking spray. In a small bowl, whisk the cayenne, eggs, cheese, spinach, evaporated milk, and green onions.

2. Add the bread cubes in one layer on the bottom of the slow cooker. Pour the egg mixture over the top and cover. Cook for 2–3 hours on high or until the edges begin to pull away from the sides of the insert. Slice and lift out each slice individually.

BREAKFAST BURRITO FILLING

Serve in a large tortilla with your favorite breakfast burrito toppings.

Serves 4

INGREDIENTS:

1¼ pounds lean boneless pork, cubed

12 ounces diced tomatoes with green chiles

1 small onion, diced

1 jalapeño, diced

½ teaspoon ground chipotle

¼ teaspoon cayenne pepper

¼ teaspoon ground jalapeño

2 cloves garlic, minced

1. Place all ingredients into a 2-quart slow cooker. Stir. Cook on low for 8 hours. Stir before serving.

HASH BROWNS

Also called home fries, this home-style dish will serve four as a main dish, or six if part of a hardy breakfast.

Serves 4

INGREDIENTS:

1 teaspoon canola oil

2 strips turkey bacon, diced

1 large onion, thinly sliced

1½ pounds red skin potatoes, thinly sliced

1. Heat oil in a nonstick skillet. Add bacon, onions, and potatoes. Sauté until just browned. The potatoes should not be fully cooked.

2. Add mixture to a 2- or 4-quart slow cooker. Cook on low for 3–4 hours or on high for 1½ hours.

PEAR OATMEAL

Cooking rolled oats overnight makes them so creamy they could be served as dessert. Cooking them with fruit is just the icing on the cake.

Serves 4

INGREDIENTS:

2 Bosc pears, cored and sliced thinly

2¼ cups pear cider or water

1½ cups old-fashioned rolled oats

1 tablespoon dark brown sugar

½ teaspoon cinnamon

1. Place all ingredients in a 4-quart slow cooker. Cook on low overnight (8–9 hours). Stir and serve.

A Quick Guide to Oatmeal

Oat groats are oats that still have the bran, but the outer husk has been removed. Rolled oats are groats that have been rolled into flat flakes for quick cooking, a process that removes the bran. Scottish oats are oat groats that have been chopped to include the bran. Quick-cooking or instant oats are more processed rolled oats.

FRENCH TOAST CASSEROLE

This recipe is great for breakfast, and it's a wonderful way to use bread that is slightly stale.

Serves 8

INGREDIENTS:

12 slices whole-meal raisin bread

6 eggs

1 teaspoon vanilla

2 cups fat-free evaporated milk

2 tablespoons dark brown sugar

1 teaspoon cinnamon

¼ teaspoon nutmeg

1. Spray a 4-quart slow cooker with nonstick spray. Layer the bread in the slow cooker.

2. In a small bowl, whisk the eggs, vanilla, evaporated milk, brown sugar, cinnamon, and nutmeg. Pour over the bread.

3. Cover and cook on low for 6–8 hours. Remove the lid and cook uncovered for 30 minutes or until the liquid has evaporated.

BREAKFAST QUINOA WITH FRUIT

Take a break from oatmeal and try this fruity quinoa instead!

Serves 4

INGREDIENTS:

1 cup quinoa

2 cups water

½ cup dried mixed berries

1 pear, thinly sliced

1 teaspoon dark brown sugar

½ teaspoon ground ginger

¼ teaspoon cinnamon

⅛ teaspoon cloves

⅛ teaspoon nutmeg

1. Place all ingredients into a 4-quart slow cooker. Stir. Cook for 2–3 hours or until the quinoa is fully cooked.

HAM AND EGG CASSEROLE

Slow cooker breakfasts ensure a hot breakfast even on the busiest of mornings. This high-protein breakfast will see you through until lunch.

Serves 6

INGREDIENTS:

6 eggs

½ teaspoon freshly ground black pepper

¼ teaspoon paprika

⅓ cup shredded sharp Cheddar

4 ounces canned diced green chiles, drained

3 ounces 98% fat-free smoked ham slice, diced

2 slices thin sandwich bread

1. In a small bowl, whisk the eggs, spices, Cheddar, and chiles. Stir in the ham. Set aside.

2. Spray a 2-quart slow cooker with nonstick cooking spray. Place the bread in a single layer on the bottom of the insert. Pour the egg mixture on top.

3. Cook for 7 hours on low. Use a spatula to separate the egg from the sides of the slow cooker. Lift the whole casserole out of the insert. Place it on a cutting board and slice it into six equal slices.

PEAR, APPLE, AND CRANBERRY PANCAKE TOPPING

Add this festive topping to pancakes to make breakfast a real treat!

Serves 8

INGREDIENTS:

3 tart apples, thinly sliced

3 Bosc pears, thinly sliced

¾ cup fresh cranberries

1 tablespoon brown sugar

½ teaspoon ground ginger

½ teaspoon cinnamon

¼ teaspoon nutmeg

¼ teaspoon mace

1. Place all ingredients into a 2-quart slow cooker. Stir. Cook on low for 2 hours.

Crantastic!

Cranberries are a superfood. High in antioxidants and fiber, they are a welcome addition to both sweet and savory dishes. They are also naturally high in pectin, which means they'll thicken any dish.

CHEESE "SOUFFLÉ"

Try this slimmed-down, no-fuss version of soufflé at your next brunch.

Serves 8

INGREDIENTS:

8 ounces reduced-fat sharp Cheddar, shredded

8 ounces skim-milk mozzarella, shredded

8 slices thin sandwich bread

2 cups fat-free evaporated milk

4 eggs

¼ teaspoon cayenne pepper

1. Mix the cheeses, and set aside. Tear the bread into large pieces, and set aside. Spray a 4-quart slow cooker with nonstick cooking spray. Alternately layer the cheese and bread in the insert, beginning and ending with bread.

2. In a small bowl, whisk the evaporated milk, eggs, and cayenne. Pour over the bread and cheese layers. Cook on low for 2–3 hours.

BREAKFAST RISOTTO

Serve this like you would cooked oatmeal: topped with additional brown sugar, raisins or other dried fruit, and milk.

Serves 6

INGREDIENTS:

¼ cup butter, melted

1½ cups Arborio rice

3 small apples, peeled, cored, and sliced

1½ teaspoons ground cinnamon

⅛ teaspoon freshly ground nutmeg

⅛ teaspoon ground cloves

⅛ teaspoon salt

⅓ cup brown sugar

1 cup apple juice

3 cups milk

1. Add the butter and rice to the slow cooker; stir to coat the rice in the butter.

2. Add the remaining ingredients and stir to combine. Cover and cook on low for 9 hours or until the rice is cooked through.

Arborio Rice

Arborio rice is a short-grain rice used in risotto because it has a creamy texture when cooked. Other varieties used in risotto are Vialone Nano and Carnaroli rice.

SLOW-COOKED OATMEAL WITH DRIED AND FRESH FRUIT

Wake up to the perfect hearty breakfast for a chilly fall morning.

Serves 2

INGREDIENTS:

1 Bosc pear, peeled and cubed

1¼ cups water

¾ cup old-fashioned rolled oats

¼ cup dried tart cherries

¼ teaspoon sugar

¼ teaspoon ground ginger

1. Place all ingredients into a 2-quart slow cooker. Cook on low for 8 hours. Stir prior to serving.

MILLET PORRIDGE WITH APPLES AND PECANS

Millet, like quinoa, is a small seed cereal crop. It's very easy to digest and makes a healthy hot breakfast.

Serves 4

INGREDIENTS:

4 cups almond milk

1 cup dried millet

1 apple, diced (and peeled if preferred)

2 teaspoons cinnamon

½ cup honey

½ cup chopped pecans

¼ teaspoon salt

1. Grease a 2.5-quart slow cooker with nonstick cooking spray.

2. Pour in almond milk, millet, the diced apple, cinnamon, honey, chopped pecans, and salt. Stir to combine.

3. Cook on high for 2½–3 hours or on low for 5–6 hours or until all of the liquid has been absorbed into the millet. Try not to overcook as it can become mushy.

A Note on Millet

Millet is particularly high in magnesium, which is a common deficiency in many with celiac disease. It also seems to help lower triglycerides and C-reactive protein (an inflammatory marker important in assessing cardiovascular risk). For more information on millet, see Cheryl Harris, RD's website: *www.harriswholehealth.com.*

PEAR CLAFOUTIS

Clafoutis is a soft pancake-like breakfast with cinnamon and pears. If you choose to use a larger slow cooker than the specified 2.5-quart, you will need to reduce the cooking time. When the sides are golden brown and a toothpick stuck in the middle comes out clean the clafoutis is done.

Serves 4

INGREDIENTS:

2 pears, stem and seeds removed, cut into chunks, and peeled if preferred

½ cup brown rice flour

½ cup arrowroot starch

2 teaspoons baking powder

½ teaspoon xanthan gum

¼ teaspoon salt

⅓ cup sugar

1 teaspoon ground cinnamon

2 tablespoons vegetable shortening, melted

2 eggs

¾ cup whole milk

1 tablespoon vanilla

1. Place cut-up pears into a greased 2.5-quart slow cooker.

2. In a large bowl whisk together the brown rice flour, arrowroot starch, baking powder, xanthan gum, salt, sugar, and cinnamon.

3. Make a well in the center of the dry ingredients and add melted shortening, eggs, milk, and vanilla. Stir to combine wet with dry ingredients.

4. Pour batter over pears. Cover slow cooker and vent lid with a chopstick or the handle of a wooden spoon.

5. Cook on high for 2½–3 hours or on low for 5–6 hours. Serve warm or cold drizzled with maple syrup.

Baking Shortcut

Don't want to mix up all these ingredients? You can replace the brown rice flour, arrowroot starch, baking powder, and xanthan gum with your favorite pancake mix.

CHAPTER 6

HOT SANDWICHES

CHEESY MELTS

You can make the sandwich filling and prepare the rolls the day before, then assemble these sandwiches right before heating.

Yields 12

INGREDIENTS:

1½ pounds extra-sharp Cheddar cheese

½ cup pitted black olives

¼ cup green chilies

1 onion

¾ cup tomato sauce

3 tablespoons olive oil

½ teaspoon black pepper

¼ teaspoon salt

12 large French rolls

1. Grate the cheese; slice the olives and chilies. Mince the onion.

2. Mix the cheese, olives, chilies, and onion with the tomato sauce, oil, pepper, and salt.

3. Cut the tops off the rolls. Stuff the rolls with the cheese mixture, replace the tops, and wrap the sandwiches in foil.

4. Arrange the wrapped sandwiches on a trivet or rack in the slow cooker. Pour water around the base of the trivet.

5. Cover and heat on a high setting for 1–2 hours.

STEAMERS

If you don't have fresh buns available, don't worry. Stale buns will soften with the steam.

Yields 8

INGREDIENTS:

1 clove garlic

1 onion

1 pound ground beef

1 pound pork sausage

2 eggs

½ teaspoon salt

1 cup bread crumbs

¼ cup milk

8 hamburger buns

½ cup sliced pickles

1. Crush and mince the garlic; mince the onion. Mix the garlic and onion with the meat, eggs, salt, crumbs, and milk.

2. Form the mixture into 8 patties.

3. Briefly sear the patties on each side in a pan over high heat. Assemble the patties on hamburger buns, with pickles on each.

4. Wrap the sandwiches in aluminum foil. Arrange the wrapped sandwiches on a trivet or rack in the slow cooker. Pour water around the base of the trivet.

5. Cover and heat on a high setting for 1–2 hours.

For Future Use

Consider every leftover for use in future cooking. Corn bread, for example, can be used in many dishes. Pop it in the freezer to use later, as crumbs for meatloaf or in meatballs, giving regular old meatballs a whole new taste and texture.

BAGEL AND MUENSTER CHEESE SANDWICH

Don't worry about getting fresh bagels. The drier your bagels are, the more juice they'll absorb from the tomatoes and cheese.

Serves 6

INGREDIENTS:

6 bagels

2 tomatoes

½ pound Muenster cheese

½ pound cream cheese

1 onion

1. Slice the bagels, tomatoes, Muenster cheese, and cream cheese. Thinly slice the onion. Arrange the slices in this order: bagel, tomato, Muenster, onion, cream cheese, bagel.

2. Wrap the sandwiches in foil and arrange on a trivet in the slow cooker. Pour water around the base of the trivet.

3. Cover and heat on a high setting for 1–2 hours.

HOT CORNED BEEF SANDWICH

Serve with big dill pickles and cold cream soda on a hot afternoon when there's nothing better to do than spend time with good friends.

Serves 6

INGREDIENTS:

2 tablespoons horseradish

½ pound cream cheese

1 pound corned beef

12 slices rye bread

1. Cream the horseradish and the cream cheese together. Thinly slice the corned beef. Arrange the sandwich layers in this order: bread, beef, cheese, bread.

2. Wrap the sandwiches in foil and arrange on a trivet in the slow cooker. Pour water around the base of the trivet.

3. Cover and heat on a high setting for 1–2 hours.

CLASSIC REUBEN

These juicy sandwiches can be made ahead and frozen, then thawed before heating. You can make half-size sandwiches, as well.

Serves 6

INGREDIENTS:

12 slices rye bread

3 tablespoons butter

1 pound corned beef

½ pound Swiss cheese

1 pound sauerkraut

1 cup Russian dressing

1. Brown one side of each slice of bread in butter in a pan over medium heat.

2. Thinly slice the beef and the cheese. Drain sauerkraut until very dry. Arrange the sandwich layers in this order: bread (browned side out), beef, sauerkraut, dressing, cheese, bread.

3. Wrap the sandwiches in foil and arrange on a trivet in the slow cooker. Pour water around the base of the trivet.

4. Cover and heat on a high setting for 1–2 hours.

Think Small

When you're hosting a party, give your guests bite-sized food they can eat without relying on a knife. To do this, and still cut down on your prep time, use, for example, spring potatoes and baby carrots instead of large ones.

CRAB AND MUSHROOM KAISER ROLL

If you happen to have some fresh lobster, use it instead of crab. Serve with a fresh green salad with vinaigrette.

Serves 6

INGREDIENTS:

1 cup crabmeat

½ pound mushrooms

1 small bunch parsley

¼ pound Parmesan cheese

¾ cup mayonnaise

1 teaspoon lemon juice

⅛ teaspoon rosemary

⅛ teaspoon thyme

⅛ teaspoon sage

6 Kaiser rolls

2 tablespoons butter

¼ cup toasted slivered almonds

1. Shred and blot dry the crabmeat, mince the mushrooms and parsley, and grate the cheese. Mix the crabmeat, mushrooms, parsley, cheese, mayonnaise, lemon juice, and herbs.

2. Split the rolls and toast the insides.

3. Arrange the sandwich layers in this order: bottom of roll (toasted side in), butter, crab mixture, almonds, butter, top of roll.

4. Wrap the sandwiches in foil and arrange on a trivet in the slow cooker. Pour water around the base of the trivet.

5. Cover and heat on a high setting for 1–2 hours.

Head for the Pantry

If you're short on time and your recipe calls for dried beans, go for the canned beans instead. For each cup of dried beans in a recipe, you can use 2½ cups canned. Likewise, 1 cup dry rice can be replaced by 3½ cups cooked rice (from your leftover takeout food, perhaps?), or 2 cups cooked rice if the recipe called for instant rice.

CHICKEN AND GHERKIN SANDWICH

Some people prefer sweet pickles, but dill pickles are the standard. Use the baby gherkins; they have a nicer texture.

Serves 6

INGREDIENTS:

12 slices rye bread

½ pound cooked chicken

6 baby dill pickles

¼ pound mozzarella cheese

2 tablespoons butter

½ teaspoon salt

½ teaspoon pepper

1. Toast the bread on one side. Thinly slice the chicken, pickles, and cheese.

2. Arrange the sandwich layers in this order: bread (toasted side out), butter, chicken, salt, pepper, pickle, cheese, butter, bread.

3. Wrap the sandwiches in foil and arrange on a trivet in the slow cooker. Pour water around the base of the trivet.

4. Cover and heat on a high setting for 1–2 hours.

Don't Forget Turnips

Turnips, common in some cultures but forgotten by others, are a naturally sweet root and are delicious in curries and soups. Avoid adding salt before cooking with turnips, as they will lose their sweetness. Add salt only at the end, to flavor.

HAM AND SWISS CROISSANT

Enhance this sandwich by using honey-baked ham, a fancy mustard, or cherry tomatoes. You can also add a few leaves of raw spinach.

Serves 6

INGREDIENTS:

6 croissants

2 tomatoes

½ pound Swiss cheese

½ pound ham

3 tablespoons mustard

1. Slice the croissants and the tomatoes. Thinly slice the cheese and ham.

2. Arrange the sandwich layers in this order: bottom of croissant, ham, cheese, mustard, ham, tomato, top of croissant.

3. Wrap the sandwiches in foil and arrange on a trivet in the slow cooker. Pour water around the base of the trivet.

4. Cover and heat on a high setting for 1–2 hours.

BACON AND TURKEY SANDWICH

Fresh slices of avocado are an excellent addition to this sandwich.

Serves 6

INGREDIENTS:

12 slices bacon

12 slices rye bread

2 tomatoes

½ pound turkey

¼ pound Gruyère cheese

¼ cup mayonnaise

1. Brown the bacon in a pan over medium heat until crispy; drain.

2. Toast the bread; slice the tomatoes. Thinly slice the turkey and cheese.

3. Arrange the sandwich layers in this order: bread, mayonnaise, turkey, bacon, tomato, cheese, bread.

4. Wrap the sandwiches in foil and arrange on a trivet in the slow cooker. Pour water around the base of the trivet.

5. Cover and heat on a high setting for 1–2 hours.

Tomato Heaven

Use dried tomato, which you can get in most grocery stores, to add intense dabs of sweet texture and bright color to any dish that calls for tomatoes. Open a bag and cut the entire batch into narrow strips or squares. After cutting and handling, store in the freezer, and they can be taken out and used as needed.

STEAMED TURKEY SANDWICH

Choose a nice, dense sourdough, then leave it out for a day to dry before toasting. Also, try substituting goose or duck for turkey.

Serves 6

INGREDIENTS:

12 slices bacon

12 slices sourdough bread

3 tomatoes

½ pound turkey

½ pound Cheddar cheese

2 tablespoons butter

2 teaspoons mustard

1. Sauté the bacon in a pan over medium heat until crispy; drain.

2. Toast the bread; slice the tomatoes. Thinly slice the turkey and the cheese.

3. Arrange the sandwich layers in this order: bread, butter, turkey, cheese, bacon, tomato, mustard, butter, bread.

4. Wrap the sandwiches in foil and arrange on a trivet in the slow cooker. Pour water around the base of the trivet.

5. Cover and heat on a high setting for 1–2 hours.

STROMBOLI

For a slight variation, substitute a nice olive relish for the chopped olives in this sandwich.

Serves 6

INGREDIENTS:

½ pound roast beef

2 tablespoons butter

12 slices French bread

½ cup olives

½ pound ham

½ pound mozzarella cheese

1. Thinly slice the beef. Sauté in butter in a pan over medium heat until lightly browned.

2. Toast the bread. Mince the olives. Thinly slice the ham and cheese.

3. Arrange the sandwich layers in this order: bread, beef, ham, olives, cheese, bread.

4. Wrap the sandwiches in foil and arrange on a trivet in the slow cooker. Pour water around the base of the trivet.

5. Cover and heat on a high setting for 1–2 hours.

BAKED HAM, GRUYÈRE, AND ROQUEFORT SANDWICH

You can make these sandwiches on whole baguettes, then slice after assembly. You can also use this trick to make lots of tiny sandwiches.

Serves 6

INGREDIENTS:

2 long French baguettes

½ pound Gruyère cheese

½ pound ham

½ pound Roquefort cheese

2 tablespoons mayonnaise

3 tablespoons dry white wine

3 tablespoons butter

1. Cut the baguettes to yield 6 pieces, each 6 to 8 inches in length. Slice each lengthwise to open, then toast the insides.

2. Thinly slice the Gruyère and ham. Mince the Roquefort and blend with the mayonnaise and white wine.

3. Arrange the sandwich layers in this order: bottom of baguette, butter, Gruyère, ham, Roquefort spread, top of baguette.

4. Wrap the sandwiches in foil and arrange on a trivet in the slow cooker. Pour water around the base of the trivet.

5. Cover and heat on a high setting for 1–2 hours.

SAUCISSON EN CROUTE

Use a nice chewy roll for this hot sandwich. Also, try lengths of French bread, or roll the sausages in pita bread.

Serves 6

INGREDIENTS:

6 spicy Italian sausages

6 long sourdough rolls

2 tablespoons Dijon mustard

1. Sauté the sausages in a pan over medium heat until browned and thoroughly cooked; drain.

2. Cut off the tips of the rolls. Use the handle of a wooden spoon to hollow out the center of the roll. Dip the sausages in the mustard and insert each into a roll.

3. Wrap the sandwiches in foil and arrange on a trivet in the slow cooker. Pour water around the base of the trivet.

4. Cover and heat on a high setting for 1–2 hours.

SAUSAGE AND SAUERKRAUT SANDWICH

Personalize this sandwich with venison, moose, or andouille sausage. Also, choose German or Hungarian sauerkraut, or make your own.

Serves 6

INGREDIENTS:

1½ pounds bulk pork sausage

1 cup spiced sauerkraut

¼ pound Gruyère cheese

6 poppy seed rolls

1. Form the sausage meat into six patties and sauté in a pan over medium heat until browned and thoroughly cooked; drain. Drain the sauerkraut and thinly slice the cheese; split and toast the rolls.

2. Arrange the sandwich layers in this order: bottom of roll, sausage, sauerkraut, cheese, top of roll.

3. Wrap the sandwiches in foil and arrange on a trivet in the slow cooker. Pour water around the base of the trivet.

4. Cover and heat on a high setting for 1–2 hours.

Why Cook Slowly?

Foods with a lot of sugar, or dried fruit, which is dense with fruit sugars, should be cooked at lower temperatures so the sugar won't scorch. Large pieces of meat should also be cooked at lower temperatures, so the heat has time to reach the center of the meat without burning the outside.

SAUERKRAUT AND BRATWURST ROLL

These can be messy, but it's worth it. You can substitute caraway rye bread for pita—just split the bratwurst lengthwise.

Serves 6

INGREDIENTS:

1 apple

1½ pounds sauerkraut

1 tablespoon caraway seeds

2 tablespoons oil

6 bratwurst

1 tablespoon butter

½ cup white wine

2 tablespoons Dijon mustard

6 whole-wheat pita loaves

1. Core and chop the apple; drain the sauerkraut. Sauté the sauerkraut, apple, and caraway seeds in the oil in a pan over medium heat until the apple is soft and the liquids are reduced.

2. Sauté the bratwurst in butter in a pan over medium heat until browned on both sides; drain. Add the wine and continue to sauté over medium heat until the liquid has evaporated.

3. Roll each bratwurst, with sauerkraut and mustard, into a pita loaf.

4. Wrap the sandwiches in foil and arrange on a trivet in the slow cooker. Pour water around the base of the trivet.

5. Cover and heat on a high setting for 1–2 hours.

CLASSIC SLOPPY JOES

Make this sandwich filling at your convenience, then chill or freeze. Reheat in your slow cooker just before your party.

Serves 8

INGREDIENTS:

2 onions

1 clove garlic

2 tablespoons oil

1 pound ground beef

1 pound ground pork

¼ cup molasses

½ cup cider vinegar

½ cup tomato paste

¼ teaspoon salt

½ teaspoon black pepper

1. Thinly slice the onions; crush and mince the garlic. Sauté the onion and garlic in oil in a pan over low heat until soft. Transfer to the slow cooker.

2. Brown the meat in the same pan over medium heat; drain. Add the meat, molasses, vinegar, tomato paste, salt, and pepper to the slow cooker.

3. Cover and heat on a low setting for 3–4 hours.

MEXICAN SLOPPY JOES

Try replacing the pinto beans with black beans or garbanzos for a different texture and flavor. Serve with tortilla chips and salsa.

Serves 8

INGREDIENTS:

1 onion

1 clove garlic

2 tablespoons oil

1 pound ground beef

1 pound ground pork

½ cup pitted black olives

¼ cup sliced jalapeño peppers

¼ cup sliced green chilies

¼ teaspoon chili pepper

¼ teaspoon salt

1 cup cooked pinto beans

½ cup red wine vinegar

½ cup tomato sauce

¼ pound Monterey jack cheese

1. Thinly slice the onion; crush and mince the garlic. Sauté the onion and garlic in oil in a pan over low heat until the onion is soft. Transfer to the slow cooker.

2. Sauté the meat in a pan over medium heat until browned; drain. Add to the slow cooker.

3. Slice the olives. Add to the slow cooker, along with the jalapeño peppers, chilies, chili pepper, salt, beans, vinegar, and tomato sauce.

4. Cover and heat on a low setting for 3–4 hours.

5. Before serving, grate the cheese and stir in.

When to Salt?

If you're in a hurry when you're cooking dried beans, add salt *after* cooking, not before. If salt is added before cooking, it will slow things down.

SESAME SLOPPY JOES

Serve this filling on sesame seed buns or in pita pockets. Provide thinly sliced pickled gingerroot and some fresh green onion shoots for toppings.

Serves 8

INGREDIENTS:

1 onion

1 clove garlic

2 tablespoons sesame oil

1 pound ground beef

1 pound ground pork

¼ cup water chestnuts

3 green onions

1 teaspoon cornstarch

2 tablespoons water

½ cup rice vinegar

¼ cup soy sauce

¼ teaspoon salt

1. Thinly slice the onion; crush and mince the garlic. Sauté the onion and garlic in the sesame oil in a pan over low heat. Transfer, with oil, to the slow cooker.

2. Sauté the meat in a pan over medium heat until browned; drain. Add to the slow cooker.

3. Slice the water chestnuts and green onions. Dissolve the cornstarch in water; stir in the vinegar, soy sauce, and salt. Add the sliced vegetables and the starch mixture to the slow cooker.

4. Cover and heat on a low setting for 2–3 hours.

FRENCH DIP SANDWICHES

Using lean bottom round not only cuts the fat, it lets you slow-cook the meat long enough that you can put it on before you go to bed and have it ready for a lunch buffet the next day. If you're serving it at a buffet, simply stir the sliced meat back into the onions and broth and serve it directly from the slow cooker.

Serves 12

INGREDIENTS:

1 large onion

1 (3-pound) beef bottom round roast

½ cup dry white or red wine or water

1 envelope au jus gravy mix

⅛ teaspoon freshly ground black pepper

Salt, to taste

Hard rolls or French bread

1. Peel, quarter, and slice the onion. Line bottom of the slow cooker with the onion slices.

2. Trim and discard any visible fat from the roast and add it to the slow cooker on top of the onion.

3. Add the wine or water, au jus mix, and black pepper to a small bowl; mix well and then pour the mixture over the roast. Cook on low for 2 hours or until the meat is very tender.

4. Remove the meat from the slow cooker and let stand for 10 minutes. Cut the meat across the grain into thin slices. Serve the meat on hard rolls or French bread.

5. Taste the broth and add salt if needed. Use the broth for dipping.

CHAPTER 7

CHICKEN

RECIPE LIST

POACHED CHICKEN

Use moist, tender poached chicken in any recipe that calls for cooked chicken. It is especially good in salads and sandwiches.

Serves 8

INGREDIENTS:

4–5 pounds whole chicken or chicken parts

1 cup water

1 carrot, peeled

1 stalk celery

1 onion, quartered

1. Place the chicken into an oval 6-quart slow cooker. Arrange the vegetables around the chicken. Add the water. Cook on low for 7–8 hours.

2. Remove the skin before eating.

Quick Chicken Salad

Stir together 2 cups cubed poached chicken breast, 3 tablespoons mayonnaise, ¼ cup diced celery, 1 minced shallot, and ¼ cup dried cranberries. Refrigerate for 1 hour. Serve on multigrain crackers or whole-wheat rolls.

CHICKEN AND GRAVY

Serve this dish along with a tossed salad and steamed vegetable and you have a complete meal.

Serves 4

INGREDIENTS:

1 (10¾-ounce) can cream of chicken soup

1 (10½-ounce) can cream of mushroom soup

Freshly ground black pepper, to taste

4 (6-ounce) skinless, boneless chicken breasts

4 medium potatoes, peeled and quartered

1. Add the soups and pepper to the slow cooker. Stir to combine. Add the chicken breasts, pushing them down into the soup mixture. Add the potatoes in a layer on top. Cover and cook on low for 4–6 hours.

CHICKEN IN LEMON SAUCE

This recipe is for a one-pot meal. By completing a simple step at the end of the cooking time, you have meat, potatoes, vegetables, and sauce all ready to serve and eat. It doesn't get much easier than that.

Serves 4

INGREDIENTS:

1 (1-pound) bag frozen cut green beans, thawed

1 small onion, peeled and cut into thin wedges

4 boneless, skinless chicken breast halves

4 medium potatoes, peeled and cut in quarters

2 cloves of garlic, peeled and minced

¼ teaspoon freshly ground black pepper

1 cup Chicken Broth (Chapter 19)

4 ounces cream cheese, cut into cubes

1 teaspoon freshly grated lemon peel

Optional: Lemon peel strips

1. Place green beans and onion in the slow cooker. Arrange the chicken and potatoes over the vegetables. Sprinkle with the garlic and pepper. Pour broth over all. Cover and cook on low for 5 or more hours or until chicken is cooked through and moist.

2. Evenly divide the chicken, potatoes, and vegetables between 4 serving plates or onto a serving platter; cover to keep warm.

3. To make the sauce, add the cream cheese cubes and grated lemon peel to the broth in the slow cooker. Stir until cheese melts into the sauce. Pour the sauce over the chicken, potatoes, and vegetables. Garnish with lemon peel strips if desired.

SCALLOPED CHICKEN

If you have leftover cooked chicken on hand, you can use it in this recipe instead of the canned chicken.

Serves 4

INGREDIENTS:

Nonstick spray

1 (5-ounce) box scalloped potatoes

1 (8-ounce) can white meat chicken

3¾ cups water

1. Treat the slow cooker with nonstick spray. Add the potatoes and sprinkle the seasoning mix over the top of them. Spread the chicken over the top of the potatoes. Pour in the water. Cover and cook on low for 5 hours.

CHICKEN STROGANOFF

You can make this recipe for 8 servings by increasing the amount of chicken breasts to 3 pounds. There will be enough stroganoff sauce to accommodate more servings.

Serves 6

INGREDIENTS:

Nonstick spray

1 (10½-ounce) can cream of mushroom soup

1 (4-ounce) can sliced mushrooms, drained

1 tablespoon Worcestershire sauce

2½ pounds skinless, boneless chicken breasts

1 (16-ounce) carton sour cream

Cooked, buttered egg noodles

1. Treat crock of the slow cooker with nonstick spray. Add the soup, mushrooms, and Worcestershire sauce; stir to mix.

2. Cut the chicken breasts into bite-sized pieces; add to the cooker and stir into the sauce. Cover and cook on low for 8 hours.

3. Stir in the sour cream; cover and continue to cook long enough to bring the sour cream sauce to temperature, or for about 30 minutes. Serve over cooked, buttered egg noodles or, if you prefer, over toast or biscuits.

CHICKEN PAPRIKASH

If you prefer not to cook with wine, replace it with an equal amount of chicken broth. You can also substitute an equal amount of drained plain yogurt for the sour cream.

Serves 8

INGREDIENTS:

1 tablespoon butter

1 tablespoon extra-virgin olive oil

1 large yellow onion, peeled and diced

2 cloves garlic, peeled and minced

3 pounds boneless skinless chicken thighs

Salt and freshly ground pepper, to taste

2 tablespoons Hungarian paprika

½ cup Chicken Broth (Chapter 19)

¼ cup dry white wine

1 (16-ounce) container sour cream

Cooked egg noodles or spaetzle

Optional: Additional paprika

1. Add the butter, oil, and onion to a microwave-safe bowl; cover and microwave on high for 1 minute. Stir, re-cover, and microwave on high for another minute or until the onions are transparent. Stir in the garlic; cover and microwave on high for 30 seconds. Add to the slow cooker.

2. Cut the chicken thighs into bite-sized pieces. Add the chicken to the Dutch oven, and stir fry for 5 minutes. Stir in the salt, pepper, paprika, broth, and wine; cover and cook on low for 8 hours.

3. Stir in the sour cream; cover and continue to cook long enough to bring the sour cream sauce to temperature, or for about 30 minutes. Serve over cooked noodles or spaetzle. Sprinkle each serving with additional paprika if desired. Serve immediately.

Thickening or Thinning

If the resulting sauce for the chicken paprikash is too thin, add more sour cream. If it's too thick, slowly whisk in some milk.

ITALIAN CHICKEN

Serve this dish with a tossed salad and garlic bread. For a lower-fat meal, remove the skin from the chicken and omit the flour.

Serves 4

INGREDIENTS:

1 (3-pound) chicken, cut into pieces

1 teaspoon Italian seasoning

2 tablespoons all-purpose flour

½ teaspoon salt

⅛ teaspoon pepper

2 tablespoons Parmesan cheese, grated

½ teaspoon paprika

1 medium zucchini, sliced

½ cup Chicken Broth (Chapter 19)

1 (4-ounce) can sliced mushrooms, drained

1. Add the chicken pieces, Italian seasoning, flour, salt, pepper, cheese, and paprika to a gallon plastic bag; seal and shake the bag to coat the chicken pieces.

2. Treat the crock of the slow cooker with nonstick spray. Arrange the zucchini slices over the bottom of the crock. Pour broth over the zucchini. Arrange chicken on top. Cover and cook on low for 8 hours or until the chicken is cooked through. Increase the heat to high, add the mushrooms, cover, and cook on high for another 15 minutes.

ORANGE CHICKEN

You can use light or dark brown sugar, depending on your preference. (Dark brown sugar will impart more molasses flavor to the dish.) Serve this dish over cooked rice or stir-fry vegetables, or with both.

Serves 8

INGREDIENTS:

Nonstick spray

3 pounds boneless, skinless chicken breasts

1 small onion, peeled and diced

½ cup orange juice

1 tablespoon orange marmalade

1 tablespoon brown sugar

1 tablespoon apple cider vinegar

1 tablespoon Worcestershire sauce

1 teaspoon Dijon mustard

1. Treat the crock of the slow cooker with nonstick spray. Cut the chicken breasts into bite-sized pieces. Add the chicken and the onion to the slow cooker.

2. In a bowl or measuring cup, mix together the orange juice, marmalade, brown sugar, vinegar, Worcestershire sauce, and mustard. Pour into the slow cooker. Stir to combine the sauce with the chicken and onions. Cover and cook on low for 8 hours.

TARRAGON CHICKEN

This rich French dish can stand on its own when served with just a tossed salad and some crusty bread.

Serves 4

INGREDIENTS:

½ cup plus 2 tablespoons all-purpose flour

½ teaspoon salt

8 chicken thighs, skin removed

2 tablespoons butter

2 tablespoons vegetable or olive oil

1 medium yellow onion, peeled and diced

1 cup dry white wine

1 cup Chicken Broth (Chapter 19)

½ teaspoon dried tarragon

1 cup heavy cream

1. Add ½ cup of the flour, the salt, and the chicken thighs to a gallon plastic bag; close and shake to coat the chicken. Add the butter and oil to a large sauté pan and bring it to temperature over medium-high heat. Add the chicken thighs; brown the chicken by cooking it on one side for 5 minutes, and then turning the pieces and frying them for another 5 minutes. Drain the chicken on paper towels and then place in the slow cooker. Cover the slow cooker. Set temperature to low.

2. Add the onion to the sauté pan; sauté until the onion is transparent. Stir in 2 tablespoons of flour, cooking the flour until the onion just begins to brown. Slowly pour the wine into the pan, stirring to scrape the browned bits off of the bottom of the pan and into the sauce. Add the broth. Cook and stir for 15 minutes or until the sauce is thickened enough to coat the back of a spoon. Stir the tarragon into the sauce, and then pour the sauce over the chicken in the slow cooker. Cover and cook for 4–8 hours.

3. Pour the cream into the slow cooker; cover and cook for an additional 15 minutes or until the cream is heated through. Test for seasoning and add additional salt and tarragon if needed. Serve immediately.

Cooking Times

After 4 hours, the chicken will be cooked through. If you want to leave the chicken cooking all day, after 8 hours the meat will fall away from the bone. You can then remove the bones before you stir in the cream.

CHICKEN CACCIATORE

If you prefer, you can remove the skin from a 3-pound chicken and cut it into 8 serving pieces and substitute that for the chicken thighs.

Serves 4

INGREDIENTS:

¾ cup all-purpose flour

½ teaspoon salt

8 chicken thighs, skin removed

3 tablespoons vegetable or olive oil

1 medium yellow onion, peeled and diced

4 cloves garlic, peeled and minced

3 tablespoons oil-packed sun-dried tomatoes

1 cup dry white wine

⅛ teaspoon dried sage

¼ teaspoon dried rosemary

Pinch dried red pepper flakes

Freshly ground black pepper, to taste

1. Add ½ cup of the flour, the salt, and the chicken thighs to a gallon plastic bag; close and shake to coat the chicken.

2. Add the oil to a large sauté pan and bring it to temperature over medium-high heat. Add the chicken thighs; brown the chicken by cooking it on one side for 5 minutes, and then turning the pieces and frying them for another 5 minutes.

3. Drain the chicken on paper towels and then place in the slow cooker. Cover the slow cooker. Set temperature to low.

4. Add the onion to the sauté pan; sauté until the onion just begins to brown. Stir in the garlic and sauté for 30 seconds. Coarsely chop the sun-dried tomatoes and add them to the pan. Slowly pour the wine into the pan, stirring to scrape the browned bits off of the bottom of the pan. Stir in the sage, rosemary, pepper flakes, and black pepper, and then pour the sauce over the chicken in the slow cooker. Cover and cook for 4–8 hours, depending on the sizes of the chicken pieces.

TERIYAKI CHICKEN

Serve Teriyaki Chicken over cooked rice.

Serves 6

INGREDIENTS:

2 pounds boneless, skinless chicken breasts

1 (16-ounce) frozen stir-fry mix vegetables, thawed

¼ cup Chicken Broth (Chapter 19)

1 cup teriyaki sauce

1. Cut the chicken breasts into strips or bite-sized pieces. Add to the slow cooker along with the vegetables, broth, and sauce. Stir to mix. Cover and cook on low for 6 hours.

CHICKEN AND ARTICHOKES

This is another dish that can be served with just a tossed salad and some crusty bread to make it a complete meal.

Serves 4

INGREDIENTS:

8 boneless, skinless chicken thighs

½ cup Chicken Broth (Chapter 19)

1 tablespoon fresh lemon juice

2 teaspoons dried thyme

1 clove garlic, peeled and minced

¼ teaspoon freshly ground black pepper

1 (13-ounce) can artichoke hearts, drained

1. Add all ingredients to the slow cooker; stir to mix. Cover and cook on low for 6 hours. If necessary, uncover and allow to cook for ½ hour or more to thicken the sauce.

Artichoke Hearts

You can use thawed frozen artichoke hearts in place of canned ones. Or, if all you have on hand are marinated artichoke hearts, drain them and add them to the recipe; simply omit the thyme and garlic if you do.

CURRIED CHICKEN IN COCONUT MILK

Chicken base is available from Minor's (www.soupbase.com) *or Redi-Base* (www.redibase.com), *or you can use chicken bouillon concentrate.*

Serves 4

INGREDIENTS:

1 small onion, peeled and diced

2 cloves garlic, peeled and minced

1½ tablespoons curry powder

1 cup coconut milk

¾ teaspoon chicken broth base

8 chicken thighs, skin removed

Cooked rice

1. Add the onion, garlic, curry powder, coconut milk, and broth base to the slow cooker. Stir to mix. Add the chicken thighs. Cover and cook on low for 6 hours. Use a slotted spoon to remove the thighs to a serving bowl. Whisk to combine the sauce and pour over the chicken. Serve immediately over rice.

ALMOND CHICKEN

The dried minced onion (sometimes sold as dried onion flakes) will absorb some of the chicken broth during the cooking process and naturally thicken the sauce. For a subtler flavor, use freeze-dried shallots available from the Spice House (www.thespicehouse.com) instead.

Serves 4

INGREDIENTS:

1 (14-ounce) can chicken broth

4 strips bacon, cooked

2 pounds boneless, skinless chicken breasts

¼ cup dried minced onion

1 (4-ounce) can sliced mushrooms, drained

2 tablespoons soy sauce

1½ cups celery, sliced diagonally

Cooked rice

1 cup toasted slivered almonds

1. Add the chicken broth to the slow cooker. Cut the bacon and chicken into bite-sized pieces; add to the slow cooker along with the dried minced onion, mushrooms, soy sauce, and celery. Stir to combine. Cover and cook on low for 6 hours. Serve over cooked rice and topped with the toasted slivered almonds.

Toasting Almonds

You can toast slivered almonds by adding them to a dry skillet over medium heat. Stir frequently until the almonds begin to brown. Alternatively, you can bake them at 400°F for about 5 minutes, stirring them occasionally. Whichever method you use, watch the almonds carefully because they quickly go from toasted to burnt.

EASY CHICKEN AND DRESSING

Serve this dish with a tossed salad or steamed vegetable.

Serves 4

INGREDIENTS:

Nonstick spray

1 (15¾-ounce) can cream of chicken soup

⅓ cup milk

4 (8-ounce) boneless, skinless chicken breasts

1 (6-ounce) package chicken-flavored stuffing mix

1⅔ cups water

1. Treat the crock of the slow cooker with nonstick spray. Add the soup and milk; stir to combine. Put the chicken in the slow cooker, pressing it down into the soup.

2. Mix together the stuffing mix and water in a bowl; spoon over the top of the chicken. Cover and cook on low for 8 hours.

CHICKEN IN PLUM SAUCE

You can use commercial plum sauce or the one in Chapter 4 for this rich, sweet entrée. Serve it over rice along with steamed broccoli.

Serves 4

INGREDIENTS:

Nonstick spray

1¼ cups plum sauce

2 tablespoons butter, melted

2 tablespoons orange juice concentrate, thawed

1 teaspoon Chinese five-spice powder

8 chicken thighs, skin removed

Optional: Toasted sesame oil

Optional: Soy sauce

1. Treat the crock of the slow cooker with nonstick spray. Add the plum sauce, butter, orange juice concentrate, and five-spice powder to the slow cooker; stir to combine.

2. Add the chicken thighs. Cover and cook on low for 6–8 hours. Top each serving with toasted sesame oil and soy sauce to taste if desired.

SWEET AND SPICY PULLED CHICKEN

Make this recipe after breakfast and it will be ready by lunchtime.

Serves 4

INGREDIENTS:

1¾ pounds boneless, skinless chicken thighs

¼ cup chili sauce

¼ cup balsamic vinegar

2 tablespoons ginger preserves

2 tablespoons pineapple juice

2 tablespoons lime juice

1 teaspoon ground cayenne pepper

½ teaspoon ground chipotle

½ teaspoon hot paprika

1 jalapeño, minced

3 cloves garlic, minced

1 teaspoon yellow hot sauce

1. Place all ingredients in a round 2- or 4-quart slow cooker. Cook on low for 3½ hours, or for 1½ hours on low and then turn it up to high for an additional hour.

2. When done, the meat should shred easily with a fork. Thoroughly shred the chicken. Toss to coat the meat evenly with the sauce.

BUFFALO CHICKEN SANDWICH FILLING

Try this on crusty rolls and top with crumbled blue cheese or low-fat blue cheese dressing.

Serves 4

INGREDIENTS:

4 boneless, skinless chicken thighs

¼ cup diced onion

1 clove garlic, minced

½ teaspoon freshly ground black pepper

⅛ teaspoon salt

2 cups buffalo wing sauce

1. Place all ingredients in a 4-quart slow cooker. Stir. Cook on high for 2–3 hours or until the chicken is easily shredded with a fork. If the sauce is very thin, cook on high uncovered for 30 minutes or until thickened.

2. Shred the chicken and toss with the sauce.

Lower-Fat Blue Cheese Dressing

In a small bowl stir 3 tablespoons reduced-fat blue cheese crumbles, 3 tablespoons fat-free buttermilk, ¼ cup reduced-fat mayonnaise, ½ tablespoon lemon juice, ⅛ teaspoon Worcestershire sauce, 1 pinch black pepper, and ½ tablespoon reduced-fat sour cream. Store in an airtight container for up to 3 days.

CHICKEN AND DUMPLINGS

Memories of bland chicken and dumplings will be banished forever after one bite of this flavorful Cajun-influenced dish.

Serves 6

INGREDIENTS:

1 tablespoon canola oil

1 onion, chopped

3 cloves garlic, minced

1 cup diced crimini mushrooms

2 carrots, diced

2 stalks celery, diced

1 parsnip, diced

1 jalapeño, seeded and diced

½ teaspoon salt

½ teaspoon ground black pepper

1 large red skin potato, diced

½ teaspoon dried dill weed

½ teaspoon ground cayenne pepper

6 cups Chicken Broth (Chapter 19)

3 cups diced, cooked chicken breast

1 tablespoon baking powder

2 cups flour

¾ cup 1% milk or fat-free buttermilk

2 eggs

¼ cup chopped green onion

1. Heat the canola oil in a small skillet, then add the onions, garlic, and mushrooms. Sauté until softened, about 2 minutes. Add to an oval 4-quart slow cooker along with the carrots, celery, parsnip, jalapeño, salt, pepper, potato, dill weed, cayenne, and broth. Cook on low for 6 hours.

2. Add the cooked chicken and turn up to high.

3. Meanwhile, whisk the baking powder and flour in a medium bowl. Stir in the buttermilk, eggs, and green onion. Mix to combine. Divide the mixture into 3" dumplings.

4. Carefully drop the dumplings one at a time into the slow cooker. Cover and continue to cook on high for 30 minutes or until the dumplings are cooked through and fluffy.

It's in the Book!

This is a great recipe to use Chicken Broth (Chapter 19) in. Make the broth the day before or overnight. You could even use leftover chicken from Slow-Roasted Chicken with Potatoes, Parsnips, and Onions (this chapter). Planning ahead saves time.

CARIBBEAN CHICKEN CURRY

Traditional Jamaican curries are cooked for long periods of time over the stove top, making them a logical fit for the slow cooker. The spices meld together and the chicken is meltingly tender.

Serves 8

INGREDIENTS:

1 tablespoon Madras curry powder

1 teaspoon allspice

½ teaspoon ground cloves

½ teaspoon ground nutmeg

1 teaspoon ground ginger

2 pounds boneless, skinless chicken thighs, cubed

1 teaspoon canola oil

1 onion, chopped

2 cloves garlic, chopped

2 jalapeños, chopped

½ pound red skin potatoes, cubed

⅓ cup light coconut milk

1. In a medium bowl, whisk together the curry powder, allspice, cloves, nutmeg, and ginger. Add the chicken and toss to coat each piece evenly.

2. Place the chicken in a nonstick skillet and quickly sauté until the chicken starts to brown. Add to a 4-quart slow cooker along with the remaining spice mixture.

3. Heat the oil in a nonstick skillet and sauté the onions, garlic, and peppers until fragrant. Add to the slow cooker.

4. Add the potatoes and coconut milk to the slow cooker. Stir. Cook 7–8 hours on low.

CHICKEN PICCATA

Serve over mashed potatoes or egg noodles.

Serves 4

INGREDIENTS:

2 boneless, skinless thin-cut chicken breasts

1 cup flour

1 teaspoon canola oil

¼ cup lemon juice

3 tablespoons nonpareil capers

¾ cup Chicken Broth (Chapter 19)

1. Dredge both sides of the chicken breasts in the flour. Discard leftover flour.

2. Heat the oil in a nonstick pan. Quickly sear the chicken on each side.

3. Place the chicken, lemon juice, capers, and broth into a 4-quart slow cooker.

4. Cook on high for 3 hours or for 6 hours on low.

MOROCCAN CHICKEN

This dish was inspired by traditional North African tagines and adapted for the slow cooker.

Serves 6

INGREDIENTS:

½ teaspoon coriander

½ teaspoon cinnamon

¼ teaspoon salt

1 teaspoon cumin

4 boneless, skinless chicken thighs, diced

½ cup water

4 cloves garlic, minced

1 onion, thinly sliced

1" knob ginger, minced

15 ounces canned chickpeas, drained and rinsed

4 ounces dried apricots, halved

1. Place all of the spices, chicken, water, garlic, onion, and ginger into a 4-quart slow cooker. Cook on low for 5 hours.

2. Stir in the chickpeas and apricots and cook on high for 40 minutes.

CHICKEN WITH FIGS

This recipe was inspired by traditional Moroccan tangines, a type of savory slow-cooked stew. Try it with whole-grain couscous or quinoa.

Serves 8

INGREDIENTS:

½ pound boneless, skinless chicken thighs

¾ pound boneless, skinless chicken breasts

¾ cup dried figs

1 sweet potato, peeled and diced

1 onion, chopped

3 cloves garlic, minced

2 teaspoons cumin

1 teaspoon coriander

½ teaspoon cayenne pepper

½ teaspoon ground ginger

½ teaspoon turmeric

½ teaspoon ground orange peel

½ teaspoon freshly ground black pepper

2¾ cups Chicken Broth (Chapter 19)

¼ cup orange juice

1. Cube the chicken. Quickly sauté the chicken in a dry nonstick skillet until it starts to turn white. Drain off any excess grease.

2. Place the chicken and remaining ingredients into a 4-quart slow cooker. Stir. Cook for 6 hours on low. Stir before serving.

PERUVIAN CHICKEN WITH AJI VERDE

Juicy chicken breasts are the perfect foil for this light, creamy, cilantro-spiked sauce. Aji Verde is often served as a dipping sauce, but in this dish it seeps into the chicken, infusing it with flavor.

Serves 4

INGREDIENTS:

5 cloves garlic, mashed

2 bone-in chicken breasts

2 tablespoons red wine vinegar

1 teaspoon cumin

1 teaspoon sugar

2 tablespoons soy sauce

2 jalapeños, chopped

½ cup cilantro

⅓ cup water

⅓ cup Cotija cheese

1 teaspoon apple cider vinegar

¼ teaspoon salt

1. Spread the cloves of garlic over the chicken pieces. Place into an oval 4-quart slow cooker. Pour the vinegar, cumin, sugar, and soy sauce over the chicken. Cook on low for 5 hours or until the chicken is thoroughly cooked.

2. In a food processor, pulse together the jalapeños, cilantro, water, cheese, cider vinegar, and salt.

3. Remove the chicken from the slow cooker. Remove and discard the skin. Spread the sauce on each breast. Return to the slow cooker and cook on low 15 minutes before serving.

¿Qué es el Queso Cotija?

Cotija cheese is a Mexican cheese made from cow's milk. It can be found in large blocks or grated. It has a flavor profile similar to Parmesan and can be rather crumbly. Use it as a topping for salads, tacos, soups, beans, or tostadas.

THAI PEANUT CHICKEN

In this healthy version of the takeout favorite, the broccoli is steamed in the broth as the chicken slow cooks.

Serves 6

INGREDIENTS:

1 pound boneless, skinless chicken breasts, cubed

2 cups broccoli florets

1 cup Chicken Broth (Chapter 19)

¼ cup coarsely chopped peanuts

3 tablespoons soy sauce

2 tablespoons minced Thai bird peppers

2 tablespoons minced garlic

2 tablespoons minced fresh ginger

¼ cup diced green onions

1. Place the chicken, broccoli, broth, peanuts, soy sauce, pepper, garlic, and ginger into a 4-quart slow cooker. Stir.

2. Cook on low for 4–5 hours or until the chicken is thoroughly cooked. Stir in the green onions prior to serving.

CHICKEN FRICASSEE

Chicken Fricassee is a dish that is easily adapted for personal taste. Fennel, mushrooms, or parsnips can be used with great success.

Serves 6

INGREDIENTS:

2 cups sliced red cabbage

2 carrots, cut into coin-sized pieces

2 stalks celery, diced

1 onion, sliced

3 bone-in chicken breasts

¾ cup Chicken Broth (Chapter 19)

2 teaspoons paprika

2 teaspoons dried thyme

2 teaspoons dried parsley

1. Place the cabbage, carrots, celery, and onions on the bottom of an oval 4-quart slow cooker.

2. Place the chicken skin-side up on top of the vegetables. Pour the broth over the chicken and sprinkle it evenly with the spices. Pat the spices onto the chicken skin.

3. Cook on low 6 hours or until the chicken is cooked through. Remove the skin prior to serving.

CHICKEN SALTIMBOCCA

Saltimbocca can refer to a number of ham- or prosciutto-wrapped meat dishes. In this version, the mild chicken takes on the strong flavors of the capers and prosciutto.

Serves 4

INGREDIENTS:

4 boneless, skinless breast tenderloins

4 paper-thin slices prosciutto

1½ cups Chicken Broth (Chapter 19)

3 tablespoons capote capers

¼ cup minced fresh sage

1. Wrap each tenderloin in prosciutto. Secure with a toothpick if necessary. Place tenderloins in a single layer in an oval 4-quart slow cooker.

2. Pour the broth over the chicken. Sprinkle with the capers and sage. Cook on low for 5 hours or until the chicken is fully cooked. Discard the cooking liquid prior to serving.

BALSAMIC CHICKEN AND SPINACH

Serve this with rice pilaf.

Serves 4

INGREDIENTS:

¾ pound boneless, skinless chicken breasts, cut into strips

¼ cup balsamic vinegar

4 cloves garlic, minced

1 tablespoon minced fresh oregano

1 tablespoon minced fresh Italian parsley

½ teaspoon freshly ground black pepper

5 ounces baby spinach

1. Place the chicken, vinegar, garlic, and spices into a 4-quart slow cooker. Stir. Cook on low for 6 hours.

2. Stir in the baby spinach and continue to cook until it starts to wilt, about 15 minutes. Stir before serving.

SLOW-ROASTED CHICKEN WITH POTATOES, PARSNIPS, AND ONIONS

Chicken made in the slow cooker is amazingly tender. The onions add a lot of flavor with no added fat needed.

Serves 6

INGREDIENTS:

4 medium onions, sliced

1 6-pound roasting chicken

6 large red skin potatoes, halved

4 parsnips, diced

1 teaspoon salt

1 teaspoon black pepper

1. Cover the bottom of a 6- to 7-quart oval slow cooker with half of the onions.

2. Place the chicken, breast-side up, on top of the onions.

3. Cover the chicken with the remaining onions.

4. Arrange the potatoes and parsnips around the chicken.

5. Cover and cook on low for 8 hours or until the chicken has an internal temperature of 165°F as measured using a food thermometer. Discard the chicken skin before serving.

A Snippet about Parsnips

Parsnips have a mild flavor and a texture that is well suited to extended cooking times. Always peel off the bitter skin before cooking. If parsnips are not available, carrots are an acceptable substitute.

CHICKEN AND SAUSAGE PAELLA

This simplified paella is an elegant addition to any dinner party; no specialty paella pan needed!

Serves 8

INGREDIENTS:

2 cups cubed cooked chicken breast

8 ounces fully cooked chicken andouille sausage, cut into 1" pieces

2½ quarts Chicken Broth (Chapter 19)

1½ cups frozen peas

2 carrots, diced

12 ounces long-grain rice

1 onion, diced

1 teaspoon crushed saffron

1 teaspoon smoked paprika

1½ cups raw shrimp

1. Place the chicken breast, sausage, broth, peas, carrots, rice, onion, saffron, and paprika in a 6- to 7-quart slow cooker. Cook on high for 2 hours.

2. Add the shrimp and continue to cook on high for 30 minutes or until the shrimp is fully cooked. Stir prior to serving.

JERK CHICKEN

Virtually no hands-on time makes this recipe a breeze.

Serves 12

INGREDIENTS:

3 pounds boneless, skinless chicken breast or thighs

3 tablespoons Jamaican jerk seasoning

1 Scotch bonnet pepper, sliced

¼ cup fresh thyme leaves

½ cup lemon juice

1 onion, chopped

1 clove garlic, minced

1 teaspoon hickory liquid smoke

½ teaspoon ground allspice

¼ teaspoon cloves

1. Place the chicken on the bottom of a 6- to 7-quart slow cooker. Pour the remaining ingredients on top. Cook on low for 5 hours.

Easy Mornings

Cut up vegetables in the evening and refrigerate them overnight. If cutting and storing meat, place it in a separate container from the vegetables to avoid cross contamination. To save even more time, you can measure out dry spices and leave them in the slow cooker insert overnight.

TWENTY CLOVES OF GARLIC CHICKEN

This is a scaled-down version of the classic dish Forty Cloves of Garlic Chicken.

Serves 2

INGREDIENTS:

20 whole cloves garlic

1 split chicken breast

⅛ teaspoon salt

⅛ teaspoon black pepper

1. Peel the garlic cloves. Sprinkle the chicken with salt and pepper.

2. Place the chicken breast and garlic cloves in a 1½- to 2-quart slow cooker. Cook on low for 6–7 hours.

Cooking Tip

If you need to cook the chicken longer than the suggested 6–7 hours, add ¼ cup chicken broth to the slow cooker at the beginning of the cooking time. This will help keep the chicken juicy. Alternately, add half an onion.

FILIPINO CHICKEN ADOBO

Adobo is the unofficial dish of the Philippines. There are many variations, but they all have a pleasant sour-tart flavor.

Serves 2

INGREDIENTS:

2 boneless, skinless chicken thighs

¼ cup water

¼ cup cane vinegar

¼ cup soy sauce

1 teaspoon whole black peppercorns

5 cloves garlic, halved

2 bay leaves

1. Place all ingredients in a 2-quart slow cooker. Cook for 6–8 hours. Discard the bay leaves before serving.

CHICKEN TACO FILLING

Perfect for a quick weeknight meal, the preparation time is short and the spices get the entire day to flavor the meat.

Serves 2

INGREDIENTS:

1 small onion, diced

1 clove garlic, minced

2 tablespoons minced jalapeño

½ pound ground chicken

½ cup diced tomato

½ teaspoon ground chipotle

½ teaspoon oregano

¼ teaspoon hot paprika

½ teaspoon hot Mexican-style chili powder

½ teaspoon ground cayenne pepper

1. In a small nonstick skillet, sauté the onions, garlic, jalapeño, and chicken until the chicken is cooked through, about 3 minutes. Drain off any grease.

2. Add the chicken mixture and the remaining ingredients to a 1½- to 2-quart slow cooker. Stir to incorporate the spices into the meat. Cook for 6–8 hours on low.

What Is Chipotle?

Chipotle peppers are smoked jalapeño peppers. Their smoky hot flavor is perfect for adding depth and heat to slow-cooked foods. Chipotles are often found as a ground spice or in adobo, a tomato-onion sauce. They are also available as whole, dried peppers.

SPICY OLIVE CHICKEN

This recipe creates a delicious sauce underneath the roasted chicken. The pan juices will add flavor to the sauce.

Serves 4

INGREDIENTS:

1 (3-pound) whole chicken, cut into 8 pieces

1 teaspoon salt

½ teaspoon ground black pepper

4 tablespoons unsalted butter

⅔ cup chopped sweet onion

2 tablespoons capers, drained and rinsed

24 green olives, pitted

½ cup Chicken Broth (Chapter 19)

½ cup dry white wine

1 teaspoon prepared Dijon mustard

½ teaspoon hot sauce

2 cups cooked white rice

¼ cup fresh chopped parsley

1. Sprinkle the chicken pieces with salt and pepper and brown them in the butter in a large skillet for about 3 minutes on each side. Sauté the onion in the same skillet for an additional 3–5 minutes. Pour chicken, onion, capers, and olives into a greased 4-quart slow cooker.

2. In a small bowl whisk together the broth, wine, and mustard. Pour over chicken in the slow cooker. Add hot sauce. Cover and cook on high for 3–3½ hours or on low for 5½–6 hours.

3. When ready to serve, place chicken over rice. Ladle sauce and olives over each serving. Garnish with parsley.

Capers

Capers are flavorful berries. Picked green, they can be packed in salt or brine. Try to find the smallest—they seem to have more flavor than the big ones do. Capers are great on their own or incorporated into sauces. They are also good in salads and as a garnish on many dishes that would otherwise be dull.

CHAPTER 8

TURKEY AND LAMB

MOCK BRATWURST IN BEER

Bavarian seasoning is a mix of a blend of Bavarian-style crushed brown mustard seeds, French rosemary, garlic, Dalmatian sage, French thyme, and bay leaves. The Spice House (www.thespicehouse.com) has a salt-free Bavarian Seasoning Blend that is appropriate for this recipe.

Serves 8

INGREDIENTS:

2 stalks celery, finely chopped

1 (1-pound) bag baby carrots

1 large onion, peeled and sliced

2 cloves garlic, peeled and minced

4 slices bacon, cut into small pieces

1 (3-pound) boneless turkey breast

1 (2-pound) bag sauerkraut, rinsed and drained

8 medium red potatoes, washed and pierced

1 (12-ounce) can beer

1 tablespoon Bavarian seasoning

Salt and freshly ground pepper, to taste

1. Add the ingredients to the slow cooker in the order given. Note that the liquid amount needed will depend on how wet the sauerkraut is when you add it. The liquid should come up halfway and cover the turkey breast, with the sauerkraut and potatoes being above the liquid line. Add more beer if necessary. Slow-cook on low for 8 hours. Taste for seasoning and adjust if necessary. Serve hot.

Bavarian Seasoning Substitution

You can substitute a tablespoon of stone-ground mustard along with ¼ teaspoon each of rosemary, garlic powder, sage, and thyme. Add a bay leaf (that will need to be removed before you serve the meal). Just before serving, taste for seasoning and adjust if necessary.

TURKEY IN ONION-MUSHROOM GRAVY

Add a tossed salad and steamed vegetable to make this dish a complete meal.

Serves 8

INGREDIENTS:

Nonstick spray

½ cup water

1 (3-pound) boneless turkey breast

1 envelope dry onion soup mix

1 small onion, peeled and thinly sliced

8 ounces fresh mushrooms, cleaned and sliced

8 medium red potatoes, peeled

1 tablespoon butter, softened

1 tablespoon all-purpose flour

1 cup heavy cream

Salt and freshly ground pepper, to taste

1. Treat the crock of the slow cooker with nonstick spray. Add the water. Place the turkey in the slow cooker and sprinkle the soup mix over the top of it. Add the onion, mushrooms, and potatoes. Cover and cook on low for 8 hours or until the turkey reaches an internal temperature of 170°F.

2. Move the turkey breast and potatoes to a serving platter; cover and keep warm.

3. Cover, increase the slow cooker to high, and cook for 15 minutes or until the liquid in the crock is bubbling around the edges. Mix the butter and flour together; dollop into the cooker. Whisk to work into the liquid, stirring and cooking for 5 minutes or until the flour taste is cooked out of the sauce and the mixture begins to thicken. Whisk in the cream and continue to cook for 15 minutes or until the cream comes to temperature and the gravy coats the back of a spoon. Taste for seasoning and add salt and pepper, to taste.

4. Slice the turkey and ladle the gravy over the slices, and serve the extra on the side.

Turkey Stroganoff

Omit the potatoes and cook the Turkey in Onion-Mushroom Gravy recipe as directed through Step 2. Stir 1 cup of sour cream into the liquid in the slow cooker, continuing to cook and stir until the mixture comes to temperature. Serve over cooked egg noodles and the sliced turkey.

HONEY-GLAZED TURKEY

If the turkey legs are large, you can remove the meat from the bone before serving and increase the number of servings to six or eight.

Serves 4

INGREDIENTS:

Nonstick spray

¼ cup apricot jam

2 tablespoons honey

1 tablespoon fresh lemon juice

1 tablespoon barbecue sauce

1 tablespoon soy sauce

1 teaspoon paprika

1 teaspoon salt

¼ teaspoon freshly ground black pepper

½ teaspoon dried rosemary

½ teaspoon dried thyme

4 turkey legs, skin removed

1 teaspoon cornstarch

1 teaspoon cold water

1. Treat the crock of the slow cooker with nonstick spray. Turn the heat setting to high. Add the jam, honey, lemon juice, barbecue sauce, and soy sauce. Once the mixture has heated enough to melt the jam and honey into the mixture, stir in the paprika, salt, pepper, rosemary, and thyme. Add the turkey legs, spooning the sauce over them. Cover, reduce the heat setting to low, and cook for 8 hours. Uncover, increase heat setting to high, and cook for ½ hour to reduce the pan juices.

2. Remove the turkey legs to a serving platter; cover and keep warm. Add the cornstarch and water in a small bowl; stir to mix, and then thin with a little of the pan juices. Stir the resulting cornstarch slurry into the slow cooker. Cook and stir for 5 minutes or until thickened enough to coat the back of a spoon. Pour the glaze over the turkey legs and serve.

Turkey Sandwiches

Complete Step 1 of the Honey-Glazed Turkey recipe. Remove the turkey legs and allow to cool enough to remove the meat from the bones while you make the cornstarch slurry. Once the glaze is thickened, stir in the turkey meat. Serve on rolls or toasted whole-grain country bread.

HOLIDAY TURKEY BREAST

Do not use jellied cranberry sauce in this recipe. Taste the whole cranberry sauce before adding it to the slow cooker. If it's sweet enough for your taste, then substitute water for the apple juice.

Serves 8

INGREDIENTS:

Nonstick spray

1 envelope onion and herb soup mix

1 (16-ounce) can whole cranberry sauce

¼ cup apple juice

1 (3-pound) boneless turkey breast

1. Treat the crock of the slow cooker with nonstick spray. Add the soup mix, cranberry sauce, and juice to the slow cooker; stir to combine.

2. Add turkey breast and spoon the cranberry sauce mixture over the turkey. Cover and cook on low for 8 hours or until the internal temperature of the turkey is 170°F.

SPICED APPLE CIDER TURKEY

This recipe makes candied sweet potatoes while it cooks the turkey in the sweetened cider sauce.

Serves 8

INGREDIENTS:

Nonstick spray

1 (3-pound) boneless turkey breast

Salt and freshly ground black pepper, to taste

2 apples

4 large sweet potatoes

½ cup apple cider or apple juice

½ teaspoon ground cinnamon

¼ teaspoon ground cloves

¼ teaspoon ground allspice

2 tablespoons brown sugar

1. Treat the crock of the slow cooker with nonstick spray. Add turkey breast and season it with salt and pepper.

2. Peel, core, and slice the apples; arrange the slices over and around the turkey.

3. Peel the sweet potatoes and cut each in half; add to the slow cooker.

4. Add the cider or juice, cinnamon, cloves, allspice, and brown sugar to a bowl or measuring cup; stir to combine and pour over the ingredients in the slow cooker.

5. Cover and cook on low for 8 hours or until the internal temperature of the turkey is 170°F.

TURKEY AND GRAVY

Season with your choice of Mrs. Dash Garlic Herb, Onion & Herb, Original, or Table Blend seasoning. For more servings, increase the size of the turkey breast; if necessary, increase the cooking time so it reaches an internal temperature of 170°F.

Serves 8

INGREDIENTS:

1¾ cups Turkey or Chicken Broth (Chapter 19)

2 stalks celery

1 large carrot

1 medium onion, peeled and quartered

1 (3-pound) boneless turkey breast

1 teaspoon Mrs. Dash Seasoning Blend

¼ cup (Wondra) instant flour

Optional: 2 tablespoons Madeira

Salt and freshly ground black pepper, to taste

1. Add the broth to the slow cooker. Cut each celery stalk in half. Scrub and cut the carrot into four pieces. Add the celery, carrot, and onion to the slow cooker. Nestle the turkey breast on top of the vegetables, and sprinkle the seasoning blend over it. Cover and cook on low for 8 hours.

2. Remove the turkey breast to a serving platter; cover and keep warm.

3. Strain the pan juices through a cheesecloth-lined colander set over a large nonstick skillet, squeezing the vegetables in the cheesecloth to release the juices.

4. Transfer ¼ cup of the broth to a bowl and mix it together with the Madeira and instant flour; stir until the flour is dissolved. Bring the broth to a boil over medium-high heat. Whisk the flour mixture into the broth, stirring constantly until the gravy is thickened and coats the back of a spoon. Taste for seasoning, and add salt and pepper if needed. Slice the turkey and pour the gravy over the top of the slices, or serve the gravy on the side.

Another Option

If you don't have instant flour on hand, you can instead strain the turkey broth into a bowl or large measuring cup. Melt ¼ cup butter in a large nonstick skillet and whisk ¼ cup all-purpose flour into the butter. Slowly whisk the broth into the resulting butter-flour roux; bring to a boil, stirring constantly, and cook until thickened.

TURKEY MOLE

For extra heat, add a few of the ancho chili seeds to the cooker. For even more heat, add a dried pasilla negro chili, too. Use this dish as filling in heated corn or flour tortillas, or serve it with rice and refried beans.

Serves 8

INGREDIENTS:

2 tablespoons olive oil

1 small onion, peeled and diced

2 cloves garlic, peeled and minced

1 tablespoon tomato paste

1 (8-ounce) can diced tomatoes

1 dried ancho chili

1½ tablespoons Mexican chocolate or semisweet chocolate chips

1 teaspoon sesame seeds

2 teaspoons slivered almonds

1 cup Turkey or Chicken Broth (Chapter 19)

4 turkey legs, skin removed

Salt and freshly ground black pepper, to taste

Optional: Cinnamon, to taste

1. Add the oil and onion to the slow cooker; cover and cook on high for 30 minutes or until the onion just begins to brown. Stir in the garlic and tomato paste; cover and cook for 15 more minutes.

2. Stir the diced tomatoes into the onion mixture. Remove the stem and seeds from the dried chili; snip it into small pieces and add it to the cooker along with the chocolate chips, sesame seeds, almonds, and broth. Stir to combine. Add the turkey; cover and cook on low for 8 hours.

3. Remove the turkey legs; allow to cool enough to remove the meat from the bones.

4. Use an immersion blender to purée the mole sauce in the slow cooker. Taste for seasoning and add salt, pepper, and cinnamon if desired. Stir the turkey into the sauce.

Sauce on the Side

The Turkey Mole recipe makes about 2 cups of sauce. You can stir the turkey into 1 cup of that sauce and reserve the remaining sauce to serve on the side.

TURKEY IN ONION SAUCE

This is an African-inspired dish. Serve it over cooked rice.

Serves 8

INGREDIENTS:

5 large onions, peeled and thinly sliced

4 cloves garlic, peeled and minced

¼ cup fresh lemon juice

1 teaspoon salt

¼ teaspoon cayenne pepper

4 turkey thighs, skin removed

Freshly ground black pepper, to taste

1. Add the onions, garlic, lemon juice, salt, and cayenne pepper to the slow cooker; stir to combine. Nestle the turkey legs into the onion mixture. Cover and cook on low for 8 hours.

2. Remove the turkey legs and allow to cool enough to remove the meat from the bone. Leave the cover off of the slow cooker and allow the onion mixture to continue to cook until the liquid has totally evaporated. (You can raise the setting to high to speed things up if you wish. Just be sure to stir the mixture occasionally to prevent the onions from burning.) Stir the turkey into the onion mixture. Taste for seasoning and add pepper if desired. For more heat, add additional cayenne pepper, too.

BARBECUE TURKEY

Dark meat turkey stays moist, even after long slow-cooking times. Left to cook long enough, it becomes tender enough to use to make "pulled" turkey sandwiches that are especially good if you add coleslaw or shredded lettuce, bacon, and tomato. An alternative is to serve Barbecue Turkey over cooked rice or noodles.

Serves 4

INGREDIENTS:

½ cup ketchup

2 tablespoons brown sugar

1 tablespoon quick-cooking tapioca

1 tablespoon apple cider vinegar

1 teaspoon Worcestershire sauce

1 teaspoon soy or steak sauce

¼ teaspoon ground cinnamon

⅛ teaspoon ground cloves

Optional: Dried red pepper flakes, to taste

2 turkey thighs, skin removed

1. Add the ketchup, brown sugar, tapioca, vinegar, Worcestershire sauce, soy or steak sauce (or both), cinnamon, cloves, and red pepper flakes, if using, to the slow cooker; stir to combine.

2. Place the turkey thighs in the slow cooker, meaty side down. Cover and cook on low for 8 or more hours or until the turkey is tender and pulls away from the bone. Remove the turkey; allow to cool enough to remove the meat from the bones. Skim any fat off of the top of the barbecue sauce in the slow cooker. Stir the turkey into the sauce and continue to cook long enough for it to come back to temperature.

FRUITED TURKEY ROAST

A pinch of dried red pepper flakes acts as a flavor enhancer. Add more if you prefer sweet and spicy sauce. You can add more kick to the sauce by substituting spicy mustard for the stone-ground.

Serves 8

INGREDIENTS:

Nonstick spray

1 (3-pound) turkey roast

1 medium onion, peeled and diced

1 cup cranberries

2 peaches, peeled, seeded, and diced

¼ cup Turkey or Chicken Broth (Chapter 19)

¼ cup brown sugar

3 tablespoons stone-ground mustard

Optional: Dried red pepper flakes, to taste

Optional: Zest of 1 orange

Optional: Salt and freshly ground black pepper, to taste

1. Treat the crock of the slow cooker with nonstick spray. Add the turkey. Pour the diced onion, cranberries, and diced peaches around the turkey. Add the broth, brown sugar, mustard, and red pepper flakes, if using, to a bowl; stir to mix, adding the orange zest if using. Pour into the slow cooker. Cover and cook on low for 8 hours or until the internal temperature of the roast reaches 170°F.

2. Remove the turkey to a serving platter. (If the turkey roast is held together with a net, you can remove it at this time. Some find it easier to carve with the net in place. Regardless, allow the turkey to "rest" for at least 10 minutes before you slice it.) Cover and keep warm.

3. Use an immersion blender to purée the pan liquids. Taste for seasoning and adjust if necessary. Transfer to a gravy boat and serve alongside the roast.

TURKEY SAUSAGE AND BEANS MEDLEY

You can serve this dish as a main course along with a salad and some crusty bread or as a baked beans alternative. Either way, it's even better if you add some diced bacon to the slow cooker when you add the other ingredients, or crumble crisp bacon and sprinkle chopped green onions over the top of each serving.

Serves 8

INGREDIENTS:

1 pound cooked smoked turkey sausage

1 (15-ounce) can black beans, rinsed and drained

1 (15-ounce) can butter beans, rinsed and drained

1 (15-ounce) can Great Northern beans, rinsed and drained

1 (15-ounce) can red kidney beans, rinsed and drained

1 (8-ounce) can tomato sauce

½ cup ketchup

1 medium red bell pepper, seeded and diced

1 large sweet onion, peeled and diced

¼ cup brown sugar

1 tablespoon Worcestershire sauce

1 teaspoon Dijon or dry mustard

Optional: Hot sauce or dried red pepper flakes, to taste

1. Dice the smoked turkey sausage and add to the slow cooker along with the other ingredients. Cover and cook on low for 8 hours.

ASIAN-SPICED TURKEY BREAST

A 3-pound turkey breast or roast will yield about 8 (4-ounce) servings. If you prefer larger portions, adjust the servings or increase the size of the roast. If you do the latter, you may need to increase the cooking time to ensure the meat gets done.

Serves 8

INGREDIENTS:

½ cup orange marmalade

1 tablespoon fresh ginger, peeled and grated

1 clove garlic, peeled and minced

½ teaspoon Chinese five-spice powder

Salt and freshly ground black pepper, to taste

¼ cup orange juice

1 (3-pound) turkey breast or roast

1. Add the marmalade, ginger, garlic, spice powder, salt, pepper, and orange juice to the slow cooker. Stir to mix. Place the turkey breast or roast into the cooker. Spoon some of the sauce over the meat. Cover and cook on low for 8 hours or until the internal temperature of the meat is 170°F.

THYME-ROASTED TURKEY BREAST

Slow-cooked turkey is so moist there's no basting required!

Serves 10

INGREDIENTS:

2 onions, thinly sliced

1 6- to 7-pound turkey breast or turkey half

½ cup minced thyme

½ tablespoon freshly ground black pepper

½ tablespoon salt

½ tablespoon dried parsley

½ tablespoon celery flakes

½ tablespoon mustard seed

1. Arrange the onion slices in a thin layer on the bottom of a 6- to 7-quart slow cooker.

2. Make a small slit in the skin of the turkey and spread the thyme between the skin and meat. Smooth the skin back onto the turkey.

3. In a small bowl, stir the pepper, salt, parsley, celery flakes, and mustard seed. Rub the spice mixture into the skin of the turkey.

4. Place the turkey in the slow cooker on top of the onion layer. Cook for 8 hours. Remove the skin and onions and discard them before serving the turkey.

HONEY-MUSTARD TURKEY

You can substitute maple syrup for the honey. Another alternative is to substitute Dijon mustard instead of stone-ground and white wine vinegar for the cider.

Serves 4

INGREDIENTS:

Nonstick spray

2 turkey thighs, skin removed

4 red potatoes, peeled and quartered

¼ cup stone-ground mustard

⅓ cup honey

1 tablespoon apple cider vinegar

1 tablespoon quick-cooking tapioca

Optional: Extra-virgin olive oil

1. Treat the crock of the slow cooker with nonstick spray. Place the thighs in the slow cooker, meaty side down. Layer the potatoes over the thighs. Add the mustard, honey, vinegar, and tapioca to a bowl; mix well, then pour into the slow cooker. Cover and cook on low for 8 hours. When serving, drizzle extra-virgin olive oil over the potatoes if desired.

TURKEY IN RED WINE SAUCE

A hearty wine like Zinfandel works well in this Coq au Vin–inspired dish. If you prefer, you can make the dish with 8 chicken thighs instead of with turkey.

Serves 4

INGREDIENTS:

4 strips bacon

2 medium carrots, diced

½ stalk celery, finely diced

1 medium onion, peeled and diced

8 ounces fresh mushrooms, cleaned and sliced

2 cloves garlic, peeled and minced

2 turkey thighs, skin removed

Salt and freshly ground black pepper, to taste

2 teaspoons dried parsley

½ teaspoon dried thyme

1 bay leaf

½ cup dry red wine

½ cup double-strength chicken or turkey broth

1 (10-ounce) package frozen artichoke hearts, thawed

Optional: 2 tablespoons butter, softened

Optional: 2 tablespoons all-purpose flour

1. Add the bacon, carrots, and celery to a microwave-safe bowl. Cover and microwave on high for 1 minute; stir, recover, and microwave on high for another minute. Stir in the onion; cover and microwave on high for 2 minutes. Stir in the mushrooms; stirring occasionally, microwave uncovered on high for 3–5 minutes or until the mushrooms have given off their liquid. Stir in the garlic, and then transfer to the slow cooker.

2. Place the turkey thighs meaty side down in the slow cooker. Sprinkle with the salt, pepper, parsley, and thyme. Add the bay leaf. Pour in the wine and chicken broth. Cover and cook on low for 7 hours.

3. Remove the turkey thighs and take the meat off the bone. Return the meat to the slow cooker. Add the artichokes; cover and cook on low for 1 hour.

4. To thicken the sauce by cooking down the pan juices, transfer the artichokes to a serving dish; cover and keep warm. Skim any fat from the surface of the pan liquids; cook, stirring occasionally, uncovered on high for 15–30 minutes or until the liquid has reduced by half. Taste for seasoning, adjust if necessary, and then pour the sauce over the chicken and vegetables.

5. To thicken the sauce using the optional butter and flour, use a slotted spoon to transfer the meat, mushrooms, and artichokes to a serving bowl; cover and keep warm. Cover and increase the heat to high. Mix the butter and flour together in a small bowl along with about ½ cup of the pan liquids. Once the liquids in the slow cooker are bubbling around the edges, remove the cover and whisk in the butter-flour mixture. Cook, stirring constantly, for 10 minutes or until the flour taste is cooked out of the sauce and it coats the back of a spoon. Taste for seasoning, adjust if necessary, and then pour the sauce over the chicken and vegetables.

LAMB CHOPS

The red currant jelly gives the gravy a fruity taste reminiscent of wine.

Serves 6

INGREDIENTS:

1 tablespoon olive or vegetable oil

6 (8-ounce) lamb rib chops, cut 1-inch thick

12 small new potatoes, scrubbed

6 medium carrots, peeled and cut into 1-inch pieces

2 cups water

½ teaspoon dried dill

½ teaspoon salt

¼ teaspoon ground black pepper

4 teaspoons butter, softened

4 teaspoons all-purpose flour

¼ cup red currant jelly

½ cup plain regular or low-fat yogurt

1. Bring the oil to temperature in a large nonstick skillet over medium-high heat. Add the lamb to the skillet; brown for 3 minutes on each side.

2. Remove a narrow strip of peel from the center of each new potato. Place potatoes, carrots, water, dill, salt, and pepper in a large slow cooker. Add the lamb to the slow cooker over the vegetables. Cover and cook on low for 8 hours.

3. Transfer the lamb chops and vegetables to a serving platter; cover and keep warm.

4. For the sauce, strain the cooking liquid; skim off any fat and discard. Pour all but ½ cup of the cooking liquid back into the slow cooker; turn the heat setting to high.

5. Whisk the butter, flour, and jelly into the reserved ½ cup of cooking liquid; remove any lumps, and then whisk the flour mixture into the liquid in the slow cooker. Cook and stir for 15 minutes or until the gravy is thickened and bubbly. Stir in the yogurt. Taste for seasoning and add additional salt, pepper, and jelly if needed. Serve chops and vegetables with the sauce.

GREEK BONELESS LEG OF LAMB

Lamb does surprisingly well in the slow cooker. It is nearly impossible to overcook, and every bite is meltingly tender.

Serves 12

INGREDIENTS:

4 pounds boneless leg of lamb

1 tablespoon crushed rosemary

1 teaspoon freshly ground black pepper

¼ teaspoon kosher salt

¼ cup lemon juice

¼ cup water

1. Slice off any visible fat from the lamb and discard. Place in a 4- or 6-quart slow cooker.

2. Add the remaining ingredients on top of the lamb. Cook on low for 8 hours.

3. Remove from the slow cooker. Discard cooking liquid. Remove any remaining visible fat from the lamb. Slice the lamb prior to serving.

Healthy Cooking with Lamb

Lamb has a reputation as a somewhat fatty meat. However, buying a leaner cut, like the boneless leg where much of the fat and bone has been removed by the butcher, and slicing off any excess at home can eliminate much of the fat. When slow cooking, the fat melts off the meat and accumulates in the bottom of the cooker where it can easily be discarded after removing the meat.

MOROCCAN LAMB STEW

Look for boneless, lean lamb chops to dice for this recipe; it is cheaper and easier than buying a whole leg of lamb.

Serves 2

INGREDIENTS:

½ pound lean boneless lamb, cubed

2 cloves garlic, minced

½ onion, chopped

2 tablespoons lemon juice

¼ cup sliced green olives

2 teaspoons honey

¼ teaspoon salt

½ teaspoon freshly ground black pepper

¼ teaspoon turmeric

2 springs fresh thyme

1. Place the lamb, garlic, onion, lemon juice, olives, honey, salt, pepper, and turmeric in a 2-quart slow cooker. Top with the sprigs of thyme. Cook on low for 8 hours.

GINGER TOMATO LAMB

You can substitute beef or pork for lamb in this recipe if you wish. Serve with triangles of fresh pita bread.

Serves 4–6

INGREDIENTS:

2 pounds lamb

2 tablespoons butter

1 onion

1 clove garlic

3 tablespoons flour

1½ tablespoons curry powder

2 tomatoes

1 inch fresh gingerroot

1 teaspoon salt

¼ cup water

1. Cube the lamb. Sauté in butter in a pan over medium heat until slightly browned. Transfer the meat to the slow cooker; set aside the pan with the juices.

2. Chop the onion; crush and mince the garlic. Add the onion and garlic to the pan used for the lamb and sauté over medium heat until the onion is tender. Stir in the flour and curry and mix while heating. When thickened, add the onion mixture to the slow cooker.

3. Chop the tomatoes. Peel and grate the gingerroot. Add the tomatoes, ginger, salt, and water to the slow cooker.

4. Cover and heat on a low setting for 4–5 hours.

MOUNTAIN HONEY LAMB WITH DATES

You can buy ghee for this recipe, or make your own (Chapter 16). Serve this with warm, fresh pita bread.

Serves 6–8

INGREDIENTS:

2 pounds lamb

1 onion

5 tablespoons Ghee (Chapter 16)

1 cup dates

1 teaspoon turmeric

1 teaspoon cinnamon

½ teaspoon salt

2 tablespoons honey

1 cup uncooked rice

2½ cups water

Rind of ¼ lemon

1. Cut the lamb into cubes; slice the onion. Sauté the lamb and onion in 3 tablespoons of the Ghee in a pan over medium heat until the meat is lightly browned.

2. Pit and chop the dates. Add the meat mixture, dates, spices, salt, honey, rice, and water to the slow cooker.

3. Cover and heat on a low setting for 4–5 hours.

4. Finely grate the lemon rind. Half an hour before serving, add the lemon rind and the remaining Ghee.

LAMB WITH GARLIC, LEMON, AND ROSEMARY

You can use the spice rub in this recipe as a marinade by applying it to the leg of lamb several hours (or up to one full day) before cooking. The red wine in this dish can be replaced with Chicken or Beef Broth (Chapter 19).

Serves 4

INGREDIENTS:

4 cloves garlic, crushed

1 tablespoon fresh rosemary, chopped

1 tablespoon olive oil

½ teaspoon salt

1 teaspoon ground pepper

1 large lemon, cut into ¼" slices

1 (3-pound) leg of lamb

½ cup red wine

1. In a small bowl mix together garlic, rosemary, olive oil, salt, and pepper. Rub this mixture onto the leg of lamb.

2. Place a few lemon slices in the bottom of a greased 4-quart slow cooker. Place spice-rubbed lamb on top of lemon slices.

3. Add remaining lemon slices on top of lamb. Pour wine around the lamb.

4. Cook on low heat for 8–10 hours, or on high for 4–6 hours.

Using Different Cuts of Affordable Meat

You could also use this spice rub on a beef rump roast, beef or lamb shanks, or any cheaper cut of meat. The flavors will infuse into the meat and make a delicious base for a stew, soup, or casserole.

LAMB AND ROOT VEGETABLE TAGINE

This exotic dish is a North African–inspired stew with curried root vegetables and apricots.

Serves 6

INGREDIENTS:

1 tablespoon olive oil

2 pounds leg of lamb, trimmed of fat and cut into bite-sized chunks

½ onion, chopped

1 clove garlic, minced

½ teaspoon pepper

½ teaspoon salt

1 cup gluten-free chicken stock

½ pound (about 2 medium) sweet potatoes, peeled and cut into 1" chunks

⅓ cup dried apricots, cut in half

1 teaspoon coriander

1 teaspoon cumin

¼ teaspoon cinnamon

1. In a large skillet, brown cubed lamb in olive oil, approximately 1–2 minutes per side. Add lamb to a greased 4-quart slow cooker. Cook onion and garlic in the same skillet for 3–4 minutes until soft and then add to slow cooker.

2. Add remaining ingredients to slow cooker. Cook on high for 4 hours or on low for 8 hours.

CHAPTER 9

BEEF

BEEF AND CABBAGE

The longer cooking time helps the flavors develop. But because the meat is already cooked, this meal is done when the cabbage is tender, or in about 4 hours on low. Serve over cooked brown rice or mashed potatoes.

Serves 4

INGREDIENTS:

1 pound cooked beef

1 small head of cabbage, chopped

1 medium onion, peeled and diced

2 carrots, peeled and thinly sliced

2 stalks celery, sliced in ½-inch pieces

1 clove garlic, peeled and minced

2 cups Beef Broth (Chapter 19)

1 (14½-ounce) can diced tomatoes

¼ teaspoon sugar

Salt, to taste

⅛ teaspoon freshly ground black pepper

1. Cut the cooked beef into bite-sized pieces and add it to the slow cooker along with the cabbage, onion, carrots, and celery; stir to mix.

2. Add the garlic, broth, tomatoes, sugar, salt, and pepper to a bowl; mix well and pour over the beef. Set the slow cooker on high and cook for 1 hour or until the cabbage has begun to wilt.

3. Reduce heat to low and cook for 4 hours. Adjust seasonings if necessary.

EASY BEEF STROGANOFF

Adding some balsamic vinegar and sugar to this recipe mimics the flavor of using beef cooked in wine. The combination of cream cheese and sour cream gives this dish a much richer flavor, but you can use all sour cream if you prefer.

Serves 4

INGREDIENTS:

1 pound cooked beef

1 small onion, peeled and thinly sliced

1 (4-ounce) can sliced mushrooms, drained

1 (10¾-ounce) can cream of mushroom soup

1 tablespoon balsamic vinegar

1 teaspoon sugar

¼ teaspoon garlic powder

1 (4-ounce) package cream cheese

½ cup sour cream

1. Dice or shred the cooked beef and add to the slow cooker along with the onion. Add the mushrooms, soup, vinegar, sugar, and garlic powder to a bowl; stir to mix and then pour into the slow cooker. Cover and cook on low for 4 hours.

2. Cut the cream cheese into small cubes; stir into the beef mixture in the slow cooker. Cover and cook on low for ½ hour or until the cheese is melted. Stir in the sour cream; cover and cook on low for 15 minutes or until the sour cream comes to temperature. Serve over hot cooked egg noodles.

NEW ENGLAND BOILED DINNER

Cutting the meat into serving-sized pieces before you add it to the slow cooker will make the meat cook up more tender, but you can keep it in one piece if you prefer to carve it at the table.

Serves 8

INGREDIENTS:

1 (3-pound) boneless beef round rump roast

2 (10¾-ounce) cans onion soup

1 teaspoon prepared horseradish

1 bay leaf

1 clove garlic, peeled and minced

6 large carrots, peeled and cut into 1-inch pieces

3 rutabagas, peeled and quartered

4 large potatoes, peeled and quartered

1 (2-pound) head of cabbage, cut into 8 wedges

2 tablespoons butter

2 tablespoons all-purpose flour

Salt and freshly ground black pepper, to taste

Optional: 1 cup sour cream

1. Cut the beef into eight serving pieces and add it along with the soup, horseradish, bay leaf, and garlic to the slow cooker. Add the carrots, rutabagas, potatoes, and cabbage wedges. Cover and cook on low for 8 hours.

2. Remove meat and vegetables to a serving platter; cover and keep warm.

3. Increase the slow cooker setting to high; cover and cook until the pan juices begin to bubble around the edges. Mix the butter and flour in a bowl together with ½ cup of the pan juices; strain out any lumps and whisk the mixture into the simmering liquid in the slow cooker. Cook and stir for 15 minutes or until the flour flavor is cooked out and the resulting gravy is thickened enough to coat the back of a spoon. Taste for seasoning and add salt and pepper if desired. Stir in the sour cream if using. Serve alongside or over the meat and vegetables.

Horseradish Gravy

If you prefer a more intense horseradish flavor with cooked beef, increase the amount to 1 tablespoon. Taste the pan juices before you thicken it with the butter and flour mixture, and add more horseradish at that time if desired. Of course, you can have some horseradish or some horseradish mayonnaise available as a condiment for those who want more.

PASTRAMI

New York–style pastrami is peppercorn-crusted smoked corned beef that is sometimes steamed before serving. Smoked paprika will impart a subtle smoky flavor. For a more intense smoked flavor, use liquid smoke, too.

Serves 12

INGREDIENTS:

1 (4-pound) corned beef brisket

2 large onions, peeled and sliced

2 cloves garlic, peeled and minced

2 tablespoons pickling spices

1½ cups water

1 tablespoon black peppercorns, crushed

¾ teaspoon freshly grated nutmeg

¾ teaspoon ground allspice

2 teaspoons smoked paprika

Optional: ¼ teaspoon liquid smoke

1. Trim any fat from the corned beef brisket. Add the brisket, onions, garlic, pickling spice, and water to the slow cooker. Cover and cook for 8 hours. Turn off the cooker and allow the meat to cool enough to handle it.

2. Preheat the oven to 350°F.

3. Add the crushed (or cracked) peppercorns, nutmeg, allspice, paprika, and liquid smoke (if using) to a small bowl; mix well. Rub the peppercorn mixture over all sides of the corned beef. Place on a roasting pan; roast on the middle shelf for 45 minutes. Let the meat rest for 10 minutes, then carve by slicing it against the grain or on the diagonal.

Deli-Style Pastrami Sandwich

Pile thin slices of pastrami on a slice of deli rye slathered with mustard. Top with another slice of rye bread. Serve with a big, crisp kosher dill pickle.

YANKEE POT ROAST

New England cooking is traditionally plain and straightforward. If your family prefers a heartier flavor, add 1 teaspoon of Mrs. Dash Garlic Herb Seasoning Blend.

Serves 8

INGREDIENTS:

¼ pound salt pork or bacon, cut into cubes

2 stalks celery, diced

1 (4-pound) chuck or English roast

Salt and freshly ground black pepper, to taste

2 large onions, peeled and quartered

1 (1-pound) bag of baby carrots

2 turnips, peeled and diced

8 medium potatoes, peeled

2 cups Beef Broth (Chapter 19)

4 tablespoons butter

4 tablespoons all-purpose flour

1. Add the salt pork or bacon and the celery to the bottom of the slow cooker. Place the roast on top of the pork; salt and pepper to taste. Add the onion, carrots, turnips, and potatoes. Pour in the broth. Cover and cook on low for 8 hours.

2. Use a slotted spoon to move the meat and vegetables to a serving platter; cover and keep warm.

3. Mix the butter and flour together with ½ cup of the broth. Increase the slow cooker heat setting to high; cover and cook until the mixture begins to bubble around the edges. Whisk the flour mixture into the broth; cook, stirring constantly, for 10 minutes, or until the flour flavor is cooked out of the gravy and it's thickened enough to coat the back of a spoon. Taste the gravy for seasoning and stir in more salt and pepper if needed. Serve over or alongside the meat and vegetables.

Mimicking the Maillard Reaction

Contrary to myth, searing meat before it's braised doesn't seal in the juices, but it does—through a process known as the Maillard reaction—enhance the flavor of the meat through a caramelization process. Using beef broth (or, even better, a combination of brown stock and water) mimics that flavor and lets you skip the browning step.

ONION POT ROAST

Turn this into two 4-serving meals by making roast beef sandwiches the next day. The meat will be tender and moist if you refrigerate leftovers in the pan juices.

Serves 8

INGREDIENTS:

1 (3-pound) boneless chuck roast

1 (1-pound) bag of baby carrots

2 stalks of celery, diced

1 green bell pepper, seeded and diced

1 large yellow onion, peeled and sliced

1 envelope onion soup mix

½ teaspoon black pepper

1 cup water

1 cup tomato juice

2 cloves garlic, peeled and minced

1 tablespoon Worcestershire sauce

1 tablespoon steak sauce

1. Cut the roast into serving-sized portions. Add the carrots, celery, green bell pepper, and onion to the slow cooker. Place the roast pieces on top of the vegetables and sprinkle with soup mix and black pepper.

2. Add the water, tomato juice, garlic, Worcestershire sauce, and steak sauce to a bowl or measuring cup; mix well and then pour into the slow cooker. Cover and cook on low for 8 hours.

POT ROAST WITH ROOT VEGETABLES

A variety of autumnal vegetables make this pot roast a complete meal in one.

Serves 12

INGREDIENTS:

1 cup water

4 russet potatoes, quartered

4 carrots, cut into thirds

4 parsnips, quartered

3 rutabagas, quartered

2 onions, sliced

1 celeriac, cubed

7 cloves garlic, sliced

4 pounds lean top round beef roast, excess fat removed

½ teaspoon salt

1 teaspoon paprika

½ teaspoon freshly ground black pepper

1. Pour the water into an oval 6-quart slow cooker. Add the potatoes, carrots, parsnips, rutabagas, onions, celeriac, and garlic. Stir.

2. Add the beef. Sprinkle with salt, paprika, and pepper. Cook on low for 8 hours.

3. Remove and slice the beef. Use a slotted spoon to serve the vegetables. Discard the cooking liquid.

MUSHROOM STEAK AND VEGETABLES

Serve this dish over mashed potatoes along with your choice of microwave steam-in-bag vegetables or a tossed salad.

Serves 8

INGREDIENTS:

2 pounds boneless beef round steak, cut ¾-inch thick

2 medium onions, peeled and sliced

3 cups sliced fresh mushrooms

1 (12-ounce) jar beef gravy

1 (1-ounce) envelope dry mushroom gravy mix

1. Trim fat from the steak; cut it into eight serving-size pieces. Spread the onions over the bottom of the crock. Add the meat on top of the onions and the mushrooms to the top of the meat.

2. Combine beef gravy and mushroom gravy mix. Pour the gravy mixture into the slow cooker; cover and cook on low for 8 hours.

BEEF IN BEER

You can thicken the pan juices with a cornstarch slurry if you wish. Serve alongside potatoes and a steamed vegetable. For a change of pace, serve pretzels instead of having bread at the table and provide beer for those who want it.

Serves 6

INGREDIENTS:

2 tablespoons butter

2 large onions, peeled and sliced

2 cloves garlic, peeled and minced

1 (3-pound) boneless chuck roast

¼ cup water

½ double-strength beef broth

½ cup lager beer

1 tablespoon light brown sugar

1 tablespoon Dijon mustard

1 tablespoon apple cider vinegar

1. Melt the butter in a large nonstick skillet over medium-high heat. Add the onions and sauté for 5 minutes or until the onions are lightly browned; stir in the garlic and sauté for 30 seconds. Pour the onions and garlic into the slow cooker.

2. Trim the roast of any fat and cut into six serving-sized pieces. Put the skillet back over the heat; add the meat to the skillet and fry for 2 minutes on each side. Move the meat to the slow cooker.

3. Put the skillet back over the heat. Add the water, stirring well to bring up any browned meat clinging to the pan. Stir in the broth, beer, brown sugar, mustard, and vinegar. Mix well, and then pour over the meat in the slow cooker. Cover and cook on low for 8 hours. Ladle onions and broth over each serving of meat.

BARBECUE WESTERN RIBS

At the end of the 8-hour cooking time, the meat will be tender and falling off of the bones. You can stretch this recipe to 8 servings if you serve barbecue beef sandwiches instead of 4 servings of beef. Add potato chips and coleslaw for a delicious, casual meal.

Serves 4

INGREDIENTS:

1 cup barbecue sauce

½ cup orange marmalade

½ cup water

3 pounds beef Western ribs

1. Add the barbecue sauce, marmalade, and water to the slow cooker. Stir to mix.

2. Add the ribs, ladling some of the sauce over the ribs. Cover and cook on low for 8 hours. To thicken the sauce, if desired, use a slotted spoon to remove the meat and bones; cover and keep warm. Skim any fat from the sauce in the cooker; increase the heat setting to high and cook uncovered for 15 minutes or until the sauce is reduced and coats the back of a spoon.

BANANA RIBS

Bananas add a subtle sweetness to the meat. If available, try tiny red bananas instead of the standard yellow.

Serves 10–12

INGREDIENTS:

4 potatoes

2 ears corn

1 bunch cilantro

1 teaspoon dried oregano

½ teaspoon salt

½ teaspoon black pepper

2 pounds beef ribs

2 onions

2 tomatoes

1 green bell pepper

3 bananas

4 cups Beef Broth (Chapter 19)

1. Peel the potatoes and cut them into 2-inch cubes. Husk and quarter the ears of corn. Put the potatoes and corn in the bottom of the slow cooker.

2. Chop the cilantro. Mix it in a small bowl with the oregano, salt, and black pepper. Sprinkle the vegetables in the slow cooker with one-third of the cilantro mixture.

3. Cut the ribs into serving-sized pieces. Arrange in the slow cooker over the potatoes and corn. Sprinkle with one-third of the cilantro mixture.

4. Chop the onions, tomatoes, and green pepper. Peel the bananas and cut them into ½-inch slices. Arrange the cut vegetables and fruit over the meat in the slow cooker. Sprinkle with the remaining cilantro mixture.

5. Add the broth.

6. Cover and heat on a low setting for 6–8 hours.

SIRLOIN DINNER

Add a tossed salad and some warm dinner rolls and this recipe makes a complete meal.

Serves 8

INGREDIENTS:

1 (4-pound) beef sirloin tip roast

2 tablespoons extra-virgin olive oil

1 teaspoon kosher or sea salt

½ teaspoon freshly ground pepper

1 teaspoon garlic powder

1 teaspoon onion powder

1 teaspoon ground cumin

1 teaspoon dried thyme leaves, crushed

½ teaspoon sweet paprika

2 turnips, peeled and cut into 2-inch pieces

2 parsnips, peeled and cut into 2-inch pieces

4 large red potatoes, peeled and quartered

1 (1-pound) bag baby carrots

8 cloves garlic, peeled and cut in half lengthwise

2 large onions, peeled and sliced

½ cup dry red wine

1 cup Beef Broth (Chapter 19)

Salt and freshly ground black pepper, to taste

1. To ensure the roast cooks evenly, tie it into an even form using butcher's twine. Rub the oil onto the meat.

2. Mix the salt, pepper, garlic powder, onion powder, cumin, thyme, and paprika together. Pat the seasoning mixture on all sides of the roast. Place the roast in the slow cooker.

3. Arrange the turnips, parsnips, potatoes, and carrots around the roast. Evenly disperse the garlic around the vegetables. Arrange the onion slices over the vegetables. Pour the wine and broth into the slow cooker. Season with salt and pepper, to taste. Cover and cook on low for 8 hours.

4. Use a slotted spoon to remove the roast and vegetables to a serving platter; cover and keep warm. Let the roast rest for at least 10 minutes before carving. To serve, thinly slice the roast across the grain. Serve drizzled with some of the pan juices.

Rare Sirloin Roast

If you prefer a rare roast, use a probe thermometer set to your preferred doneness setting (130°F for rare). You'll need to be close by so that you hear the thermometer alarm when it goes off. Remove the roast to a platter; cover and keep warm. Cover and continue to cook the vegetables if necessary.

SWISS STEAK

Minute steaks are usually tenderized pieces of round steak. You can instead buy 2½ pounds of round steak, trim it of fat, cut it into 6 portions, and pound each portion thin between two pieces of plastic wrap. Serve Swiss Steak over mashed potatoes.

Serves 6

INGREDIENTS:

½ cup all-purpose flour

1 teaspoon salt

¼ teaspoon freshly ground black pepper

6 (6-ounce) beef minute steaks

2 tablespoons vegetable oil

2 teaspoons butter

½ stalk celery, finely diced

1 large yellow onion, peeled and diced

1 cup Beef Broth (Chapter 19)

1 cup water

1 (1-pound) bag baby carrots

Optional: Worcestershire or steak sauce, to taste

1. Add the flour, salt, pepper, and minute steaks to a gallon plastic bag; seal and shake to coat the meat.

2. Add the oil and butter to a large skillet and bring it to temperature over medium-high heat. Add the meat and brown it for 5 minutes on each side. Transfer the meat to the slow cooker.

3. Add the celery to the skillet and sauté while you add the onion to the plastic bag; seal and shake to coat the onion in flour. Add the flour-coated onions to the skillet and, stirring constantly, sauté for 10 minutes or until the onions are lightly browned. Add the broth to the skillet and stir to scrape up any browned bits clinging to the pan. Add the water and continue to cook until the liquid is thickened enough to lightly coat the back of a spoon. Pour into the slow cooker. Add the carrots. Cover and cook on low for 8 hours.

4. Transfer the meat and carrots to a serving platter. Taste the gravy for seasoning, and add Worcestershire or steak sauce to taste if desired. Serve alongside or over the meat and carrots.

Swiss Steak and Pasta

If instead of mashed potatoes, you'd prefer the serve the Swiss Steak over cooked pasta, stir 2 tablespoons of tomato paste into the onions before you make the gravy in Step 3. Or, you can substitute 1 cup of diced tomatoes for the water.

HORSERADISH ROAST BEEF AND POTATOES

Horseradish gives this beef dish an extra flavor dimension.

Serves 6–8

INGREDIENTS:

⅓ cup prepared horseradish

2 tablespoons extra-virgin olive oil

1 teaspoon freshly ground black pepper

1 teaspoon dried thyme, crushed

½ teaspoon salt

1 (3-pound) boneless beef chuck roast

2 celery stalks, cut in half

¼ cup dry white wine or Beef Broth (Chapter 19)

1¼ cups Beef Broth (Chapter 19)

2 pounds (about 12–16) small red potatoes

Optional: Water

1 (1-pound) package baby carrots

Optional: 2 tablespoons all-purpose flour

Optional: 2 tablespoons butter

1. In a small bowl, mix together the horseradish, oil, pepper, thyme, and salt. Trim the fat from the roast and cut it into 2-inch cubes. Rub the horseradish mixture into meat. Add the seasoned roast, celery, white wine, and broth to a 4-quart slow cooker. Cover and cook for 1–2 hours on high or until the celery is limp. Discard the celery. Add water or more broth, if necessary, to bring the liquid level up to just the top of the meat.

2. Wash the potatoes. Add the potatoes and carrots to the cooker. Cover and cook on low for 6 hours, or until meat is tender and the vegetables are cooked through. Serve warm.

3. Optional: If you wish to thicken the pan juices, remove the meat and vegetables to a serving platter. Cover and keep warm. Turn the slow cooker to the high setting; cover and cook until the juices bubble around the edges. Mix the flour together with the butter and ½ cup of the pan juices; whisk into the slow cooker. Cook, stirring constantly, for 15 minutes or until the flour taste is cooked out of the gravy and it is thickened enough to coat the back of a spoon.

Improvised Beef Stew

If you have leftovers, you can make a hearty beef stew by cutting the beef, potatoes, and carrots into bite-sized pieces and stirring them into the thickened pan juices. Add a tablespoon or two of ketchup or some hot sauce for an extra punch of flavor if desired. Reheat and serve with hard rolls, or over biscuits.

POT ROAST IN FRUIT-INFUSED GRAVY

You can substitute 8 medium red potatoes, washed and halved or quartered, for the parsnips. To truly infuse the fruit flavors into the gravy, use an immersion blender to purée the fruit before you begin making the gravy in Step 3.

Serves 8

INGREDIENTS:

2 cloves garlic, peeled and minced

1 teaspoon dried sage, crushed

½ teaspoon salt

½ teaspoon freshly ground black pepper

⅛ teaspoon cayenne pepper

1 (3-pound) boneless beef chuck roast

2 tablespoons vegetable oil

1 cup Beef Broth (Chapter 19)

1 large onion, peeled and diced

1 cup pitted prunes (dried plums), cut in half

2 large apples, peeled, cored, and cut into thick slices

1 pound parsnips, peeled and cut into ½-inch pieces

1 (1-pound) bag of baby carrots

¼ cup butter

¼ cup all-purpose flour

1 tablespoon balsamic vinegar

1. In a small bowl, stir together garlic, sage, salt, black pepper, and cayenne. Spread the garlic mixture over both sides of the meat. Add the oil to a large skillet and bring it to temperature over medium-high heat; add the roast and brown it on both sides. Add the browned roast to the slow cooker. Pour the broth over the roast. Add the onion, prunes, apples, parsnips, and baby carrots. Cover and cook on low for 8 hours.

2. With a slotted spoon transfer the meat and vegetables to a serving platter; cover and keep warm.

3. Skim the fat off the juices that remain in the pan. Add water if necessary to bring the pan juices to 1½ cups. Increase the heat setting to high; cover and cook until the liquid bubbles around the edges. In a bowl, mix the butter, flour, and ½ cup of the pan juices together, and then whisk into the slow cooker. Cook, stirring constantly, for 15 minutes or until the flour taste is cooked out of the gravy and it's thickened enough to coat the back of a spoon. Taste for seasoning and add salt and pepper if necessary. Stir in the balsamic vinegar. Serve the gravy over the roast, vegetables, and fruit.

Adding a German Influence

Stir several finely crushed ginger snaps into the pan juices before you add the flour mixture. Once it's thickened, substitute red wine or apple cider vinegar for the balsamic vinegar.

BEEF BOURGUIGNON

For a complete fine-dining experience, serve Beef Bourguignon over mashed potatoes or buttered noodles and with a salad, steamed vegetable, and warm dinner rolls.

Serves 8

INGREDIENTS:

8 slices of bacon, diced

1 large yellow onion, peeled and diced

3 cloves garlic, peeled and minced

1 (3-pound) boneless English or chuck roast

16 ounces fresh mushrooms, cleaned and sliced

2 tablespoons tomato paste

2 cups Beef Broth (Chapter 19) or water

4 cups burgundy

½ teaspoon thyme

1 bay leaf

Salt and freshly ground black pepper, to taste

1 large yellow onion, peeled and thinly sliced

Optional: ½ cup butter, softened

Optional: ½ cup all-purpose flour

1. Add the bacon to a large nonstick skillet; fry the bacon over medium heat until it renders its fat. Use a slotted spoon to remove the bacon and reserve it for another use or use it in the tossed salads you serve with the meal. Add the onion to the skillet and sauté for 5 minutes or until the onion is transparent. Stir in the garlic, sauté for 30 seconds, and then transfer the onion mixture to the slow cooker. Cover the cooker.

2. Trim the roast of any fat and cut it into bite-sized pieces; add the beef pieces to the skillet and brown the meat over medium-high heat for 5 minutes. Transfer the meat to the slow cooker. Cover the cooker. Add half of the sliced mushrooms to the skillet; stir-fry for 5 minutes or until the mushroom liquids have evaporated; transfer to the slow cooker and replace the cover.

3. Add the tomato paste to the skillet and sauté for 3 minutes or until the tomato paste just begins to brown. Stir in the broth or water, scraping the bottom of the pan to remove any browned bits and work them into the sauce. Remove the pan from the heat and stir in the burgundy, thyme, bay leaf, salt, and pepper; stir to combine. Pour into the slow cooker. Add the remaining mushrooms and sliced onion to slow cooker. Cover and cook on low for 8 hours.

4. Optional: To thicken the sauce, use a slotted spoon to transfer the meat and much of the cooked onions and mushrooms to a serving platter; cover and keep warm. In a small bowl or measuring cup, mix the butter together with the flour to form a paste; whisk in some of the pan liquid a little at a time to thin the paste. Strain out any lumps if necessary. Increase the heat of the cooker to high. When the pan liquids begin to bubble around the edges, whisk in the flour mixture. Cook, stirring constantly, for 15 minutes or until the flour taste is cooked out of the sauce and it has thickened enough to coat the back of a spoon. Taste for seasoning and add additional salt and pepper if needed. Pour over the meat, mushrooms, and onions on the serving platter.

APPLE-MUSTARD BEEF BRISKET

Serve Apple-Mustard Beef Brisket with a crusty bread and a tossed salad with honey-mustard dressing. If you wish, you can add some peeled and quartered root vegetables (carrots, parsnips, or turnips) to the cooker, too.

Serves 8

INGREDIENTS:

1 (3-pound) beef brisket

1 large yellow onion, peeled and quartered

2 large cloves garlic, peeled and minced

4 large cloves garlic, peeled and left whole

1 (10-ounce) jar apple jelly

3 tablespoons Dijon mustard

Salt and freshly ground pepper, to taste

¾ teaspoon curry powder

⅓ cup dry white wine

1 cup apple juice

1 cup water

Optional: 2 apples

1. Add all ingredients to the slow cooker in the order given. If using, peel, core, and slice the apples and put them in a layer on top of the meat. Cover and cook on low for 8 hours or until meat is tender.

Delayed Satisfaction

Brisket will become even more moist and tender if you allow it to cool in the broth, so this makes a good dish to make the day before. To reheat it, bake it for 45 minutes at 325°F. Baste it with some additional sauce and put it under the broiler for a few minutes to allow the meat to develop a glaze.

BEEF BARBECUE

An English roast tends to pull apart easier, which makes it perfect for beef barbecue sandwiches. You can speed up the cooking process by cutting the roast into smaller pieces.

Serves 8

INGREDIENTS:

1 (3-pound) beef English roast

1 cup water

½ cup red wine

½ cup ketchup

1 tablespoon red wine vinegar

2 teaspoons Worcestershire sauce

2 teaspoons mustard powder

2 tablespoons dried minced onion

1 teaspoon dried minced garlic

1 teaspoon cracked black pepper

1 tablespoon brown sugar

1 teaspoon chili powder

½ teaspoon ground cinnamon

¼ teaspoon ground cloves

¼ teaspoon ground ginger

Pinch ground allspice

Pinch dried pepper flakes, crushed

1. Add the roast to the slow cooker. Mix all remaining ingredients together and pour over the beef. Cover and cook on low for 8 hours.

2. Use a slotted spoon to remove the beef from the slow cooker; pull it apart, discarding any fat or gristle. Taste the meat and sauce and adjust seasonings if necessary.

3. To thicken the sauce, increase the heat of the cooker to high, skim any fat off the surface of the sauce (or blot it with a paper towel), and let cook uncovered while you pull apart the beef.

Barbecue Spaghetti

Serve beef barbecue over your favorite cooked pasta. Top with some grated Cheddar cheese and diced sweet or green onion.

COTTAGE PIE WITH CARROTS, PARSNIPS, AND CELERY

Cottage pie is similar to the more familiar shepherd's pie, but it uses beef instead of lamb. This version uses lots of vegetables and lean meat.

Serves 6

INGREDIENTS:

1 large onion, diced

3 cloves garlic, minced

1 carrot, diced

1 parsnip, diced

1 stalk celery, diced

1 pound 94% lean ground beef

1½ cups Brown Stock (Chapter 19)

½ teaspoon hot paprika

½ teaspoon crushed rosemary

1 tablespoon Worcestershire sauce

½ teaspoon dried savory

⅛ teaspoon salt

¼ teaspoon freshly ground black pepper

1 tablespoon cornstarch and 1 tablespoon water, mixed (if necessary)

¼ cup minced fresh parsley

2¾ cups plain mashed potatoes

1. Sauté the onions, garlic, carrots, parsnips, celery, and beef in a large nonstick skillet until the ground beef is browned. Drain off any excess fat and discard it. Place the mixture into a round 4-quart slow cooker. Add the stock, paprika, rosemary, Worcestershire sauce, savory, salt, and pepper. Stir.

2. Cook on low for 6–8 hours. If the meat mixture still looks very wet, create a slurry by mixing together 1 tablespoon cornstarch and 1 tablespoon water. Stir this into the meat mixture.

3. In a medium bowl, mash the parsley and potatoes using a potato masher. Spread on top of the ground beef mixture in the slow cooker. Cover and cook on high for 30–60 minutes or until the potatoes are warmed through.

Save Time in the Morning

Take a few minutes the night before cooking to cut up any vegetables you need for a recipe. Place them in an airtight container or plastic bag and refrigerate until morning. Measure any dried spices and place them in a small container on the counter until needed.

ROULADEN

Rouladen is a German dish that has many variations; this one is simply delicious!

Serves 4

INGREDIENTS:

¼ cup red wine

1 cup water

4 very thin round steaks (about ¾ pound total)

2 tablespoons grainy German-style mustard

Optional: 1 tablespoon lean bacon crumbles

4 dill pickle spears

1. Pour the wine and water into the bottom of an oval 4-quart slow cooker.

2. Place the steaks horizontally on a platter. Spread ½ tablespoon mustard on each steak and sprinkle with one-quarter of the bacon crumbles. Place one of the pickle spears on one end of each steak. Roll each steak toward the other end, so it looks like a spiral. Place on the skillet seam-side down. Cook for 1 minute, then use tongs to flip the steaks carefully and cook the other side for 1 minute.

3. Place each roll in a single layer in the water-wine mixture. Cook on low for 1 hour. Remove the rolls, discarding the cooking liquid.

Roulade Rules

Roulade, the generic term for steak wrapped around a savory filling, works best with steaks that are approximately ⅛" thick, 8"–10" long, and 5" wide. Look for them in the meat section labeled as "rolling steaks," or ask the butcher to specially cut some. They are a great way to enjoy red meat in small portions.

SLIMMED-DOWN MOUSSAKA

This version of moussaka uses lean beef instead of higher-fat lamb, baked eggplant instead of fried, and a lighter version of béchamel sauce to create a dish that is authentic tasting but much lower in fat.

Serves 6

INGREDIENTS:

2 1-pound eggplants, peeled

Salt, as needed

1 teaspoon olive oil

1 large onion, diced

2 cloves garlic, minced

20 ounces whole tomatoes in purée

1 tablespoon tomato paste

½ teaspoon cinnamon

1 tablespoon oregano, minced

1 tablespoon flat-leaf parsley, minced

1 pound 94% lean ground beef

1 cup fat-free evaporated milk

1 tablespoon butter

1 egg

2 tablespoons flour

1. Slice the eggplants vertically into ¼"-thick slices. Place in a colander and lightly salt the eggplant. Allow to drain for 15 minutes. Meanwhile, preheat the oven to 375°F. Rinse off the eggplant slices and pat them dry. Arrange the slices in a single layer on two parchment paper–lined baking sheets. Bake for 15 minutes.

2. While prepping the eggplant, heat the oil in a nonstick skillet. Sauté the onion and garlic for 1 minute, then add the tomatoes, tomato paste, cinnamon, oregano, parsley, and ground beef. Break up the tomatoes into small chunks using the back of a spoon. Simmer, stirring occasionally, until the meat is browned and most of the liquid evaporates.

3. Ladle half of the sauce onto the bottom of a 4- or 6-quart oval slow cooker. Top with a single layer of eggplant, taking care to leave no gaps between slices. Top with remaining sauce. Top with another layer of eggplant. Cover with the lid and cook for 2½–3 hours on high or up to 6 hours on low.

4. In a small saucepan, whisk together the evaporated milk, butter, egg, and flour. Bring to a boil and then reduce the heat. Whisk until smooth.

5. Pour the sauce over the eggplant and cook an additional 1–1½ hours on high.

Slow Cooking with Eggplant

Salting eggplant draws out any extra liquid that might dilute the dish. It is not necessary to salt eggplant in all recipes, but if it is called for, don't skip that step. Similarly, some dishes will call for baking the eggplant. This also helps to dry out the eggplant and ensures a velvety texture.

BETTER-THAN-TAKEOUT MONGOLIAN BEEF

This homemade version of the Chinese takeout favorite is lower in fat and sodium. Serve it over rice and sprinkle with diced green onion before serving.

Serves 6

INGREDIENTS:

3 pounds lean beef bottom roast, extra fat removed

3 cloves garlic, grated

1" knob peeled fresh ginger, grated

1 medium onion, thinly sliced

½ cup water

½ cup low-sodium soy sauce

2 tablespoons black vinegar

2 tablespoons hoisin sauce

1 tablespoon five-spice powder

1 tablespoon cornstarch

1 teaspoon red pepper flakes

1 teaspoon sesame oil

1. Place all ingredients in a 4-quart oval slow cooker. Cover and cook for 5 hours on low or until the meat is thoroughly cooked through and tender.

2. Remove the roast to a cutting board. Slice thinly and return it to the slow cooker. Cook for an additional 20 minutes on high. Stir the meat and the sauce before serving.

BRACIOLE

Look for steaks that are approximately ⅛" thick, 8"–10" long, and 5" wide to make this Italian roulade.

Serves 8

INGREDIENTS:

½ teaspoon olive oil

½ cup diced onions

2 cloves garlic, minced

32 ounces canned diced tomatoes

8 stalks rapini

8 very thin-cut round steaks (about 1¼ pounds total)

4 teaspoons bread crumbs

4 teaspoons grated Parmesan

1. Heat the oil in a nonstick pan. Sauté the onions and garlic until the onions are soft, about 5 minutes. Place in a 6-quart oval slow cooker. Add the tomatoes and stir.

2. Cut the stems off the rapini. Place the steaks on a platter horizontally. Sprinkle each steak with ½ teaspoon bread crumbs and ½ teaspoon Parmesan. Place a bunch of rapini leaves on one end of each steak. Roll each steak toward the other end. It should look like a spiral. Place in the skillet seam-side down. Cook for 1 minute, use tongs to flip the steaks carefully, and cook the other side for 1 minute.

3. Place each roll in a single layer on top of the tomato sauce. Cook on low for 1–2 hours or until the steaks are cooked through.

STEAK CARNITAS

Carnitas are delicious wrapped in tortillas. Serve with shredded iceberg lettuce, diced tomatoes, diced onion, and cilantro.

Serves 10

INGREDIENTS:

1½ pounds lean bottom round, cubed

3 cloves garlic, minced

1 jalapeño, minced

¼ cup habanero salsa

¼ teaspoon salt

¼ teaspoon freshly ground black pepper

2 teaspoons ground chipotle

1 teaspoon New Mexican chili powder

½ teaspoon oregano

2 tablespoons lime juice

2 tablespoons orange juice

1 tablespoon lime zest

1. Quickly brown the beef in a nonstick skillet. Add to a 4-quart slow cooker.

2. In a small bowl, whisk the rest of the ingredients. Pour over the beef. Stir.

3. Cook on low for 6 hours, remove the cover, and cook on high for 30 minutes. Stir before serving.

Juice Citrus with Ease

Here are a few tips to get the most juice out of citrus. Microwave the whole fruit for 20 seconds before juicing. Roll the fruit on the countertop before you squeeze it. After squeezing the fruit the first time, use a knife to slice the membranes and squeeze it again to extract even more juice.

PORTOBELLO TRI-TIP

Lean, often overlooked cuts of beef like the tri-tip are perfect for the slow cooker. The long, moisture-rich environment creates tender meat, despite the lack of fat.

Serves 12

INGREDIENTS:

3 pounds tri-tip, excess fat removed

6 Portobello mushroom caps, sliced

1 onion, diced

1 tablespoon Canadian Steak Seasoning

¼ cup Beef Broth (Chapter 19)

1 tablespoon Worcestershire sauce

1 tablespoon balsamic vinegar

1. In a dry skillet, sear each side of the tri-tip. Place in a 6- to 7-quart slow cooker.

2. Spray a nonstick pan with cooking spray. Sauté mushrooms and onions until the onions are soft but not browned. Add to the slow cooker, along with the remaining ingredients.

3. Cook on low for 6–8 hours or until the meat is falling apart and tender.

Make Your Own Canadian Steak Seasoning

In a small bowl, stir 2 tablespoons each black pepper, kosher salt, caraway seeds, paprika, granulated garlic, and dehydrated mushrooms. Store in an airtight container. Mix into hamburgers or meatloaf or use as a dry rub on steaks.

BARBECUE BRISKET

This brisket turns out moist and tender as it is slow cooked in the sauce. Serve on sandwich buns or sliced on a platter.

Serves 15–18

INGREDIENTS:

5 pound beef brisket (not corned beef)

4 teaspoons liquid smoke

½ teaspoon salt

¼ teaspoon pepper

1 cup chili sauce

½ cup barbecue sauce

1. Season the brisket with liquid smoke, salt, and pepper. Place in the slow cooker.

2. Combine chili sauce and barbecue sauce and pour over the brisket.

3. Cover and cook 8–10 hours or until brisket is tender. Thinly slice meat against the grain and serve.

SAUSAGE AND CABBAGE

This hearty recipe is satisfying on a cold winter night. Serve it with dark crusty bread, toasted and spread with butter.

Serves 6

INGREDIENTS:

1½ pounds bratwurst

1 onion, chopped

4 cloves garlic, minced

2 cups chopped red cabbage

2 cups chopped green cabbage

¼ cup sugar

¼ cup red wine vinegar

½ teaspoon salt

⅛ teaspoon pepper

¼ cup English mustard

1. In large skillet, cook bratwurst over medium heat until it begins to brown. Remove from heat. Add onion and garlic; cook and stir until onion is crisp-tender, about 4 minutes.

2. In 4- or 5-quart slow cooker, combine onion, garlic, cabbages, sugar, wine vinegar, salt, and pepper and mix. Top with bratwurst and spread bratwurst with mustard. Cover and cook on low for 7–8 hours or until cabbage is tender and sausage is thoroughly cooked.

CHAPTER 10

PORK

APPLE CIDER PORK LOIN

Pork loin can dry out in the slow cooker. The pork will be juicier if you let it cool completely in the pan juices before you remove it and slice it. Return the slices to the pan juices when you reheat it. Serve the loin with the cider sauce ladled over the slices.

Serves 8

INGREDIENTS:

1 (4-pound) pork loin

¼ cup Dijon mustard

1 teaspoon dried thyme

¼ cup light brown sugar

1 cup apple cider

4 cups unsweetened applesauce

Optional: 1 medium onion, peeled and sliced

1. Trim any fat from the pork loin.

2. Add the mustard, thyme, and brown sugar to a bowl; mix it to make a paste and then rub it into the pork loin.

3. Add the cider and then the loin to the slow cooker. Pour the applesauce over the loin. If using, add the onion slices in a layer on top of the applesauce. Cover and cook on low for 6 hours or until the internal temperature of the loin is 160°F. If serving immediately, remove the pork loin, cover it to keep warm, and allow it to rest for 10 minutes before you slice it into servings. Skim any fat from the surface of the cider-applesauce sauce from the slow cooker and then ladle it over the slices.

Sauced-Up Applesauce

To add an extra kick to the pan juices from the Apple Cider Pork Loin recipe, stir in 3 tablespoons of prepared horseradish and 2 teaspoons of fresh lemon juice.

APRICOT PORK SIRLOIN ROAST

A pork sirloin roast is low in fat, yet it cooks up tender and moist. If you prefer gravy instead of sauce, simply mix the reduced pan juices with some heavy cream.

Serves 8

INGREDIENTS:

15 pitted prunes (dried plums)

12 dried apricots, pitted

½ cup boiling water

1 cup Chicken Broth (Chapter 19)

1 cup dry white wine or apple juice

1 (3½-pound) pork sirloin roast, trimmed of fat and silver skin

4 large sweet potatoes, peeled and quartered

Salt and freshly ground pepper, to taste

1 tablespoon cornstarch

2 tablespoons cold water

1. Add the prunes and apricots to the slow cooker. Pour the boiling water over the dried fruit; cover and let set for 15 minutes.

2. Add the chicken broth, wine, pork sirloin roast, and sweet potatoes. Cover and cook on low for 5–6 hours or until the internal temperature of the roast is 160°F.

3. Remove the meat and sweet potatoes from the cooker; cover and keep warm.

4. Turn the cooker to high. Use an immersion blender to purée the fruit. In a small bowl, mix the cornstarch into the cold water. Once the liquid in the slow cooker begins to bubble around the edges, slowly whisk in the cornstarch liquid. Reduce the heat to low and simmer the sauce for several minutes, stirring occasionally, until thickened. Place the pork roast on a serving platter and carve into eight slices. Arrange the sweet potatoes around the pork. Ladle the sauce over the meat. Serve immediately.

HAM AND SWEET POTATOES

Serve this dish with a tossed salad, some applesauce, a steamed vegetable, and some warm dinner rolls or buttered rye bread toast.

Serves 6

INGREDIENTS:

1 (20-ounce) can pineapple tidbits

1 (2-pound) boneless ham steak

3 large sweet potatoes, peeled and diced

1 large sweet onion, peeled and diced

½ cup orange marmalade

2 cloves garlic, peeled and minced

¼ teaspoon freshly ground black pepper

½ teaspoon dried parsley

Optional: 1 tablespoon brown sugar

1. Drain the pineapple, reserving 2 tablespoons of the juice.

2. Trim the ham of any fat and cut it into bite-sized pieces. Add the pineapple, 2 tablespoons pineapple juice, and ham to the slow cooker along with the sweet potatoes, onion, marmalade, garlic, black pepper, parsley, and brown sugar if using. Stir to combine. Cover and cook on low for 6 hours.

ROAST PORK WITH CINNAMON CRANBERRIES AND SWEET POTATOES

You can substitute Peach Marmalade (Chapter 4) for the orange marmalade and orange juice called for in this recipe. Doing so will add a subtle taste of peaches and pineapple to the dish, too.

Serves 6

INGREDIENTS:

1 (3-pound) pork butt roast

Salt and freshly ground pepper, to taste

1 (16-ounce) can sweetened whole cranberries

1 medium onion, peeled and diced

¼ cup orange marmalade

½ cup orange juice

¼ teaspoon ground cinnamon

¼ teaspoon ground cloves

3 large sweet potatoes, peeled and quartered

Optional: 1 tablespoon cornstarch

Optional: 2 tablespoons cold water

1. Place the pork, fat side up, in the slow cooker. Salt and pepper to taste. Combine the cranberries, onion, marmalade, orange juice, cinnamon, and cloves in a large measuring cup; stir to mix and then pour over the pork roast. Arrange the sweet potatoes around the meat. Cover and cook on low for 6 hours or until the pork is tender and pulls apart easily.

2. To serve with a thickened sauce, transfer the meat and sweet potatoes to a serving platter. Cover and keep warm. Skim any fat off of the pan juices. (You'll want about 2 cups of juice remaining in the cooker.) Cover and cook on the high setting for 30 minutes, or until the pan liquids begin to bubble around the edges.

3. In a coffee cup, combine the cornstarch with the water. Whisk into the liquid in the slow cooker. Reduce temperature setting to low and continue to cook and stir for an additional 2 minutes or the cornstarch flavor has cooked out of the sauce and it is thickened and bubbly.

BRATWURST IN BEER

You can serve the bratwurst and sauerkraut over mashed potatoes or on warmed bakery hot dog buns slathered with stone-ground mustard. The beer you use is your choice, or you can substitute apple juice or cider if you prefer.

Serves 8

INGREDIENTS:

8 precooked bratwurst sausages

2 large sweet onions, peeled and sliced

1 (2-pound) bag of sauerkraut, rinsed and drained

1 (12-ounce) bottle of beer

1. Add the sausages and onions to the slow cooker. Cover and cook on high for 30 minutes or until the sausage begins to render its fat and the onions are limp.

2. Add the sauerkraut and beer to the slow cooker. Cover and cook on low for 3 hours.

3. Optional cooking step: For added flavor, you can brown the bratwurst on the grill or under the broiler before serving.

To Prick or Not to Prick

Using a fork to prick the skin of each bratwurst allows it to render some of its fat during the cooking process and to absorb more of the beer flavor. Not piercing the skin lets the bratwurst retain that crisp pop when you bite into the sausage. The choice is yours, depending on your taste preference.

PORK STEAKS IN APPLE AND PRUNE SAUCE

Serve this dish over some mashed potatoes (available premade in most supermarket refrigerator or freezer cases) and alongside some steam-in-the-bag green beans.

Serves 6

INGREDIENTS:

12 pitted prunes (dried plums)

3 pounds boneless pork steaks, trimmed of fat

2 Granny Smith apples, peeled, cored, and sliced

¾ cup dry white wine or apple juice

¾ cup heavy cream

Salt and freshly ground pepper, to taste

1 tablespoon red currant jelly

Optional: 1 tablespoon butter

1. Add the prunes, pork steak, apple slices, wine or apple juice, and cream to a 4-quart or larger slow cooker. Salt and pepper to taste. Cover and cook on low for 6 hours.

2. Now you have a choice: You can either remove the meat and fruit to a serving platter and keep warm or you can remove the meat, skim the fat from the liquid in the slow cooker, and use an immersion blender to blend the fruit into the creamy broth.

3. Cook uncovered on high for 30 minutes or until the pan juices begin to bubble around the edges. Reduce the setting to low or simmer, and cook for 15 more minutes or until the mixture is reduced by half and thickened. Whisk in the red currant jelly. Taste for seasoning and add more salt and pepper if needed. Whisk in the butter a teaspoon at a time if you want a richer, glossier sauce. Ladle the sauce over the meat or pour it into a heated gravy boat.

MEXICAN PORK ROAST

Serve this pork over rice and with Fat-Free Refried Beans (Chapter 23) on the side, or in burritos (see sidebar).

Serves 4

INGREDIENTS:

1 tablespoon olive oil

1 large sweet onion, peeled and sliced

1 medium carrot, peeled and finely diced

1 jalapeño pepper, seeded and minced

1 clove of garlic, peeled and minced

Salt, to taste

¼ teaspoon dried Mexican oregano

¼ teaspoon ground coriander

¼ teaspoon freshly ground black pepper

1 (3-pound) pork shoulder or butt roast

1 cup Chicken Broth (Chapter 19)

1. Add the olive oil, onion, carrot, and jalapeño to the slow cooker. Stir to coat the vegetables in the oil. Cover and cook on high for 30 minutes or until the onions are softened. Stir in the garlic.

2. Add the salt, oregano, coriander, and black pepper to a bowl; stir to mix. Rub the spice mixture into the pork roast. Add the pork roast and broth to the slow cooker. Cover and cook on low for 6 hours or until the pork is tender and pulls apart easily.

3. Use a slotted spoon to remove the pork and vegetables to a serving platter. Cover and let rest for 10 minutes.

4. Increase the temperature of the slow cooker to high. Cook and reduce the pan juices by half.

5. Use two forks to shred the pork and mix it in with the cooked onion and jalapeño. Ladle the reduced pan juices over the pork.

Mexican Pork Roast Burritos

Warm 4 large flour tortillas. Spread refried beans on each tortilla. Divide the pork between the tortillas and top with salsa and, if desired, grated cheese, shredded lettuce, and sour cream. Roll and serve.

ASIAN PORK RIBS

If hoisin sauce isn't available, you can use all ketchup instead. If you prefer a hotter kick to the barbecue sauce, add more dried red pepper flakes or hot sauce to taste.

Serves 6

INGREDIENTS:

4 pounds country pork ribs

1¾ cups ketchup

¼ cup hoisin sauce

2 tablespoons honey

2 tablespoons white wine or rice vinegar

2 tablespoons soy sauce

¼ teaspoon five-spice powder

1 large sweet onion, peeled and diced

2 teaspoons fresh ginger, minced

1 clove garlic, peeled and minced

2 teaspoons toasted sesame oil

Pinch dried red pepper flakes

Optional: 1 teaspoon cornstarch

Optional: 1 tablespoon cold water

1. Cut the ribs into individual rib portions. Optional cooking step: Position the broiler rack about 6 inches from the source of the heat and preheat the broiler. Broil the ribs for 5 minutes on each side or until browned.

2. Add the ketchup, hoisin sauce, honey, white wine or vinegar, soy sauce, five-spice powder, onion, ginger, garlic, sesame oil, and dried red pepper flakes to the slow cooker; stir to mix. Transfer the ribs to the slow cooker, coating the ribs with the sauce as you do so. Cover and cook on low for 8 hours or until the ribs are tender.

3. Optional: If you want thicker sauce available to serve over the ribs, transfer the ribs to a platter and keep warm. Skim any surface fat from the sauce in the slow cooker. Cook, stirring occasionally, uncovered on high until the sauce is reduced to about 1 cup. Mix the cornstarch together with the cold water in a small bowl. Whisk into the sauce, and cook, gently stirring constantly, for 5 minutes or until the cornstarch taste is cooked out of the sauce and it is thickened enough to coat the back of a spoon. Either serve the sauce on the side or pour it over the ribs.

COLA PORK ROAST DINNER

Using soda adds a sweet background note to the taste of the cooked pork. If you prefer, you can substitute 1½ cups of water for the Coca-Cola or Dr. Pepper.

Serves 4

INGREDIENTS:

1 (3-pound) pork sirloin or butt roast

1 envelope dry onion soup mix

1 (12-ounce) can Coca-Cola or Dr. Pepper

1 medium sweet onion, peeled and slice

1 (1-pound) bag baby carrots

4 medium potatoes, peeled

1. Place the pork roast in the slow cooker. Sprinkle the soup mix over the pork. Pour in the soda. Add the onion, carrots, and potatoes. Cover and cook on low for 6 hours or until the internal temperature of the roast reaches 160°F.

STICKY SPICY SPARE RIBS

Broiling the ribs removes most of the fat, but they still get very tender in the slow cooker.

Serves 8

INGREDIENTS:

4 pounds lean pork spare ribs

2 tablespoons dark brown sugar

½ cup chili sauce

¼ cup rice vinegar

¼ cup garlic-chili sauce

1 shallot, minced

1. Place the ribs on a broiler-safe platter. Broil on high until much of the fat has been rendered. Place in a 6- to 7-quart slow cooker.

2. In a small bowl, whisk the brown sugar, chili sauce, rice vinegar, garlic-chili sauce, and shallot. Pour over the ribs. Cook for 8 hours.

3. Remove spare ribs from the slow cooker. Place them on a baking sheet in a cold oven to keep warm. Transfer sauce to a small bowl. Drain off fat. Pour over the ribs before serving.

COUNTRY PORK RIBS

The heat in this sauce comes from the cinnamon, ginger, and allspice. If you prefer a more hot and sweet sauce, add ⅛ teaspoon or more of cayenne pepper or dried red pepper flakes.

Serves 4

INGREDIENTS:

3 pounds country pork ribs

1 medium sweet onion, peeled and diced

½ cup maple syrup

2 tablespoons light brown sugar

2 tablespoons soy sauce

½ teaspoon ground cinnamon

½ teaspoon ground ginger

½ teaspoon ground allspice

3 cloves garlic, peeled and minced

¼ teaspoon freshly ground black pepper

Optional: Cayenne pepper or dried red pepper flakes, to taste

1. Cut the ribs into individual ribs. Add the ribs and onion to the slow cooker.

2. Add the maple syrup, brown sugar, soy sauce, cinnamon, ginger, allspice, garlic, black pepper, and cayenne pepper or red pepper flakes, if using, to a bowl; stir to mix. Pour the maple syrup mixture into the slow cooker.

3. Cover and cook on low for 8 hours or until the meat is tender enough to pull away from the bone.

A Finger Foods Meal

Forgo the silverware and serve Country Pork Ribs along with potato chips and an assortment of crudités (raw fresh vegetables like green onions, celery stalks, carrot sticks, bell pepper slices, etc.) and dip. Provide plenty of napkins!

NORTH CAROLINA–INSPIRED BARBECUE

Cooking the pork in beer with apples adds a German influence to these sandwiches. The North Carolina influence comes from the ketchup-based coleslaw served as the condiment on the sandwiches. To continue the comfort-food theme, serve with baked beans and warm German potato salad.

Serves 12

INGREDIENTS:

3 pounds pork Western ribs

1 (12-ounce) can beer

2 large Golden Delicious apples

1 large sweet onion, peeled and sliced

2 tablespoons brown sugar

Optional: 1 cup Peach Marmalade (Chapter 4)

½ teaspoon freshly ground black pepper

Salt, to taste

12 hamburger buns

1. Add the pork to the slow cooker. (Do not trim the fat from the ribs; it's what helps the meat cook up moist enough to shred for sandwiches. A lot of the fat will melt out of the meat as it cooks.)

2. Pour the beer over the pork. Peel, core, and slice the apples and add them to the slow cooker along with the onion, brown sugar, marmalade (if using), black pepper, and salt. Cover and cook on low for 6 hours or until the pork is cooked through and tender.

3. Use a slotted spoon to move the pork to a cutting board. Remove and discard any fat still on the meat. Use two forks to shred the meat.

4. Spoon the meat onto hamburger buns. Top the meat with a heaping tablespoon of North Carolina–Style Coleslaw (see sidebar).

5. Optional: Have the onion slices that were cooked in with the meat available for those who want to add them to their sandwiches.

North Carolina–Style Coleslaw

Add ¾ cup cider vinegar, 1 tablespoon ketchup, 1 tablespoon brown sugar, 1 teaspoon salt, ⅛ teaspoon dried red pepper flakes, and ¾ teaspoon freshly ground black pepper to a large bowl. Whisk to mix, and then stir in a 2-pound bag of coleslaw mix. Add hot sauce, to taste. (This coleslaw is tart by itself; to best decide how to adjust the seasoning, taste it with some of the meat. Stir in some mayonnaise or extra-virgin olive oil if you think it's too tart.)

PORK CASSOULET

If you need more than 4 servings, a 4-quart slow cooker is large enough to hold all of the ingredients if you double the recipe.

Serves 4

INGREDIENTS:

1 pound boneless pork shoulder

2 slices bacon

1 large onion, peeled and diced

2 cloves garlic, peeled and minced

1 cup Chicken Broth (Chapter 19)

1 (15-ounce) can diced tomatoes

1 (15-ounce) can cannellini beans, rinsed and drained

1 (1-pound) bag baby carrots

2 stalks celery, thinly sliced

Salt and freshly ground black pepper, to taste

Optional: 1½ teaspoons Mrs. Dash Onion and Herb Blend

1. Trim the pork of any fat, and cut it into bite-sized pieces. Cut the bacon into 1-inch pieces. Add the bacon to a nonstick skillet; cook over medium-high heat for 2 minutes or until it begins to render its fat. Add the pork and sauté for 5 minutes or until the pork is browned on all sides. Transfer the meat to the slow cooker.

2. Add the onion to the skillet; sauté for 3 minutes or until the onion is transparent. Add the garlic and sauté for 30 seconds. Transfer the onion and garlic to the slow cooker.

3. Add the remaining ingredients to the slow cooker. Cover and cook on low for 6 hours or until the pork is tender.

Skip the Browning

If you have Brown Stock (Chapter 19) on hand, you can substitute ¼ cup of the chicken broth for an equal amount of the Brown Stock. This will impart the browned meat flavor to the Cassoulet. Likewise, if you have pork broth made from pork that had been browned prior to slow cooking it, you can substitute ¼ cup of that instead.

PORK ADOBADA

Adobada is Spanish for "marinated," but you can achieve a similar effect by cooking the pork loin for a very long time over low heat.

Serves 8

INGREDIENTS:

1 teaspoon canola oil

3 pounds pork loin

1 medium onion, diced

5 cloves garlic, minced

1½ cups water

½ cup apple cider vinegar

¼ cup orange juice

3 tablespoons light brown sugar

1 tablespoon ground cumin

1 tablespoon ground Anaheim chile

1 teaspoon ground cayenne pepper

1. Heat the oil in a large skillet. Cook the pork for 1 minute on each side. Place it in a 4-quart slow cooker, and pour the remaining ingredients over the meat. Cover and cook on low for 6 hours.

2. If the sauce is very thin, pour it into a saucepan and cook until it reduces. Pour the sauce over the roast and shred the meat with a fork. Toss to distribute the sauce evenly over the meat.

PORK SAUSAGES BRAISED IN SAUERKRAUT

This is a great meal for a party; the sausages can be kept warm for hours without overcooking.

Serves 6

INGREDIENTS:

6 reduced-fat smoked pork sausages

4 pounds sauerkraut

½ tablespoon caraway seeds

1 tablespoon yellow mustard seeds

1 small onion, thinly sliced

2 tablespoons apple cider vinegar

1. Prick each sausage with a fork at least once. Quickly sear in a dry skillet to brown all sides for about 1 minute. Remove from the skillet and cut a slit down the middle of each sausage vertically ¼" deep.

2. Place the sauerkraut, caraway seeds, mustard seeds, onions, and vinegar into a 4- or 6-quart slow cooker. Stir to distribute all ingredients evenly.

3. Add the sausage. Toss. Cover and cook for 3–4 hours on low.

RED COOKED PORK

Red Cooked Pork, although not red at all, is an excellent example of homestyle Chinese cooking. Serve with rice and steamed vegetables.

Serves 6

INGREDIENTS:

1½ pounds boneless pork loin

¼ cup Shaoxing (Chinese cooking wine)

4 cloves garlic

1 cup water

2 tablespoons dark brown sugar

2 tablespoons dark soy sauce

3 whole star anise

1. Heat a nonstick skillet. Quickly sear the meat on all sides.

2. Place all ingredients into a 4-quart slow cooker. Stir. Cook on low for 8–9 hours.

3. Remove the roast from the slow cooker and slice or cube. Pour the sauce into a small saucepan and cook until it reduces and thickens. Discard the star anise and drizzle the sauce over the meat.

How to Braise

Braising is a technique that is well suited to the slow cooker. The first step is to sear the meat to enhance flavor. Then transfer it to the slow cooker to simmer slowly until it is fork tender.

SOUR CHERRY–GLAZED PORK

Ginger preserves are a shortcut to a flavorful sauce without a lot of fuss. Look for ginger preserves near the jams and jellies at any supermarket.

Serves 4

INGREDIENTS:

3 tablespoons ginger preserves

¼ cup dried sour cherries

⅔ cup water

¼ teaspoon freshly ground black pepper

¼ teaspoon salt

⅛ teaspoon ground nutmeg

1¼ pounds pork loin

1. In a small bowl, whisk the preserves, sour cherries, water, pepper, salt, and nutmeg.

2. Place the pork loin into a 4-quart slow cooker. Pour the glaze over the pork. Cook on low for 8 hours.

CHINESE-STYLE BRAISED PORK

This Chinese-inspired pork is perfect served sliced over rice and garnished with chopped green onion.

Serves 4

INGREDIENTS:

1⅓ pounds pork loin

2 cloves minced garlic

1 tablespoon red pepper flakes

1 small onion, minced

1 teaspoon ground ginger

1 teaspoon ground garlic

½ teaspoon cinnamon

½ teaspoon ground star anise

1 tablespoon rice vinegar

3 tablespoons soy sauce

1 teaspoon sesame oil

1. Heat a large nonstick skillet. Cook the pork for 1 minute on each side.

2. Place the pork in a 4-quart slow cooker. Pour the remaining ingredients over the meat. Cover and cook on low 8 hours.

JAMAICAN HAM

This pleasantly spiced ham is the perfect weekday version of the Jamaican holiday dish.

Serves 4

INGREDIENTS:

20 ounces canned pineapple chunks in juice

1½ pounds boneless smoked ham quarter

1 tablespoon ground cloves

1 teaspoon allspice

1 teaspoon ground ginger

1. Use toothpicks to attach half the pineapple chunks to the ham. Place it into a 4-quart slow cooker.

2. Pour the remaining pineapple chunks, juice, and spices over the ham. Cook for 6–8 hours on low.

3. Remove the ham from the slow cooker. Remove the toothpicks, placing the pineapple chunks back into the slow cooker. Stir the contents of the slow cooker.

4. Slice the ham and return it to the slow cooker. Toss with the juices prior to serving.

Banish Dull Flavors

Store herbs and spices in a cool, dark cabinet to preserve freshness and flavor. Label each bottle with the date it was opened. Discard herbs and spices 1 year after first use.

PORK TENDERLOIN WITH FENNEL

Slightly sweet fennel accents the pork's natural sweetness.

Serves 10

INGREDIENTS:

4 pounds pork tenderloin, excess fat removed

4 bulbs fennel, cubed

1½ cups Caramelized Onions (Chapter 26)

1 teaspoon freshly ground black pepper

½ teaspoon salt

1. Place the pork into an oval 6- to 7-quart slow cooker. Top with remaining ingredients. Cook on low for 8 hours.

BLACKBERRY PULLED PORK

The blackberry seeds are very soft after the long cooking time, but if you want a smoother sauce, press the blackberries through a mesh sieve before adding them to the slow cooker. Discard the seeds.

Serves 12

INGREDIENTS:

6 pounds boneless pork roast, excess fat removed

2 cups fresh blackberries

½ cup chili sauce

½ cup balsamic vinegar

¼ teaspoon lime juice

1 tablespoon ginger preserves

2 teaspoons mesquite liquid smoke

2 teaspoons freshly ground black pepper

1 teaspoon ground cayenne pepper

1 teaspoon chili powder

1 teaspoon hot paprika

2 large onions, diced

5 cloves garlic, minced

¼ teaspoon salt

1. Place all ingredients in a 6-quart slow cooker. Cook on low for 8–9 hours or on high for 6 hours.

2. When done, the meat should shred easily with a fork. Remove the pork from the slow cooker. Shred with a fork and set aside. Mash any solid bits of the sauce in the slow cooker with a potato masher. Return the pork to the slow cooker, and toss to coat the pork evenly with the sauce.

PINEAPPLE PORK CHOPS

Serve these sweet and hot chops with rice.

Serves 2

INGREDIENTS:

1 small onion, sliced

3 ¼" thick fresh pineapple slices

½ pound thick-cut boneless pork chops

2 tablespoons soy sauce

1 teaspoon fresh ginger, grated

3 Thai bird peppers, minced

1. Place the onion slices on the bottom of a 1½- to 2-quart slow cooker. Top with a pineapple slice. Center 1 pork chop over the pineapple slice. Top with a second pineapple slice. Center the second pork chop over the pineapple. Top with the last pineapple slice.

2. Add the soy sauce, ginger, and peppers. Cook on low for 8–10 hours.

Substitution Suggestion

If you can't find Thai bird peppers or if you want a dish with less heat, substitute 1 jalapeño. Habanero peppers or Scotch bonnet peppers are quite hot and fruity tasting and would also make good substitutions. A tablespoon of hot sauce could be used in a pinch.

PORK TENDERLOIN WITH SWEET AND SAVORY APPLES

The tart apples sweeten over the long cooking time and nearly melt into the pork.

Serves 2

INGREDIENTS:

⅛ teaspoon salt

¼ teaspoon freshly ground black pepper

¾–1 pound boneless pork tenderloin

½ cup onions, sliced

5 fresh sage leaves

2 cups Granny Smith apples, peeled and diced

1. Sprinkle salt and pepper on the tenderloin. Place the onion slices on the bottom of a 1½- to 2-quart slow cooker. Add the tenderloin. Place the sage on top of the meat. Top with the diced apples.

2. Cover and cook on low for 8–10 hours.

Pork Tenderloin Tip

Lean, boneless pork tenderloin is often sold in very large packages containing 2 or more tenderloins, with a combined weight that is frequently over 15 pounds. As a result, it can be very expensive. Buy pork tenderloin on sale, and cut the meat into meal-sized portions. Label and freeze the portions until they are needed.

PORK AND TOMATILLO BURRITO FILLING

Serve with tomatoes, lettuce, and avocado in large tortillas.

Serves 2

INGREDIENTS:

½ pound boneless lean pork tenderloin roast

¾ cup tomatillos, diced

¼ cup onions, sliced

½ jalapeño, diced

1 tablespoon lime juice

1. Place all ingredients into a 2-quart slow cooker. Stir. Cook on low for 8–10 hours.

2. Use a fork to shred all of the contents. Toss to distribute the ingredients evenly.

HONEY-MUSTARD PORK LOIN

A mixture of mustard and honey keep the pork from drying out during the long cooking time.

Serves 2

INGREDIENTS:

3 tablespoons Dijon mustard

1 tablespoon mild honey

½ pound pork tenderloin

1. In a small bowl, mix the mustard and honey. Spread the mixture on the pork tenderloin in an even layer.

2. Place into a 2-quart slow cooker. Cook on low for 6 hours.

RHUBARB PULLED PORK

Rhubarb adds a tartness that contrasts with the sweetness of the pork.

Serves 2

INGREDIENTS:

½ pound pork loin

½ cup rhubarb, chopped

1 small onion, diced

1 tablespoon ginger preserves

1 tablespoon chili sauce

1. Quickly sear the pork on all sides in a nonstick skillet. Place into a 2-quart slow cooker. Add remaining ingredients. Cook on high for 5 hours.

2. Remove the pork from the slow cooker. Shred with a fork. Mash the rhubarb in the slow cooker with a potato masher until smooth. Add the pork back into the slow cooker and stir to distribute the sauce evenly.

SAN FRANCISCO GINGER PORK CHOPS

This is a variation of the classic San Francisco recipe. The subtle hint of ginger goes very well with the tangy red wine sauce.

Serves 4

INGREDIENTS:

4 center-cut pork chops

2 tablespoons olive oil

1 clove garlic, chopped

1 onion, cut into rings

½ cup soy sauce

½ cup red wine

¼ teaspoon crushed red pepper flakes

1 teaspoon ground ginger

3 tablespoons brown sugar

1 tablespoon honey

1. In skillet, brown pork chops in olive oil over medium-high heat for 3–4 minutes per side. Remove chops to cool. In same skillet, sauté the chopped garlic for 1–2 minutes until garlic is a light golden brown. Place pork chops and garlic in a freezer bag.

2. Layer onion rings on top of chops.

3. In a food processor, mix soy sauce, red wine, red pepper flakes, ginger, brown sugar, and honey. Blend well and pour over pork chops.

PULLED PORK

Serve this pork with sweet barbecue sauce, garlic toast, and a salad for a delicious meal.

Serves 6–8

INGREDIENTS:

3 pounds lean pork roast

Salt and pepper to taste

1 teaspoon onion powder

2 medium onions, sliced

3 cloves garlic, minced

Water to cover

1. Season pork with salt, pepper, and onion powder and set aside.

2. Lay ⅔ of sliced onions in bottom of slow cooker, and add ½ of minced garlic evenly over onions. Place seasoned pork roast on top of onions, and lay remaining onion and garlic on top of roast.

3. Cover with water. Cook on low for 8 hours and remove to a plate.

4. Remove any fat and pull meat apart using two forks.

Gravy in the Slow Cooker

Once you remove the pork from the cooker, you can make gravy out of the juices. Remove the onions and set aside. In a small bowl, combine ½ cup cold water with 3 tablespoons cornstarch. Stir until cornstarch is completely dissolved. Pour into the slow cooker and stir until mixture thickens. Add onions to gravy, cool, and freeze in a plastic container or freezer bag.

SWEET AND SOUR PORK ROAST

This pork roast comes out of the slow cooker full of flavor, and tastes even better after being frozen with the sauce. Serve this tangy roast with white rice and green beans.

Serves 6–8

INGREDIENTS:

4-pound lean pork roast

Salt and pepper to taste

3 cups sweet and sour sauce

1 (20-ounce) can pineapple chunks

1. Season the pork with salt and pepper and put in the bottom of the slow cooker.

2. Pour the sweet and sour sauce over the top of the roast.

3. Cook on low for 7–8 hours.

4. Remove pork from slow cooker and shred.

5. Return shredded pork to the slow cooker and stir in can of pineapple chunks. Cook additional 30 minutes.

ITALIAN PORK WITH CANNELLINI BEANS

This is an incredibly simple one-dish meal that is packed with flavor.

Serves 4

INGREDIENTS:

1½ pounds pork loin

28 ounces crushed tomatoes

1 head roasted garlic

1 onion, minced

2 tablespoons capers

2 teaspoons Italian seasoning

15 ounces canned cannellini beans, drained and rinsed

1. Place the pork loin into a 4-quart slow cooker. Add the tomatoes, garlic, onion, capers, and seasoning. Cook on low for 7–8 hours.

2. One hour before serving, add the cannellini beans and continue to cook on low for the remaining time.

How to Make Roasted Garlic

You can easily make your own roasted garlic in the oven. Simply cover a small baking sheet with aluminum foil and place 2–4 whole (unpeeled) heads of garlic on the pan. Drizzle 2 tablespoons of olive oil over the garlic and bake at 350°F for about 45 minutes. Allow to cool for 5–10 minutes and then gently squeeze garlic cloves out of the "paper" surrounding them. Alternately you could place the same ingredients in a 1½- to 2½-quart slow cooker. Cover and cook on high for 2 hours. Store roasted garlic cloves in the fridge for up to 2 weeks.

TEX-MEX PULLED PORK

This easy dish is great alone or in sandwich buns.

Serves 8

1 (15-ounce) can tomato sauce

1 cup barbecue sauce

1 onion, diced

1 (4.5-ounce) can diced green chile peppers

1 tablespoon chili powder

2 teaspoons ground cumin

1 teaspoon dried oregano

2½ pounds boneless pork loin roast, trimmed

¼ cup chopped fresh cilantro

1. In a 3-quart or larger slow cooker, mix tomato sauce, barbecue sauce, onion, green chile peppers, chili powder, cumin, and oregano. Place pork in slow cooker, and spoon sauce over meat to coat.

2. Cover, and cook on low 8–10 hours, or until pork is tender.

3. Use 2 forks to shred the meat. Pour sauce into a serving dish; stir in cilantro and shredded pork.

TOMATO-BRAISED PORK

In this recipe pork is gently cooked in tomatoes to yield incredibly tender meat.

Serves 4

INGREDIENTS:

28 ounces canned crushed tomatoes

3 tablespoons tomato paste

1 cup loosely packed fresh basil

½ teaspoon freshly ground black pepper

½ teaspoon marjoram

1¼ pounds boneless pork roast

1. Place the tomatoes, tomato paste, basil, pepper, and marjoram into a greased 4-quart slow cooker. Stir to create a uniform sauce. Add the pork.

2. Cook on low for 7–8 hours or until the pork easily falls apart when poked with a fork. Serve pork and sauce over cooked rice or polenta with a salad on the side.

GLAZED LEAN PORK SHOULDER

Apples and apple cider form a glaze over a long cooking time that is both flavorful and light. Use crisp, in-season apples for best results.

Serves 8

INGREDIENTS:

3 pounds bone-in pork shoulder, excess fat removed

3 apples, thinly sliced

¼ cup apple cider

1 tablespoon brown sugar

1 teaspoon allspice

½ teaspoon cinnamon

¼ teaspoon nutmeg

1. Place the pork shoulder into a 4-quart slow cooker. Top with the remaining ingredients. Cook on low for 8 hours. Remove the lid and cook on high for 30 minutes or until the sauce thickens.

POLYNESIAN PORK CHOPS

You can substitute pork steaks for the pork chops. (Because pork steaks tend to have more marbling, there's actually less chance of pork steaks drying out when prepared this way.)

Serves 6

INGREDIENTS:

6 (6-ounce) boneless pork chops

1 green bell pepper, seeded and diced

1 large onion, diced

2 cups converted rice

1 teaspoon sea salt

1 (20-ounce) can crushed pineapple

1 cup gluten-free honey-mustard barbecue sauce

3 cups water

½ teaspoon ground black pepper

1. Treat the slow cooker with nonstick cooking spray. Trim and discard any fat from the pork chops and then cut them into bite-sized pieces.

2. Arrange half of the pork on the bottom of the slow cooker. Top with the bell pepper, onion, and rice. Sprinkle with salt and place the remaining pork over the rice.

3. In a small bowl, combine the entire can of pineapple, barbecue sauce, water, and black pepper; stir to mix and then pour into the slow cooker. Cover and cook on low for 8 hours or until the pork is cooked through and the rice is tender.

4. Stir the mixture in the slow cooker to fluff the rice. Taste for seasoning and add additional salt, barbecue sauce, and pepper if needed.

RED WINE–BRAISED PORK TENDERLOIN ROAST

This roast is simmered in red wine and beef broth for a tender and delicious meal. Serve with Rosemary-Garlic Mashed Potatoes (Chapter 26) and sautéed fennel or steamed broccoli.

Serves 6

INGREDIENTS:

2 pounds boneless pork tenderloin roast

1 tablespoon dried onion flakes

¼ teaspoon freshly ground black pepper

¼ teaspoon salt

2 teaspoons garlic powder

1 cup warm water

¾ cup red wine

1 teaspoon beef bouillon granules or 1 cube beef bouillon

1. Place the pork roast into a greased 4-quart slow cooker.

2. In a large bowl whisk together the dried onion flakes, black pepper, salt, and garlic powder. Pour in the water, red wine, and bouillon and whisk everything together thoroughly.

3. Pour red wine mixture over the pork roast. Cover and cook on low for 4 hours or on high for 3 hours. Because pork tenderloin is such a lean cut you do not want to overcook this meat.

Sautéed Fennel

Fennel is delicious as a savory, yet slightly sweet side dish. Heat a cast-iron skillet until almost smoking and add 3 tablespoons of olive oil. When the oil is hot stir in 2 cloves of sliced garlic. Add in 2 heads of finely sliced fennel with ½ teaspoon salt and ¼ teaspoon finely ground pepper. Sauté for an additional 3–4 minutes until fennel begins to caramelize (turns golden brown). Add about a tablespoon of water and cover with a lid to allow fennel to steam for about a minute. Serve immediately.

BUBBLE AND SQUEAK

Adding some ham and bacon to this traditional British dish makes it a complete meal, even if you choose to serve it without a salad.

Serves 6

INGREDIENTS:

6 strips bacon, cut into pieces

2 stalks celery, finely diced

3 large carrots, peeled and grated

1 medium yellow onion, peeled and diced

2 zucchini, grated and squeezed dry

3 large potatoes, peeled and diced

½ cup ham, chopped

3 cups coleslaw mix

1 teaspoon salt

½ teaspoon freshly ground black pepper

1. Place bacon, celery, carrots, onion, zucchini, potatoes, and ham into a 4-quart slow cooker. Cover and cook on high for 3 hours or until the potatoes are soft enough to mash down. Use the back of a large spoon or ladle to press the mixture down into the slow cooker to compress it.

2. Spread the coleslaw mix over the ham mixture. Cover and continue to cook on high for 30 minutes or until the cabbage is tender. If necessary, leave the pan over the heat until any excess moisture from the cabbage and zucchini evaporates. Season with salt and pepper. To serve, spoon portions directly from the slow cooker.

ORANGE HONEY–GLAZED HAM

Many people are intimidated by making ham. Using the slow cooker makes it super easy and the homemade orange honey glaze is a breeze to mix up.

Serves 6

INGREDIENTS:

1 (4-pound) bone-in ham

½ cup seltzer water

½ cup orange juice

¼ cup honey

1–2 tablespoons orange zest

1 teaspoon ground cloves

¼ teaspoon cinnamon

1. Place ham, seltzer water, and orange juice in a greased 4- to 6-quart slow cooker. Cook on low for 6–8 hours or on high for 3–4 hours.

2. In a small bowl mix together honey, orange zest, ground cloves, and cinnamon. Spread over ham. Cook for an additional 45 minutes to an hour, venting the slow cooker lid with a chopstick or spoon handle. The ham should become golden brown and glazed. If necessary, finish off ham in 350°F oven for 15–20 minutes to get a shiny glaze.

Orange Soda or Seltzer?

You can use 1 cup of orange soda in place of the seltzer water and orange juice called for in this recipe. Orange juice was used here because the recipe also calls for fresh orange zest. In a pinch though, use what you have on hand! If you don't have orange zest you can add a splash of lime juice to the honey glaze instead.

EASY BROWN SUGAR SPIRAL-SLICED HAM

Making a holiday meal doesn't have to be hard or require a ton of ingredients! This super-easy ham is simply rubbed with brown sugar which beautifully caramelizes during slow cooking.

Serves 16

INGREDIENTS:

1 (8-pound) spiral-sliced ham

1 cup brown sugar

1. Remove ham from packaging. Rub entire ham with the brown sugar. Place ham on the bottom of a greased 6-quart (or larger) oval slow cooker. Cook on low for 6–8 hours or on high for 3–4 hours.

Make Your Own Brown Sugar

Out of brown sugar? Simply cream together 1 cup of sugar with 2–3 tablespoons of dark molasses. Mix well with a fork until mixture has the appearance of regular brown sugar. Store in an airtight container.

CHAPTER 11

GROUND MEAT

TURKEY MEATLOAF

Instead of making the meatloaf entirely from ground turkey, you can use a combination of ground beef, ground pork, and ground turkey.

Serves 6

INGREDIENTS:

2 pounds ground turkey

1 large yellow onion, peeled and diced

2 stalks celery, finely diced

1 green bell pepper, seeded and diced

2 cloves garlic, peeled and minced

2 large eggs

1 cup fresh bread crumbs or cracker crumbs

Salt and freshly ground black pepper, to taste

6 slices bacon

½ cup ketchup

1 tablespoon brown sugar

Optional: Chili powder, to taste

1. Add the ground turkey, onion, celery, bell pepper, garlic, eggs, bread crumbs, salt, and pepper to a large bowl; mix well with your hands. Form into a loaf to fit the size (round or oval) of your slow cooker.

2. Line the slow cooker with two pieces of heavy-duty aluminum foil long enough to reach up both sides of the slow cooker and over the edge, crossing one piece over the other. Place a piece of nonstick foil the size of the bottom of the slow cooker crock inside the crossed pieces of foil to form a platform for the meatloaf. (This is to make it easier to lift the meatloaf out of the slow cooker.)

3. Place three pieces of bacon over the top of the nonstick foil. Put the meatloaf over the top of the bacon. Spread the ketchup over the top of the meatloaf. Sprinkle the brown sugar and chili powder, if using, over the top of the ketchup. Place the remaining three slices of bacon over the top of the seasoned ketchup. Cover and cook on low for 7 hours or until the internal temperature of the meatloaf registers 165°F.

4. Lift the meatloaf out of the slow cooker and place it on a cooling rack. Allow it to rest for 20 minutes before transferring it to a serving platter and slicing it.

Slow Cooker Liner

Instead of placing two pieces of heavy-duty aluminum foil across each other and over the sides of the slow cooker, you can instead line it with a Reynolds Slow Cooker Liner (*www.reynoldspkg.com*) and then place the nonstick foil piece inside the liner.

BARBECUE MEATLOAF

This recipe assumes you're using commercial barbecue sauce, which is usually thicker than homemade sauce. The brown sugar sprinkled over the top of the meatloaf helps caramelize the sauce.

Serves 8

INGREDIENTS:

2 pounds lean ground beef

½ pound lean ground pork

2 large eggs

1 large yellow onion, peeled and diced

Salt and freshly ground pepper, to taste

1½ cups quick-cooking oatmeal

1 teaspoon dried parsley

1½ cups barbecue sauce

1 tablespoon brown sugar

Optional: Mrs. Dash Extra Spicy Seasoning Blend, to taste

1. Add the ground beef, ground pork, eggs, onion, salt, pepper, oatmeal, parsley, and 1 cup of the barbecue sauce to a large bowl; mix well with your hands. Form into a loaf to fit the size (round or oval) of your slow cooker.

2. Line the slow cooker with two pieces of heavy-duty aluminum foil long enough to reach up both sides of the slow cooker and over the edge, crossing one piece over the other. Place a piece of nonstick foil the size of the bottom of the slow cooker crock inside the crossed pieces of foil or slow cooker liner to form a platform for the meatloaf. (This is to make it easier to lift the meatloaf out of the slow cooker.)

3. Put the meatloaf over the top of the nonstick foil. Spread the remaining ½ cup of barbecue sauce over the top of the meatloaf. Sprinkle the brown sugar and Mrs. Dash Extra Spicy Seasoning Blend, if using, over the top of the ketchup. Cover and cook on low for 8 hours or until the internal temperature of the meatloaf registers 165°F.

4. Lift the meatloaf out of the slow cooker and place it on a cooling rack. Allow it to rest for 20 minutes before transferring it to a serving platter and slicing it.

ZESTY MEATLOAF

As an alternative, you can form the meatloaf mixture into about fifty cocktail-size meatballs, bake at 350°F for 18 minutes, and then add them with the sauce (in Step 2) to the slow cooker; cover and cook on low for 3 hours.

Serves 8

INGREDIENTS:

2 pounds lean ground beef

1 large egg

1 (10½-ounce) can condensed French onion soup

Salt and freshly ground pepper, to taste

2 cups herb-seasoned stuffing mix or crushed seasoned croutons

1 (15-ounce) can tomato sauce

2 tablespoons Worcestershire sauce

⅓ cup brown sugar, packed

2 tablespoons red wine or balsamic vinegar

Optional: Mrs. Dash Extra Spicy Seasoning Blend, to taste

1. Add the ground beef, egg, onion soup, salt, pepper, and stuffing mix or crushed croutons to a large bowl; mix well with your hands. Form into a loaf to fit the size (round or oval) of your slow cooker.

2. Put the meatloaf in the slow cooker. Add the tomato sauce, Worcestershire sauce, brown sugar, vinegar, and Mrs. Dash Extra Spicy Seasoning Blend, if using, to a bowl and stir to mix. Pour over the meatloaf.

3. Cover and cook on low for 7 hours or until the internal temperature of the meatloaf registers 165°F. Slice and serve with the sauce from the slow cooker.

COUNTRY MEATLOAF

The grated carrots and butter-style crackers make this a sweeter-tasting meatloaf.

Serves 6

INGREDIENTS:

1 pound lean ground beef

½ pound lean ground pork

¾ teaspoon salt

¼ teaspoon ground black pepper

1 medium yellow onion, peeled and finely chopped

1 stalk celery, very finely chopped

½ cup carrot, grated

1 small green pepper, seeded and finely chopped

1 large egg

½ cup ketchup

½ cup tomato sauce

½ cup quick-cooking oatmeal

½ cup butter-style crackers, crumbled

Nonstick spray

⅓ cup ketchup

2 tablespoons brown sugar

1 tablespoon prepared mustard

1. Add the ground beef and pork, salt, pepper, onion, celery, carrot, green pepper, egg, ketchup, tomato sauce, oatmeal, and cracker crumbs into a large bowl and mix well.

2. Treat the slow cooker with nonstick spray. Add the meat mixture and shape the meatloaf to fit the crock of the slow cooker.

3. In a small bowl, mix together the ketchup, brown sugar, and mustard; spread it over the top of the meatloaf. Cover and cook on low for 7 hours or until the meat is cooked through. Use paper towels to blot and remove any fat that's rendered from the meat. Let the meatloaf sit for 30 minutes and then slice and serve.

One-Pot Meatloaf Meal

There will be room on top of the Country Meatloaf to add 3 large peeled and sliced carrots and 6 medium peeled potatoes. You may need to increase the cooking time to 8 hours if you add the vegetables.

PINEAPPLE SAUSAGE MEATBALLS

If you slow-cook meatballs in sauce for longer than 3 hours, you run the risk that they'll break apart and become a part of the sauce. Serve this dish over cooked rice.

Serves 8

INGREDIENTS:

1 (20-ounce) can crushed pineapple, packed in juice, drained

¼ cup dried minced onion

1 cup ketchup

2 cups barbecue sauce

1 tablespoon brown sugar

1 teaspoon chili powder

Optional: Mrs. Dash Extra Spicy Seasoning Blend, to taste

1 pound lean ground beef

1 pound lean ground pork

2 large eggs

1 large yellow onion, peeled and diced

Salt and freshly ground pepper, to taste

1½ cups quick-cooking oatmeal

1 teaspoon dried parsley

1. Add the drained crushed pineapple, dried onion, ketchup, 1 cup of the barbecue sauce, brown sugar, chili powder, and Mrs. Dash Extra Spicy Seasoning Blend, if using, to the slow cooker. Cover and cook on low while you make the meatballs.

2. Preheat the oven to 425°F. Add the remaining cup of barbecue sauce, ground beef, ground pork, egg, diced onion, oatmeal, and parsley to a large bowl; use hands to mix. Form into twenty-four meatballs. Place on a baking sheet; bake for 10 minutes or until browned on the outside but still rare on the inside.

3. Add the browned meatballs to the sauce. Cover and cook on low for 3 hours.

MEATBALLS IN CHIPOTLE SAUCE

Serve these meatballs with some of the sauce over cooked rice. Top with guacamole and sour cream, if desired, or serve along with an avocado salad.

Serves 6

INGREDIENTS:

1 tablespoon vegetable oil

1 large onion, thinly sliced

1½ teaspoons garlic powder

1 tablespoon chili powder

¼ teaspoon dried Mexican oregano

2 canned chipotle chili peppers in adobo sauce

1 (28-ounce) can crushed tomatoes

1 cup Chicken Broth (Chapter 19)

Salt and freshly ground black pepper, to taste

1½ pounds lean ground beef

½ pound ground pork

1 large egg

1 small white onion, peeled and diced

1 tablespoon chili powder

1½ teaspoons garlic powder

10 soda crackers, crumbled

1. Add the vegetable oil and sliced onions to the slow cooker; stir to coat the onions in the oil. Cover and cook on high for 30 minutes or until the onions are transparent.

2. Stir in the garlic powder, chili powder, and oregano. Cover and cook on high for 15 minutes. Stir in the chipotles in adobo sauce, tomatoes, broth, salt, and pepper. Cover and cook on high while you prepare the meatballs.

3. Preheat the oven to 425°F. Add the ground beef, ground pork, egg, diced onion, chili powder, garlic powder, and crumbled crackers to a large bowl; use hands to mix. Form into eighteen meatballs. Place on a baking sheet; bake for 10 minutes or until browned on the outside but still rare on the inside.

4. Use an immersion blender to purée the sauce in the slow cooker. Add the browned meatballs to the sauce. Cover and cook on low for 3 hours.

For Hotter Sauce

You can add extra heat to the sauce by adding more than 2 of the canned chipotles or some Mrs. Dash Extra Spicy Seasoning Blend.

COLA-CRAVIN' GROUND BEEF

Browning ground beef before it's added to the slow cooker lets you improve its flavor by rendering and removing the fat out of the meat and replacing it with extra-virgin olive oil. Serve this sauce over macaroni or rigatoni; it's perfect for those who prefer to top pasta dishes with grated Cheddar cheese.

Serves 8

INGREDIENTS:

3 pounds lean ground beef

2 tablespoons extra-virgin olive oil

1 large sweet onion, peeled and diced

2 cloves garlic, peeled and minced

1 cup Coca-Cola

1 (26-ounce) jar pasta sauce

1. Brown the ground beef in a large nonstick skillet over medium heat, breaking apart the meat as you do so. Remove and discard any fat rendered from the meat.

2. Stir in the oil and onion; sauté for 5 minutes or until the onion is transparent. Stir in the garlic. Transfer the meat mixture to the slow cooker.

3. Add the cola and pasta sauce. Stir to combine. Cover and cook on low for 4 hours or longer.

TAMALE PIE

For a flavor boost, drizzle some extra-virgin olive oil over each serving.

Serves 8

INGREDIENTS:

2 pounds lean ground beef

1 large white onion, peeled and diced

3 tablespoons chili powder

Nonstick spray

1½ cups cornmeal

2½ cups whole milk

4 large eggs

Salt, freshly ground black pepper, and ground cumin, to taste

2 (16-ounce) cans stewed tomatoes

2 (14-ounce) cans pitted black olives, drained

4 cups frozen whole kernel corn, thawed

2 cups (8 ounces) Cheddar cheese, grated

1 cup (4 ounces) Monterey jack cheese, grated

1. Brown the ground beef together with the onion in a large nonstick skillet over medium heat, breaking apart the meat as you do so. Remove and discard any fat rendered from the meat. Stir in the chili powder; sauté for 2 minutes.

2. Treat the crock of the slow cooker with nonstick spray. Transfer the ground beef mixture to the slow cooker.

3. Add the cornmeal, milk, eggs, salt, pepper, and cumin to a large bowl and whisk until smooth. Coarsely chop the tomatoes and drained black olives. Stir the tomatoes, black olives, and corn into the cornmeal mixture. Pour into the slow cooker. Stir to mix together with the ground beef. Cover and cook on high for 5 hours or until the mixture is set in the center.

4. Sprinkle the cheeses over the top of the tamale pie. Cover and cook on high for 10 minutes or until the cheese is melted. Spoon directly from the slow cooker to serve.

Hot Tamale Pie

Add heat to the Tamale Pie by including seeded and diced jalapeño or other hot peppers to taste when you fry the ground beef and onions in Step 1.

FRITO PIE

You can easily increase the number of servings in this recipe by adding another can of pinto beans or serving it over a large helping of Fritos. Choose mild, medium, or sharp Cheddar according to your preference.

Serves 12

INGREDIENTS:

3 cups lean ground beef

2 tablespoons extra-virgin olive oil

1 large white onion, peeled and diced

2½ teaspoons garlic powder

3 tablespoons chili powder

4 teaspoons ground cumin

Salt and freshly ground black pepper, to taste

2 (28-ounce) cans diced tomatoes

1 (15-ounce) can pinto beans, rinsed and drained

1 (12-ounce) bag Fritos original corn chips

4 cups (1 pound) Cheddar cheese, grated

Optional: Green onions, diced

1. Brown the ground beef in a large nonstick skillet over medium heat, breaking apart the meat as you do so. Remove and discard any fat rendered from the meat.

2. Stir in the oil and onion, garlic powder, chili powder, cumin, salt, and pepper; sauté for 5 minutes or until the onion is transparent. Transfer the ground beef mixture to the slow cooker.

3. Stir in the tomatoes and pinto beans. Cover and cook on low for 5–8 hours. (When you taste the chili for seasoning, keep in mind that it'll be served over salty corn chips.)

4. To serve, place a (1-ounce or more) handful of Fritos on each plate. Ladle the chili over the Fritos. Top with grated cheese and diced green onion if desired.

Restaurant-Style Taco Pie

For each serving, tear open (on the side, not the top) an individual serving–sized (1-ounce) bag of Fritos and place it flat on a serving plate. Ladle the chili into the bag and over the corn chips.

ITALIAN MEATBALLS

There are no eggs and only a small amount of bread crumbs in these meatballs so they'll stand up to the long cooking time without falling apart. You can serve these meatballs and the sauce over cooked rice or pasta, or in meatball sandwiches.

Serves 8

INGREDIENTS:

4 tablespoons extra-virgin or light olive oil

1 large sweet onion, peeled and diced

4 cloves garlic, peeled and minced

2 (28-ounce) cans plum tomatoes, drained and chopped

1 (6-ounce) can tomato paste

1 cup Chicken Broth (Chapter 19)

Salt and freshly ground black pepper, to taste

½ teaspoon sugar

Pinch dried red pepper flakes

1 pound lean ground beef

½ pound ground veal

½ pound lean ground pork

⅓ cup fresh bread crumbs

¼ cup freshly grated Parmesan-Reggiano or Romano cheese

6 tablespoons fresh Italian parsley, minced

1. Add the oil and onion to the slow cooker; stir to coat the onions in the oil. Cover and cook on high for 30 minutes or until the onion is transparent. Stir in 2 cloves of the minced garlic, tomatoes, tomato paste, broth, salt, pepper, sugar, and dried red pepper flakes. Cover and cook on high while you make the meatballs.

2. Add the remaining 2 cloves of minced garlic, beef, veal, pork, bread crumbs, cheese, parsley, and salt and pepper, to taste, to a bowl; use your hands to mix. Shape into sixteen equal-sized meatballs. Add the meatballs to the slow cooker. Reduce the temperature of the slow cooker to low; cover and cook for 7 hours or until the internal temperature of the meatballs is 160°F.

Dealing with the Fat

Some fat will be rendered from the Italian meatballs during the slow-cooking process. It will rise to the surface, so skim it from the sauce and discard. Carefully ladle the meatballs from the slow cooker before you whisk the sauce to evenly distribute the onions and other ingredients, or use an immersion blender if you prefer a smoother sauce.

GREEK-STYLE MEATBALLS AND ARTICHOKES

Mediterranean flavors abound in this dish. Serve it with an orzo pilaf.

Serves 10

INGREDIENTS:

2 thin slices white sandwich bread

½ cup 1% milk

2¾ pounds lean ground pork

2 cloves garlic, minced

1 egg

½ teaspoon lemon zest

¼ teaspoon freshly ground pepper

16 ounces frozen artichoke hearts, defrosted

3 tablespoons lemon juice

2 cups Chicken Broth (Chapter 19)

¾ cup frozen chopped spinach

⅓ cup sliced Greek olives

1 tablespoon minced fresh oregano

1. Preheat the oven to 350°F. Place the bread and milk in a shallow saucepan. Cook on low until the milk is absorbed, about 1 minute. Place into a large bowl and add the pork, garlic, egg, zest, and pepper.

2. Mix until all ingredients are evenly distributed. Roll into 1" balls. Line two baking sheets with parchment paper. Place the meatballs in a single layer on the baking sheets. Bake for 15 minutes, and then drain on paper towel–lined plates.

3. Add the meatballs to a 6- to 7-quart slow cooker. Add the remaining ingredients.

4. Cook on low for 6–8 hours.

STUFFED ONIONS

Serve with a salad and a steamed vegetable.

Serves 4

INGREDIENTS:

4 medium onions, peeled

1 pound ground beef or lamb

¼ teaspoon ground allspice

¼ teaspoon dried dill

3 tablespoons fresh lemon juice

2 teaspoons dried parsley

Salt and freshly ground black pepper, to taste

1 large egg

1–2 tablespoons all-purpose flour

2 tablespoons extra-virgin olive oil

1 cup Chicken Broth (Chapter 19)

1. Cutting across the onions (not from bottom to top), cut the onions in half. Scoop out the onion cores.

2. Chop the onion cores and add to the ground beef or lamb, allspice, dill, 2 tablespoons of the lemon juice, parsley, salt, pepper, and egg; mix well.

3. Fill the onion halves with the meat mixture. (The meat will overflow the onions and form a mound on top.) Sprinkle the flour over the top of the meat.

4. Add the oil to a deep 3½-quart nonstick skillet or electric skillet and bring it to temperature over medium heat. Add the onions to the pan, meat side down, and sauté for 10 minutes or until browned.

5. Arrange the onions in the slow cooker so that the meat side is up. Mix the other tablespoon of lemon juice into the broth; pour the broth around the onions. Cover and cook on high for 4 hours or low for 8 hours or until the onion is soft and the meat is cooked through.

CHAPTER 12

FISH AND SEAFOOD

POACHED SALMON

To add more flavor to the poached salmon, you can replace ½ cup of the water with an equal amount of dry white wine. Another option is to add some fresh parsley stems (without the leaves) to the poaching liquid.

Serves 4

INGREDIENTS:

1 tablespoon butter

4 thin slices sweet onion

1½ cups water

1 tablespoon lemon juice

1 sprig fresh dill

4 (6-ounce) salmon fillets

Sea salt, to taste

Optional: 1 lemon, quartered

Optional: Dill Sauce (see sidebar)

1. Use the butter to grease the bottom and halfway up the side of the slow cooker. Arrange the onion slices over the bottom of the slow cooker, pressing them into the butter so that they stay in place. Pour in the water. Cover and cook on high for 30 minutes.

2. Place a salmon fillet over each onion slice. Cover and cook on high for 30 minutes or until the salmon is opaque. Transfer the (well-drained) fillets to individual serving plates or to a serving platter. Garnish with lemon wedges and serve with Dill Sauce (see sidebar) if desired.

Dill Sauce

Peel and grate 1 English cucumber; add the grated cucumber to a bowl, lightly salt it, and set it aside for 1 hour. Drain any liquid off the cucumber and then squeeze it dry with paper towels. Stir in 1½ cups sour cream, ½ cup mayonnaise, 1 tablespoon fresh lemon juice, 1 small minced clove of garlic, sea salt to taste, and ⅔ cup fresh, finely chopped dill. Cover with plastic wrap, chill for an hour, and then serve alongside the Poached Salmon.

CRAB SUPREME

You can serve Crab Supreme directly from the slow cooker as a dip. Or you can use it as a warm sandwich filling by slathering it on slices of French bread. Serve the sandwiches along with a tossed greens and cucumber salad or coleslaw mix dressed with Lemon Dill Dressing (see sidebar).

Yields 8 cups

INGREDIENTS:

1 quart (full-fat) mayonnaise

2 cups (full-fat) sour cream

¼ cup dry sherry or Chicken Broth (Chapter 19)

3 tablespoons fresh lemon juice

¼ cup fresh Italian parsley, minced

2 pounds fresh crabmeat

Salt and freshly ground white pepper, to taste

Hot sauce, to taste

1. Add the mayonnaise, sour cream, sherry or broth, and lemon juice to the slow cooker. Whisk to mix. Cover and cook on low for 2 hours.

2. Stir in the parsley. Pick over the crabmeat to remove any shells and cartilage, and then stir it into the mayonnaise mixture in the slow cooker. Cover and cook on low for 30 minutes or until the crab is heated through. Taste for seasoning and add salt, white pepper, and hot sauce if desired.

Lemon Dill Dressing

To make 1½ cups of dressing, in a bowl whisk together 1 cup mayonnaise, ¼ cup buttermilk, 2 tablespoons chopped fresh dill, 1 tablespoon minced fresh Italian parsley, 1 tablespoon grated lemon zest, 2 teaspoons fresh lemon juice, 1 small minced clove of garlic, and salt and freshly ground pepper to taste. Cover bowl and refrigerate until chilled. (The dressing will thicken as it chills.)

FISH "BAKE"

The stewed tomatoes help prevent the fish from overcooking and makes a sauce perfect for serving the fish over cooked couscous, pasta, rice, or steamed cabbage, or alongside polenta.

Serves 4

INGREDIENTS:

2 tablespoons olive oil

4 flounder or cod fillets

1 clove garlic, peeled and minced

1 small onion, peeled and thinly sliced

1 green bell pepper, seeded and diced

1 (14½-ounce) can stewed tomatoes

½ teaspoon dried basil

½ teaspoon dried oregano

1 teaspoon dried parsley

Salt and freshly ground black pepper, to taste

2 tablespoons freshly grated Parmesan-Reggiano cheese

1. Add the oil to the slow cooker. Use the oil to coat the bottom of and the sides of the crock.

2. Rinse the fish fillets and pat dry with paper towels. Add in a single layer over the oil.

3. Evenly distribute the garlic, onion, and green bell pepper over the fish. Pour the stewed tomatoes over the fish. Evenly sprinkle the basil, oregano, parsley, salt, pepper, and cheese over the tomatoes.

4. Cover and cook on low for 6 hours or until the fish is opaque and flakes apart.

SALMON LOAF

If you're using saltine crackers, add dill pickles to Salmon Loaf. If you prefer butter-style crackers, use sweet pickles. Serve it as you would meatloaf, topped with Creamy Dill Sauce (see sidebar) instead of gravy.

Serves 4

INGREDIENTS:

2 (7½-ounce) cans red sockeye salmon, drained, skin removed

¼ cup crackers, finely crushed

1 small onion, peeled and minced

1 large egg

2 tablespoons mayonnaise

1 tablespoon fresh lemon juice

1 tablespoon fresh parsley, minced

1 tablespoon fresh dill, chopped

½ teaspoon freshly ground black pepper

Optional: 2 tablespoons pickles, finely minced

1. Add the salmon, crackers, onion, egg, mayonnaise, lemon juice, parsley, dill, pepper, and pickles, if using, to a bowl. Gently mix with a fork until evenly combined.

2. Place two long pieces of heavy-duty aluminum foil across each other in the crock of the slow cooker. Press into the crock and top with a piece of nonstick foil shaped to hold the salmon loaf. Use your hands to shape the salmon loaf and place it on top of the nonstick foil.

3. Cover the slow cooker, tucking the ends of the heavy-duty foil under lid. Cook on low for 6–8 hours or on high for 3–4 hours or until the salmon loaf is cooked through and set. Turn off the slow cooker, remove the lid, and let the salmon loaf stand for 15 minutes. Use the heavy-duty foil as handles to lift the loaf out of the slow cooker. Transfer the loaf to a serving plate. Slice and serve with Creamy Dill Sauce if desired.

Creamy Dill Sauce

Melt 1 tablespoon of butter in a nonstick skillet over medium heat. Whisk in 1 tablespoon flour, ¼ teaspoon sea salt, and ¼ teaspoon freshly ground black pepper. Slowly whisk in 1 cup milk and 2 tablespoons minced fresh dill. Stirring constantly, bring to a boil and boil for 1 minute; lower heat and simmer and stir until the mixture is thick enough to coat the back of a spoon. Serve over the salmon loaf.

CIOPPINO

Serve Cioppino with warm sourdough bread or ladled over cooked spaghetti. You can substitute any non-oily fish (such as red snapper fillets with the skin removed) for the cod.

Serves 6

INGREDIENTS:

2 tablespoons olive oil

1 large sweet onion, peeled and diced

2 stalks celery, finely diced

2 cloves garlic, peeled and minced

3 cups bottled clam juice or Fish Stock (Chapter 19)

2 cups water

1 (28-ounce) can diced or peeled Italian tomatoes

1 cup Zinfandel or other dry red wine

2 teaspoons dried parsley

1 teaspoon dried basil

1 teaspoon dried thyme

Dried red pepper flakes, to taste

1 teaspoon sugar

1 bay leaf

1 pound cod, cut into 1-inch pieces

½ pound raw shrimp, peeled and deveined

½ pound scallops

Sea salt and freshly ground black pepper, to taste

1. Add the oil, onion, and celery to the slow cooker. Stir to mix the vegetables together with the oil. Cover and cook on high for 30 minutes or until the onions are transparent.

2. Add the clam juice or stock, water, tomatoes, wine, parsley, basil, thyme, red pepper flakes, sugar, and bay leaf. Stir to combine. Cover, reduce the slow cooker setting to low, and cook for 5 hours.

3. If you used whole peeled tomatoes, use a spoon to break them apart. Gently stir in the cod, shrimp, and scallops. Increase the slow cooker setting to high. Cover and cook for 30 minutes or until the seafood is cooked through. Discard bay leaf. Ladle into soup bowls and serve immediately.

ALMOND-STUFFED FLOUNDER

Making this dish in the slow cooker lets you layer the fish and stuffing rather than stuffing and rolling the fillets. You can substitute sole for the flounder. Serve with warm dinner rolls, a tossed salad, and cooked wild rice.

Serves 4

INGREDIENTS:

Nonstick spray

4 (4-ounce) fresh or frozen flounder fillets

1 cup (4 ounces) Swiss cheese, grated

½ cup slivered almonds

Optional: 1 tablespoon freeze-dried chives

Sweet paprika, to taste

Optional: ¼ cup dry white wine

1 tablespoon butter

½ cup carrot, grated

1 tablespoon all-purpose flour

¼ teaspoon dried tarragon

Sea salt, to taste

White pepper, to taste

½ cup milk

½ cup heavy cream

1. Treat the crock of the slow cooker with nonstick spray. Rinse the fish and pat dry with paper towels. Lay 2 fillets flat in the slow cooker. Sprinkle the grated cheese, almonds, and chives (if using) over the fillets. Place the remaining fillets on top. Sprinkle paprika over the fish fillets. Pour the wine around the fish.

2. Add the butter and carrots to a microwave-safe bowl or measuring cup. Cover and microwave on high for 1 minute; stir and microwave on high for 1 more minute. Stir in the flour, tarragon, salt, and pepper. Whisk in the milk. Cover and microwave on high for 1 minute. Stir in the cream. Pour the sauce over the fish.

3. Cover and cook on low for 2 hours or until the fish is cooked through, the cheese is melted, and the sauce is thickened. Sprinkle with additional paprika before serving, if desired. Turn off the slow cooker and let rest for 15 minutes. To serve, use a knife to cut through all layers into four wedges. Spoon each wedge onto a plate (so that there is fish and filling in each serving).

ETOUFFÉE

Serve Etouffé over cooked rice.

Serves 6

INGREDIENTS:

2 tablespoons vegetable oil

1 large onion, peeled and diced

6 scallions

2 stalks celery, finely diced

1 green bell pepper, seeded and diced

1 jalapeño, seeded and diced

2 cloves garlic, peeled and minced

3 tablespoons tomato paste

3 (15-ounce) cans diced tomatoes

Salt, to taste

½ teaspoon dried basil

½ teaspoon dried oregano

½ teaspoon dried thyme

¼ teaspoon cayenne pepper

1 pound raw shrimp, peeled and deveined

1 pound scallops, quartered

2 teaspoons cornstarch

1 tablespoon cold water

Hot sauce, to taste

1. Add the oil and onion to the slow cooker. Clean the scallions and chop the white parts and about 1 inch of the greens. Add to the slow cooker along with the celery, green bell pepper, and jalapeño. Stir to coat the vegetables in the oil. Cover and cook on high for 30 minutes or until the vegetables are soft.

2. Stir in the garlic and tomato paste. Cover and cook on high for 15 minutes.

3. Stir in the tomatoes, salt, basil, oregano, thyme, and cayenne pepper. Reduce the heat setting of the slow cooker to low; cover and cook for 6 hours.

4. Stir in the shrimp and scallops. Increase the heat setting of the slow cooker to high, cover, and cook for 15 minutes.

5. Add the cornstarch and water to a small bowl. Stir to mix. Remove any lumps if necessary. Uncover the slow cooker and stir in the cornstarch mixture. Cook and stir for 5 minutes, or until the mixture is thickened and the cornstarch flavor is cooked out. Stir in hot sauce, to taste.

JAMBALAYA

This is a one-pot main dish that you can serve along with a tossed salad and garlic toast, crackers, or corn bread. Have hot sauce at the table for those who wish to add it.

Serves 8

INGREDIENTS:

2 tablespoons olive oil

8 ounces kielbasa sausage, diced

1 large onion, peeled and diced

1 large red bell pepper, seeded and diced

2 stalks celery, finely diced

2 cloves garlic, peeled and minced

1 cup converted long-grain rice

8 ounces boneless, skinless chicken thighs

1 (15-ounce) can diced tomatoes

1 cup bottled clam juice or Fish Stock (Chapter 19)

1 cup water or Chicken Broth (Chapter 19)

1 tablespoon Worcestershire sauce

½ teaspoon dried thyme

½ teaspoon dried oregano

½ teaspoon sugar

Dried red pepper flakes, to taste

¼ teaspoon freshly ground black pepper

8 ounces raw shrimp, peeled and deveined

8 ounces scallops, cut in half

Sea salt, to taste

1. Add the oil, kielbasa, onion, red bell pepper, and celery to the slow cooker. Stir to coat the vegetables in the oil. Cover and, stirring halfway through, cook on high for 45 minutes, or until the onion is transparent. Stir in the garlic and rice.

2. Cut the chicken into bite-sized pieces and stir in with the other ingredients in the slow cooker. Cover and cook on high for 15 minutes.

3. Add the tomatoes, clam juice or stock, water or broth, Worcestershire sauce, thyme, oregano, sugar, dried red pepper flakes, and black pepper. Stir to mix. Reduce the heat setting of the slow cooker to low, cover, and cook for 6 hours or until the rice is tender.

4. Increase the temperature of the slow cooker to high. Stir in the shrimp and scallops. Cover and cook for 15 minutes or until the shrimp and scallops are cooked through. Taste for seasoning and add salt if needed.

HALIBUT IN WHITE WINE SAUCE

You can omit the wine in the sauce and replace it with milk. Then, when you taste the sauce for seasoning before you pour it over the fish, whisk in a little white wine or champagne vinegar and mayonnaise.

Serves 4

INGREDIENTS:

Nonstick spray

2 (12-ounce) packages frozen halibut fillets, thawed

¼ cup butter

2 tablespoons all-purpose flour

1 tablespoon sugar

¼ teaspoon sea salt

⅓ cup dry white wine

⅔ cup milk

Optional: Fresh dill

Optional: Lemon wedges

1. Treat the inside of the slow cooker with nonstick spray. Rinse the halibut and pat dry with paper towels. Place them in the slow cooker.

2. Melt the butter in a small saucepan. Stir in the flour, sugar and salt. When well blended, whisk in the wine and milk. Cook and stir for 5 minutes (allowing the sauce to boil for at least 1 minute), or until thickened. Taste for seasoning and add additional salt if needed.

3. Pour the sauce over the fish. Cover and cook on high for 3 hours or until the fish is opaque and flakes easily with a fork. Garnish with fresh dill and lemon wedges if desired.

SHRIMP IN CREOLE SAUCE

Serve Shrimp in Creole Sauce over cooked white or brown long-grain rice.

Serves 8

INGREDIENTS:

3 tablespoons olive or vegetable oil

1 large yellow onion, peeled and diced

3 stalks celery, diced

1 large red bell pepper, seeded and diced

1 tablespoon butter

¼ cup all-purpose flour

1 (6-ounce) can tomato paste

2 (28-ounce) cans diced tomatoes

½ teaspoon dried thyme

1 bay leaf

⅛ teaspoon dried red pepper flakes

½ teaspoon light brown sugar

1 cup Chicken Broth (Chapter 19)

2 pounds raw shrimp, peeled and deveined

Sea salt and freshly ground black pepper, to taste

Optional: Hot sauce

1. Add 2 tablespoons of the oil and the onion, celery, and red bell pepper to the slow cooker. Stir to coat the vegetables in oil. Cover and cook on high for 30 minutes, or until the onion is transparent.

2. Add the remaining tablespoon of oil and the butter to a skillet over medium heat. When the butter is melted into the oil, stir in the flour. Stirring constantly, cook for 5 minutes or until the flour mixture turns a light golden brown.

3. Stir the browned flour mixture and the tomato paste into the slow cooker. Reduce the heat setting to low and add the tomatoes, thyme, bay leaf, dried red pepper flakes, brown sugar, and broth. Stir to combine. Cover and cook on low for 6–8 hours.

4. Remove and discard the bay leaf. Increase the heat setting to high. Stir in the shrimp, cover, and cook for 15 minutes or until the shrimp are pink and cooked through. Taste for seasoning; add salt and pepper, if needed, and hot sauce if desired. Serve immediately.

POACHED SWORDFISH WITH LEMON-PARSLEY SAUCE

Swordfish steaks are usually cut thicker than most fish fillets, plus they're a firmer fish so it takes longer to poach them. You can speed up the poaching process a little if you remove the steaks from the refrigerator and put them in room-temperature water during the 30 minutes of Step 1.

Serves 4

INGREDIENTS:

1 tablespoon butter

4 thin slices sweet onion

2 cups water

4 (6-ounce) swordfish steaks

Sea salt, to taste

1 lemon

2 tablespoons extra-virgin olive oil

2 teaspoons fresh lemon juice

¼ teaspoon Dijon mustard

Optional: Freshly ground white or black pepper, to taste

1 tablespoon fresh flat-leaf parsley, minced

1. Use the butter to grease the bottom and halfway up the side of the slow cooker. Arrange the onion slices over the bottom of the slow cooker, pressing them into the butter so that they stay in place. Pour in the water. Cover and cook on high for 30 minutes.

2. Place a swordfish steak over each onion slice. Thinly slice the lemon; discard the seeds and place the slices over the fish. Cover and cook on high for 45 minutes or until the fish is opaque. Transfer the (well-drained) fish to individual serving plates or to a serving platter.

3. Add the oil, lemon juice, mustard, and white or black pepper, if using, to a bowl; whisk to combine. Immediately before serving the swordfish, fold in the parsley. Evenly divide the sauce between the swordfish steaks.

Swordfish Salad

Triple the amount of lemon-parsley sauce and toss ⅔ of it together with 8 cups of salad greens. Arrange 2 cups of greens on each serving plate. Place a hot or chilled swordfish steak over each plate of the dressed greens. Spoon the additional sauce over the fish.

HAWAIIAN-STYLE MAHI-MAHI

The fish is gently poached in a flavorful liquid, which infuses it with flavor.

Serves 6

INGREDIENTS:

6 4-ounce mahi-mahi fillets

12 ounces pineapple juice

3 tablespoons grated fresh ginger

¼ cup lime juice

3 tablespoons ponzu sauce

1. Place the fillets in a 6-quart slow cooker. Top with the remaining ingredients. Cook on low 5 hours or until the fish is fully cooked.

2. Remove the fillets and discard the cooking liquid.

Slow Cooking with Fish

Fish is fabulous in the slow cooker. The fish stays moist and cooks evenly as long as there is at least some liquid in the insert.

GINGER-LIME SALMON

The slow cooker does all the work in this recipe, creating a healthy yet impressive dish that requires virtually no hands-on time.

Serves 12

INGREDIENTS:

3-pound salmon fillet, bones removed

¼ cup minced fresh ginger

¼ cup lime juice

1 lime, thinly sliced

1 onion, thinly sliced

1. Place the salmon skin-side down in an oval 6- to 7-quart slow cooker. Pour the ginger and lime juice over the fish. Arrange the lime and then the onion in single layers over the fish.

2. Cook on low for 3–4 hours or until the fish is fully cooked and flaky. Remove the skin before serving.

Cracked!

Before each use, check your slow cooker for cracks. Even small cracks in the glaze can allow bacteria to grow in the ceramic insert. If there are cracks, replace the insert or the whole slow cooker.

LOW COUNTRY BOIL

Popular in Georgia and the Carolinas, Low Country Boil is the perfect one-pot meal for a summer day.

Serves 8

INGREDIENTS:

4 ears corn, halved

1½ pounds baby red skin potatoes

¼ cup Chesapeake Bay seasoning or shrimp boil seasoning

1 tablespoon yellow mustard seeds

2 large onions, thinly sliced

1 bay leaf

Water, as needed

1½ pounds medium shrimp

1. Place the corn, potatoes, seasoning, mustard seeds, onions, and bay leaf into a 6- or 7-quart slow cooker. Fill the insert with water until it is about 2½" below the top edge of the insert.

2. Cook for 2½ hours on high or until the corn and potatoes are tender. Add the shrimp and continue to cook on high for 20 minutes or until thoroughly cooked. Remove bay leaf before serving.

CATFISH SMOTHERED IN ONIONS

This simple Cajun-inspired dish is wonderful when paired with Stewed Okra (Chapter 26).

Serves 2

INGREDIENTS:

½ teaspoon canola oil

2 onions, sliced

2 cloves garlic, minced

1 jalapeño, diced

2 catfish fillets

1 small tomato, diced

½ teaspoon hot sauce

½ teaspoon Creole seasoning

1. Heat the oil in a nonstick pan. Sauté the onions, garlic, and jalapeño until softened.

2. Place the catfish in a 2-quart slow cooker. Top with remaining ingredients. Cook on low for 2½ hours or until the fish is fully cooked through.

Homemade Creole Seasoning

In a small bowl, whisk 1 tablespoon each of garlic powder, onion powder, dried oregano, dried basil, and ½ tablespoon each of freshly ground black pepper, white pepper, cayenne, celery seed, and paprika. Store in an airtight container up to 1 year.

AROMATIC PAELLA

This is a fun dish for a slow cooker. The mussels and clams open during the cooking and flavor the rice.

Serves 10–12

INGREDIENTS:

2 onions

1 pound bulk spicy sausage

1 tablespoon olive oil

4 cloves garlic

2 pounds tomatoes

16 ounces clam juice

2 cups Chicken Broth (Chapter 19)

1 cup dry vermouth

2½ cups uncooked rice

2 teaspoons coriander

½ teaspoon cumin

1 teaspoon saffron

¼ teaspoon white pepper

¼ teaspoon salt

1 pound fish

1 pound shrimp

2 tablespoons olive oil

1 pound fresh mussels

1 pound fresh clams

1 green pepper

1 cup fresh green peas

1. Thinly slice the onions. Sauté with the sausage in oil in a pan over low heat until the sausage is crumbled and browned, then drain and transfer to the slow cooker.

2. Crush the garlic and dice the tomatoes; stir in with the sausage and onions. Add the liquids, rice, spices, and salt.

3. Cover and heat on a low setting for 4–6 hours.

4. Cube the fish. Sauté the fish and shrimp in the remaining oil. Clean the mollusk shells. Do not steam them.

5. Dice the green pepper. An hour before serving, add the seafood, green pepper, and peas to the slow cooker.

SALMON AND WILD RICE

Wild rice pilaf is slowly cooked in the slow cooker, then salmon fillets are added at the end to steam to perfection.

Serves 6

INGREDIENTS:

1 tablespoon olive oil

1 tablespoon butter

1 onion, chopped

3 cloves garlic, minced

4 cups Chicken Broth (Chapter 19)

1 teaspoon salt

⅛ teaspoon pepper

½ teaspoon dried oregano leaves

2 cups wild rice

1 (16-ounce) package baby carrots

½ cup heavy cream

1 cup sour cream

¼ cup Dijon mustard

1 teaspoon dried basil leaves

6 (5-ounce) salmon fillets

1. In large saucepan, combine olive oil and butter over medium heat. Add onion and garlic; cook and stir until tender, about 6 minutes. Add chicken broth, salt, pepper, and oregano and remove from heat.

2. Rinse wild rice and drain; place in 4- or 5-quart slow cooker. Top with baby carrots and pour chicken broth mixture over all. Cover and cook on low for 7–8 hours or until wild rice is tender. Stir mixture in slow cooker and add cream.

3. In small bowl, combine sour cream, mustard, and basil. Spread over salmon fillets. Place salmon in slow cooker, layering with the wild rice mixture. Cover and cook on low for 40–55 minutes or until salmon flakes when tested with fork. Serve salmon with wild rice mixture.

Keep It Safe

If you're bringing this dish to a party, make sure that you add the salmon to the slow cooker when you're already there. The wild rice mixture will keep quite well in the slow cooker, even if you have to travel an hour to get to the party. Just plug the cooker in and let it cook for about 30 minutes, add the salmon, and dinner will be ready in about an hour.

CHAPTER 13

WILD GAME

BING CHERRY PHEASANT

Cherries have a rich, savory taste that is especially delicious when coupled with a buttery pheasant.

Serves 8

INGREDIENTS:

4 pounds pheasant

½ teaspoon salt

½ teaspoon pepper

2 tablespoons flour

¼ cup butter

1 pound fresh Bing cherries

1 cup red wine

6 whole cloves

½ cup water

½ cup sugar

1 cup cream

1. Cut the pheasant into serving-size pieces. Combine the salt, pepper, and flour. Roll the pheasant pieces in the flour mixture; sauté in butter in a pan over medium heat until browned. Transfer to the slow cooker.

2. Pit and halve the cherries. Add half of the cherries, half of the wine, the cloves, and the water to the slow cooker. Cover and heat on a low setting for 4–6 hours.

3. Mix the sugar, remaining cherries, and remaining wine in a saucepan over low heat; stir until partly reduced.

4. An hour before serving, add the cream to the slow cooker.

5. When serving, provide the reduced cherry mixture as a sauce.

PHEASANT WITH ORANGE

As a side dish, cream some orange pulp into a soft spread and serve it with crusty French bread.

Serves 6

INGREDIENTS:

3 pounds pheasant

⅔ cup flour

½ teaspoon salt

¼ teaspoon pepper

2 tablespoons butter

2 tablespoons olive oil

1 cup orange juice

½ cup white raisins

2–4 sprigs fresh rosemary

1 small bunch fresh parsley

1 cup white wine

1. Cut the pheasant into serving-size pieces and remove the skin. Shake the pieces in flour, salt, and pepper to coat; sauté in butter and olive oil in a pan over medium heat until browned. Transfer to the slow cooker.

2. Add the orange juice and raisins to the meat.

3. Cover and heat on low for 4–6 hours.

4. Coarsely chop the rosemary and parsley. Half an hour before serving, add the herbs and wine to the slow cooker.

Fresh Herbs or Dried?

Most recipes assume dried herbs will be used. However, if you happen to have fresh herbs, use them. For each teaspoon of dried herbs a recipe calls for, you can substitute a tablespoon of fresh ones.

PHEASANT WITH SAUERKRAUT

Pheasant can be very dry, but the sauerkraut in this recipe keeps the meat moist and tender.

Serves 4–6

INGREDIENTS:

2 pounds pheasant

1 onion

2 tablespoons vegetable oil

2 pounds sauerkraut

2 bay leaves

6 cloves

16 ounces beer

1. Cut the pheasant meat into serving-size pieces; thinly slice the onion. Sauté the meat and onion in oil in a pan over medium heat until lightly browned.

2. Drain the sauerkraut. Layer the meat, sauerkraut, and spices in the slow cooker. Pour the beer over the top.

3. Cover and heat on low for 4–6 hours. Remove bay leaves before serving.

CINNAMON APPLE PHEASANT

Use good baking apples, like Rome or Granny Smith, for some extra tartness. You can leave the peels on for a little more color.

Serves 8

INGREDIENTS:

4 pounds pheasant

½ teaspoon salt

½ teaspoon black pepper

¼ cup butter

4 apples

2 cups apple cider

2 sticks cinnamon bark

1. Cut the pheasant into serving-sized pieces and roll in the salt and pepper. Sauté in butter in a pan over medium heat until lightly browned.

2. Core and slice the apples. Layer the pheasant with the apple slices in the slow cooker. Add the cider and cinnamon.

3. Cover and heat on low for 4–6 hours.

REINDEER STEW

Reindeer is actually domesticated caribou. This recipe can also be made with venison if you don't have any reindeer on hand.

Serves 10–12

INGREDIENTS:

1 pound baby potatoes

1 pound mushrooms

2 tablespoons olive oil

5 pounds reindeer

½ teaspoon salt

½ teaspoon pepper

¼ cup butter

¼ cup flour

1 cup water

2 cups red wine

1 bouquet garni

1. Halve the baby potatoes and mushrooms. Sauté them in oil in a pan over medium heat until the mushrooms are slightly browned. Transfer to the slow cooker.

2. Cube the meat. Roll in the salt and pepper, then sauté in the butter in a pan over medium heat until lightly browned. Add the flour and stir over medium heat until the flour browns, then stir in the water and mix while the sauce thickens. Transfer the meat and sauce to the slow cooker.

3. Add the wine and bouquet garni to the meat.

4. Cover and heat on low for 4–6 hours.

COUNTRY HARE STEW

This recipe takes some advance planning, but it's a sure way to impress your guests. Serve this with small black bread rolls.

Serves 4–6

INGREDIENTS:

2 pounds rabbit

1 carrot

1 onion

1 cup white wine

1 cup water

1 bouquet garni

1 teaspoon whole black peppercorns

½ pound butter

2 tablespoons flour

1 cup water

¼ pound salt pork

10 pearl onions

½ pound mushrooms

1 tablespoon chopped parsley

1. Cut the rabbit meat into pieces. Scrub, peel, and chop the carrot and peel and chop the onion. Marinate the meat in the refrigerator with the carrot, onion, wine, 1 cup water, bouquet garni, and peppercorns. After 2 days, remove the meat; strain the marinade and save the juice, discarding the vegetables and spices.

2. Melt the butter in a pan over medium heat and mix in the flour until blended. Add the marinated meat, stir for a few minutes, then slowly stir in the strained marinade and the remaining 1 cup of water. Transfer to the slow cooker. Cover and heat on a low setting for 4–6 hours.

3. Cube the salt pork and peel the onions. Heat the pork with the onions in water in a covered pot over high heat until boiling; drain and discard the liquid.

4. Halve the mushrooms. Sauté the boiled pork, boiled onions, and mushrooms in a pan over medium heat until the pork is browned. Drain, then transfer to the slow cooker with the meat.

5. Cover the slow cooker and heat on low another 2 hours. Before serving, stir in the parsley.

HUNGARIAN RABBIT

Rabbit and paprika are a delicious combination. This dish goes well with fresh sourdough bread or a simple rice.

Serves 8

INGREDIENTS:

1 egg

1 teaspoon milk

4 pounds rabbit

⅓ cup flour

1 tablespoon paprika

½ teaspoon salt

¼ teaspoon pepper

2 onions

3 tablespoons butter

1 cup white wine

¼ cup water

1 cup sour cream

2 teaspoons paprika

1. Beat the egg and milk together.

2. Cut the rabbit meat into pieces. Dip the pieces in the egg mixture, then coat the pieces by shaking them in a mixture of the flour, 1 tablespoon paprika, salt, and pepper.

3. Thinly slice the onions. Sauté the meat and onions in butter in a pan over medium heat until the meat is lightly browned. Transfer the meat and onions to the slow cooker. Add the wine and water.

4. Cover and heat on low for 4–6 hours.

5. Half an hour before serving, add the sour cream and remaining 2 teaspoons paprika to the slow cooker.

Rainbow of Olives

Not all olives are green, and those little red pimentos are optional. Try wrinkly black Turkish olives or giant green olives. Make olive paste to use as a sandwich garnish, or throw a handful of olive slices in your soup.

SIMPLE VENISON

Most cooked meats wrapped in foil or placed in sealable plastic freezer bags can be stored in the freezer for 3 months, or up to 2 years if frozen in vacuum-sealed plastic containers.

Serves 8

INGREDIENTS:

2¼-pound lean venison roast, trimmed of fat and cut into pieces

Water, as needed

¼ teaspoon Minor's Low-Sodium Beef Base

⅛ teaspoon Minor's Roasted Mirepoix Flavor Concentrate

1 tablespoon cider vinegar

1. Put the venison in a ceramic-lined slow cooker, add enough water to cover the roast, and set the cooker on high. Dissolve the bases in the vinegar and add to the cooker. Once the mixture begins to boil, reduce temperature to low. Allow the meat to simmer for 8 hours or until tender.

2. Drain off and discard the resulting broth from the meat. Remove any remaining fat from the meat and discard that as well. Weigh the meat and separate it into 4-ounce servings. The meat can be kept for 1 or 2 days in the refrigerator, or freeze portions for use later.

VENISON WITH GINGERED SAUERKRAUT

Serve big, buttery pumpernickel croutons with this dish. Cube the bread, dunk in melted butter, sprinkle with herbs, and toast.

Serves 4–6

INGREDIENTS:

2 pounds venison

1 pound mushrooms

2 tablespoons vegetable oil

1 onion

1½ pounds sauerkraut

½ cup water

2 tablespoons brown sugar

½ cup red wine vinegar

1 teaspoon soy sauce

½ teaspoon ground ginger

1. Cube the meat and quarter the mushrooms. Sauté meat and mushrooms in oil in a pan over medium heat until the meat is lightly browned.

2. Thinly slice the onion. Drain the sauerkraut. Mix the water, sugar, vinegar, soy sauce, and ginger in a small mixing bowl.

3. Layer the meat mixture, onion, and sauerkraut in the slow cooker. Pour the vinegar mixture over the top.

4. Cover and heat on low for 4–6 hours.

VENISON ROAST IN ORANGE

If you don't have access to venison, substitute beef or pork. Use an inexpensive cut; the acidic orange juice will tenderize it during cooking.

Serves 9

INGREDIENTS:

1 slice bacon

2 cloves garlic

3 pounds venison roast

½ teaspoon salt

½ teaspoon pepper

1 bay leaf

2 whole cloves

1 cup orange juice

1. Cut the bacon into small pieces; crush and mince the garlic. Cut the meat into serving-sized pieces.

2. Sauté the meat with the bacon, garlic, salt, and pepper over medium heat until the meat is lightly browned.

3. Transfer the meat and juices, bay leaf, cloves, and orange juice to the slow cooker.

4. Cover and heat on low for 6–8 hours. Open the slow cooker twice to baste, but no more. Remove the bay leaf before serving.

Go for the Garlic

Garlic is good added just before serving a dish. It has a whole different flavor than garlic that has been cooking for a while. Depending on the tastes of your guests, you can mince it finely or leave it in large, coarse pieces.

CAMPFIRE DUCK

Fresh duck should hang to age for about six days in the cold before cooking. Ask a butcher or hunter for help with this.

Serves 6–8

INGREDIENTS:

3 pounds duck, aged

1 teaspoon seasoning salt

½ cup flour

4 slices bacon

½ cup water

½ cup heavy cream

1. Cut the meat into serving-sized pieces. Rub with the salt and roll in the flour. Mince the bacon. Sauté the duck and bacon in a pan over high heat until browned. Adjust the heat to low. Stir in the water and mix to thicken.

2. Transfer the meat and juices to the slow cooker. Cover and heat on low for 4–6 hours. Half an hour before serving, stir in the cream.

SLOW VENISON

As with wild poultry, the secret to cooking wild game is to age the meat. Do this by marinating it in your refrigerator for an extra-long time.

Serves 6–8

INGREDIENTS:

3 pounds venison roast

3 cups red wine

3 tablespoons olive oil

3 bay leaves

10 whole cloves

1. Slice the meat. Cover with wine and marinate in the refrigerator for 3 to 4 days. Strain and save 1 cup of marinade. Sauté the meat in oil in a pan over medium heat until browned. Transfer to the slow cooker with saved marinade and spices.

2. Cover and heat on low for 4–6 hours. Baste twice.

Fresh Is Not Always Best

Fresh wild game such as venison and rabbit should be aged in a cool, dry place for several days before cooking. Check with your local meat locker or other source of wild game to be sure they do this, or for guidance on how to do this yourself for different types of game.

HOT BBQ SQUIRREL

If you don't have squirrel, you could substitute chicken or pork. But if you can get squirrel meat, give it a try.

Serves 8–10

INGREDIENTS:

4 pounds squirrel

2 slices bacon

1 clove garlic

1 cup ketchup

½ cup water

½ cup brown sugar

⅓ cup Worcestershire sauce

1 teaspoon chili powder

3 drops red pepper sauce

1. Cut the squirrel meat into pieces. Cut the bacon into 1-inch pieces, and crush the garlic.

2. Sauté the meat, bacon, and garlic in a pan over medium heat until the meat is lightly browned. Transfer to the slow cooker.

3. Add the ketchup, water, sugar, and Worcestershire sauce.

4. Cover and heat on low for 4–6 hours.

5. An hour before serving, add the chili powder and pepper sauce.

DOVE WITH HERBS

Dove has a dark, rich flavor. Complement this by providing your guests with mild sides like Wild Rice with Mixed Vegetables (Chapter 25) or fresh cherries.

Serves 6

INGREDIENTS:

1 onion

1 pound mushrooms

3 tablespoons butter

12 dove breasts

3 tablespoons flour

½ cup water

2 cups red wine

2 sprigs fresh thyme

2 sprigs fresh sage

1. Chop the onion and slice the mushrooms. Sauté the onion and mushrooms in butter in a pan over medium heat until the onion is soft. Add the dove and sauté over medium heat until the meat is lightly browned.

2. Transfer the meat and vegetables to the slow cooker, leaving the juices in the pan. Add the flour to the pan. Stir over low heat to blend and thicken, then mix in the water. Transfer to the slow cooker with half the wine.

3. Cover and heat on low for 4–6 hours.

4. Coarsely chop the herbs. Half an hour before serving, add the herbs and the remaining wine to the slow cooker.

Cleaning Wild Game

Check your wild game carefully before cooking and remove any pellets or stones. Not even slow cooking will soften these. The pellets may be from shotgun shells, while stones may have been eaten by the animal. For example, birds do this as a digestive aid.

PEPPER DUCK

This goes well with fresh whole-wheat bread, or sections of whole-wheat pita loaves. Also, use wild mushrooms, if possible.

Serves 6–8

INGREDIENTS:

3 pounds duck

½ cup flour

1 teaspoon salt

1 teaspoon pepper

1 onion

½ pound mushrooms

¼ cup butter

1 cup water

½ cup dry red wine

2 bay leaves

1 green pepper

1. Remove the bones and skin from the duck; cube the meat. Shake the meat in flour, salt, and pepper to coat. Thinly slice the onion and halve the mushrooms.

2. Sauté the duck, onion, and mushrooms in butter in a pan over medium heat until the duck is lightly browned. Put the duck mixture, water, wine, and bay leaves in the slow cooker.

3. Cover and heat on low for 4–6 hours.

4. Mince the green pepper. Half an hour before serving, stir in the green pepper. Remove the bay leaf before serving.

SHERRY DUCK WITH DILL

Use fresh dill if possible, and add it at the end for the best flavor.

Serves 4–6

INGREDIENTS:

2 pounds duck

1 cup cider vinegar

½ cup water

2 tablespoons olive oil

1 teaspoon salt

¼ teaspoon pepper

¼ cup flour

3 tablespoons butter

¼ cup flour

½ cup olives

1 tablespoon sugar

½ cup white wine

2 sprigs fresh dill weed

½ cup dry sherry

1. Cut the meat into serving-sized pieces and marinate for 24 hours, refrigerated, in the vinegar, water, oil, salt, and pepper. Strain the marinade and set aside.

2. Coat the meat with ¼ cup flour, then sauté in butter in a pan over medium heat until lightly browned. Transfer the meat to the slow cooker.

3. Add the remaining ¼ cup flour to the juices in the pan and, while heating, stir until thick. Add the marinade slowly to this and mix until smooth. Mince the olives. Add the marinade sauce, sugar, white wine, and olives to the meat in the slow cooker.

4. Cover and heat on low for 4–6 hours.

5. Coarsely chop the dill. Half an hour before serving, add the dill and sherry.

Tastes of Wild Game

Wild duck can taste too wild. Let the meat soak in buttermilk overnight in the refrigerator to tame the flavor. Drain off and discard the buttermilk two hours before you start to cook.

MANGO DUCK BREAST

Slow-cooked mangoes soften and create their own sauce in this easy duck dish. If you prefer, you can use 1½ cups of frozen precut mango instead of fresh. Serve the duck with roasted winter vegetables and steamed asparagus.

Serves 4

INGREDIENTS:

2 boneless, skinless duck breasts

1 large mango, peeled and cubed

¼ cup Chicken Broth (Chapter 19)

1 tablespoon finely grated fresh ginger

1 tablespoon minced hot pepper

1 tablespoon minced shallot

1. Place all ingredients into a 4-quart slow cooker.

2. Cook on low for 4 hours, or on high for 2 hours.

DUCK WITH SAUERKRAUT

Duck is a rich, dark meat; it goes well with the light tang of sauerkraut. You can also substitute goose in this recipe.

Serves 8–10

INGREDIENTS:

4 pounds duck

½ teaspoon salt

½ teaspoon pepper

3 tablespoons sugar

½ cup water

8 cups sauerkraut

1. Cut the duck into serving-sized pieces. Wash and dry with paper towels. Rub the meat with salt and pepper.

2. Dissolve the sugar in the water. Layer the duck and sauerkraut in the slow cooker; add the water mixture.

3. Cover and heat on low for 4–6 hours.

HASSENPFEFFER

Hassenpfeffer, or "pepper rabbit" in German, is a classic rabbit dish. Be sure to use whole peppercorns when cooking this.

Serves 6–8

INGREDIENTS:

3 pounds rabbit meat

1 onion

10 peppercorns

1½ cups vinegar

1½ cups water

½ teaspoon salt

6 cloves

2 bay leaves

3 tablespoons butter

1 cup sour cream

1. Cut the rabbit into serving-sized pieces. Slice the onion, and crack (but do not crush) the peppercorns.

2. Marinate the rabbit in the onion, vinegar, water, salt, peppercorns, cloves, and bay leaves for 2 days, turning the meat several times. Save 1 cup of the marinade, including the onion slices and spices.

3. Sauté the meat in butter in a pan over medium heat until lightly browned; transfer to the slow cooker with the reserved 1 cup of marinade.

4. Cover and heat on low for 4–6 hours.

5. Half an hour before serving, add the sour cream and remove the bay leaves.

ELK IN WINE SAUCE

If a member of your family happens to hunt elk, this is a great way to use it. But if you don't have elk on hand, you can substitute beef.

Serves 6–8

INGREDIENTS:

3 pounds boneless elk roast

¼ cup flour

½ teaspoon salt

¼ teaspoon white pepper

¾ cup butter

2 onions

1 pound mushrooms

¼ pound leeks

1 cup dry wine

1. Trim the meat and cut into serving-sized pieces; pat dry with a paper towel. Coat in a mixture of the flour, salt, and pepper. Sauté in half of the butter in a pan over high heat until browned. Set aside the meat, leaving the juices in the pan.

2. Finely chop the onions. Add the remaining butter to the pan and sauté the onions over medium heat until brown. Lift out the onions with a slotted spoon, leaving the juices in the pan, and transfer to the slow cooker. Put the meat over the onions.

3. Chop the mushrooms and leeks (white parts only) and add to the pan; sauté over low heat until soft, then transfer to the slow cooker.

4. Cover and heat on low for 4–6 hours.

5. Half an hour before serving, add the wine.

RABBIT IN COCONUT SAUCE

The flavors of rabbit and coconut work wonderfully together in this dish. Serve with a side of rice.

Serves 6–8

INGREDIENTS:

1 coconut

1 cup water

3 tomatoes

2 onions

1 teaspoon salt

½ teaspoon pepper

3 pounds rabbit meat

1. Puncture and drain the coconut, setting aside the milk. Crack the coconut; remove the meat. Pare off the brown lining and cut the coconut meat into chunks.

2. Put the coconut meat, coconut milk, and water into a blender; blend until smooth. Heat to a boil in a large saucepan and simmer 15 minutes to thicken slightly. Transfer to the slow cooker.

3. Mince the tomatoes and onions. Add the tomatoes, onions, salt, and pepper to the coconut.

4. Cut the rabbit meat into serving-sized pieces. Add to the coconut mixture. Cover and heat on low for 4–6 hours, basting often.

WILD DUCK GUMBO

You can substitute other dark, rich wild fowl for duck in this recipe. Serve with wild rice, barley, or polenta.

Serves 6

INGREDIENTS:

3 pounds duck

1½ teaspoons salt

1 teaspoon black pepper

½ teaspoon Tabasco sauce

¼ cup oil

3 tablespoons butter

3 tablespoons flour

1 onion

4 cloves garlic

6 cups water

2 dozen oysters, with liquid

1. Cut the duck into serving-sized pieces. Roll the pieces in the salt and pepper and sprinkle with Tabasco. Sauté the duck in the oil in a pan over medium heat until the meat is browned, then transfer to the slow cooker.

2. Melt the butter in a pan over low heat. Blend in the flour and stir until lightly browned.

3. Mince the onion and garlic. Add to the browned flour mixture and stir over low heat until the onion is soft.

4. Add the onion mixture and water to the slow cooker. Cover and heat on low for 4–5 hours.

5. Half an hour before serving, take out the pieces of duck and remove the bones, then put the meat back in the slow cooker. Add the oysters and oyster liquid.

CHAPTER 14

VEGETARIAN DISHES

MEATLESS MOUSSAKA

If you get your eggplant at the supermarket and suspect that it's been waxed, peel it before dicing it and adding it to the slow cooker.

Serves 8

INGREDIENTS:

¾ cup dry brown or yellow lentils, rinsed and drained

2 large potatoes, peeled and diced

1 cup water

1 stalk celery, diced fine

1 medium sweet onion, peeled and diced

3 cloves garlic, peeled and minced

½ teaspoon salt

¼ teaspoon ground cinnamon

Pinch freshly ground nutmeg

¼ teaspoon freshly ground black pepper

¼ teaspoon dried basil

¼ teaspoon dried oregano

¼ teaspoon dried parsley

1 medium eggplant, diced

12 baby carrots, each cut into 3 pieces

1 (14½-ounce) can diced tomatoes

1 (8-ounce) package cream cheese, softened

2 large eggs

1. Add the lentils, potatoes, water, celery, onion, garlic, salt, cinnamon, nutmeg, pepper, basil, oregano, and parsley to the slow cooker; stir. Top with eggplant and carrots. Cover and cook on low for 6 hours or until the lentils are cooked through.

2. Stir in undrained tomatoes. Mix cream cheese and eggs together; dollop over lentil mixture. Cover and cook on low for an additional ½ hour.

VEGETABLE CASSEROLE

This vegetable casserole, which is an adaptation of the Romanian vegetable stew known as ghivisu, can be served as a vegetarian main course or as a side dish with chicken or grilled sausage.

Serves 8

INGREDIENTS:

1 medium eggplant, diced

2 medium zucchini, sliced

1 teaspoon salt

¾ cup extra-virgin olive oil

3 cloves garlic, peeled and minced

1 tablespoon Dijon mustard

1½ teaspoons dried marjoram

½ teaspoon red pepper flakes

2 medium potatoes, peeled and diced

2 medium carrots, peeled and sliced

2 celery stalks, diced

2 medium onions, peeled and sliced

½ small head cabbage, cored and thinly sliced

1 (15-ounce) can peeled tomatoes, drained and chopped

1. Add the eggplant and zucchini to a colander. Salt the vegetables, and let stand for an hour. Rinse well under cold running water. A handful at a time, squeeze the vegetables to release the moisture, and then pat dry with paper towels.

2. Add the oil, garlic, mustard, marjoram, red pepper flakes, and salt to taste to a bowl or measuring cup; whisk to mix.

3. In the following order, layer the vegetables in the slow cooker, drizzling each layer with some of the oil mixture: eggplant and zucchini, potatoes, carrots, celery, onion, cabbage, and tomatoes. Cover and cook on low for 8 hours or until all vegetables are tender. Stir well before serving.

MEATLESS MINCEMEAT

Serve this mincemeat as a chutney or use as a filling in a mincemeat pie that's succulent enough to be a special occasion meal's main dish.

Yields about 2 quarts

INGREDIENTS:

2 cups fresh apple cider

2 cups light brown sugar, lightly packed

½ cup (1 stick) butter, cubed

1 medium orange

1 cup raisins

1 cup dried currants

8 ounces dried figs

6 ounces dried apricots

2 medium cooking apples

2 Bosc pears

⅓ cup and ¼ cup brandy, divided

⅓ cup dark rum

1 teaspoon salt

1 teaspoon ground cinnamon

1 teaspoon ground cloves

1 teaspoon ground allspice

1 teaspoon ground nutmeg

1. Add the cider, brown sugar, and butter to the slow cooker; cover and, stirring occasionally, cook on high while you prepare the fruit for the recipe.

2. Cut the orange into quarters, remove the seeds and add to a food processor along with the raisins, currants, figs, and apricots; pulse to coarsely chop. Stir into the other ingredients already in the slow cooker.

3. Peel, core, and seed the apples and pears. Add to the food processor and pulse until finely grated; alternatively, you can feed through the food processor using the grater attachment. Add to the slow cooker along with ⅓ cup of the brandy, rum, salt, cinnamon, cloves, allspice, and nutmeg. Cover and cook on high for 1 hour or until mixture reaches a simmer.

4. Uncover, and stirring occasionally, continue to cook for 2–3 hours or until the mixture is reduced to about 2 quarts. Ladle the mincemeat into two sterilized 1-quart canning jars. Top the mincemeat in each jar with 2 tablespoons of brandy. Screw on the two-piece lids; allow to cool to room temperature. Refrigerate for at least 1 week, or for up to 6 months.

Mincemeat without Alcohol

To make mincemeat without alcohol, replace ⅓ cup of the brandy and the rum with cider. Reduce the amount of brown sugar to 1½ cups. Then, after you've ladled the mincemeat into the jars, spoon 2 tablespoons of honey into each jar instead of the brandy.

MOROCCAN ROOT VEGETABLES

Moroccan Root Vegetables is good served with couscous and Cucumber-Yogurt Salad (see sidebar).

Serves 8

INGREDIENTS:

1 pound parsnips, peeled and diced

1 pound turnips, peeled and diced

2 medium onions, chopped

1 pound carrots, peeled and diced

6 dried apricots, chopped

4 pitted prunes, chopped

1 teaspoon ground turmeric

1 teaspoon ground cumin

½ teaspoon ground ginger

½ teaspoon ground cinnamon

¼ teaspoon ground cayenne pepper

1 tablespoon dried parsley

1 tablespoon dried cilantro

1¾ cups Vegetable Stock (Chapter 19)

1. Add the parsnips, turnips, onions, carrots, apricots, prunes, turmeric, cumin, ginger, cinnamon, cayenne pepper, parsley, and cilantro to the slow cooker. Pour in the stock. Cover, and cook on low for 9 hours or until the vegetables are cooked through.

Cucumber-Yogurt Salad

In a serving bowl, mix together 3 cups of drained plain yogurt (or a mixture of drained yogurt and sour cream for a salad that's less tart) and 2 or 3 peeled, seeded, and thinly sliced cucumbers. Add 12 fresh chopped mint leaves, 2 peeled and minced cloves of garlic, and some salt to a small bowl, and crush them together. Stir the mint mixture into the salad. Add more salt if needed. Chill until ready to serve.

WILD RICE CASSEROLE

Using instant rice mixes in this recipe takes away the worry about whether or not the rice will get done.

Serves 8

INGREDIENTS:

2 medium onions, peeled and chopped

3 stalks celery, thinly sliced

2 (6-ounce) packages dry instant long-grain and wild rice mix

2½ cups water

1 (10.75-ounce) can condensed cream of mushroom soup

1 stick (½ cup) butter, melted

½ pound processed American cheese, shredded

½ cup fresh mushrooms, cleaned and sliced

Salt and freshly ground black pepper, to taste

1. Add the onions, celery, rice mix, water, condensed cream of mushroom soup, butter, American cheese, and mushrooms to the slow cooker; stir to mix. Cover and cook on low 8 hours or until all of the water has been absorbed by the rice. Stir the mixture; test for seasoning and add salt and pepper as desired.

SPICY BLACK BEAN CHILI

Serve this rich chili over noodles or rice cooked with a pinch of turmeric. It's good topped with some diced avocado, chopped green onion, and sour cream.

Serves 4

INGREDIENTS:

1 tablespoon extra-virgin olive oil

1 large yellow onion, peeled and diced

1 medium red bell pepper, seeded and diced

2 cloves garlic, peeled and minced

2 tablespoons chili powder, or to taste

1 (28-ounce) can crushed tomatoes

2 (15.5-ounce) cans black beans, drained and rinsed

1 cup water

1 (4-ounce) can diced green chilies

Salt and freshly ground black pepper, to taste

1. Add the oil, onion, and bell pepper to a microwave-safe bowl; cover and microwave on high for 1 minute or until the onions are transparent and the bell pepper is soft. Add the garlic and chili powder to the bowl, stir, and microwave on high for 30 seconds.

2. Add the onion mixture to the slow cooker along with the tomatoes, beans, water, and chilies. Cover and cook on low for 8 hours or until the chili is thick. Taste for seasoning, and add salt and pepper to taste.

LENTIL SOUP

In this Lentil Soup recipe, you can substitute cooked collards, chard, or other dark greens for the kale. The greens are cooked separately (see sidebar) because cooking the raw greens directly in the soup can impart a bitter flavor.

Serves 6

INGREDIENTS:

1 tablespoon extra-virgin olive oil

1 celery stalk, diced

1 large carrot, peeled and diced

1 large yellow onion, peeled and diced

2 cloves garlic, peeled and minced

1¼ cups dried brown lentils, rinsed and drained

6 cups Vegetable Stock (Chapter 19) or water

1 tablespoon tamari sauce

5 large cooked kale leaves, tough stems removed

Salt and freshly ground black pepper, to taste

1. Add the oil, celery, and carrot to a microwave-safe bowl; cover and microwave on high for 2 minutes. Stir in the onion; cover and microwave on high for 1 minute or until the onion is transparent. Add the garlic; cover and microwave on high for 30 seconds.

2. Add to the slow cooker along with the lentils, stock or water, and tamari sauce. Cover and cook on low for 8 hours. Stir the cooked greens into the soup, and season with salt and pepper, to taste.

Cooking the Greens

Remove the tough stems from the kale leaves, and then tightly roll them like a cigar; cut them crosswise into thin ribbons. Cook the kale in a pot of boiling salted water until tender. Drain and stir into the soup immediately before serving.

VEGETABLE-CHEESE SOUP

Instead of serving this soup with crackers, ladle it over biscuits or corn bread instead.

Serves 8

INGREDIENTS:

1 (15-ounce) can creamed corn

4 large potatoes, peeled and diced

1 cup baby carrots, chopped

1 small onion, peeled and diced

1 teaspoon celery seed

½ teaspoon freshly ground black pepper

3½ cups Vegetable Stock (Chapter 19)

1 (15-ounce) can cooked lentils

1 (16-ounce) jar processed cheese sauce

1. Add the corn, potatoes, carrots, onion, celery seeds, pepper, stock, and lentils to the slow cooker. Stir to combine. Cover and cook on low 8 hours.

2. Stir in the cheese; cover and cook an additional 30 minutes or until the cheese is melted and creates a sauce for the vegetables.

VEGETARIAN GRAVY

This recipe makes a cream gravy. For a rich, dark gravy, stir 1 tablespoon of tomato paste into the onions before you add the mushrooms.

Yields about 4 cups

INGREDIENTS:

2 tablespoons extra-virgin olive oil

1 large sweet onion, peeled and diced

Optional: 1 stalk celery, finely diced

Optional: 1 carrot, finely diced

8 ounces fresh mushrooms, cleaned and sliced

1 clove garlic, peeled and minced

2 cups Vegetable Stock (Chapter 19)

¼ cup butter, softened

¼ cup all-purpose flour

½-1 cup heavy cream

1. Add the oil and onion and, if using, the celery and carrot to the slow cooker. Stir to combine. Cover and cook on high for 1 hour or until the onion is transparent.

2. Stir the mushrooms and garlic into the onion mixture in the slow cooker. Add the stock. Cover and cook on low for 2 hours.

3. Uncover the slow cooker and increase the heat setting to high. In a small bowl, mix the butter together with the flour. When the broth in the slow cooker begins to bubble around the edges, drop the butter-flour mixture into the cooker a teaspoon at a time. Whisk to blend the butter-flour mixture into the broth. Continue to cook on high, stirring occasionally, for 5 minutes or until the broth is thickened. Taste to make sure the flour taste has cooked out; if not, continue to cook and stir for another few minutes.

4. Whisk in the cream; the amount you add will depend on how thick or thin you want the gravy. Stir until the cream comes to temperature. Serve immediately.

Vegetarian Gravy Base

If, for example, you only need about 1 cup of gravy for your meal, before completing Step 4 you can ladle out 3 cups of the thickened mushroom-broth mixture into three 1-cup, freezer-appropriate containers. (Allow to cool to room temperature and then cover and freeze for later.) Add cream to taste to the gravy base remaining in the slow cooker.

CASHEWS AND LENTILS LOAF

This recipe is for the vegetarian equivalent of a meatloaf. Serve it alongside a steamed vegetable. It's good topped with the Vegetarian Gravy (this chapter).

Serves 6

INGREDIENTS:

1 tablespoon cumin seed

1 tablespoon vegetable oil

2 stalks celery, diced

1 large onion, peeled and diced

2 cups carrots, shredded

2 cloves garlic, peeled and minced

1 red bell pepper, seeded and diced

Optional: 1 chili pepper, seeded and diced

Sea salt, to taste

½ teaspoon cracked or freshly ground black pepper

2 cups cooked lentils

3 cups Cheddar cheese, shredded

1 cup cashews, coarsely chopped

3 large eggs, beaten

Optional: Nonstick spray

Boiling water

1. Toast the cumin seeds in a dry pan over medium heat until they start to brown and release their aroma. Either in a spice grinder or using a mortar and a pestle, grind to a powder and set it aside.

2. Add the oil and celery to a large microwave-safe bowl; cover and microwave on high for 1 minute. Add the onion, carrots, red bell pepper, and chili pepper, if using, to the bowl; stir, cover, and then microwave on high in 1-minute increments, until the onions are transparent and the bell pepper is soft. (Uncover and stir between each 1-minute microwave cooking session.) Stir in salt and cracked pepper.

3. Add the lentils, cheese, and cashews to the bowl and stir into the cooked vegetables. Add the eggs and mix well.

4. Put the cooking rack into the crock of the slow cooker. Create a loaf pan out of two layers of heavy-duty aluminum foil. Line with a piece of nonstick aluminum foil or spray with nonstick spray. Shape the loaf in the pan created out of foil and place it on the cooking rack. Pour enough boiling water into the slow cooker to reach just under the top of the rack. Cover and cook on high for 4–5 hours or until the loaf has set. Remove from the slow cooker and allow loaf to rest for 15 minutes before slicing and serving.

Loaf Pan Handles

Create handles to make it easier to lift the loaf out of the slow cooker by crossing doubled strips of foil long enough to span the cooking rack and both sides of the cooker under the foil packet holding the nut loaf. When the nut loaf is done, you can cross the strips over the top of the nut loaf, and grabbing them with one hand use a wide spatula to reach under the loaf to lift it out of the slow cooker.

PEANUTS AND POTATOES LOAF

This meatloaf substitute is good served topped with marinara sauce or mushroom-tomato sauce.

Serves 6

INGREDIENTS:

6 medium potatoes

1 cup roasted unsalted peanuts, chopped

¼ cup green onion, finely chopped

¼ cup fresh parsley, finely chopped

2 sun-dried tomatoes, reconstituted and finely chopped

½ teaspoon sea salt

½ teaspoon chili powder

Freshly ground black pepper, to taste

2 large eggs, beaten

½ cup chili sauce

4 ounces cream cheese, softened

¼ cup plus 2 tablespoons freshly grated Parmesan-Reggiano cheese

Optional: Nonstick spray

Boiling water

1. Peel, dice, and cook the potatoes until tender. Add the cooked potatoes to a large bowl along with the peanuts, green onions, parsley, sun-dried tomatoes, salt, chili powder, pepper, eggs, chili sauce, cream cheese (cut into cubes), and ¼ cup of the Parmesan cheese. Mix well.

2. Put the cooking rack into the crock of the slow cooker. Create a loaf pan out of two layers of heavy-duty aluminum foil that are long enough to bring up and over the top of the loaf. Line with a piece of nonstick aluminum foil or spray with nonstick spray. Shape the loaf in the pan created out of foil and sprinkle the additional 2 tablespoons of Parmesan cheese over the top of the loaf. Bring the foil edges up and over the top of the loaf, and crimp it to close it. Place the foil-enclosed loaf on the cooking rack. Pour enough boiling water into the slow cooker to reach just under the top of the rack. Cover and cook on low for 8 hours or high for 4 hours.

NUT LOAF

This meatloaf substitute is good served with the Vegetarian Gravy (this chapter).

Serves 8

INGREDIENTS:

2 large onions, peeled and finely diced

8 ounces fresh mushrooms, cleaned and chopped

1 small green bell pepper, seeded and finely diced

2 tablespoons butter

3 cups carrots, grated

1½ cups celery, finely diced

5 large eggs, beaten

½ cup walnuts, chopped

¼ cup unsalted sunflower kernels

½ teaspoon sea salt

½ teaspoon dried basil

½ teaspoon dried oregano

¼ teaspoon freshly ground black pepper

3 cups soft whole-wheat bread crumbs

Optional: Nonstick spray

Boiling water

1. Add the onions, mushrooms, green bell pepper, and butter to a large microwave-safe bowl; cover and microwave on high for 1 minute. Stir, re-cover, and microwave on high for 1 more minute or until the onions are transparent and the green bell pepper is tender. Stir in the carrots, celery, eggs, walnut, sunflower kernels, salt, basil, oregano, pepper, and bread crumbs.

2. Put the cooking rack into the crock of the slow cooker. Create a loaf pan out of two layers of heavy-duty aluminum foil. Line with a piece of nonstick aluminum foil or spray with nonstick spray. Shape the loaf in the pan created out of foil and place it on the cooking rack. Pour enough boiling water into the slow cooker to reach just under the top of the rack. Cover and cook on high for 4–5 hours or until the loaf has set. Remove from the slow cooker and allow loaf to rest for 15 minutes before slicing and serving.

Temperature Check

A nut loaf (or other baked goods containing eggs) is usually done when the internal temperature reaches 160°F. You can check the temperature by inserting an instant-read meat thermometer into the center of the loaf. Or, use a programmable food thermometer that has a probe attached with a cord; set it for 160°F and an alarm will go off when the food reaches that temperature.

QUINOA PILAF

Asafetida is an herb with a foul smell raw, but it imparts a flavor similar to leeks when it's cooked. If you're uncertain about using it, cook the quinoa as instructed and then do a test sample using a sprinkling of the herbs and spices on a small portion.

Serves 4

INGREDIENTS:

1 cup quinoa

1 cup celery, diced

½ cup red bell pepper, seeded and diced

2 tablespoons extra-virgin olive oil

Pinch asafetida or 1 clove garlic, peeled and minced

½ cup raw cashews

1 bay leaf

½ teaspoon dried thyme

¼ teaspoon turmeric

½ teaspoon ground coriander

½ teaspoon ground cumin

¼ teaspoon ground ginger

½ teaspoon salt

1¾ cups boiling water

¼ cup fresh parsley or cilantro, minced

Freshly ground black pepper, to taste

1. Soak quinoa in water for 5 minutes; rinse twice, then drain.

2. Add the celery, bell pepper, and oil to a microwave-safe bowl; cover and microwave on high for 1 minute or until the celery is tender. Stir in the asafetida, cashews, and bay leaf. Cover and microwave on high for 2 minutes, or until cashews begin to take on a golden color. Let rest covered for 5 minutes.

3. Add the contents of the microwave-safe bowl to the slow cooker along with the quinoa, thyme, turmeric, coriander, cumin, ginger, and salt. Stir to combine. Pour in the boiling water, cover, and cook on low for 2 hours, or until all of the water is absorbed. Discard the bay leaf. Stir in the chopped parsley or cilantro, pepper, and serve.

What Is Quinoa?

Although it's usually thought of as a grain, quinoa (pronounced keen-wah) is technically an herb. Its high oil content makes uncooked quinoa perishable, so it should be stored in the refrigerator; it will keep refrigerated for up to a month, or it can be frozen. Quinoa is high in protein and can be used in place of bulgur, couscous, or rice.

STUFFED BELL PEPPERS

For this stuffed peppers recipe, you can use red, green, orange, or yellow bell peppers and hot or mild salsa, according to your preference.

Serves 4

INGREDIENTS:

4 large bell peppers

2½ cups cooked white or brown rice

1 (15.5-ounce) can red kidney beans, drained and rinsed

1 cup tomato salsa

3 scallions, chopped

Salt and freshly ground black pepper

1 (14½-ounce) can crushed tomatoes

½ teaspoon ground cumin

¼ teaspoon dried oregano

½ teaspoon sugar

Salt and freshly ground black pepper, to taste

1. Cut the tops off of the bell peppers. Remove and discard the stems. Scrape out the seeds and membranes in the peppers and discard.

2. Add the rice, beans, salsa, scallions, salt, and pepper to a bowl and mix well. Evenly fill the pepper cavities with the rice mixture, packing it lightly. Replace the pepper tops. Arrange the peppers upright in the slow cooker.

3. In the bowl, mix the tomatoes together with the cumin, oregano, sugar, and some additional salt and pepper. Pour over the peppers in the slow cooker. Cover and cook on low for 4 hours or until the peppers are tender but still hold their shape.

CURRIED CAULIFLOWER AND POTATOES

If you only need 6 servings, you can omit the wheat berries. Reduce the amount of water by a cup and go a bit lighter on the seasoning if you do.

Serves 8

INGREDIENTS:

½ cup wheat berries

2¼ cups water

6 medium potatoes, peeled and quartered

1 small cauliflower, cut into florets

Pinch asafetida

¾ teaspoon ground turmeric

½ teaspoon chili powder

1½ teaspoons ground cumin

¾ teaspoon salt

Pinch sugar

2 tomatoes, chopped

½ teaspoon Garam Masala Powder (Chapter 16)

1. Add the wheat berries to the slow cooker. Bring 1 cup of the water to a boil and pour it over the wheat berries. Cover and cook on high for 1 hour.

2. Add the remaining ingredients, reduce the heat setting to low, cover, and cook for 6 hours or until the potatoes are cooked through.

VEGETARIAN LASAGNA

Frozen Ground Burger Crumbles are a soy-based meat substitute available from BOCA (www.bocaburger.com).

Serves 8

INGREDIENTS:

1 (26-ounce) jar marinara sauce

1 (14.5-ounce) can diced tomatoes

Nonstick spray

1 (8-ounce) package no-boil lasagna noodles

1 (15-ounce) container part-skim ricotta cheese

1 (8-ounce) package shredded Italian cheese blend or 8 ounces shredded mozzarella cheese

1 (10-ounce) package frozen chopped spinach, thawed and squeezed dry

1 cup frozen ground (veggie) burger crumbles, thawed

1. Mix the marinara sauce and tomatoes with their juice together in a bowl.

2. Spray the inside of the crock in the slow cooker with nonstick spray. Spoon 1 cup of the sauce-tomato mixture into slow cooker. Arrange ¼ of the noodles over sauce, overlapping the noodles and breaking them into pieces so they are sized to cover as much sauce as possible. Spoon about ¾ cup sauce over the noodles, and then top that with ½ cup ricotta and ½ cup shredded cheese. Spread half of the spinach over cheese. Repeat layering two more times beginning with noodles, but in middle layer, replace the spinach with the thawed ground burger crumbles. Place remaining noodles over spinach, then top with remaining sauce and shredded cheese.

3. Cover and cook on low for 3 hours or until the noodles are cooked and the cheese is melted.

NEW MEXICAN POT PIE

Serve this dish with an avocado salad. Have chopped jalapeño and green onions available for those who want to add them.

Serves 4

INGREDIENTS:

2 tablespoons light olive oil, divided

1 small onion, peeled and diced

1 medium carrot, chopped

1 bell pepper, seeded and diced

2 cloves garlic, peeled and minced

1 cup frozen corn, thawed

2 (15.5-ounce) cans pinto beans, rinsed and drained

1 jalapeño, seeded and minced

¾ cup Vegetable Stock (Chapter 19)

1 tablespoon tamari or other soy sauce

2 tablespoons fresh cilantro, chopped

Salt and freshly ground black pepper, to taste

½ cup cornmeal

½ cup all-purpose flour

2 teaspoons baking powder

½ teaspoon baking soda

½ cup milk or soymilk

1. Add 1 tablespoon of the oil to the slow cooker. Stir in the onion and carrot. Cover and cook on high for 30 minutes or until the onions are transparent and the carrots are softened. Stir in the bell pepper, garlic, corn, pinto beans, jalapeño, stock, tamari or soy sauce, cilantro, salt, and pepper. Cover and cook on low for 5 hours. Taste for seasoning and add more salt and pepper if needed.

2. To make the top crust for the pot pie, add the cornmeal, flour, baking powder, and baking soda to a bowl, and mix well. Stir in the remaining tablespoon of oil and milk or soymilk, and mix until just combined. On a lightly floured surface, roll or pat the resulting dough into a shape about the same size as your cooker. Place the crust on top of the cooked bean mixture in the slow cooker, and cover and cook on high for 1 hour more or until crust is cooked through.

Try a Different Crust

Instead of making a top crust for the New Mexican Pot Pie, you can mix a corn muffin mix according to package directions and drop teaspoon-sized dollops of the batter on top of the bean mixture in the slow cooker. Or, you can reduce the amount of salt that you add to the bean mixture and serve it over corn chips or baked tortilla chips instead.

VEGETARIAN CHILI

You can alter the seasoning for this chili by using a specialty chili powder, like a chipotle pepper blend, or by adding some smoked paprika in addition to or instead of some of the chili powder.

Serves 6

INGREDIENTS:

2 tablespoons vegetable oil

1 medium green bell pepper, seeded and diced

¾ cup baby carrots, cut into thirds

1 large onion, peeled and diced

2 cloves garlic, peeled and minced

1 (16-ounce) can pinto beans, undrained

1 (15.5-ounce) can red kidney beans, undrained

2 (15-ounce) cans crushed tomatoes

1 pound firm tofu, rinsed, patted dry, and crumbled

2 cups water

2 cups frozen whole kernel corn, thawed

Salt, to taste

1–2 tablespoons chili powder

1 tablespoon cumin

¼ teaspoon cayenne pepper

1. Add the oil, green pepper, carrots, and onion to the slow cooker; stir to coat the vegetables in the oil. Cover and cook on high for 30 minutes or until the onion is transparent and the carrots are softened.

2. Stir in the garlic, beans, crushed tomatoes, tofu, water, corn, salt, chili powder, cumin, and cayenne pepper. Cover and cook on high for 1 hour or on low for 2 hours.

VEGETABLE STEW WITH DUMPLINGS

The cornmeal dumplings perfectly complement the fall vegetables in this hearty stew, making it a complete meal in one pot.

Serves 6

INGREDIENTS:

1 teaspoon olive oil

3 russet potatoes, peeled and diced

3 carrots, cut into ½" chunks

2 stalks celery, diced

1 onion, diced

1 rutabaga, diced

1 cup celeriac, diced

1 cup cauliflower florets

2 quarts Vegetable Stock (Chapter 19)

1 tablespoon fresh thyme

1 tablespoon fresh parsley

⅔ cup water

2 tablespoons canola oil

½ cup cornmeal

2 teaspoons baking powder

½ teaspoon salt

1. Heat the olive oil in a nonstick skillet. Add all the vegetables. Sauté until the onions are soft and translucent. Add to a 4-quart slow cooker.

2. Add the stock, thyme, and parsley. Stir. Cook for 6 hours or until the vegetables are fork tender. Stir.

3. In a medium bowl, stir the water, oil, cornmeal, baking powder, and salt. Drop in ¼-cup mounds in a single layer on top of the stew. Cover and cook on high for 20 minutes without lifting the lid. The dumplings will look fluffy and light when fully cooked.

CAULIFLOWER CHOWDER

In this rich chowder, puréed cauliflower takes the place of heavy cream.

Serves 6

INGREDIENTS:

2 pounds cauliflower florets

2 quarts Vegetable Stock (Chapter 19) or water

1 onion, chopped

3 cloves garlic, minced

1 teaspoon white pepper

¼ teaspoon salt

1½ cups broccoli florets

2 carrots, cut into coins

1 stalk celery, diced

1. Place the cauliflower, stock, onions, garlic, pepper, and salt into a 4-quart slow cooker. Stir. Cook on low for 6 hours or until the cauliflower is fork tender.

2. Use an immersion blender to purée the cauliflower in the slow cooker until very smooth. Add the broccoli, carrots, and celery. Cook for 30 minutes or until the vegetables are fork tender.

EGGPLANT CAPONATA

Serve this on small slices of Italian bread as an appetizer or use as a filling in sandwiches or wraps.

Serves 8

INGREDIENTS:

2 1-pound eggplants

1 teaspoon olive oil

1 red onion, diced

4 cloves garlic, minced

1 stalk celery, diced

2 tomatoes, diced

2 tablespoons nonpareil capers

2 tablespoons toasted pine nuts

1 teaspoon red pepper flakes

¼ cup red wine vinegar

1. Pierce the eggplants with a fork. Cook on high in a 4- or 6-quart slow cooker for 2 hours.

2. Allow to cool. Peel off the skin. Slice each in half and remove the seeds. Discard the skin and seeds.

3. Place the pulp in a food processor. Pulse until smooth. Set aside.

4. Heat the oil in a nonstick skillet. Sauté the onion, garlic, and celery until the onion is soft. Add the eggplant and tomatoes. Sauté 3 minutes.

5. Return to the slow cooker and add the capers, pine nuts, red pepper flakes, and vinegar. Stir. Cook on low 30 minutes. Stir prior to serving.

HERB-STUFFED TOMATOES

Serve these Italian-influenced stuffed tomatoes with a simple salad for an easy, light meal.

Serves 4

INGREDIENTS:

4 large tomatoes

1 cup cooked quinoa

1 stalk celery, minced

1 tablespoon minced fresh garlic

2 tablespoons minced fresh oregano

2 tablespoons minced fresh Italian parsley

1 teaspoon dried chervil

1 teaspoon fennel seeds

¾ cup water

1. Cut out the core of each tomato and discard. Scoop out the seeds, leaving the walls of the tomato intact.

2. In a small bowl, stir together the quinoa, celery, garlic, and spices. Divide evenly among the four tomatoes.

3. Place the filled tomatoes in a single layer in an oval 4-quart slow cooker. Pour the water into the bottom of the slow cooker. Cook on low for 4 hours.

CHICKPEA CURRY

This slow cooker version of chole, a traditional Indian curry, is very low in fat but high in fiber and flavor.

Serves 8

INGREDIENTS:

1 cup dried chickpeas

Water, as needed

1 teaspoon olive oil

1 onion, diced

3 cloves garlic, minced

1 tablespoon minced fresh ginger

1 large tomato, diced

2 tablespoons tomato paste

1 tablespoon cumin

1 teaspoon turmeric

1 teaspoon coriander

1 teaspoon asafetida powder

1 teaspoon cayenne pepper

¼ teaspoon cinnamon

1. Place the chickpeas into a 4-quart slow cooker. Fill the rest of the insert with water. Allow the chickpeas to soak overnight. Drain and return to the slow cooker.

2. Heat the oil in a nonstick pan. Sauté the onions, garlic, and ginger until the onions are soft and translucent. Add to the slow cooker.

3. Add the remaining ingredients. Stir. Cook on low for 8–10 hours. Stir before serving.

Quick Raita

In a small bowl, stir ½ grated English cucumber, 1 cup fat-free Greek yogurt, ¼ cup minced fresh mint, ½ teaspoon cumin, and ¼ teaspoon cayenne. Refrigerate for 2 hours. Serve cold as a condiment with Indian curries to cut the heat.

CHAPTER 15

VEGAN DISHES

TOFU RANCHERO

Bring Mexican cuisine to the breakfast table with an easy tofu ranchero.

Serves 4

INGREDIENTS:

3 tablespoons olive oil

1 (16-ounce) package firm tofu, drained and crumbled

½ onion, diced

2 cloves garlic, minced

1 lemon, juiced

½ teaspoon turmeric

1 teaspoon salt

¼ teaspoon black pepper

1 cup cooked pinto beans

8 corn tortillas

½ cup chipotle salsa

1. Add the olive oil, tofu, onion, garlic, lemon juice, turmeric, salt, black pepper, and pinto beans to a 4-quart slow cooker. Cover and cook on low heat for 4 hours.

2. When the ranchero filling is nearly done, brown the tortillas on both sides in a small sauté pan over medium heat, about 3 minutes on each side.

3. Serve by scooping a little bit of the tofu mixture onto each tortilla and topping with salsa.

Choosing Salsa

Salsa comes in many delicious and unique varieties. Most are clearly labeled mild, medium, or hot, but one's interpretation of those words can vary greatly. Chipotle salsa has a deep, earthy spice, but you can also use plain tomato salsa or tomatillo salsa in this recipe.

EASY TOFU "EGGS"

Tofu "eggs" are a great form of protein and taste delicious. They contain very little fat and no cholesterol. Build upon this basic recipe to create a variety of tofu scrambles.

Serves 4

INGREDIENTS:

2 tablespoons olive oil

1 (16-ounce) package firm tofu, drained and crumbled

¼ cup onion, diced

2 cloves garlic, minced

1 teaspoon turmeric

1 teaspoon salt

¼ teaspoon black pepper

1 lemon, juiced

1. Add all ingredients, except for the lemon juice, to a 4-quart slow cooker. Cover, and cook on medium heat for 2–4 hours.

2. About 3 minutes before the "eggs" are finished, stir in the lemon juice.

SPICY SEITAN BUFFALO STRIPS

Most bottled buffalo wing sauces contain butter, so be sure to read the label or make your own by following these steps.

Serves 6

INGREDIENTS:

⅓ cup Earth Balance Original Buttery Spread

⅓ cup hot sauce

1 tablespoon vinegar

1 teaspoon garlic powder

2 (7-ounce) packages Gardein Chick'n Strips

1. Place the Earth Balance in a small bowl and microwave for 30 seconds, or until melted.

2. Add the hot sauce, vinegar, and garlic powder, and stir well.

3. In a 4-quart slow cooker, add the prepared hot sauce mixture and Chick'n Strips, and cook over low heat for 1 hour.

Serving Strips

Faux buffalo chicken strips can be added to sandwiches or salads, but if you'd like to serve them as an appetizer or snack, place in a small basket lined with parchment paper and add a side of celery sticks, carrot sticks, and vegan ranch.

EDAMAME-MISO DIP

The Asian flavors of this unique dip are both subtle and satisfying.

Serves 4

INGREDIENTS:

½ pound frozen shelled edamame

3 cups water

1 tablespoon soy sauce

2½ tablespoons miso paste

2 green onions, thinly sliced

⅛ teaspoon salt

1. Add all ingredients to a 4-quart slow cooker, stir, cover, and cook on low heat for 2 hours, or until the edamame is tender.

2. Using a slotted spoon, remove the edamame and place it in a food processor or blender. Purée the edamame, adding enough of the cooking liquid to create a smooth consistency. Serve cold or at room temperature.

PUMPKIN-ALE SOUP

Use fresh pumpkin in place of the canned pumpkin purée when the ingredient is in season. You'll need 3¾ cups of cooked, puréed fresh pumpkin.

Serves 6

INGREDIENTS:

2 (15-ounce) cans pumpkin purée

¼ cup diced onion

2 cloves garlic, minced

2 teaspoons salt

1 teaspoon pepper

¼ teaspoon dried thyme

5 cups Vegetable Stock (Chapter 19)

1 (12-ounce) bottle pale ale beer

1. In a 4-quart slow cooker, add the pumpkin purée, onion, garlic, salt, pepper, thyme, and stock. Stir well. Cover and cook over low heat for 4 hours.

2. Allow the soup to cool slightly, then process in a blender or with an immersion blender until smooth.

3. Pour the soup back into the slow cooker, add the beer, and cook for 1 hour over low heat.

TOFU NOODLE SOUP

Even firm tofu is quite soft, so for added texture, freeze the tofu and bake before adding to the soup.

Serves 4

INGREDIENTS:

2 tablespoons olive oil

1 medium onion, diced

3 cloves garlic, minced

2 ribs celery, sliced in ½-inch pieces

7 ounces extra-firm tofu, cubed

5 cups Vegetable Stock (Chapter 19)

1 bay leaf

1 teaspoon salt

1 lemon, juiced

2 teaspoons fresh parsley, chopped

2 teaspoons fresh thyme, chopped

8 ounces cooked noodles or linguine

1. In a large sauté pan heat the olive oil over medium heat. Add the onion, garlic, and celery, and sauté for 3 minutes.

2. Add the tofu and cook 5 additional minutes.

3. In a 4-quart slow cooker, pour the sautéed vegetables, tofu, stock, bay leaf, and salt. Cover and cook on low for 8 hours.

4. Add the lemon juice, parsley, thyme, and pasta. Cover and cook for an additional 20 minutes. Discard bay leaf before serving.

Herbal Options

A variety of herbs can work well in Tofu Noodle Soup. Try substituting basil, rosemary, or even dill in this recipe.

VEGAN VICHYSSOISE

Vichyssoise is traditionally served cold (and is made using cream, too), but this warm vegan version will leave you satisfied on a cold day.

Serves 6

INGREDIENTS:

2 tablespoons Earth Balance Original Buttery Spread

3 leeks (white part only), sliced

1 white onion, sliced

3 Idaho potatoes, peeled and diced

4 cups Vegetable Stock (Chapter 19)

1 bay leaf

½ teaspoon pepper

¼ teaspoon dried thyme

1 cup unsweetened soymilk

¼ teaspoon salt

2 tablespoons chopped chives

1. Melt the Earth Balance in a large pan over medium heat. Add the leeks and onions and sauté for 10 minutes. Transfer to a 6-quart slow cooker.

2. Add the potatoes, stock, bay leaf, pepper, and thyme. Cover and cook over low heat for 6 hours. Remove the bay leaf when done.

3. Add the soymilk and purée using an immersion blender or traditional blender.

4. Season with salt to taste, and top with chives before serving.

Earth Balance

Earth Balance Original Buttery Spread is a popular brand of vegan buttery spread that has a delicious flavor and acts similarly to butter in cooking. Many types of margarine don't melt easily or have a rubbery texture, but Earth Balance Original is very creamy and can be used in all types of recipes.

SOUTHWEST VEGETABLE CHILI

Southwest cuisine is similar to Mexican food and includes a wide variety of peppers, such as the jalapeños, bell peppers, and chipotle (smoked jalapeño), and chili powder, found in this recipe.

Serves 4

INGREDIENTS:

1 (28-ounce) can diced tomatoes

1 (15-ounce) can red kidney beans

1 onion, chopped

1 green bell pepper, chopped

1 red bell pepper, chopped

1 medium zucchini, chopped

1 squash, chopped

¼ cup chopped pickled jalapeños

2 tablespoons chili powder

2 tablespoons garlic powder

2 tablespoons cumin

1 teaspoon chipotle powder

⅛ teaspoon dried thyme

¼ teaspoon black pepper

1. Add all ingredients to a 4-quart slow cooker. Cover and cook on low heat for 5 hours.

GINGER-LIME TOFU

The slow cooker does all the work in this recipe, creating a healthy yet impressive dish that requires virtually no hands-on time.

Serves 8

INGREDIENTS:

2 (14-ounce) packages extra-firm tofu, pressed and sliced into fourths

¼ cup minced fresh ginger

¼ cup lime juice

1 lime, thinly sliced

1 onion, thinly sliced

1. Place the tofu fillets in an oval 6- to 7-quart slow cooker. Pour the ginger and lime juice over the tofu, then arrange the lime and then the onion in a single layer over the top.

2. Cook on low for 3–4 hours.

MAPLE-GLAZED TOFU

Simple and sweet, like this recipe, is sometimes all you need for a delicious dish!

Serves 4

INGREDIENTS:

4 cloves garlic, minced

1 tablespoon minced ginger

½ cup maple syrup

¼ cup soy sauce

½ cup water

2 tablespoons brown sugar

1 lemon, juiced

¼ teaspoon black pepper

1 (14-ounce) package extra-firm tofu, pressed and quartered

1. In a large bowl, combine all the ingredients, except for the tofu. Pour the mixture into a 4-quart slow cooker and add the tofu.

2. Set the slow cooker to high and cook for 1–2 hours, flipping the tofu at the halfway point.

SPICY SEITAN TACOS

Hard or soft taco shells work well with this tasty recipe.

Serves 8

INGREDIENTS:

2 tablespoons olive oil

1 (16-ounce) package seitan, chopped into small pieces

2 cloves garlic, minced

½ cup soy sauce

1 tablespoon chili powder

¼ teaspoon chipotle powder

¼ teaspoon garlic powder

¼ teaspoon crushed red pepper flakes

¼ teaspoon onion powder

2 teaspoons cumin

½ teaspoon paprika

1 teaspoon black pepper

8 taco shells

1 cup shredded lettuce

1 tomato, diced

1. Add all the ingredients, except for shells, lettuce, and tomatoes, to a 4-quart slow cooker. Cover and cook on low heat for 4 hours.

2. Serve the seitan in the shells and top with lettuce and tomato.

Fresh Tortillas

For an extra-special treat, try fresh tortillas. You may have to do a little hunting around, but they can often be found at international farmers' markets and Latino stores.

RED WINE "POT ROAST"

A little bit of wine goes a long way in flavoring this simple one-crock meal.

Serves 6

INGREDIENTS:

⅓ cup red wine

½ cup water

4 red skin potatoes, quartered

3 carrots, cut into thirds

2 bulbs fennel, quartered

2 rutabagas, quartered

1 onion, sliced

4 cloves garlic, sliced

1½ pounds seitan, cubed

½ teaspoon salt

½ teaspoon freshly ground black pepper

1. Pour the wine and water into a 4-quart slow cooker. Add the potatoes, carrots, fennel, rutabagas, onion, and garlic. Stir.

2. Add the seitan. Sprinkle with salt and pepper. Cover and cook on low for 8 hours.

ITALIAN HERB SEITAN

Serve this simple Italian dish over a bed of angel hair pasta and use the remaining liquid as a sauce to dress your pasta.

Serves 6

INGREDIENTS:

1 (16-ounce) package seitan, cut into bite-sized pieces

6 cloves garlic, minced

¼ cup rice wine vinegar

½ cup Vegetable Stock (Chapter 19)

½ cup chopped rosemary

½ cup chopped parsley

1 teaspoon salt

¼ teaspoon black pepper

1. Add all of the ingredients to a 4-quart slow cooker. Cover and cook on low heat for 6 hours.

The Power of Seitan

Seitan, otherwise known as wheat gluten, is a powerful source of protein and a great alternative to meat. One serving has a whopping 18 grams of protein, and the benefits don't stop there—it's also a great source of iron.

SRIRACHA AND SOY TEMPEH

Sriracha is sometimes affectionately referred to as "rooster sauce" because of the drawing on the bottle of Huy Fong's sriracha sauce, but don't let the cute name fool you. This sauce packs a spicy punch.

Serves 4

INGREDIENTS:

1 (13-ounce) package tempeh, cut into bite-sized squares

4 cloves garlic, minced

1 teaspoon minced ginger

1 tablespoon olive oil

½ cup soy sauce

¼ cup water

2 tablespoons brown sugar

1 teaspoon sriracha sauce

1. Add all ingredients to a 4-quart slow cooker. Cover and cook on high heat for 2 hours.

TEMPEH BRAISED IN SAUERKRAUT

Sauerkraut is fermented cabbage that is often sold canned or in jars in grocery stores nationwide.

Serves 6

INGREDIENTS:

3 cups sauerkraut

½ tablespoon caraway seeds

1 tablespoon yellow mustard seeds

1 small onion, thinly sliced

2 tablespoons apple cider vinegar

1 pound tempeh, cut into 1½-inch cubes

1. Place the sauerkraut, caraway seeds, mustard seeds, onion, and vinegar into a 4- or 6-quart slow cooker. Stir to distribute all ingredients evenly.

2. Add the tempeh and toss.

3. Cover and cook for 3–4 hours on low.

SWEET AND SOUR TOFU

This recipe is not only kid-friendly but vegan and gluten-free. Serve it over rice and garnish with diced green onions.

Serves 6

INGREDIENTS:

12 ounces extra-firm tofu, cubed

¼ cup rice vinegar

3 tablespoons water

1 tablespoon sesame seeds

1 tablespoon brown sugar

1 tablespoon tamari

1 tablespoon pineapple juice

1 teaspoon ground ginger

¾ cup pineapple chunks

1 cup snow peas

½ cup sliced onion

1. Spray a nonstick skillet with cooking spray. Sauté the tofu until it is lightly browned on each side. Add to a 4-quart slow cooker.

2. In a small bowl, whisk together the vinegar, water, sesame seeds, brown sugar, tamari, pineapple juice, and ginger until the sugar fully dissolves. Pour over the tofu.

3. Add the remaining ingredients. Cook on low for 4 hours. Remove the lid and cook on low for 30 minutes.

WHITE BEAN CASSOULET

The longer you cook this cassoulet, the creamier it gets.

Serves 8

INGREDIENTS:

1 pound dried cannellini beans

2 cups boiling water

1 ounce dried porcini mushrooms

2 leeks, sliced

1 teaspoon canola oil

2 parsnips, diced

2 carrots, diced

2 stalks celery, diced

½ teaspoon ground fennel

1 teaspoon crushed rosemary

1 teaspoon dried chervil

⅛ teaspoon cloves

¼ teaspoon salt

¼ teaspoon freshly ground black pepper

2 cups Vegetable Stock (Chapter 19)

1. The night before making the soup, place the beans in a 4-quart slow cooker. Fill with water to 1" below the top of the insert. Soak overnight.

2. Drain the beans and return them to the slow cooker. Pour the boiling water over the dried mushrooms in a heat-proof bowl and soak for 15 minutes. Slice only the white and light green parts of the leek into ¼" rounds. Cut the rounds in half.

3. Heat the oil in a nonstick skillet. Add the leeks, parsnips, carrots, and celery. Sauté for 1 minute, just until the color of the vegetables brightens. Add to the slow cooker along with the spices. Add the mushrooms, their soaking liquid, and the stock. Stir.

4. Cook on low for 8–10 hours.

PALAK TOFU

Palak tofu is a fresh-tasting, protein-rich Indian dish that is only slightly spicy.

Serves 4

INGREDIENTS:

14 ounces extra-firm tofu

1 tablespoon canola oil

1 teaspoon cumin seeds

2 cloves garlic, minced

2 jalapeños, minced

¾ pound red skin potatoes, diced

½ teaspoon ground ginger

¾ teaspoon Garam Masala Powder (Chapter 16)

1 pound frozen cut-leaf spinach

¼ cup fresh cilantro

1. Cut the tofu into ½" cubes. Set aside.

2. Heat the oil in a nonstick skillet. Sauté the cumin seeds for 1 minute, then add the garlic and jalapeños. Sauté until fragrant, then add the tofu and potatoes. Sauté for 3 minutes. Add the ginger, Garam Masala, frozen spinach, and cilantro. Sauté 1 minute.

3. Pour the mixture into a 4-quart slow cooker and cook for 4 hours on low.

KOREAN-STYLE HOT POT

Serve this hot and spicy main dish with sides of steamed rice and kimchi.

Serves 8

INGREDIENTS:

3 bunches baby bok choy

8 cups water

8 ounces sliced crimini mushrooms

12 ounces extra-firm tofu, cubed

3 cloves garlic, thinly sliced

¼ teaspoon sesame oil

1 tablespoon crushed red pepper flakes

7 ounces enoki mushrooms

1. Remove the leaves of the baby bok choy. Wash thoroughly. Place them whole in a 4-quart slow cooker. Add the water, crimini mushrooms, tofu, garlic, sesame oil, and crushed red pepper. Stir.

2. Cook on low for 8 hours. Add the enoki mushrooms and stir. Cook an additional ½ hour before serving.

GREEN CHILE AND HOMINY STEW

This spicy yet comforting stew is packed with flavor

Serves 6

INGREDIENTS:

1 teaspoon canola oil

2 cubanelle peppers, diced

4 ounces canned diced green peppers

2 jalapeños, diced

1 onion, diced

4 cloves garlic, minced

3¾ cups water

24 ounces canned hominy

¼ teaspoon salt

½ teaspoon freshly ground black pepper

½ teaspoon ground jalapeño

3 zucchini, diced

1. Heat the oil in a nonstick pan. Sauté the cubanelle peppers, canned green peppers, jalapeños, onion, and garlic until fragrant.

2. Add the mixture to a 4-quart slow cooker. Add the water, hominy, salt, pepper, and ground jalapeño. Stir. Cook on low for 7 hours.

3. Add the zucchini and cook on high for 1 hour. Stir prior to serving.

MISO SOUP WITH TOFU AND WAKAME

Traditionally, miso is never heated to boiling while making soup, making it a perfect dish to make in the slow cooker. Adding tofu and wakame seaweed makes it a complete meal.

Serves 6

INGREDIENTS:

2 quarts water

3–4 tablespoons white miso paste

12 ounces extra-firm tofu, diced

1 cup broken, dried wakame seaweed

1 bunch green onions, diced

1. Pour the water into a 4-quart slow cooker. Whisk in the miso paste until it is fully dissolved. Add the tofu. Cook on low for up to 8 hours.

2. Add the seaweed and green onion. Cook for 15 minutes on high. Stir before serving.

CHOCOLATE "MUD" CAKE

Slow cooker mud cake might not look pretty, but the taste more than makes up for it.

Serves 8

INGREDIENTS:

1 cup flour

½ cup sugar

2 teaspoons baking powder

¼ teaspoon salt

3 tablespoons cocoa powder

3 tablespoons softened Earth Balance Original Buttery Spread

1 teaspoon vanilla

⅓ cup soymilk

½ cup vegan chocolate chips

1 cup vegan chocolate icing

1. In a large mixing bowl, combine the flour, sugar, baking powder, salt, and cocoa powder.

2. In a medium bowl, combine the Earth Balance, vanilla, and soymilk until well blended.

3. Add the wet mixture and the chocolate chips to the large mixing bowl and stir until just combined. Pour the batter into a greased 4-quart slow cooker. Cover and cook on high heat for 2½ hours.

4. Once done, allow the cake to cool slightly, then top with chocolate icing.

Vegan Chocolate Icing

There are many vegan icings available in your local grocery store, and you might be surprised that they are made by brands such as Duncan Hines and Pillsbury. They are "accidentally vegan" though, which means they aren't advertised as such. Be sure to read the label before buying.

CHAPTER 16

INDIAN FAVORITES

GHEE

Store this in glass jars in the refrigerator. If the recipe you're using it in calls for liquid ghee, warm the ghee before using.

Yields about 3 cups

INGREDIENTS:

2 pounds butter, unsalted

1. Cut the butter into large cubes.

2. Cover and heat on a low setting for 2–3 hours. The butter should separate. Don't let it brown.

3. Skim off the clear liquid on the top; this is ghee. Store refrigerated and covered. Discard the butter solids, or use in cooking as a butter substitute.

HOT CILANTRO CHUTNEY

This is a very popular North Indian chutney used as a dip here, but it can also be used as a base for several Indian recipes.

Yields ½ cup

INGREDIENTS:

1½ packed cups cilantro

4–6 Thai green chilies, roughly chopped

2 fresh garlic cloves

1½" piece of gingerroot

½ tablespoon cumin seeds

Optional: 1 tablespoon skinless roasted peanuts

Salt, to taste

2 tablespoons fresh lemon juice

1. Blend all the ingredients in a food processor to a smooth paste. To aid in the blending process, you can add 1 tablespoon of water if needed. Chill for about 30 minutes. Serve as a dipping sauce. This chutney will keep, refrigerated, for 4 days.

GARAM MASALA POWDER (WARM SPICE MIX)

You can vary this recipe a bit—experiment with various spices until you find the combination that works for you.

Yields 2 tablespoons

INGREDIENTS:

8 cloves

4 teaspoons cumin seeds

3 green whole cardamom pods

2 black whole cardamom pods

1 (2") cinnamon stick

2 teaspoons coriander seeds

1 teaspoon black peppercorns

1 bay leaf

Optional: Pinch of grated nutmeg

1. Heat a small skillet on medium heat. Add all the spices except the nutmeg and dry roast the spices, stirring constantly. After about 5 minutes, the spices will darken and begin to release a unique aroma.

2. Remove the skillet from the heat, then add the nutmeg. Transfer the spice mix to a bowl and allow to cool for about 5 minutes.

3. Using a spice grinder, grind the spices to a fine powder. Store in an airtight jar. The spice mixture will keep for up to 3 months.

TANDOORI SPICE MIX (TANDOORI MASALA)

This recipe is quintessential North India. You can also try adding red chili to it.

Yields about 2 tablespoons

INGREDIENTS:

½ teaspoon carom seeds

1 tablespoon Garam Masala Powder (this chapter)

½ teaspoon ginger powder

¼ teaspoon black salt

½ teaspoon dried fenugreek leaves

¼ teaspoon dried mango powder

1. Place the carom seeds in a resealable plastic bag and crush with a rolling pin.

2. Combine all the ingredients in a bowl and mix thoroughly. Transfer to an airtight jar and store.

Packaged Spice Mixes

If you need a spice mix in a hurry, you can buy most packaged spice mixes (like the garam masala, tandoori masala, and chaat masala) at your local Indian grocery stores instead of making them yourself.

PERFECT SLOW COOKER BASMATI RICE

Cooking basmati rice can get a little tricky in a slow cooker, but a couple of small tips and practice can take you a long way. The first trick is not to go overboard with water since very little evaporates. Second, and most important, add some grease to prevent sticking.

Serves 4–6

INGREDIENTS:

2 cups long-grain white basmati rice

3 cups water

1½ tablespoons Ghee (this chapter)

Salt, if needed

1. Rinse the rice with water. Immediately put it in the slow cooker, not letting it soak in water for long as it will turn mushy.

2. Add the water, ghee, and salt, if needed. Cover and cook on high for 1½ hours. Turn off the heat; check to see if the rice is cooked to your liking. If not, replace the lid and let the steam complete the rest of the cooking. Fluff the rice with a fork after 20 minutes. Serve hot with your favorite lentil soup or curry.

Adding Grease

Adding some kind of grease or oil or butter or ghee can serve two purposes: first, it keeps the rice from sticking to the sides and, second, it helps keep the grains fluffy.

PERFECT SLOW COOKER WHITE RICE

Parboiled or converted rice, which is widely used in India, can be made to perfection in a slow cooker.

Yields approximately 4 cups

INGREDIENTS:

2 cups parboiled rice

2 cups water

1. Combine all the ingredients together in a 5-quart slow cooker and cook on high for 3 hours or until the rice is cooked through.

COCONUT RICE

Try adding white raisins or small pieces of fresh pineapple to this dish during the last hour of cooking.

Serves 4–6

INGREDIENTS:

1 lemon

1 cup uncooked rice

2 cups coconut milk

½ cup water

½ teaspoon salt

½ teaspoon turmeric

¼ cup toasted pistachios

1. Squeeze the juice from the lemon. Put the lemon juice, rice, coconut milk, water, salt, and turmeric in the slow cooker.

2. Cover and heat on a low setting for 3–4 hours.

3. Chop the pistachios into coarse pieces. An hour before serving, stir in the pistachios.

ROASTED CHICKPEAS

Dry snacks, or as they're called namkeen or chakna, are hugely popular all across India. Every state and region has their variety of namkeen, which are served with beverages and drinks.

Yields 3 cups

INGREDIENTS:

2 (14-ounce) cans garbanzo beans

1 tablespoon lime juice

1½ teaspoons curry powder

1 teaspoon cumin powder

1. Drain garbanzo beans. In a large mixing bowl, combine all the ingredients and mix well.

2. Transfer mixture to a 5-quart slow cooker. Cover, but prop the lid open on the side for the steam to escape. Turn the heat to high and cook for 5–6 hours, or on low for 10 hours, or until the beans are dry and crunchy.

Canned Beans

Canned beans are already salty, so you do not need to add extra salt. But if you rinse them, then add a teaspoon of salt.

CURRY PASTE

Curry paste is the base of many Indian dishes including a spicy biryani and chicken curry. The secret to a perfect curry paste is slow cooking. You can store this curry paste for 2–3 weeks in a refrigerator and for months in a freezer.

Yields 2½ cups

INGREDIENTS:

2 cups sliced onion

1½" piece fresh gingerroot

5–6 cloves garlic

4–5 green Thai chili peppers

2 (14-ounce) cans of tomatoes, drained

3 tablespoons coriander powder

1 teaspoon turmeric powder

3 teaspoons Garam Masala Powder (this chapter)

3 tablespoons cooking oil

1 tablespoon Ghee (this chapter)

Salt, to taste

1. Grind onion, ginger, garlic, chili, and tomatoes in a blender to make a smooth paste.

2. To the wet paste add the dry spices except for Garam Masala. Mix it all together.

3. Add oil and Ghee to a 3- or 4-quart slow cooker. Transfer the prepared wet paste. Stir everything together. Place the lid on, turn the heat to high, and cook for 2–3 hours.

4. After 1 hour stir in the salt, turn the heat to low, and cook for 4–5 hours. Stir every couple of hours and scrape down the sides of the cooker. In the last 30 minutes, add garam masala. Cook for another 30 minutes.

5. Wait for the curry paste to cool down. Transfer the prepared curry paste to a glass container or an air tight container. Can be stored in the refrigerator for 2–3 weeks.

Hold Your Water
Try not to add water while grinding the wet ingredients.

MURGHI KA SHORBA (CHICKEN SOUP)

You can use any part of the chicken breasts, thighs, or even drumsticks if you can manage to get the bone out. Cut it into 1" chunks.

Serves 8–10

INGREDIENTS:

1 tablespoon Ghee (this chapter), or butter

1½ teaspoons cumin seeds

1 teaspoon turmeric powder

2 pounds boneless chicken

1 (8-ounce) can diced tomatoes, drained

5 cups Chicken Broth (Chapter 19)

1½ teaspoons Garam Masala Powder (this chapter)

1 teaspoon cayenne pepper

Salt, to taste

Optional: 1 cup thick hung yogurt

1. Add the Ghee to a large slow cooker. Add the cumin seeds and turmeric. Turn the slow cooker to high setting. Cover. As soon as the Ghee melts, add the rest of the ingredients except for the yogurt. Cover again and cook for 4 hours on high, or for 7–8 hours on low, or until the chicken is well cooked. Stir occasionally.

2. Serve hot with a dollop of yogurt.

Tips

Do not forget to brown the chicken on the stovetop for 5 minutes before dropping in the slow cooker.

BENGAL GRAM DAL AND BOTTLE GOURD SOUP (CHANA DAL LAUKI)

Bengal gram dal (or chana dal as Indians call it) is one of the most fibrous legumes and a great source of protein. When mixed with bottle gourd and some basic Indian spices, it is not only good but is very good for you.

Serves 6–8

INGREDIENTS:

2 cups dry Bengal gram dal

4 cups water

1 teaspoon turmeric powder

Salt, to taste

4 cups bottle gourd (peeled, deseeded, and cut into bite-sized chunks)

1 cup diced roma tomatoes

1 tablespoon gingerroot, coarsely chopped

1 teaspoon chopped green chili

1 teaspoon Ghee (this chapter)

1 pinch asafetida

1 teaspoon cumin seeds

1 tablespoon coriander powder

1 tablespoon chopped cilantro

1. Wash the dal and transfer it to a 5–6 quart slow cooker. Add water, salt, and turmeric powder. Cook on high for 1 hour.

2. Place the diced bottle gourd, tomatoes, ginger, and green chili into the slow cooker. Cook on low for 5 hours, or until everything is cooked through. With a spatula, stir everything together well.

3. Heat the Ghee in a pan for tempering. Add the asafetida and cumin seeds. Once the cumin seeds pop, add the coriander powder. Turn heat off immediately. Stir with a spoon and then add it to the soup along with the cilantro. Mix well and serve with rice or warm bread.

Tomato Options

You can use any kind of tomatoes for this dish. For a tangy soup, try using green tomatoes.

RESTAURANT-STYLE DAL FRY

When you ask for dal in most North Indian restaurants, you will be served fried yellow lentils. But you can use this same recipe to make a dal fry for any other kind of lentil.

Serves 4–6

INGREDIENTS:

1½ cups yellow lentils, washed (toor dal)

4 cups water, and more if needed

½ teaspoon turmeric powder

Salt, to taste

4–5 tablespoons oil or Ghee (this chapter)

1 teaspoon cumin seeds

1 teaspoon garlic, minced

3–4 dried whole red chilies

¼ cup red onion, chopped

½ cup tomato, diced

Pinch asafetida

3 tablespoons cilantro, chopped

1. In a slow cooker, combine the lentils, water, turmeric powder, salt, and 1 tablespoon of the oil. Cover and cook on high for 2–2½ hours, or on low for 4–5 hours, or until the lentils are soft. If the water begins to dry up, add up to ½ cup more. (The consistency should be like a creamy soup.)

2. Using a spoon, mash the cooked lentils to a creamy consistency. Set aside.

3. In a medium pan, heat the remaining vegetable oil. Add the cumin seeds. When they begin to sizzle, add the garlic and red chilies. Sauté for about 20 seconds. Add the red onion and sauté until it turns light brown. Add the tomato and cook uncovered on low 5 minutes or until the tomato melts.

4. Add the tomato mixture to the cooked dal. Garnish with cilantro and the pinch of asafetida and serve hot over Perfect Slow Cooker Basmati Rice (this chapter).

INDIAN LENTILS

Look for orange lentils in your local market or an international grocery. Brown lentils give an entirely different taste and texture.

Serves 6

INGREDIENTS:

1 onion

3 cloves garlic

1 green pepper

1 teaspoon cumin

2 tablespoons Ghee (this chapter)

2 cups tomatoes, cubed

1½ cups orange lentils

3 cups water

2 teaspoons honey

¼ teaspoon salt

1. Slice the onion and garlic; dice the green pepper. Sauté the onion, garlic, and green pepper with cumin in Ghee in a pan over medium heat until the onion is soft.

2. Add the tomatoes, onion mixture, lentils, water, honey, and salt to the slow cooker.

3. Cover and heat on a low setting for 3–4 hours.

All about Aroma

Once they're opened, slow cookers full of food will release a strong aroma. Try putting different slow cookers in different areas of your entertaining space, even in separate rooms. Have a "dessert room," a "spicy room," and a "bakery" room and let your guests move freely between them.

SIMPLE MUNG BEAN CURRY (TADKA DAL)

Tadka in Indian cooking means "seasoning." This yellow dal is a North Indian favorite. Serve atop steamed Indian basmati rice.

Serves 6

INGREDIENTS:

2 cups yellow split mung beans (yellow moong dal), well rinsed

6 cups water, more as needed

½ teaspoon turmeric powder

4–5 tablespoons vegetable oil, divided

1 teaspoon cumin seeds

1 small red onion, minced

1 teaspoon ginger, grated

1 serrano green chili, seeded and minced

Optional: 1 small tomato, minced

Salt, to taste

Optional: 1 tablespoon minced cilantro

1. In a slow cooker, combine the beans, water, turmeric, and 1 tablespoon of the vegetable oil. Cover and cook on high for 2½–3 hours, or on low for 4–5 hours, or until the beans are very soft. If the water starts to dry up, you can add another ½–1 cup of water. Turn off the heat and set aside.

2. In a medium-sized skillet, heat the remaining vegetable oil. Add the cumin seeds; when they begin to sizzle, add the red onion. Sauté for 7–8 minutes or until the onions are well browned.

3. Add the ginger, green chili, and tomato (if using). Cook for another 8 minutes or until the tomato is soft.

4. Add the salt and cilantro and mix well. Add the onion mixture to the beans and mix well. Reheat gently and serve hot.

GINGER-FLAVORED CHICKEN CURRY (MURGH ADRAKI)

Use fresh tender ginger for this recipe. Serve with plain Naan.

Serves 4–5

INGREDIENTS:

2 tablespoons gingerroot, grated

1 teaspoon coriander powder

1 teaspoon Garam Masala Powder (this chapter)

½ teaspoon red chili powder

¾ cup plain yogurt, whipped

4 tablespoons vegetable oil, divided

8 skinless chicken thighs

½ teaspoon cumin seeds

1 black cardamom pod

1 bay leaf

2 medium-sized fresh tomatoes, puréed

Salt, to taste

Water, as needed

1. In a large bowl or resealable plastic bag, combine the ginger, coriander powder, Garam Masala, red chili powder, yogurt, and 2 tablespoons of the vegetable oil; mix well. Add the chicken and coat all pieces evenly with the marinade. Set aside.

2. In a large skillet, heat the remaining 2 tablespoons of vegetable oil. Add the cumin seeds, cardamom pod, and bay leaf. When the seeds begin to sizzle, add the tomato purée.

3. Sauté over medium heat until the tomatoes are cooked and the oil begins to separate from the tomato mixture, about 3–4 minutes.

4. Add the chicken and the marinade to the tomato mixture, along with the salt. Transfer to the slow cooker. Add up to ½ cup of water. Cover and cook 2½–3 hours, or on low for 5–6 hours, or until the chicken is completely cooked and the juices run clear. Stir occasionally. If you like a thinner gravy, add some more water. Remove the black cardamom pod and bay leaf before serving. Serve hot.

Indian Cooking Oils

Indian cooking uses peanut, vegetable, mustard, sesame, and corn oil for cooking. There are two varieties of ghee that are used, vanaspathi (vegetable) and usli (clarified butter). Indian cooking does not use any animal fat or lard as a cooking medium.

TANDOORI CHICKEN

For a crispier outer skin broil the chicken for 5–10 minutes under a broiler after cooking in the slow cooker.

Serve 6

INGREDIENTS:

¼ cup Tandoori Masala (this chapter)

½ cup yogurt

¼ teaspoon red food coloring

1½ tablespoons ginger-garlic paste

1 tablespoon Garam Masala Powder (this chapter)

3 tablespoons oil

Salt, to taste

1½ cups onion, sliced

1 whole chicken (washed well and skinned)

1. Mix all the ingredients (except for the onion and chicken) together in a bowl making a thick, bright-colored marinade. Make a few incisions in the chicken and rub the marinade all over the chicken. If there is some marinade left, pour it inside the cavity of the bird. Tuck the bird tight (place the loose ends of its legs and wings inside to prevent it from burning during the prolonged cooking process).

2. Add the onion to the slow cooker, forming a bottom layer. Place the chicken on top of the onion. Cover and cook on high for the first 1½ hours. Then reduce the heat to low and continue cooking for 4–5 hours or until the chicken is cooked through.

3. Cooking time will depend on the size of the chicken. Cut through the meatier part of the bird and if the juice comes out clear, then the chicken is cooked. Serve hot with Hot Cilantro Chutney (this chapter).

MACCHI DUM PUKHT (SLOW-COOKED FISH)

Even if you are not a fan of fish, the moment you put this dish in your mouth you will turn into one! Tastes best with naan.

Serves 6

INGREDIENTS:

4 fish steaks, scaled and cut into 3" pieces

1 tablespoon turmeric

Salt, to taste

¼ cup oil, preferably mustard oil

1 cup onion paste (grind onion in a food processor)

2 inches gingerroot

3 Thai green chilies

¼ cup blanched almonds, skins off

1 teaspoon Kashmiri lal mirch

1 teaspoon Garam Masala Powder (this chapter)

Water, as needed

½ cup yogurt

1. Rub the fish with turmeric and salt. Set aside for 30 minutes. Heat the oil in a pan and pan-fry the fish steaks until they turn golden brown on all sides, about 5–8 minutes. Set aside on a paper towel to drain the excess oil.

2. In your food processor, grind together the onion paste, gingerroot, chilies, and blanched almonds.

3. In the remaining oil from the fried fish, add the onion-ginger-chili, almond, and chili paste. Add salt to the paste. Cook it on the stovetop until all the water is cooked off and the onion starts to separate from the oil, about 10 minutes.

4. Transfer this masala mixture to the slow cooker. Add Kashmiri lal mirch and Garam Masala. Add up to 1½ cup of water. Cover and cook on high for 1 hour, or on low for 2 hours, or until the sauce simmers down to a thicker consistency.

5. Stir in the yogurt and carefully place the fish pieces into the sauce. Cover and cook for another 30 minutes or until the sauce is thickened to a consistency of your liking and the fish flakes with a fork.

6. Once cooked, turn the slow cooker off and let the lid stay in place for 15–20 minutes before serving.

GOAN CHICKEN CURRY

This Indian dish is made easily in the slow cooker. Try it over rice or with some naan.

Serves 10

INGREDIENTS:

1 teaspoon canola oil

2 medium onions, diced

4 cloves garlic, minced

3 pounds boneless, skinless chicken thighs, cubed

1 tablespoon fresh ginger, minced

2 cups toasted unsweetened coconut

1 teaspoon cinnamon, ground

¼ teaspoon nutmeg, ground

½ teaspoon cloves, ground

½ teaspoon salt

1 teaspoon cumin seeds

1 teaspoon black mustard seeds

2 tablespoons red pepper flakes

1½ cups water

1. In a large nonstick skillet, heat the oil. Sauté the onions and garlic for 3 minutes.

2. Place all ingredients in a 6-quart slow cooker. Stir. Cover and cook for 6–8 hours on low. Stir before serving.

How to Toast Coconut

Preheat the oven to 350°F. Arrange shredded coconut on a single layer on a cookie sheet. Bake for 10–15 minutes or until light golden brown. Stir the coconut and check it frequently to prevent burning. Remove it from the oven and allow it to cool before using.

CARROT AND CHEESE PUDDING (GAJAR PANEER KA HALWA)

Quintessential India. Serve this warm, and garnished with your choice of unsalted nuts. This dish also freezes well.

Serves 4

INGREDIENTS:

6–7 cups carrots, peeled and grated

1 (14-ounce) can sweetened condensed milk

4–5 tablespoons butter, or Ghee (this chapter)

¼ cup raisins

¼ cup slivered almonds

¾ cup scrambled or grated paneer

½ teaspoon cardamom powder

1. Combine the carrots and condensed milk together in a slow cooker. Cover and cook on low for 4 hours and then prop the lid open on the side by 1". Turn the slow cooker to high and cook for 2–3 hours (stirring occasionally) or until the carrots are completely cooked.

2. Heat 1 tablespoon butter or Ghee in a large pan, wok, or skillet. Pan-fry the raisins and almonds. Take them out of the pan and set aside.

3. Transfer the contents from the slow cooker into the hot pan. Cook on medium heat, stirring every 2–3 minutes for 10–15 minutes to make sure 80 percent of the liquid is evaporated.

4. Add the rest of the butter or Ghee and the paneer to the pudding along with cardamom powder. Stir. This will make it look shiny and rich. Cook for another 4–5 minutes. Turn off the heat and serve hot.

Banana Pudding

Very popular in western India, this nutritious pudding is quite filling. Mash a banana, add 1 cup of milk, and sugar to taste. Top with raisins and serve chilled.

CHAI PUDDING

Any tea lover would delight in this creamy tapioca pudding.

Serves 6

INGREDIENTS:

2 chai tea bags

2 cups fat-free evaporated milk

⅓ cup brown sugar

½ teaspoon cinnamon

½ teaspoon ground star anise

½ teaspoon mace

½ teaspoon ground cardamom

¼ cup small pearl tapioca

1 egg

1. In a bowl, steep the tea bags in the evaporated milk for 20 minutes. Discard the bags. Whisk in the sugar, spices, and tapioca.

2. Pour the mixture into a 2- or 4-quart slow cooker and cook on low for 1½ hours. Stir in the egg and continue to cook for 30 minutes. Let it cool and then place it into the refrigerator to slightly chill before serving.

CREAMY MILK PUDDING (BASOONDI)

Tangy and sweet cold pineapple transforms this Indian favorite into a tropical delight. The sweetened, thickened milk dessert layered over the pineapple is mouthwatering.

Serves 4

INGREDIENTS:

2 cups ricotta cheese

1 cup whole milk

1 cup heavy cream

1 cup condensed milk

Sugar, if needed

¼ teaspoon saffron

1 (14-ounce) can crushed pineapple, drained and chilled

1. In a medium bowl, combine the ricotta cheese, milk, heavy cream and condensed milk. Mix well by hand or with a hand blender. Taste to check sweetness and add sugar if needed.

2. Transfer the mixture to a 3- to 4-quart slow cooker. Cover and cook on low for about 40 minutes, stirring frequently. The mixture will become creamy and have a very pale yellow color. The final consistency should be that of a creamy custard.

3. Remove from heat. Add the kesar. Stir well. Cool to room temperature, about 1 hour.

4. Fold in the chilled pineapple and serve.

Vark, or Silver Foil

You will often notice Indian sweets are covered with what appears to be shining silver. It is what it appears—silver! Silver is beaten into very thin sheets and used as a decorative ingredient in desserts. It is edible and provides a majestic touch to dishes. It is not easily available—check with your Indian grocer.

CHAPTER 17

KOSHER CLASSICS

SUMMER BORSCHT

Serve this cooling beet soup with a dollop of sour cream or vegan sour cream. Try Tofutti's Sour Supreme.

Serves 6

INGREDIENTS:

3½ cups cooked beets, shredded

¼ cup onion, diced

½ teaspoon salt

1 teaspoon sugar

¼ cup lemon juice

½ tablespoon celery seed

2 cups kosher vegetable broth

2 cups water

1. In a 4-quart slow cooker, place all of the ingredients. Cover and cook on low for 6–8 hours, or on high for 4 hours.

2. Refrigerate the soup for 4 hours or overnight. Serve cold.

Can't Beat Beets

Beets, also known as beetroot, can be peeled, steamed, cooked, pickled, and shredded; they are good hot or cold. They are high in folate, vitamin C, potassium, and fiber. Although they have the highest sugar content of all vegetables, beets are very low in calories; one beet is only 35 calories.

SIMPLE BRISKET

After a few minutes of browning, the brisket can be left to cook by itself while you pay more attention to all those other Passover preparations.

Serves 6–8

INGREDIENTS:

Cooking spray

2 tablespoons vegetable oil

1 large onion, diced

2 cloves garlic, minced

1 (3-pound) brisket, trimmed of excess fat

1 teaspoon powdered pareve beef bouillon

1 cup water

2 tablespoons balsamic vinegar

1 teaspoon ground ginger

½ teaspoon pepper

1. Lightly spray the inside of a 6-quart slow cooker with cooking spray.

2. Heat vegetable oil in a large skillet over medium heat. Add onion and garlic; stir frequently for 3–4 minutes or until onions just start to brown. Push to the sides of the pan and add brisket. Let sear undisturbed for 4 minutes, then carefully use tongs to turn brisket over. Let sear for another 4 minutes.

3. Transfer brisket and onions to prepared slow cooker.

4. In a medium bowl, stir together the bouillon, water, balsamic vinegar, ginger, and pepper. Pour mixture over brisket. Cover and cook on low for 7–8 hours or until brisket is very tender.

5. Turn off the slow cooker. When safe to handle, remove insert and allow contents to cool for 30 minutes. Transfer to a heat/refrigerator-safe covered dish and refrigerate overnight.

6. The next day, place brisket on cutting board. Slice as thinly as possible across the grain. Return to covered dish. Heat in preheated 350°F oven for 30 minutes or until hot.

What's Kosher?

To be considered kosher, meat has to come from animals that have cloven hooves and chew their cud. Kosher meat comes from animals including (but not limited to) cows, bison, goats, and sheep. Although the Bible doesn't specify the signs by which one can recognize kosher birds, it does provide a list of kosher fowl, including chicken, pigeon, and domesticated duck, goose, and turkey. Birds of prey, such as vultures and owls, are not kosher. To be considered kosher, fish must have fins and scales. So, while tuna is a kosher fish, sharks are not. Shellfish, such as clams, shrimp, octopus, and lobster, are also not permitted.

APPLE-MUSTARD BEEF BRISKET

Serve this dish with a crusty bread and a tossed salad with honey-mustard dressing. If you wish, you can add some peeled and quartered root vegetables (carrots, parsnips, or turnips) to the cooker, too.

Serves 8

INGREDIENTS:

1 (3-pound) beef brisket

1 large yellow onion, peeled and quartered

2 large cloves garlic, peeled and minced

4 large cloves garlic, peeled and left whole

1 (10-ounce) jar apple jelly

3 tablespoons Dijon mustard

Salt and freshly ground pepper, to taste

¾ teaspoon curry powder

⅓ cup dry white wine

1 cup apple juice

1 cup water

2 apples (optional)

1. Add all ingredients to 5- or 6-quart slow cooker in the order given. If using apples, peel, core, and slice them and put them in a layer on top of the meat. Cover and cook on low for 8 hours or until meat is tender.

Delayed Satisfaction

Brisket will become even more moist and tender if you allow it to cool in the broth, so this is a good dish to make the day before. To reheat it, bake it for 45 minutes at 325°F. Baste it with some additional sauce and put it under the broiler for a few minutes to allow the meat to develop a glaze.

TZIMMES

This traditional long-cooking sweet vegetable stew is served at Passover as well as other Jewish holidays.

Serves 12–16

INGREDIENTS:

Cooking spray

4 large carrots, peeled and cut into 1" chunks

1 medium onion, peeled and diced

5 large sweet potatoes, peeled and cut into large chunks

1 (8-ounce) package pitted prunes, halved

1 cup (4 ounces) dried apricots, halved

¼ cup raisins

2 tablespoons honey

½ teaspoon ground cinnamon

½ teaspoon ground ginger

1 teaspoon kosher salt

⅛ teaspoon ground pepper

½ cup orange juice

¾ cup apple juice

1. Lightly spray the inside of a 6-quart slow cooker with the cooking spray. Add the carrots, onion, sweet potatoes, prunes, dried apricots, raisins, and honey to the slow cooker. Stir to combine.

2. Sprinkle in the cinnamon, ginger, salt, and pepper.

3. Pour in the orange and apple juices. Cover and cook on high for 10–12 hours.

BRISKET TZIMMES

If there's room in the slow cooker, at the beginning of Step 3 you can add a 1-pound bag of thawed frozen cut green beans along with the sweet potatoes.

Serves 8

INGREDIENTS:

1 (3-pound) beef brisket

1 large yellow onion, peeled and diced

Salt and freshly ground black pepper, to taste

2 stalks celery, diced

1 large carrot, peeled and diced

1 (12-ounce) box pitted prunes (dried plums)

1 tablespoon dried or freeze-dried parsley

3 cups Beef Broth (Chapter 19)

3 tablespoons fresh lemon juice

¼ teaspoon ground cloves

1 teaspoon ground cinnamon

1 tablespoon honey

2 tablespoons white or white wine vinegar

4 large sweet potatoes, peeled and quartered

1. Add the brisket, onion, salt, pepper, celery, carrot, prunes, and parsley to a 5- or 6-quart slow cooker.

2. In a large bowl, mix the broth, lemon juice, cloves, cinnamon, honey, and vinegar together and then pour over the meat. Cover and cook on low for 6 hours or until the meat is cooked through.

3. Add the sweet potatoes. Cover and cook on low for another 2 hours or until the brisket and sweet potatoes are tender.

4. Use a slotted spoon to move the vegetables and meat to a serving platter. Tent with foil or otherwise cover and keep warm. Allow the meat to rest for 15 minutes before you carve it, slicing it against the grain.

A Touch More Cinnamon?

Taste the broth at the end of Step 2. That's the ideal time to add more ground cloves and cinnamon to taste if you think it could use more.

BEEF TZIMMES

Tzimmes are served at many Jewish holidays.

Serves 8

INGREDIENTS:

2 tablespoons vegetable oil

1 medium onion, peeled and diced

2 pounds beef stew meat, cut into 1" cubes

2 cups kosher beef broth

2 tablespoons tomato paste

1 tablespoon minced fresh rosemary

2 carrots, peeled and cut into 1" chunks

2 sweet potatoes, peeled and cut into 1" chunks

1 cup prunes, cut into halves

1 (8-ounce) can pineapple chunks or tidbits, drained

1 teaspoon kosher salt

¼ teaspoon black pepper

1. Heat oil in a large skillet. Sauté onion for 5 minutes or until it softens and starts to brown. Transfer to a 4- or 6-quart slow cooker and set aside.

2. Add meat cubes to skillet and brown for 3 minutes per side. Transfer to slow cooker and add all remaining ingredients except salt and pepper.

3. Cover and cook on low for 8–10 hours. Add salt and pepper. Taste and add more if needed.

MATZOH BALL SOUP

Although it is not strictly traditional, adding dill or parsley to the matzoh balls adds a fresh note to this slow-cooked soup.

Serves 6

INGREDIENTS:

2 quarts kosher chicken stock

1 stalk celery, diced

2 carrots, cut into coin-sized pieces

1 parsnip, diced

1 onion, diced

1½ cups diced cooked chicken

2 tablespoons vegetable oil

2 large eggs, slightly beaten

½ cup matzoh meal

2 tablespoons seltzer

1 teaspoon kosher salt

1½ tablespoons minced fresh dill or parsley

1. Put the stock, celery, carrots, parsnip, and onion into a 4-quart slow cooker. Cook on low for 6–8 hours. Add the chicken 1 hour before serving.

2. About 45 minutes before serving, mix the oil, eggs, matzoh meal, seltzer, salt, and dill (or parsley) in a large bowl until matzoh meal is completely moistened. Refrigerate mixture for 15 minutes.

3. Rinse hands in cold water (repeat as necessary), then form mixture into 1" balls. Drop them into the soup, cover, and cook for 20 minutes.

Matzoh Meal Year-Round

Leftover matzoh meal can be used year-round. Use in place of crushed crackers or bread crumbs to bread fish or chicken before frying, for Chanukah potato latkes, or in meatballs.

CHANUKAH CARROT "COINS"

These "coins" are a play on the chocolate gelt (money) children receive for Chanukah.

Serves 4

INGREDIENTS:

Cooking spray

1 pound carrots, peeled and sliced into ¼"-thick coins

½ cup orange marmalade

2 tablespoons orange juice

2 tablespoons honey

2 tablespoons unsalted butter or margarine, melted

¼ teaspoon ground ginger

½ teaspoon ground cinnamon

½ teaspoon kosher salt

1. Lightly spray the inside of a 4-quart slow cooker with cooking spray. Add carrots and set aside.

2. In a small bowl whisk together the remaining ingredients. Pour over carrots. Cover and cook on high for 4 hours.

LAG B'OMER SWEET AND SOUR RED CABBAGE

This cabbage dish is great alongside barbecued foods.

Serves 6

INGREDIENTS:

½ head red cabbage, shredded

1 medium onion, shredded

1½ tablespoons dark brown sugar

1 teaspoon margarine

¼ cup water

½ cup apple cider vinegar

1 tablespoon white wine vinegar

½ teaspoon freshly ground black pepper

¼ teaspoon salt

⅛ teaspoon ground cloves

½ teaspoon thyme

1. Place all ingredients into a 4-quart slow cooker. Stir to distribute all ingredients evenly.

2. Cook on low for 4–6 hours or until the cabbage is very soft. Stir before serving.

Lag B'Omer

Lag B'Omer is the 33rd day of the Omer (the counting of the 49 days from the second night of Passover to the day before Shavuot). Thousands of students of Rabbi Akiva, a great rabbi of the Torah, died from a great plague that occurred during one such counting of the Omer. Lag B'Omer commemorates the one day when no one died. It is celebrated with outdoor activities such as picnics, barbecues, and bonfires.

PASSOVER POTATOES AU GRATIN

Serve this dairy dish with a simple salad for lunch.

Serves 4

INGREDIENTS:

Cooking spray

2 tablespoons margarine, divided

1 medium onion, peeled and diced

1 (5-ounce) box scalloped potatoes (any variety)

2 cups hot water

4 ounces Cheddar or Swiss cheese (or a combination of both), shredded

1. Spray the inside of a 4-quart slow cooker with cooking spray.

2. Melt margarine in a sauté pan over medium-high heat. Add diced onion. Cook, stirring occasionally, until onions soften and start to brown, about 5–8 minutes. Transfer to prepared slow cooker.

3. Add the potatoes and sprinkle the seasoning mix over the top of them. Dot with the remaining margarine. Pour in the water. Cover and cook on low for 5 hours.

4. Uncover and sprinkle on the cheese. Re-cover and continue to cook for another 15 minutes or until cheese has melted.

PASSOVER SCALLOPED CHICKEN

Here's an easy meal that's delicious enough to serve year-round.

Serves 4

INGREDIENTS:

Cooking spray

2 tablespoons margarine, divided

1 medium onion, peeled and diced

1 (5-ounce) box scalloped potatoes (any variety)

1 cup cooked diced chicken

2 cups hot water

1. Spray the inside of a 4-quart slow cooker with cooking spray.

2. Melt margarine in a sauté pan over medium-high heat. Add diced onion. Cook, stirring occasionally, until onions soften and start to brown, about 5–8 minutes. Transfer to prepared slow cooker.

3. Add the potatoes and sprinkle the seasoning mix over the top of them. Spread the chicken on top of the potatoes. Dot with remaining margarine. Pour in the water. Cover and cook on low for 5 hours.

POTATO KUGEL

Kugel means pudding, sweet or savory, with or without noodles. This version is a noodle-free savory version.

Serves 8

INGREDIENTS:

Cooking spray

6 Yukon gold potatoes, peeled and grated

1 medium onion, diced

½ cup boiling water

3 eggs

1 teaspoon kosher salt

¼ teaspoon black pepper

1 teaspoon pareve chicken bouillon powder

2 tablespoons vegetable oil

1. Spray the inside of a 4-quart slow cooker with cooking spray.

2. In a large mixing bowl, combine the grated potatoes, diced onion, and boiling water. Transfer to prepared slow cooker.

3. In the same mixing bowl, whisk together the eggs, salt, pepper, bouillon powder, and oil. Stir egg mixture into potato mixture.

4. Cover slow cooker and cook on high for 1 hour, then on low for 6–8 more hours.

ALMOND CAKE WITH HONEY LEMON SYRUP

The long cooking time softens up the matzoh meal.

Serves 12

INGREDIENTS:

HONEY LEMON SYRUP

¼ cup honey

2 tablespoons granulated sugar

¼ cup water

2 tablespoons fresh lemon juice

ALMOND CAKE

Cooking spray

1 (6-ounce) package ground almonds

½ cup matzoh cake meal

1 cup sugar, divided

1 teaspoon ground cinnamon

¼ teaspoon kosher salt

4 large eggs, room temperature

2 tablespoons fresh lemon juice

1 teaspoon grated lemon peel

¼ cup vegetable oil

¼ cup sliced almonds

1. Make the Honey Lemon Syrup: Heat honey, sugar, water, and lemon juice in a 1-quart saucepan over medium-high heat, stirring constantly until sugar is dissolved. Bring to a boil, then remove from heat and let cool. Set aside.

2. Line a 4-quart slow cooker with aluminum foil, allowing the foil to come at least 4" up the sides. Spray with cooking spray. Set aside.

3. In a medium bowl, whisk together the ground almonds, matzoh cake meal, ½ cup sugar, cinnamon, and salt. Set aside.

4. In a large bowl, using an electric mixer on medium speed, beat the eggs, remaining ½ cup sugar, lemon juice, and grated lemon peel for 2 minutes, then increase to high speed (for handheld mixer) or medium-high speed (for a stand mixer such as KitchenAid) for 6–8 more minutes until batter turns pale in color and thickens. Reduce speed back to medium and beat in vegetable oil for another minute. Use a spatula to fold in dry mixture until completely moistened.

5. Scrape batter into prepared slow cooker. Cook on high for 2–2½ hours or until cake starts to pull away from sides of pan and a toothpick inserted into center comes out clean.

6. Holding foil by edges, lift and remove cake from slow cooker; place on cooling rack. Let cool for 10 minutes; cake will sink slightly. Carefully peel foil from cake and place on serving dish. Slice cake into 12 squares. Sprinkle evenly with sliced almonds. Spoon cooled syrup over cake. Let cake absorb syrup for 30 minutes before serving.

NEW YORK–STYLE CHEESECAKE

Making cheesecake in the slow cooker might sound odd, but it is actually the perfect appliance for the job. The constant low heat and moist environment keep it from drying out or cracking, even when using low-fat ingredients.

Serves 8

INGREDIENTS:

¾ cup low-fat chocolate or cinnamon graham cracker crumbs

1½ tablespoons butter, melted

8 ounces sour cream, at room temperature

8 ounces cream cheese, at room temperature

⅔ cup sugar

1 egg, at room temperature

2 teaspoons vanilla extract

1½ tablespoons flour

1 tablespoon lemon juice

1 tablespoon lemon zest

1 cup hot water

1. In a small bowl, mix together the graham cracker crumbs and butter. Press into the bottom and sides of a 6" springform pan.

2. In a large bowl, mix the sour cream, cream cheese, sugar, egg, vanilla, flour, lemon juice, and zest until completely smooth. Pour into the springform pan.

3. Pour the water into the bottom of a 6-quart slow cooker. Place a trivet in the bottom of the slow cooker. Place the springform pan onto the trivet.

4. Cook on low for 2 hours. Turn off the slow cooker and let the cheesecake steam for 1 hour and 15 minutes with the lid on. Remove the cheesecake from the slow cooker. Refrigerate for 6 hours or overnight before serving.

Shavuot and Dairy Products

Shavuot celebrates the giving of the Torah to the Jewish people. Dairy foods, a symbol of modesty, were considered appropriate for such a celebration.

SUKKOT APPLE AND PEAR SPREAD

Make the most of in-season apples and pears in this easy alternative to apple or pear butter.

Yields 3 quarts

INGREDIENTS:

4 Winesap apples, cored and sliced

4 Bartlett pears, cored and sliced

1 cup water or pear cider

¼ packed cup brown sugar

¼ cup sugar

¼ teaspoon ginger

¼ teaspoon cinnamon

¼ teaspoon nutmeg

¼ teaspoon allspice

1. Place all ingredients into a 4-quart slow cooker. Cook on low for 10–12 hours.

2. Uncover and cook on low for an additional 10–12 hours or until thick and most of the liquid has evaporated.

3. Allow to cool completely, then pour into the food processor and purée. Pour into clean glass jars. Refrigerate for up to 6 weeks.

Sukkot

Sukkot is a fall harvest festival. Jewish people celebrate by eating most, if not all, their meals in small outdoor huts (called sukkahs or sukkot), symbolizing the tents workers lived in while harvesting foods.

MATZOH CHEESE KUGEL

Don't substitute matzoh farfel for the crumbled matzoh, because the small pieces will "melt" into the cheese.

Serves 4–6

INGREDIENTS:

Cooking spray

6 matzohs

5 eggs

¾ cup milk, regular or low-fat

¼ cup half-and-half

1 pound small-curd cottage cheese

1 teaspoon kosher salt

¼ cup granulated sugar, plus another ¼ cup for garnish

1 teaspoon ground cinnamon

3 tablespoons butter, melted

1. Spray the inside of a 4-quart slow cooker with cooking spray.

2. Coarsely crumble matzohs into small pieces, ½" or less; place in the slow cooker and set aside.

3. In a large mixing bowl, whisk together the eggs, the milk, and the half-and-half.

4. Then add in the cottage cheese, salt, ¼ cup of the sugar, cinnamon, and melted butter and use a spatula to combine. Pour mixture evenly over matzoh pieces. Do not stir. Use a spatula if necessary to make sure the matzoh pieces are moistened.

5. Cover and cook on low for 3 hours. Turn off cooker, set cover slightly ajar, and let center firm up for 15–30 minutes. Serve warm, sprinkled with additional sugar.

CHAPTER 18

GLUTEN-FREE OPTIONS

GLUTEN-FREE BLUEBERRY FRENCH TOAST CASSEROLE

Store-bought gluten-free bread is too expensive to waste if it becomes stale. This recipe shows you how to make a frugal but delicious breakfast or dessert using leftover or stale gluten-free bread.

Serves 6

INGREDIENTS:

7 cups gluten-free bread, cubed

1⅓ cups almond milk

5 eggs, whisked

1 tablespoon vanilla

1 tablespoon maple syrup

½ teaspoon salt

2 tablespoons butter (melted) or coconut oil

2 teaspoons cinnamon

3 tablespoons sugar

1½ cups blueberries, fresh or frozen

1. In a large bowl mix together the cubed gluten-free bread, almond milk, whisked eggs, vanilla, maple syrup, and salt.

2. Pour mixture into a greased 4-quart slow cooker.

3. Drizzle melted butter or coconut oil over the casserole. Sprinkle cinnamon and sugar evenly over the bread. Top with blueberries.

4. Cover slow cooker and vent with a wooden spoon handle or chopstick. Cook on high for 2½–3 hours or on low for 5–6 hours.

5. Remove lid and allow liquids to evaporate the last 20 minutes of cooking. Serve warm.

GLUTEN-FREE BREAKFAST GRANOLA

Finding gluten-free granola can be a challenge in most grocery stores, but it's super easy to make your own in the slow cooker. Make sure to stir the ingredients about every 30 minutes to prevent uneven cooking or overbrowning.

Serves 10

INGREDIENTS:

2½ cups gluten-free rolled oats

¼ cup ground flaxseeds

½ cup unsweetened shredded coconut

½ cup pumpkin seeds

½ cup walnuts, chopped

½ cup sliced almonds

1 cup dried cranberries

¾ cup brown sugar

⅓ cup coconut oil

¼ cup honey

½ teaspoon salt

1 teaspoon ground cinnamon

1. Mix all ingredients together and place in a greased 4-quart slow cooker.

2. Cover slow cooker and vent with a wooden spoon handle or a chopstick. Cook on high for 4 hours, or on low for 8 hours, stirring every hour or so.

3. When granola is toasty and done, pour it onto a cookie sheet that has been lined with parchment paper. Spread the granola out evenly over the entire sheet of parchment paper. Allow granola to cool and dry for several hours.

4. Once cooled, break granola up and place in an airtight container or a tightly sealed glass jar and store in pantry for up to 1 month. For longer storage keep granola in freezer for up to 6 months.

Change It Up

Don't like pumpkin seeds, walnuts, or dried cranberries? Use the seeds, nuts, and dried fruit that you prefer in your own granola. Use raisins, sunflower seeds, cocoa nibs, dried cranberries, or even dried bananas. The different variations are endless. You can even add chocolate chips if you'd like, but only after the granola has been cooked and cooled!

GLUTEN-FREE PULL-APART CINNAMON RAISIN BISCUITS

Who ever thought you could make gluten-free biscuits in the slow cooker? Well you can and they turn out light and soft with a perfect crumb! To prevent the biscuits on the edge from browning too quickly you can line the slow cooker with parchment paper.

Serves 9

INGREDIENTS:

1 cup brown rice flour

1 cup arrowroot starch

1 tablespoon baking powder

1 teaspoon xanthan gum

½ teaspoon salt

⅓ cup sugar

½ teaspoon ground cinnamon

⅓ cup vegetable shortening

2 eggs

¾ cup whole milk

½ cup raisins

1. In a large bowl whisk together the brown rice flour, arrowroot starch, baking powder, xanthan gum, salt, sugar, and cinnamon.

2. Cut in the vegetable shortening using a fork and knife, until it resembles small peas within the gluten-free flour mixture.

3. In a small bowl whisk together eggs and milk. Pour into the flour mixture and mix with a fork to combine, until the dough is like a very thick, sticky cake batter. Fold in the raisins.

4. Grease a 4-quart slow cooker and/or line with parchment paper.

5. Drop biscuit dough in balls about the size of a golf ball into the bottom of the greased slow cooker. The biscuits will touch each other and may fit quite snugly.

6. Cover slow cooker and vent lid with the handle of a wooden spoon or a chopstick. Cook biscuits on high for about 2–2½ hours or on low for around 4–4½ hours. Biscuits around the edge of the slow cooker will be more brown than those in the center. The biscuits should have doubled in size during cooking. The biscuits are done when a toothpick inserted in the center of the middle biscuit comes out clean.

7. Turn the slow cooker off and remove the insert to a heat-safe surface such as the stovetop or on top of potholders. Allow the biscuits to cool for several minutes before removing from slow cooker insert. They will "pull apart" individually.

Quick Vanilla Glaze

Impress your family by making a quick powdered sugar glaze for these lightly sweetened biscuits/buns. Mix together 1 cup of powdered sugar with 1½ tablespoons of water or milk and ½ teaspoon of vanilla extract. Drizzle artistically over warm buns and serve immediately.

GLUTEN-FREE CORN BREAD

When you're gluten-free one of the hardest foods to replace can be bread. This easy recipe for gluten-free corn bread is baked right in your slow cooker. Perfect as a side for weeknight meals or to use in stuffing for the holidays!

Serves 12

INGREDIENTS:

⅓ cup brown rice flour

⅔ cup arrowroot starch

⅔ cup gluten-free cornmeal

1 teaspoon xanthan gum

2 teaspoons baking powder

½ teaspoon salt

3 tablespoons sugar

¼ cup oil

2 eggs

1 cup milk or dairy-free substitute

1. In a large bowl whisk together brown rice flour, arrowroot starch, and cornmeal. Add xanthan gum, baking powder, salt, and sugar. Mix together thoroughly.

2. In a smaller bowl mix together the oil, eggs, and milk or dairy-free substitute.

3. Mix wet ingredients into dry ingredients with a fork, until you have a thick batter.

4. Grease 3 emptied and cleaned (15-ounce) aluminum cans and place ⅓ of the corn bread batter into each can. The cans will be about half full.

5. Place the cans in a 4-quart slow cooker. Pour ½ cup of water around the cans.

6. Cover the slow cooker and vent the lid with a chopstick. Cook on high for 3–3½ hours or on low for 6–7 hours. Bread should rise and double in size and become golden brown on top when done.

7. Remove cans of bread carefully from slow cooker and allow bread to cool before removing from cans. Slice each loaf into 4 round pieces of bread. Serve warm.

Gluten-Free Cornmeal

Many companies that process cornmeal also make mixes that include wheat flour. It's important to find a company that makes cornmeal that has been tested to have less than 20 ppm (parts per million) of gluten. This recipe was tested using Bob's Red Mill brand gluten-free cornmeal.

GLUTEN-FREE SWEET AND SOUR MINI HOT DOG SNACKERS

Sometimes it can be difficult to make sure certain brands of sandwich meats and hot dogs are gluten-free. To make it easier, instead of searching high and low for mini gluten-free hot dogs, simply use a brand of regular gluten-free hot dogs you trust and cut them into bite-sized pieces.

Serves 4

INGREDIENTS:

1 package gluten-free hot dogs, cut into bite-sized pieces

½ cup grape jelly

½ cup gluten-free barbecue sauce

2 tablespoons orange juice

½ teaspoon ground white pepper

1 tablespoon gluten-free Worcestershire sauce

½ teaspoon ground mustard

1. Place cut-up hot dogs into a greased 2.5-quart slow cooker.

2. In a bowl mix together the jelly, barbecue sauce, orange juice, pepper, Worcestershire sauce, and mustard. Pour over the hot dogs in the slow cooker.

3. Cover and cook on high for 3–4 hours or on low for 6–8 hours.

GLUTEN-FREE "SHAKE IT AND BAKE IT" DRUMSTICKS

Remember that wonderful chicken seasoning from your childhood? You can now make it gluten-free for crispy chicken drumsticks right in your slow cooker!

Serves 6

INGREDIENTS:

1 cup gluten-free corn tortilla chips, finely crushed

1½ tablespoons olive oil

½ teaspoon salt

½ teaspoon paprika

¼ teaspoon celery seeds

¼ teaspoon ground black pepper

¼ teaspoon garlic powder

½ teaspoon dried onion flakes

¼ teaspoon dried basil

¼ teaspoon dried parsley

¼ teaspoon dried oregano

6 chicken drumsticks

1. In a heavy-duty gallon-sized zip-top bag mix together the seasoning ingredients: crushed tortilla chips, olive oil, salt, paprika, celery seeds, pepper, garlic powder, onion flakes, basil, parsley, and oregano.

2. To prepare the slow cooker either wrap 4 to 5 small potatoes in foil and place them in the bottom of a greased 4-quart slow cooker, or make 4 to 5 foil balls about the size of a small potato and place them in the bottom of the slow cooker. (This will help the chicken to get a little bit crispy in the slow cooker instead of cooking in its juices.)

3. Place 2 drumsticks in the bag with the seasoning mix, seal it tightly, and shake the bag to coat the chicken. Place coated chicken drumsticks on top of the foil balls. Repeat with remaining drumsticks, 2 at a time.

4. Cover slow cooker and vent the lid with a chopstick to help release extra moisture. Cook on high for 4 hours or on low for 8 hours.

Make It and Shake It for Later

Double or triple the batch of the seasoned coating ingredients so in the future you can prepare this delicious gluten-free appetizer or light meal in a snap.

GLUTEN-FREE LASAGNA WITH SPINACH

There is no need to precook the gluten-free noodles in this recipe.

Serves 10

INGREDIENTS:

28 ounces low-fat ricotta cheese

1 cup defrosted and drained frozen cut spinach

1 egg

½ cup part-skim shredded mozzarella cheese

8 cups (about 2 jars) marinara sauce

½ pound uncooked gluten-free lasagna noodles

1. In a medium bowl, stir the ricotta, spinach, egg, and mozzarella.

2. Ladle a quarter of the marinara sauce along the bottom of a greased 6-quart slow cooker. The bottom should be thoroughly covered in sauce. Add a single layer of lasagna noodles on top of the sauce, breaking noodles if needed to fit in the sides.

3. Ladle an additional quarter of sauce over the noodles, covering all of the noodles. Top with half of the cheese mixture, pressing firmly with the back of a spoon to smooth. Add a single layer of lasagna noodles on top of the cheese, breaking noodles if needed to fit in the sides.

4. Ladle another quarter of the sauce on top of the noodles, and top with the remaining cheese. Press another layer of noodles onto the cheese and top with the remaining sauce. Take care that the noodles are entirely covered in sauce.

5. Cover and cook for 4–6 hours until cooked through.

GLUTEN-FREE EASY ITALIAN SPAGHETTI

It doesn't get any easier than this. Because this meal cooks so quickly, you can put it together as soon as you get home from work.

Serves 4

INGREDIENTS:

1 pound ground beef, browned

1 (16-ounce) jar marinara sauce

1 cup water

8 ounces gluten-free pasta, uncooked

½ cup grated Parmesan cheese

1. Add browned ground beef, marinara sauce, and water to a greased 4-quart slow cooker. Cook on high for 2 hours or on low for 4 hours. 45 minutes prior to serving stir dry gluten-free pasta into meat sauce. The pasta will cook in the sauce. Serve with Parmesan cheese sprinkled on top of each serving.

GLUTEN-FREE RETRO TUNA PASTA CASSEROLE

The popular tuna casserole can now be made gluten-free! In this recipe the pasta is cooked separately, so it doesn't become overcooked in the casserole.

Serves 4

INGREDIENTS:

2 cans water-packed white tuna, drained and flaked

1 cup heavy cream

¾ cup mayonnaise

4 hard-boiled eggs, chopped

1 cup finely diced celery

½ cup finely minced onion

1 cup frozen garden peas

¼ teaspoon ground black pepper

1½ cups crushed potato chips, divided

2 cups gluten-free pasta, cooked

1. In a large bowl combine tuna, cream, mayonnaise, eggs, celery, onion, peas, ground pepper, and ¾ cup crushed potato chips.

2. Pour tuna mixture into a greased 4-quart slow cooker. Top with remaining potato chips. Cover and cook on low for 3 hours or on high for 1½ hours.

3. To serve: Place tuna casserole on top of ½ cup of pasta per person.

GLUTEN-FREE BISCUIT-TOPPED CHICKEN PIE

Pure comfort food! This creamy chicken and vegetable pie is topped with homemade gluten-free buttermilk drop biscuits. To make the pie extra rich, drizzle a few tablespoons of melted butter over the biscuit topping right before cooking.

Serves 6

INGREDIENTS:

4 tablespoons brown rice flour

4 tablespoons butter

1 cup whole milk

1 cup gluten-free chicken broth

1 teaspoon salt

½ teaspoon ground black pepper

2 cups cooked chicken breast, cut or torn into bite-sized pieces

1 (12-ounce) can mixed vegetables, drained

1 prepared batch of dough for Gluten-Free Buttermilk Drop Biscuits (this chapter)

1. In a small saucepan over medium heat, whisk together flour and butter. When butter has melted, slowly stir in milk, chicken broth, salt, and pepper. Cook on medium heat for 5–10 minutes, whisking constantly until mixture is thick, with a gravy consistency.

2. Add chicken and vegetables to a greased 4-quart slow cooker. Pour cream soup mixture into the slow cooker and mix with chicken and vegetables.

3. Using an ice cream scoop, drop biscuit dough over chicken, vegetables, and sauce.

4. Cover slow cooker and vent lid with a chopstick. Cook on high for 3–4 hours or on low for 6–8 hours until chicken sauce is bubbling up around the biscuits, and the biscuits are cooked through.

Gluten-Free Baking Mixes

Instead of homemade biscuits, you can also use your favorite gluten-free biscuit baking mix. It must be an all-purpose mix that includes xanthan gum and a leavening ingredient such as baking powder or baking soda. Use a recipe on the package that will make 8–10 gluten-free biscuits as a topping for chicken pie.

GLUTEN-FREE CHICKEN ALFREDO PASTA

Quartered artichokes add a tangy flavor to this easy pasta casserole.

Serves 4

INGREDIENTS:

1 pound boneless skinless chicken thighs, cut into ¾-inch pieces

1 (14-ounce) can quartered artichokes, drained

1 (16-ounce) jar gluten-free Alfredo pasta sauce

1 cup water

½ cup sun-dried tomatoes, drained and chopped

8 ounces gluten-free pasta, uncooked

2 tablespoons shredded Parmesan cheese

1. In a greased 4-quart slow cooker, mix chicken, artichokes, Alfredo sauce, and water. Cover and cook on high for 3 hours or on low for 6 hours.

2. 45 minutes before serving, stir tomatoes and uncooked pasta into chicken mixture.

3. Cover lid and continue to cook until pasta is al dente. Sprinkle Parmesan cheese over individual servings.

Make Your Own Alfredo Sauce

Most Alfredo sauces are naturally gluten-free: They're usually made with butter, cheese, cream, and spices. To make your own, whisk together over medium heat: ½ cup butter, 8 ounces of light cream cheese, 1 cup whole milk or half-and-half, ⅓ cup Parmesan cheese, and 1 tablespoon of garlic powder. Allow the mixture to cool. It will thicken as it cools.

GLUTEN-FREE CHEESY POTATO WEDGES

Who doesn't like fries? Kids are especially fond of these salty, usually crispy treats. While these potatoes don't crisp up as much as fried ones, they are definitely a salty, cheesy, and delicious treat that's much healthier than fast food!

Serves 4

INGREDIENTS:

2 pounds red potatoes

2 teaspoons dried onions

1 teaspoon oregano

½ teaspoon garlic salt

½ teaspoon black pepper

2 tablespoons olive oil

¼ cup grated Parmesan cheese

1. Wash and scrub potatoes. Pat dry and cut into ½" wedges.

2. Place dried onions, oregano, garlic salt, and pepper in a gallon-sized zip-top bag. Add the potatoes to the bag and shake to coat the potatoes.

3. Pour the potatoes into a greased 4-quart slow cooker. Drizzle with olive oil.

4. Cover and cook on high for 4 hours or on low for 6–8 hours. Midway through the cooking process lift the lid of the slow cooker and carefully pour out any liquids that have collected at the bottom. Cover and resume cooking until potatoes are fork tender.

5. Place potatoes on a platter and sprinkle with Parmesan cheese and additional salt and pepper if needed.

GLUTEN-FREE SHORTCUT CHICKEN PARMESAN

With a savory Italian sauce and lots of gooey mozzarella cheese, you'll never miss the breading in this recipe! Serve it with gluten-free garlic bread and steamed broccoli.

Serves 4

INGREDIENTS:

2 pounds boneless, skinless chicken breasts

1 (15-ounce) can tomato sauce

1 (4-ounce) can tomato paste

1 tablespoon Italian seasoning

½ teaspoon dried basil

½ teaspoon garlic powder

½ teaspoon salt

½ teaspoon ground pepper

2 cups shredded mozzarella

½ cup grated Parmesan cheese

1. Place chicken in the bottom of a greased 4-quart slow cooker.

2. In a large bowl mix together tomato sauce, tomato paste, Italian seasoning, basil, garlic powder, salt, and pepper. Pour sauce over chicken. Cook on high for 3–4 hours or on low for 5–6 hours.

3. An hour prior to serving sprinkle cheeses on top of the tomato sauce. Cook for 45 minutes to an hour until cheeses are melted and gooey.

GLUTEN-FREE SLOW COOKER YEAST BREAD

Did you know you can make gluten-free sandwich bread right in your slow cooker? If using the loaf pan for this bread, make sure to use the size recommended in the recipe. Otherwise, your bread can rise too high and then fall while baking.

Serves 12

INGREDIENTS:

⅓ cup arrowroot starch

⅓ cup blanched almond flour

3 tablespoons millet flour

1½ cups brown rice flour

1 teaspoon salt

1 tablespoon xanthan gum

2 teaspoons bread machine yeast (try: Saf, Red Star, or Fleischmann's)

3 tablespoons sugar

1 egg, plus 2 egg whites, room temperature

1⅓ cups whole milk, heated to 110°F

3 tablespoons olive oil

1. In a large bowl whisk together arrowroot starch, blanched almond flour, millet flour, brown rice flour, salt, xanthan gum, yeast, and sugar.

2. In a smaller bowl whisk together the egg, egg whites, milk, and oil.

3. Pour wet ingredients into whisked dry ingredients. Stir with a wooden spoon or a fork for several minutes until dough resembles a thick cake batter. First it will look like biscuit dough, but after a few minutes it will appear thick and sticky.

4. Line an 8½" × 4½" metal or glass loaf pan with parchment paper or spray with nonstick cooking spray. Pour bread dough into the pan. Using a spatula that's been dipped in water or coated with oil or nonstick cooking spray, spread the dough evenly in the pan. Continue to use the spatula to smooth out the top of the bread dough. Place the loaf pan in a 6-quart or larger oval slow cooker.

5. Cover the slow cooker and vent the lid with a chopstick or the handle of a wooden spoon. Cook on high for 3½–4 hours. The bread will rise and bake at the same time. The bread should be about double in size and the sides should be a light golden brown; the bread will not "brown" as much as it would in the oven.

6. Remove the bread from the pan and cool on a wire rack. Slice and keep in an airtight plastic bag on the counter for 2 days. Freeze any remaining bread.

Free-Form Oval Bread

If you don't have a large 6-quart slow cooker, simply line a 2.5-quart or a 4-quart slow cooker with parchment paper. Spray it with non-stick cooking spray. Coat your hands or a large spoon with cooking spray or olive oil and shape the dough into an oval loaf. Place loaf in the middle of the parchment paper and bake. You will need to keep a close eye on the loaf as it can burn around the edges since it's closer to the heating element.

GLUTEN-FREE SLOW COOKER YEAST ROLLS

This recipe proves how versatile gluten-free yeast dough can be, even in the slow cooker! You will need 2 4-quart slow cookers or 1 6-quart slow cooker for this recipe.

Serves 12

INGREDIENTS:

1 recipe Gluten-Free Slow Cooker Yeast Bread dough (in this chapter)

3 tablespoons olive oil or melted butter

½ teaspoon garlic powder

½ teaspoon toasted sesame seeds

½ teaspoon Italian seasoning

1. Using an ice cream scoop, scoop dough into 12 balls and place each ball in a greased cupcake liner. Place the cupcake liners on the bottom of one large or two smaller slow cookers.

2. Brush rolls with melted butter and sprinkle garlic powder, sesame seeds, and/or Italian seasoning over the tops.

3. Cover and vent the lid with a chopstick or the handle of a wooden spoon. Cook on high for 1½–2½ hours until dough has almost doubled in size and the rolls are cooked through. You will need to watch the rolls at the end of the cooking period as they can get overdone on the edges since they are so close to the cooking element.

Drop Rolls

Instead of using cupcake liners you can simply line the slow cooker with parchment paper. Spray the parchment paper with nonstick cooking spray and drop the scoops of dough onto the parchment paper. Bake as directed.

GLUTEN-FREE BUTTERMILK DROP BISCUITS

Buttermilk adds a tangy flavor to these fluffy gluten-free biscuits.

Serves 12

INGREDIENTS:

2 cups brown rice flour

¼ cup sorghum flour

½ cup arrowroot starch

¼ cup potato starch or cornstarch

2 tablespoons sugar

4 teaspoons baking powder

1 teaspoon salt

1 teaspoon baking soda

1 teaspoon xanthan gum

½ cup chilled butter

1¼ cups buttermilk

1 egg

1. In a large bowl whisk together all dry ingredients. Cut butter into the dry ingredients with two knives or with a pastry cutter until it resembles small peas throughout the dry ingredients.

2. In a smaller bowl mix together buttermilk and egg. Pour buttermilk mixture into the dry ingredients and mix with a fork. Biscuit dough will be slightly stiff when thoroughly mixed.

3. Line a 6-quart slow cooker with parchment paper and spray it with nonstick cooking spray.

4. Using an ice cream scoop, scoop out 10–12 drop biscuits and place them on the parchment paper on the bottom of the slow cooker.

5. Cover and vent the lid of the slow cooker with a chopstick or the end of a wooden spoon. Cook on high for 2–2½ hours until the biscuits have risen by about half and are cooked through.

Dairy-Free "Buttermilk"

For a dairy-free buttermilk alternative mix 2 tablespoons of lemon juice or apple cider vinegar with 1¼ cups almond milk or coconut milk.

GLUTEN-FREE CHOCOLATE BREAD PUDDING

Fat-free evaporated milk gives this bread pudding a creamy texture, but it has several dozen fewer calories than heavy cream.

Serves 10

INGREDIENTS:

4 cups cubed gluten-free bread, day-old and toasted

2⅓ cups fat-free evaporated milk

2 eggs

⅓ cup light brown sugar

¼ cup cocoa

1 teaspoon vanilla extract

1. Grease a 4-quart slow cooker with nonstick cooking spray. Add the bread cubes.

2. In a medium bowl, whisk the evaporated milk, eggs, brown sugar, cocoa, and vanilla until the sugar and cocoa are dissolved. Pour over the bread cubes.

3. Cover and cook on low for 5 hours or until the pudding no longer looks wet.

CHAPTER 19

SOUPS

CHICKEN BROTH

When you remove the meat from the bones, save the dark meat for use in a casserole and the white meat for chicken salad. (To keep the chicken moist, return it to the strained broth and let it cool overnight in the refrigerator before you chop it for the salad.)

Yields 4 cups

INGREDIENTS:

3 pounds bone-in chicken pieces

1 large onion, peeled and quartered

2 large carrots, scrubbed

2 stalks celery

1 teaspoon salt

½ teaspoon freshly ground black pepper

4½ cups water

1. Add the chicken pieces and onion to a 4–6-quart slow cooker.

2. Slice the carrot and cut the celery into pieces that will fit in the slow cooker and add them. Add the salt, pepper, and water. Cover and cook on low for 6–8 hours. (Cooking time will depend on the size of the chicken pieces.) Allow to cool to room temperature.

3. Strain, discarding the cooked vegetables. Remove any meat from the chicken bones and save for another use. Refrigerate the (cooled) broth overnight. Remove and discard the hardened fat. The resulting concentrated broth can be kept for 1 or 2 days in the refrigerator or frozen for up to 3 months.

Schmaltz

The chicken fat that will rise to the top of the broth and harden overnight in the refrigerator is known as schmaltz. You can save that fat and use it instead of butter for sautéing vegetables.

TURKEY BROTH

This method makes a concentrated turkey broth. The amount of concentration will depend on how much meat is on the turkey wings and the amount of time you simmer them in the water. As a general rule, for regular turkey broth you can usually mix ½ cup of this broth with ½ cup water.

Yields about 4 cups

INGREDIENTS:

3 pounds bone-in turkey wings

1 large onion, peeled and quartered

2 large carrots, scrubbed

2 stalks celery

Salt and freshly ground black pepper, to taste

4½ cups water

1. Add the turkey and onion to the slow cooker. Slice the carrot and cut the celery into pieces that will fit in the slow cooker and add them. Add the salt, pepper, and water. Cover and cook on low for 6–8 hours. (Cooking time will depend on the size of the turkey wings.) Allow to cool to room temperature.

2. Strain, discarding the cooked vegetables. Remove any meat from the bones and save for another use; discard the skin. Refrigerate the (cooled) broth overnight. Remove and discard the hardened fat. The resulting concentrated broth can be kept for 1 or 2 days in the refrigerator or frozen for up to 3 months.

Saving Time Later

Lightly coat pieces of turkey skin in all-purpose flour. Fry the skin in oil or butter in a nonstick skillet for about 6 minutes or until it's crispy. Add to the slow cooker along with the other ingredients for the broth. Use the resulting broth when you want to impart the added flavor achieved from browning turkey pieces, but want to skip that step before adding the turkey to the slow cooker.

BEEF BROTH

Unlike chicken or turkey broth, beef broth requires a larger ratio of meat to the amount of bones used to make it. This method makes a concentrated broth. As a general rule, for regular beef broth you can usually mix ½ cup of this broth with ½ cup water.

Yields about 4 cups

INGREDIENTS:

1 (2-pound) bone-in chuck roast

1 pound beef bones

1 large onion, peeled and quartered

2 large carrots, scrubbed

2 stalks celery

1 teaspoon salt

½ teaspoon freshly ground black pepper

4½ cups water

1. Add the chuck roast, beef bones, and onion to a 4-quart or larger slow cooker. Slice the carrots and cut the celery into pieces that will fit in the slow cooker and add them. Add the salt, pepper, and water. Cover and cook on low for 8 hours.

2. Use a slotted spoon to remove the roast and beef bones. Reserve the roast and the meat removed from the bones for another use; discard the bones.

3. Once the broth has cooled enough to make it easier to handle, strain it; discard the cooked vegetables. Refrigerate the (cooled) broth overnight. Remove and discard the hardened fat. The resulting concentrated broth can be kept for 1 or 2 days in the refrigerator or frozen for up to 3 months.

Boiling Broth

You don't want to let broth come to a boil during the initial cooking process because fat will render from the meat, incorporate into the broth, and make it cloudy. However, after you have strained the broth and removed the fat, you can keep it in the refrigerator longer if you bring it to a boil every other day; cool it and return it to the refrigerator until needed.

BROWN STOCK

When you add ¼ cup of this concentrated broth to a slow-cooked beef dish, you'll get the same succulent flavor as if you first seared the meat in a hot skillet before adding it to the slow cooker. The broth also gives a delicious flavor boost to slow-cooked tomato sauce or tomato gravy.

Yield: About 4 cups

INGREDIENTS:

2 large carrots, scrubbed

2 stalks celery

1½ pounds bone-in chuck roast

1½ pounds cracked beef bones

1 large onion, peeled and quartered

Salt and freshly ground black pepper, to taste

4½ cups water

1. Preheat the oven to 450°F. Cut the carrots and celery into large pieces. Put them along with the meat, bones, and onion into a roasting pan. Season with salt and pepper. Put the pan in the middle part of the oven and, turning the meat and vegetables occasionally, roast for 45 minutes or until evenly browned.

2. Transfer the roasted meat, bones, and vegetables to the slow cooker. Add the water to the roasting pan; scrape any browned bits clinging to the pan and then pour the water into the slow cooker. Cover and cook on low for 8 hours. (It may be necessary to skim accumulated fat and scum from the top of the pan juices; check the broth after 4 and 6 hours to see if that's needed.)

3. Use a slotted spoon to remove the roast and beef bones. Reserve the roast and the meat removed from the bones for another use; discard the bones.

4. Once the broth has cooled enough to handle, strain it; discard the cooked vegetables. Refrigerate the (cooled) broth overnight. Remove and discard the hardened fat. The resulting concentrated broth can be kept for 1 or 2 days in the refrigerator, or frozen for up to 3 months.

HAM BROTH

In the same way that adding a ham bone to the cooking liquid for ham and bean soup improves the soup's flavor, ¼ cup of ham broth for every ¾ cup of chicken broth can give a boost to potato soup, too.

Yields about 4 cups

INGREDIENTS:

1 (3-pound) bone-in ham or 3 pounds of ham bones

1 large onion, peeled and quartered

12 baby carrots

2 stalks celery, cut in half

4½ cups water

1. Add all ingredients to a 4–6-quart slow cooker. Cover and cook on low for 6 hours or until the ham pulls away from the bone.

2. Strain; discard the celery and onion. Reserve any ham removed from the bones and the carrots for another use.

3. Once cooled, cover and refrigerate the broth overnight. Remove and discard any hardened fat. The broth can be kept for 1 or 2 days in the refrigerator or frozen up to 3 months.

PORK BROTH

Pork broth is seldom called for in recipes, but it can add layers of flavor when mixed with Chicken and/or Ham Broth (this chapter) in bean or vegetable soups.

Yields about 4 cups

INGREDIENTS:

1 (3-pound) bone-in pork butt roast

1 large onion, peeled and quartered

12 baby carrots

2 stalks celery, cut in half

4½ cups water

1. Add all ingredients to the slow cooker. Cover and cook on low for 6 hours or until the pork is tender and pulls away from the bone.

2. Strain; discard the celery and onion. Reserve the pork roast and carrots for another use. Once cooled, cover and refrigerate the broth overnight. Remove and discard the hardened fat. The broth can be kept for 1 or 2 days in the refrigerator, or frozen up to 3 months.

Pork Roast Dinner

To make concentrated broth and a pork roast dinner at the same time, increase the amount of carrots, decrease the water to 2½ cups, and add 4 peeled medium potatoes or sweet potatoes (cut in half) on top. Cook according to the instructions. (White potatoes will cloud the broth, but the starch from them will naturally thicken it a little.)

FISH STOCK

Chefs use fish heads to make Fish Stock. Most home cooks simply use whitefish. You can add a French flair by substituting 1 cup of dry white wine or ¾ cup of dry vermouth for an equal amount of water.

Yields about 4 cups

INGREDIENTS:

2 pounds bone-in whitefish (flounder, halibut, etc.)

1 large onion, peeled and thinly sliced

1 tablespoon fresh lemon juice

4 cups water

¼ teaspoon sea salt

1. Add the fish, onion, lemon juice, water, and salt to the slow cooker. Cover and cook on low for 4–8 hours.

2. Strain through a fine sieve or fine wire-mesh strainer. Reserve the cooked fish for another use if desired. Discard the bones and onions. Refrigerate in a covered container and use within 2 days, or freeze for up to 3 months.

Warm Fish Fillet and Potato Salad

If you use meaty bone-in fish pieces to make Fish Stock, you can shred and cube the fish removed from those bones and add that fish over the top of some warm, boiled sliced red potatoes, diced red onion, and minced parsley. Dress with commercial red wine vinaigrette or one made using fresh lemon juice, Dijon mustard, salt, pepper, and extra-virgin olive oil.

SEAFOOD STOCK

This recipe calls for using the shells only because the amount of time it takes to slow-cook the stock would result in seafood that would be too tough to eat.

Yields about 4 cups

INGREDIENTS:

2 pounds shrimp, crab, or lobster shells

1 large onion, peeled and thinly sliced

1 tablespoon fresh lemon juice

4 cups water

¼ teaspoon sea salt

1. Add the seafood shells, onion, lemon juice, water, and salt to the slow cooker. Cover and cook on low for 4–8 hours.

2. Strain through a fine sieve or fine wire-mesh strainer. Discard the shells and onions. Refrigerate in a covered container and use within 2 days or freeze for up to 3 months.

Fish or Seafood Stock in a Hurry

For each cup of seafood or fish stock called for in a recipe, you can substitute ¼ cup of bottled clam juice and ¾ cup of water. Just keep in mind that the clam juice is very salty, so adjust any recipe in which you use it accordingly.

VEGETABLE STOCK

This is a great recipe for using up leftover vegetables and peelings. Vegetable stock is a healthy ingredient to keep in the fridge to make quick soups or to cook starches such as rice and potatoes.

Yields 6 cups

INGREDIENTS:

2 carrots, roughly chopped

1 onion, quartered

3 cloves garlic

2 ribs celery, roughly chopped

2 red potatoes, quartered, peeled or unpeeled

6 cups water

1 teaspoon salt

1 teaspoon ground pepper

1. Place chopped vegetables in a 4- to 6-quart slow cooker.

2. Pour water over the vegetables and add salt and pepper.

3. Cover and cook on high for 4–6 hours or on low for 8–10 hours.

4. Allow broth to cool slightly and then strain out vegetables. Pour stock into clean glass jars and refrigerate for up to a week or freeze for several months until needed. If you plan to freeze the stock either store in zip-top bags or leave 2 inches of room in each glass jar to allow liquids to expand.

Reducing Stocks

A simple way to add more flavor to your stock is to simply cook it down (reduce it by half) in a pot on the stove. Reduced stocks have a great depth of flavor and can be used as a sauce, gravy, or as the liquid to cook rice, potatoes, or pasta.

CHICKEN NOODLE SOUP

You can substitute a cut-up 3-pound whole chicken for the chicken pieces in this recipe. Bone-in chicken adds additional flavor to the soup broth. Stirring in the beaten eggs when you add the chicken back into the soup will give it a homemade noodles taste.

Serves 8

INGREDIENTS:

4 bone-in chicken thighs, skin removed

2 bone-in chicken breasts, skin removed

4 large carrots, peeled and sliced

1 large sweet onion, peeled and diced

2 stalks celery, diced

1 teaspoon salt

2 teaspoons dried parsley

¾ teaspoon dried marjoram

½ teaspoon dried basil

¼ teaspoon poultry seasoning

¼ teaspoon freshly ground black pepper

1 bay leaf

8 cups water

2½ cups medium egg noodles, uncooked

2 large eggs

1. Add the chicken thighs and breasts, carrots, onion, celery, salt, parsley, marjoram, basil, poultry seasoning, black pepper, bay leaf, and 6 cups of the water to the slow cooker. Cover and cook on low for 8 hours. Move the chicken to a cutting board. Remove and discard the bay leaf.

2. Increase the temperature of the slow cooker to high. Add the remaining 2 cups of water. Stir in the noodles and cook, covered, on high for 20 minutes or until the noodles are cooked through.

3. While the noodles cook, remove the meat from the bones. Cut the chicken into bite-sized pieces or shred it with two forks.

4. Ladle about ½ cup of the broth from the slow cooker into a bowl. Add the eggs and whisk to mix; stir the egg mixture into the slow cooker along with the chicken. Cover and cook for 15 minutes.

MINESTRONE SOUP

Minestrone is a classic Italian vegetable soup. The zucchini and cabbage are added at the end for a burst of fresh flavor.

Serves 8

INGREDIENTS:

3 cloves garlic, minced

15 ounces canned fire-roasted diced tomatoes

28 ounces canned crushed tomatoes

2 stalks celery, diced

1 medium onion, diced

3 medium carrots, diced

3 cups Vegetable Stock (this chapter) or Chicken Broth (this chapter)

30 ounces canned kidney beans, drained and rinsed

2 tablespoons tomato paste

2 tablespoons minced basil

2 tablespoons minced oregano

2 tablespoons minced Italian parsley

1½ cups shredded cabbage

¾ cup diced zucchini

1 teaspoon salt

½ teaspoon pepper

8 ounces small cooked pasta

1. Add the garlic, diced and crushed tomatoes, celery, onion, carrots, stock, beans, tomato paste, basil, and spices to a 4-quart slow cooker. Cook on low heat for 6–8 hours. Add shredded cabbage and zucchini and turn to high for the last hour. Stir in the salt, pepper, and pasta before serving.

Suggested Pasta Shapes for Soup

Anchellini, small shells, hoops, alfabeto, or ditaletti are all small pasta shapes suitable for soup. For heartier soups, try bow ties or rotini. Thin rice noodles or vermicelli are better for Asian-style soups.

MUSHROOM BARLEY SOUP

Using three types of mushrooms adds a lot of flavor to this soup.

Serves 8

INGREDIENTS:

1 ounce dried porcini mushrooms

1 cup boiling water

1½ teaspoons butter

5 ounces sliced fresh shiitake mushrooms

4 ounces sliced fresh button mushrooms

1 large onion, diced

1 clove garlic, minced

⅔ cup medium pearl barley

¼ teaspoon ground black pepper

6 cups Beef Broth (this chapter)

1. Place the dried porcini mushrooms in a heat-safe bowl. Pour the boiling water over the mushrooms. Soak for 15 minutes.

2. Meanwhile, melt the butter in a medium skillet. Sauté the fresh mushrooms, onion, and garlic until the onions are soft.

3. Drain the porcini mushrooms and discard the water. Add all of the mushrooms, onions, garlic, barley, pepper, and the broth to a 4-quart slow cooker. Stir. Cook 6–8 hours on low.

Hearty Vegetarian Variation

Add 1 diced carrot, 1 diced celery stalk, and 1 diced red potato with the rest of the ingredients. Use Vegetable Stock (this chapter) instead of Beef Broth. Stir in some fresh thyme prior to serving.

HERBED CHICKEN AND VEGETABLE SOUP

This soup is also delicious if you use a roux to thicken the broth and serve it pot pie–style: ladled over split buttermilk biscuits. If you need to let the soup cook all day so that it's done when you get home, it's okay to add the green beans, corn, and peas when you add the other ingredients.

Serves 8

INGREDIENTS:

7 large carrots

2 stalks celery, finely diced

1 large sweet onion, peeled and diced

8 ounces fresh mushrooms, cleaned and sliced

1 tablespoon extra-virgin olive oil

1 teaspoon butter, melted

1 clove garlic, peeled and minced

4 cups Chicken Broth (this chapter)

6 medium potatoes, peeled and diced

1 tablespoon dried parsley

¼ teaspoon dried oregano

¼ teaspoon dried rosemary

1 bay leaf

2 strips orange zest

Salt and freshly ground black pepper, to taste

8 chicken thighs, skin removed

1 (10-ounce) package frozen green beans, thawed

1 (10-ounce) package frozen whole kernel corn, thawed

1 (10-ounce) package frozen baby peas, thawed

Optional: Fresh parsley

1. Peel the carrots. Dice six of the carrots and grate one. Add the grated carrot, celery, onion, mushrooms, oil, and butter to the slow cooker. Stir to coat the vegetables in the oil and butter. Cover and cook on high for 30 minutes or until the vegetables are soft.

2. Stir in the garlic. Add the broth, diced carrots, potatoes, dried parsley, oregano, rosemary, bay leaf, orange zest, salt, pepper, and chicken thighs. Cover and cook on low for 6 hours.

3. Use a slotted spoon to remove the thighs, cut the meat from the bone and into bite-sized pieces, and return it to the pot. Remove and discard the orange zest and bay leaf. Stir in the green beans, corn, and peas; cover and cook on low for 1 hour or until the vegetables are heated through. Taste for seasoning and add additional salt, pepper, and herbs if needed.

Try It with a Tomato Base

Transform the Herbed Chicken and Vegetable Soup recipe into a tomato-based meal by substituting 2 (15-ounce) cans diced tomatoes for the chicken broth.

MANHATTAN SCALLOP CHOWDER

Serve this chowder with oyster crackers or warm dinner rolls and a tossed salad.

Serves 6

INGREDIENTS:

2 tablespoons butter, melted

2 stalks celery, finely diced

1 medium green bell pepper, seeded and diced

1 large carrot, peeled and finely diced

1 medium onion, peeled and diced

2 large potatoes, scrubbed and diced

1 (15-ounce) can diced tomatoes

1 (15-ounce) can tomato purée

2 cups (bottled) clam juice

1 cup dry white wine

¾ cup water

1 teaspoon dried thyme

1 teaspoon dried parsley

1 bay leaf

¼ teaspoon freshly ground black pepper

1½ pounds bay scallops

Salt, to taste

Optional: Fresh parsley, minced

Optional: Fresh basil

1. Add the butter, celery, bell pepper, and carrot to the slow cooker; stir to coat the vegetables in the butter. Cover and cook on high for 15 minutes. Stir in the onion. Cover and cook on high for 30 minutes, or until the vegetables are soft.

2. Stir in the potatoes, tomatoes, tomato purée, clam juice, wine, water, thyme, dried parsley, bay leaf, and pepper. Cover, reduce the temperature to low, and cook for 7 hours or until the potatoes are cooked through.

3. Cut the scallops so that they are each no larger than 1-inch pieces. Add to the slow cooker, increase the temperature to high, cover, and cook for 15 minutes or until the scallops are firm. Remove and discard the bay leaf. Taste for seasoning and add salt or adjust other seasoning if necessary. Ladle into soup bowls. If desired, sprinkle minced fresh parsley over each serving and garnish with fresh basil.

CLAM CHOWDER

This chowder is even better if you sauté 1 small diced red pepper along with the carrots and celery. Serve the chowder with oyster crackers and a tossed salad.

Serves 8

INGREDIENTS:

8 strips bacon

2 large carrots, peeled and finely diced

2 stalks celery, finely diced

2 large yellow onions, peeled and diced

2 tablespoons all-purpose flour

6 (6½-ounce) cans baby clams

8 medium red potatoes, scrubbed and diced

1 tablespoon dried parsley

1 bay leaf

1 tablespoon Worcestershire sauce

2 teaspoons dried thyme

5 cups water

3 cups heavy cream

1 cup whole milk

Salt and freshly ground black pepper, to taste

Hot sauce, to taste

Optional: Fresh parsley, minced

1. Cut the bacon into bite-sized pieces and add to the slow cooker along with the carrots and celery. Cover and cook on high for 15 minutes. Stir in the onions; cover and cook on high for 30 minutes or until the onion is transparent. Stir in the flour; gradually add 1 can of the (undrained) clams; stir and cook to remove any lumps.

2. Add the remaining (undrained) clams, potatoes, parsley, bay leaf, Worcestershire sauce, thyme, and water to the slow cooker. Cover and cook on high for 4 hours.

3. Stir in the cream, milk, salt, pepper, and hot sauce. Cover, reduce the slow cooker heat setting to low, and cook for 30 minutes or until the soup is heated through. (You do not want to bring it to a boil after you've added the cream and milk.) Taste for seasoning and adjust if necessary. Ladle into soup bowls and sprinkle minced fresh parsley over each serving if desired.

Speed Things Up

It'll dirty another pan, but you can speed up the cooking process for the Clam Chowder recipe if you fry the bacon in a nonstick skillet over medium-high heat and then sauté the carrots, celery, and onion in the rendered bacon fat. If you do, stir in the flour and cook it in with the sautéed vegetables on the stove for 2 minutes before you add it to the slow cooker.

CHICKEN MULLIGATAWNY SOUP

When serving this dish, also provide toasted strips of fresh coconut and white raisins.

Serves 6–8

INGREDIENTS:

1 pound boneless, skinless chicken breast

3 tablespoons butter

2 apples

2 onions

¼ cup flour

1½ tablespoons curry powder

6 cups Chicken Broth (this chapter)

1 cup uncooked rice

½ teaspoon salt

1. Cube the chicken. Sauté in butter in a pan over medium heat until lightly browned.

2. Core and cube the apples and mince the onions. Add the apples and onions to the chicken in the pan over medium heat and stir until the onions are soft. Add the flour and curry powder and stir to blend in.

3. Put the sautéed mixture, broth, rice, and salt in the slow cooker.

4. Cover and heat on a low setting for 4–6 hours.

HUNGARIAN GOULASH

This dish freezes well. Keep a batch set aside for unexpected company, then reheat and add a fresh parsley garnish.

Serves 6–8

INGREDIENTS:

2 onions

3 tablespoons butter

1 pound beef

1 pound pork

2 tablespoons flour

½ teaspoon salt

½ teaspoon pepper

2 tablespoons paprika

¼ cup celery

3 potatoes

1 cup Brown Stock (this chapter)

1 cup tomato sauce

½ teaspoon salt

½ teaspoon thyme

1 bay leaf

2 whole cloves

¼ cup parsley

1. Chop the onions and sauté in butter in a pan over medium heat until browned. Cube the meat and add to the onions. Sauté over medium heat until browned.

2. Mix the flour with ½ teaspoon salt, pepper, and paprika. Stir the flour mixture into the meat and onions. Transfer the meat mixture to the slow cooker.

3. Chop the celery into ½-inch lengths; cut the potatoes into 1-inch cubes.

4. Add the celery, potatoes, stock, tomato sauce, ½ teaspoon salt, and spices to the slow cooker. Cover and heat on a low setting for 4–6 hours.

5. Chop the parsley. Before serving, remove the bay leaf and stir in the parsley.

BEEF-VEGETABLE SOUP

Add a bit more flavor to this soup by substituting several strips of bacon cut into bite-sized pieces for the oil. Another alternative is substituting canned French Onion Soup for some of the beef broth.

Serves 8

INGREDIENTS:

7 large carrots

2 stalks celery, finely diced

1 large sweet onion, peeled and diced

8 ounces fresh mushrooms, cleaned and sliced

1 tablespoon extra-virgin olive oil

1 teaspoon butter, melted

1 clove garlic, peeled and minced

4 cups Beef Broth (this chapter)

6 medium potatoes, peeled and diced

1 tablespoon dried parsley

¼ teaspoon dried oregano

¼ teaspoon dried rosemary

1 bay leaf

Salt and freshly ground black pepper, to taste

1 (3-pound) chuck roast

1 (10-ounce) package frozen green beans, thawed

1 (10-ounce) package frozen whole kernel corn, thawed

1 (10-ounce) package frozen baby peas, thawed

Optional: Fresh parsley

1. Peel the carrots. Dice six of the carrots and grate one. Add the grated carrot, celery, onion, mushrooms, oil, and butter to the slow cooker. Stir to coat the vegetables in the oil and butter. Cover and cook on high for 30 minutes or until the vegetables are soft.

2. Stir in the garlic. Add the broth, diced carrots, potatoes, dried parsley, oregano, rosemary, bay leaf, salt, and pepper. Trim the roast of any fat, cut into bite-sized pieces and add to slow cooker. Cover and cook on low for 6 hours or until the beef is tender and the potatoes are cooked through.

3. Remove and discard the bay leaf. Stir in the green beans, corn, and peas; cover and cook on low for 1 hour or until the vegetables are heated through. Taste for seasoning and add additional salt, pepper, and herbs if needed.

It Works with Tomato, Too

Make Beef-Vegetable Soup a tomato-based dish by substituting 2 (15-ounce) cans of diced tomatoes for the Beef Broth.

FRESH VEGETABLE SOUP

If fresh herbs are available, you can replace the dried herbs with a bouquet garni made by tying a small bunch of parsley and a stalk each of thyme, basil, and marjoram together with kitchen twine and suspending it in the soup.

Serves 8

INGREDIENTS:

6 cups water or Chicken Broth (this chapter)

1 large yellow onion, peeled and diced

2 leeks—white part only, rinsed and sliced

1 (28-ounce) can whole plum tomatoes, crushed

4 large carrots, peeled and diced

1 acorn squash, peeled, seeded, and diced

2 large potatoes, peeled and diced

2 (15-ounce) cans garbanzo or white beans, rinsed and drained

¼ teaspoon dried thyme

¼ teaspoon dried basil

¼ teaspoon dried marjoram

2 teaspoons dried parsley

2 stalks celery, sliced

½ cup celery leaves, chopped

½ pound green beans, ends trimmed and cut into 2-inch pieces

½ pound zucchini, sliced

1 small cabbage, cored and shredded

Salt and freshly ground black pepper, to taste

1. Add the water or broth, onion, leeks, tomatoes, carrots, acorn squash, potatoes, beans, thyme, basil, marjoram, and parsley to the slow cooker. Cover and cook on low for 6 hours or until the acorn squash and potatoes are tender.

2. Stir in the celery, celery leaves, green beans, zucchini, cabbage, and salt and pepper. Add additional water or broth if needed. Cover and cook for 1 hour or until the newly added vegetables are cooked through. Ladle into soup bowls.

Notes on Fresh Vegetable Soup

This recipe is an adaptation of a French country soup that is served with toasted croutons or slices of French bread spread with (basil and Parmesan cheese) pesto and crème fraîche floating on top. You can replace the beans with other seasonal fresh vegetables (peas, corn cut from the cob, etc.) if you wish.

OATMEAL SOUP

This recipe is a way to add fiber to your diet. You have the option of adding the cooked chicken breast back into the soup or into the tossed salad you serve with the soup.

Serves 4

INGREDIENTS:

½ cup oatmeal

2 tablespoons oat bran

2 tablespoons butter

1 small carrot, peeled and grated

½ stalk celery, finely diced

1 medium sweet onion, peeled and diced

2 bone-in chicken breasts, cut in half

Salt and freshly ground black pepper, to taste

4 cups water

1 cup heavy cream

Optional: ¼ cup fresh parsley, minced

1. Preheat oven to 350°F. Add the oatmeal and oat bran to a baking sheet lined with nonstick foil. Stirring the oatmeal mixture every 2 minutes, bake for 6 minutes or until the oatmeal is toasted and lightly browned. (Watch carefully, because it will go from browned to burnt in an instant!)

2. Melt the butter in a nonstick skillet over medium heat. Add the carrot and celery; sauté for 3 minutes or until the vegetables begin to soften. Stir in the onion and sauté for 5 minutes or until the onion is transparent. Remove the skin from the chicken breast pieces; place meat side down in the skillet and fry for 5 minutes. Transfer the meat and vegetables to the slow cooker. Season to taste with salt and pepper. Add the water. Cover and cook on low for 7 hours or until the chicken and oats are cooked through.

3. Use a slotted spoon and remove the chicken breast pieces from the slow cooker. Use an immersion blender to purée the vegetables and oatmeal into the broth if you wish. Stir in the cream. Cover and cook on low for 30 minutes, or until the soup is brought to temperature. Ladle into bowls. Garnish each serving with a tablespoon of minced fresh parsley if desired.

Oatmeal Choices

Use your choice of quick-cook oatmeal, old fashioned oatmeal, or steel-cut oats, according to your preference. Just keep in mind that you may need to add additional water during the cooking process if you use steel-cut oats.

POTATO SOUP

This soup is a meal in itself.

Serves 4

INGREDIENTS:

4 strips bacon

1 small carrot, peeled and grated

½ stalk celery, finely diced

1 large sweet onion, peeled and diced

1 (4-ounce) cooked ham steak, diced

Optional: 4 slices Canadian bacon

4 large potatoes, peeled and diced

5 cups Chicken Broth (this chapter)

Salt and freshly ground black pepper, to taste

1. Cut the bacon into 1-inch pieces and add it to the slow cooker along with the carrot, celery, and onion. Cover and cook on high for 15 minutes.

2. Stir in the diced ham. If using, cut the Canadian bacon into bite-sized pieces and stir into the vegetables. Cover and cook on high for 15 more minutes or until the fat begins to render from the bacon and the onion is transparent.

3. Stir the diced potatoes into the onion mixture. Cover and cook on high for 15 more minutes. Add the broth, salt, and pepper; reduce heat setting to low, cover, and cook for 4 hours or until the potatoes are cooked through.

Deluxe Cream of Potato Soup

Once the potatoes are cooked through, add 1 cup heavy cream, 4 ounces of cream cheese cut into cubes, and 1 cup (4 ounces) grated medium or sharp Cheddar cheese to the slow cooker. Stirring occasionally, cover and cook on low for 30 minutes or until the cheeses are melted and can be stirred into the soup.

BUTTERNUT SQUASH SOUP

The apple will sweeten the soup a little, but you can add maple syrup if you want it sweeter. You can turn this into a cream soup by stirring in 1 cup of heavy cream after you've puréed the soup. Preheat the cream if you want to save yourself the step of needing to reheat the soup.

Serves 6

INGREDIENTS:

2 tablespoons butter, melted

1 medium onion, peeled and diced

1 stalk celery, thinly diced

1 butternut squash, peeled, seeded, and diced

1 small Granny Smith apple, peeled, cored, and diced

2 (3-inch) cinnamon sticks

6 whole cloves

6 allspice berries

6 cups Chicken Broth (this chapter)

Salt and freshly ground black pepper, to taste

Optional: 1 or 2 tablespoons maple syrup

Freshly grated nutmeg

1. Add the butter, onion, and celery to the slow cooker. Cover and, stirring occasionally, cook on high for 30 minutes or until the onions begin to soften or are transparent. Add the diced squash (about 3 cups), apple, and cinnamon sticks. Place the cloves and allspice in a muslin cooking bag or tie them inside a piece of cheesecloth; add to the slow cooker along with the broth, salt, and pepper. Cover and cook on low for 6 hours or until the squash is tender.

2. Remove the cinnamon sticks, cloves, and allspice. Use an immersion blender to purée the soup. Taste for seasoning and adjust, adding maple syrup to taste if desired. Ladle into bowls. Grate fresh nutmeg to taste over each serving.

Easier Than Peeling and Dicing the Butternut Squash

Some supermarkets sell butternut squash that's already peeled and diced. Or, you can use a knife to pierce the squash several times, place it on a baking sheet, and bake it in a 350°F oven for an hour. Once it's cool enough to handle, cut it lengthwise. Scrape out and discard the seeds. Use a spoon to scrape the cooked flesh from the inside of the peel.

CREAM OF BROCCOLI SOUP

You can convert this to a rich broccoli-cheese soup by adding 2 to 4 ounces of cream cheese cut into cubes and 1 cup (4 ounces) of grated Cheddar cheese when you add the cream.

Serves 4

INGREDIENTS:

1 (12-ounce) bag frozen broccoli florets, thawed

1 small onion, peeled and diced

4 cups Chicken Broth (this chapter)

Salt and freshly ground black pepper, to taste

Optional: 4 slices white bread, crusts removed

1 cup heavy cream

1. Add the broccoli, onion, broth, salt, and pepper to the slow cooker; cover and cook on low for 4 hours. If you prefer a thickened cream soup, tear the bread into pieces and stir them into the broth.

2. Use an immersion blender to purée the soup. Stir in the cream. Cover and, stirring occasionally to ensure that the bread remains blended in with the soup, cook on low for 30 minutes, or until the soup is brought to temperature.

CREAM OF MUSHROOM SOUP

For a thicker soup, use crème fraîche instead of cream. If you do, watch the soup carefully while you bring it back to temperature because if the soup comes to a boil, it can separate.

Serves 4

INGREDIENTS:

8 ounces fresh mushrooms, cleaned and sliced

1 small onion, peeled and diced

4 cups Chicken Broth (this chapter)

Salt and freshly ground black pepper, to taste

1 cup heavy cream or crème fraîche

1. Add the mushrooms, onion, broth, salt, and pepper to the slow cooker; cover and cook on low for 4 hours.

2. (Optional step: If you want to purée the cooked diced onion, first use a slotted spoon to remove some of the mushrooms and set aside. Use an immersion blender to purée and then return the reserved mushrooms to the slow cooker.)

3. Stir in the cream or crème fraîche. Cover and cook on low for 30 minutes or until the soup is brought to temperature.

SPLIT PEA SOUP

The combination of chicken broth and the different meats in this soup gives it a distinctive flavor. Because the sodium content in the broth and meats can affect the flavor, wait until the soup is cooked and, when you taste it for seasoning, add salt if it's needed.

Serves 6

INGREDIENTS:

6 strips bacon, diced

2 stalks celery, finely diced

3 large carrots, peeled

1 large sweet onion, peeled and diced

2 cups dried split peas, rinsed and drained

4 cups Chicken Broth (this chapter)

3 cups water

2 large potatoes, peeled and diced

1 smoked ham hock

4 ounces smoked sausage or ham, diced

Salt and freshly ground black pepper, to taste

1. Add the bacon and celery to the slow cooker; cover and cook on high while you prepare the carrots. Grate half of one of the carrots and dice the remaining carrots. Add the grated carrot and diced onion to the slow cooker; stir to mix them in with the bacon and celery. Cover and cook on high for 30 minutes or until the onions are transparent.

2. Add the diced carrots, split peas, broth, water, potatoes, ham hock, and smoked sausage or ham to the slow cooker. Cover and cook on low for 8 hours or until the peas are soft. Use a slotted spoon to remove the ham hock; remove the meat from the bone and return it to the slow cooker. Taste for seasoning and add salt and pepper if needed.

Adjustments to the Split Pea Soup Recipe

If you have homemade Ham Broth (this chapter) available, you can substitute ½ cup of it for an equal amount of the water and omit the smoked ham hock. This is a soup that can also be enhanced by adding ½ cup of Pork Broth (this chapter) instead of that much of the water, too.

THAI-SPICED CHICKEN SOUP

Thai red curry paste is a mixture of red chili peppers, shallots, garlic, galangal, lemongrass, coriander roots, peppercorns, salt, shrimp paste, and Kaffir lime zest. Fish sauce is a salty condiment and, much like soy sauce, a flavoring in Thai cuisine; it is made from fermented fish.

Serves 8

INGREDIENTS:

2 tablespoons peanut or vegetable oil

2 carrots, peeled and thinly sliced

4 stalks celery, thinly sliced

1 small onion, thinly sliced

8 ounces fresh mushrooms, cleaned and sliced

2 cloves garlic, peeled and minced

2 pounds boneless, skinless chicken breasts

8 cups Chicken Broth (this chapter)

2 cups frozen cross-cut green beans, thawed

1 tablespoon fresh ginger, grated

2 tablespoons red Thai curry paste

1 tablespoon fresh lemon juice

1 tablespoon fresh lime juice

½ teaspoon ground cumin

¼ teaspoon ground cardamom

¼ teaspoon ground cinnamon

¼ teaspoon ground dried coriander

⅛ teaspoon ground anise seed

1 tablespoon fish sauce

Optional: Fresh cilantro, minced

1. Add the oil, carrots, celery, and onion to the slow cooker; stir to coat the vegetables in the oil. Cover and cook on high for 30 minutes or until the onion is transparent. Stir in the mushrooms and garlic; cover and cook on high for 15 minutes.

2. Cut the chicken breast into bite-sized pieces. Add to the slow cooker along with all of the remaining ingredients except for the fresh cilantro, if using. Cover and cook on low for 7 hours. Taste for seasoning, and add more Thai red curry paste (if you think the soup needs more heat) or more fish sauce (if you think the soup needs more salt). Ladle into soup bowls; sprinkle each serving with minced fresh cilantro if desired.

CAULIFLOWER AND CHEESE SOUP

Be sure to save any leftovers. This rich soup tastes even better when it's reheated and served the next day. Just remember to reheat it over low heat so that the cheese doesn't separate.

Serves 6

INGREDIENTS:

1 (12-ounce) bag frozen cauliflower, thawed

1 small onion, peeled and diced

5 cups Chicken Broth (this chapter)

Salt and freshly ground black pepper, to taste

4 ounces cream cheese, cut into cubes

1 cup (4 ounces) medium Cheddar cheese, grated

1 cup heavy cream

1. Add the cauliflower, onion, broth, salt, and pepper to the slow cooker; cover and cook on low for 4 hours. Use an immersion blender to purée the soup if desired.

2. Stir in the cream cheese, Cheddar cheese, and cream. Cover and, stirring occasionally, cook on low for 30 minutes or until the soup is brought to temperature.

BORSCHT

When available, you can substitute about a pound of diced vine-ripened tomatoes for the canned.

Serves 6–8

INGREDIENTS:

1½ tablespoons extra-virgin olive oil

1 clove garlic, peeled and minced

½ pound chuck roast, cut into ½-inch pieces

1 small yellow onion, peeled and diced

1 pound red beets

1 small head cabbage, cored and chopped

1 (15-ounce) can diced tomatoes

7 cups Beef Broth (this chapter)

¼ cup red wine vinegar

2 bay leaves

1 tablespoon lemon juice

Beet greens

Salt and freshly ground black pepper, to taste

Sour cream

Optional: Fresh dill

1. Add the oil, garlic, beef, and onion to the slow cooker; stir to coat the beef and vegetables in the oil. Cover and cook on high for 30 minutes or until the onion is transparent.

2. Peel and dice the beets. (You may wish to wear gloves; beet juice can stain your hands and fingernails. Be careful, because it can also stain some countertops.) Save the beet greens; rinse well and cover them with cold water until needed.

3. Add the beets, cabbage, tomatoes, broth, vinegar, bay leaves, and lemon juice to the slow cooker. Cover and cook on low for 7 hours.

4. Chop the reserved beet greens and add to the soup; cover and cook on low for another 15 minutes, or until the greens are wilted. Discard bay leaves. Taste for seasoning and add salt and pepper to taste. Ladle the soup into bowls and garnish each bowl with a heaping tablespoon of sour cream and some fresh dill if using.

SOUTHWESTERN CHEESE SOUP

Serve this soup with a tossed salad and corn chips. Use hot or mild green chilies, according to your personal preference.

Serves 8

INGREDIENTS:

2 pounds lean ground beef

1 envelope taco seasoning mix

1 (15¼-ounce) can whole kernel corn

1 (15-ounce) can kidney beans

1 (15-ounce) can diced tomatoes

2 (15-ounce) cans stewed tomatoes

1 (7-ounce) can green chilies, minced and drained

2 pounds Velveeta cheese, cut into cubes

1. Fry the ground beef in a large nonstick skillet over medium-high heat, breaking it apart as you do so. Drain and discard any fat rendered from the beef.

2. Transfer the ground beef to the slow cooker and stir the taco seasoning mix into the meat. Add the corn, beans, diced tomatoes, stewed tomatoes, and chilies to the slow cooker. Cover and cook on low for 4 hours.

3. Stir the cheese into the soup. Cover, and stirring occasionally, continue to cook on low for 30 minutes or until the cheese is melted and blended into the soup.

BAKED BEANS SOUP

You can increase the number of servings of this soup to 8 by adding 2 cans of stewed tomatoes. Serve over corn bread with a tossed salad.

Serves 6

INGREDIENTS:

2 (16-ounce) cans baked beans

1 tablespoon molasses

1 tablespoon brown sugar

6 strips bacon, diced

1 large sweet onion, peeled and diced

1 (15-ounce) can stewed tomatoes

1 (2-pound) chuck roast

Salt and freshly ground pepper, to taste

1. Add the baked beans, molasses, brown sugar, bacon, onion, and stewed tomatoes to the slow cooker; stir to mix.

2. Trim the beef of any fat and cut it into 1-inch cubes. Add to the slow cooker and stir it into the beans. Cover and cook on low for 8 hours or until the beef is tender. Taste for seasoning; add salt and pepper if needed.

BLACK BEAN SOUP

This is excellent served with Corn Bread (Chapter 23).

Serves 8

INGREDIENTS:

3 slices turkey bacon

1 teaspoon canola oil

1 medium onion, diced

1 habanero pepper, seeded and minced

3 cloves garlic, minced

1 stalk celery, diced

1 carrot, diced

30 ounces canned black beans, drained and rinsed

3 cups Chicken Broth (this chapter) or Turkey Broth (this chapter)

1. Cook the turkey bacon in a nonstick skillet until crisp. Drain on paper towel–lined plates. Crumble the bacon into small pieces.

2. Heat the oil in a nonstick skillet. Add the onion, habanero, garlic, celery, and carrot. Sauté until the onions are soft, about 2–4 minutes.

3. Put the beans, onion mixture, and bacon crumbles into a 4-quart slow cooker. Add the broth and stir. Cook on low for 8–10 hours or on high for 4 hours.

Hints about Habaneros

Green habanero peppers are not ripe; when they are ready to eat, they range in color from yellow to bright red. Habanero peppers have a spicy, fruity flavor and are quite hot. If you prefer a milder dish, you can substitute an equal number of jalapeños.

ITALIAN WEDDING SOUP

This is a main-course soup that you can serve with garlic bread and a tossed salad. Have additional Parmesan-Reggiano available at the table to grate over the soup.

Serves 4

INGREDIENTS:

1 pound frozen meatballs, thawed

6 cups Chicken Broth (this chapter)

1 pound curly endive or escarole, coarsely chopped

2 large eggs

2 tablespoons freshly grated Parmesan-Reggiano cheese

Salt and freshly ground black pepper, to taste

1. Add the meatballs, broth, and endive or escarole to the slow cooker; cover and cook on low for 4 hours. Use a slotted spoon to remove the meatballs to a serving bowl; cover and keep warm. Increase the setting of the slow cooker to high; cook uncovered while you whisk the eggs.

2. Add the eggs, cheese, salt, and pepper to a small bowl; whisk to blend. Stir the soup in the slow cooker in a circular motion, and then drizzle the egg mixture into the moving broth. Use a fork to separate the eggs into thin strands. Once the eggs are set, pour the soup over the meatballs.

Wedding Soup Varieties

Wedding soup consists of some sort of greens (endive, escarole, cabbage, lettuce, kale, or spinach) and meat served in a broth.

CREAM OF WINTER VEGETABLES SOUP

Serve this soup with a tossed salad, smoked sausage, and French or artisan whole-grain bread.

Serves 6

INGREDIENTS:

2 tablespoons butter

4 leeks

1 large yellow onion, peeled and diced

4 medium carrots, peeled and sliced

4 medium potatoes, peeled and diced

2 large turnips, peeled and diced

6 cups boiling water or Chicken Broth (this chapter)

Salt and freshly ground black pepper, to taste

1¼ cups crème fraîche

1. Coat the inside of the crock of the slow cooker with the butter. Slice the white parts of the leeks and about an inch of the green parts into ½-inch thick slices; rinse well and drain. Add to the slow cooker along with the onion, carrots, potatoes, and turnips. Pour the boiling water or broth over the vegetables. Cover and cook on low for 8 hours or until all the vegetables are tender.

2. Use an immersion blender to purée the soup. Taste for seasoning and add salt and pepper if desired. Stir in the crème fraîche; cover and cook on low for 15 minutes, or until the soup is brought back to temperature.

Crème Fraîche

Add 1 cup of heavy cream, ⅓ cup sour cream, and 2 tablespoons plain yogurt (with active acidophilus cultures) to a sterilized glass container. Mix, cover with plastic wrap, and let sit for 8 hours at room temperature. Refrigerate until ready to use or for up to a week.

ROASTED RED PEPPER SOUP

If you have a grill, try preparing your own sweet red peppers. Cut 3 peppers, brush with oil, and grill until tender.

Serves 4

INGREDIENTS:

1 onion

1 tablespoon vegetable oil

1 tablespoon flour

2 7½-ounce jars roasted red bell peppers

1 teaspoon sugar

3½ cups Vegetable Stock (this chapter)

½ teaspoon salt

½ teaspoon black pepper

2 tablespoons dry sherry

¼ cup heavy cream

1. Chop the onion and sauté in oil in a pan over medium heat until soft, then stir in the flour. Add mixture to the slow cooker.

2. Drain and chop the red bell peppers. Combine with the sugar, stock, salt, and pepper in the slow cooker.

3. Cover and heat on a low setting for 2–3 hours.

4. Use a slotted spoon to remove some of the onion and peppers from the slow cooker. Purée them in a blender or food processor and return them to the slow cooker.

5. Half an hour before serving, stir in the sherry and cream.

LENTIL AND BARLEY SOUP

As with all soup bones, ask your butcher for some bones that have some meat remaining. This adds flavor and nutrients.

Serves 8

INGREDIENTS:

1 onion

3 cloves garlic

1½ pounds lamb bones

8 cups water

½ teaspoon salt

2 bay leaves

¼ teaspoon black pepper

1 cup brown lentils

½ cup pearl barley

1 bunch fresh parsley

1. Coarsely chop the onion and mince the garlic.

2. Combine the onion, garlic, bones, water, salt, and spices in the slow cooker.

3. Rinse the lentils and remove any stones. Add the lentils and barley to the slow cooker.

4. Cover and heat on a low setting for 4–5 hours.

5. Coarsely chop the parsley and provide as a garnish for individual servings. Remove the bay leaves before serving.

A Garlic Project

Some evening while you're sitting at home talking on the phone or watching television, peel a dozen or so cloves of garlic and put them in a small jar of olive or vegetable oil. This will keep the garlic fresh and give the oil a nice flavor for future use in recipes or salad dressings.

TACO SOUP

Serve this soup with a variety of toppings, just like a taco! Cheddar cheese, sour cream, jalapeño peppers, and tortilla chips all taste delicious paired with this soup.

Serves 8

INGREDIENTS:

1½ pounds ground beef

1 (15-ounce) can whole kernel corn, with liquid

1 (15-ounce) can cream corn

1 (15-ounce) can hominy, with liquid

1 (15-ounce) can kidney beans, with liquid

1 (15-ounce) can pinto beans, with liquid

2 (14.5-ounce) cans diced tomatoes, with liquid

1 (1.25-ounce) package taco mix

1 (1-ounce) package dry ranch dressing mix

1. Brown ground beef in skillet. Drain.

2. Add beef and remaining ingredients to the slow cooker and mix well.

3. Cover and cook on low for 6–7 hours.

Portion Control Your Soup

Line your favorite microwavable soup mug with a quart-sized freezer bag. Pour the soup into the lined mug and flash freeze. Once the soup is frozen, lift the bag of soup from the mug, and return the soup to the freezer. Now you have a perfectly shaped portion of soup that can go from the freezer straight to your mug. To heat, defrost, microwave, and serve soup in the same cup!

GREEK-STYLE ORZO AND SPINACH SOUP

Lemon zest adds a bright, robust flavor to this simple soup.

Serves 6

INGREDIENTS:

2 cloves garlic, minced

3 tablespoons lemon juice

1 teaspoon lemon zest

5 cups Chicken Broth (this chapter)

1 small onion, thinly sliced

1 cup cubed cooked chicken breast

⅓ cup dried orzo

4 cups fresh baby spinach

1. Add the garlic, lemon juice, zest, broth, and onions to a 4-quart slow cooker. Cover and cook on low for 6–8 hours.

2. Stir in the chicken and cook for 30 minutes on high. Add the orzo and spinach. Stir and continue to cook on high for an additional 15 minutes. Stir before serving.

Quick Tip: Zesting

There are many tools on the market that are for zesting citrus, but all you really need is a fine grater. Be sure to take off the outermost part of the peel, where the aromatic essential oils that hold the flavor are located. The white pith underneath is bitter and inedible.

TORTILLA SOUP

This soup tastes even better the next day. Have it for dinner one day and lunch the next.

Serves 8

INGREDIENTS:

1 teaspoon cumin

1 teaspoon chili powder

1 teaspoon smoked paprika

⅛ teaspoon salt

25 ounces canned crushed tomatoes

14 ounces canned fire-roasted diced tomatoes

3 cups Chicken Broth (this chapter) or Turkey Broth (this chapter)

2 cloves garlic, minced

1 medium onion, diced

4 ounces canned diced green chiles, drained

2 habanero peppers, diced

1 cup fresh corn kernels

2 cups cubed cooked chicken or turkey breast

1. Place the spices, tomatoes, broth, garlic, onions, and peppers in a 4-quart slow cooker. Cover, and cook on low for 6 hours.

2. After 6 hours, add the corn and turkey or chicken. Cover and cook for an additional 45–60 minutes.

Put the Tortilla in Tortilla Soup

Slice 4 corn tortillas in half, then into ¼" strips. Heat ½ teaspoon canola oil in a shallow skillet. Add the tortilla strips and cook, turning once, until they are crisp and golden. Drain on paper towel–lined plates. Blot dry. Divide evenly among the bowls of soup before serving.

PUMPKIN BISQUE

This simple soup is a perfect first course at a holiday meal or as a light lunch.

Serves 4

INGREDIENTS:

2 cups puréed pumpkin

4 cups water

1 cup fat-free evaporated milk

¼ teaspoon ground nutmeg

2 cloves garlic, minced

1 onion, minced

1. Place all ingredients into a 4-quart slow cooker. Stir. Cook on low for 8 hours.

2. Use an immersion blender or blend the bisque in batches in a standard blender until smooth. Serve hot.

Make Your Own Pumpkin Purée

Preheat the oven to 350°F. Slice a pie pumpkin or an "eating" pumpkin into wedges and remove the seeds. Place the wedges on a baking sheet and bake until the flesh is soft, about 40 minutes. Scoop out the flesh and allow it to cool before puréeing it in a blender.

OLD-FASHIONED ONION SOUP

Make your own croutons to serve with this soup. Cut thick slices of black bread into cubes. Sprinkle with grated Parmesan and pepper, then broil until browned.

Serves 8

INGREDIENTS:

6 yellow onions

6 tablespoons butter

4 cups Beef Broth (this chapter)

½ teaspoon salt

½ teaspoon black peppercorns

¼ pound fresh Parmesan cheese

1. Thinly slice the onions. Slowly sauté in butter in pan over low heat until browned.

2. Add onions, broth, salt, and peppercorns to the slow cooker.

3. Cover and heat on a low setting for 3–4 hours.

4. Grate the Parmesan. Before serving, stir ¼ cup grated cheese into the soup. Set out the remainder to garnish individual servings.

CATFISH CIOPPINO

This hearty and delicious seafood stew is best served with crusty sourdough bread to sop up all the juices.

Serves 8

INGREDIENTS:

1 onion, chopped

2 stalks celery, diced

6 cloves garlic, minced

28 ounces canned diced tomatoes

8 ounces clam juice

¾ cup water or Fish Stock (this chapter)

6 ounces tomato paste

1 teaspoon red pepper flakes

2 tablespoons minced oregano

2 tablespoons minced Italian parsley

1 teaspoon red wine vinegar

10 ounces catfish nuggets

10 ounces peeled raw shrimp

6 ounces diced cooked clams

6 ounces lump crabmeat

¾ cup diced lobster meat

¼ cup diced green onion

1. Place the onions, celery, garlic, tomatoes, clam juice, water or stock, tomato paste, red pepper flakes, oregano, parsley, and vinegar in a 4-quart slow cooker. Stir vigorously. Cook on low for 8 hours.

2. Add the seafood and green onion and cook on high for 30 minutes. Stir prior to serving.

Save Your Shells

Save your shrimp shells to make shrimp stock. Simply follow the recipe for Chicken Broth (this chapter) and use the shells instead of chicken bones. Add a couple of extra pieces of celery, onion, and carrot for extra flavor. Use in seafood dishes instead of fish or chicken stock.

HAMBURGER-POTATO SOUP

Serve this with a tossed salad and a steamed vegetable.

Serves 6

INGREDIENTS:

1½ pounds lean ground beef

2 cloves garlic, peeled and minced

¼ teaspoon freshly ground black pepper

½ teaspoon dried thyme

1 tablespoon butter

6 medium potatoes, peeled and sliced

Salt, to taste

2 large onions, peeled and diced

1 (10¾-ounce) can condensed cream of mushroom soup

½ cup milk

1. Add the ground beef to a nonstick skillet over medium-high heat; breaking apart the meat as you do so, fry for 5 minutes or until the beef is lightly browned. Stir in the garlic, pepper, and thyme; sauté for 30 seconds. Remove and discard any excess fat rendered from the meat.

2. Butter the inside of the slow cooker. Put half of the sliced potatoes in a layer over the bottom of the slow cooker; lightly salt the potatoes. Top the potatoes with half of the diced onions. Add half of the browned beef. Add the remaining potatoes, another light sprinkling of salt, remaining onions, and remaining browned beef.

3. Add the mushroom soup and milk to a bowl or measuring cup; stir to combine. Pour the soup mixture over the contents of the slow cooker. Cover and cook on low for 8 hours or until the potatoes are cooked through.

Cheeseburger-Potato Casserole

After the 8 hours of cooking time, or when the potatoes are cooked through, sprinkle 1 cup (4 ounces) of grated Cheddar cheese over the top of the casserole. Cover and cook on low for 30 minutes or until the cheese is melted.

JAPANESE CUSTARD

This delicate custardlike soup goes well with grilled fish and vegetables, or as part of a light meal with a green salad.

Serves 4

INGREDIENTS:

2 eggs

2 cups Chicken Broth (this chapter)

¼ teaspoon salt

¼ pound mushrooms

¼ pound boneless, skinless chicken

4 green onions

1 teaspoon rice oil

¼ cup cooked rice

1. Beat the eggs well. Mix with the chicken broth and salt in a mixing bowl.

2. Dice the mushrooms, chicken, and green onions; sauté in rice oil in a pan over low heat until the mushrooms are soft.

3. Distribute the mushroom mixture and rice between 4 custard cups. Divide the broth mixture between the same custard cups; top each with a lid of glass.

4. Arrange the dishes on a trivet in the slow cooker. Pour water around the base.

5. Cover and heat on a high setting for 1–2 hours.

Try Something New

Perhaps you've noticed an ethnic grocery store down the street or near your office. Go in and take a look. Even if you can't read the labels, there might be a picture, or you could be brave and try something you can't identify. This is an excellent way to find new ingredients unavailable in standard grocery stores, like wide varieties of olives, flatbreads, chili powders, curries, coconut milk, exotic fruits, and much more.

COCONUT SOUP

This dish is simple but smooth and creamy. You can also add rice, chicken, or seafood to add other flavors and textures.

Serves 6–8

INGREDIENTS:

1 onion

2 tablespoons butter

3 tablespoons flour

5 cups Chicken Broth (this chapter)

1¼ cups coconut milk

1. Finely chop the onion. Sauté in butter in a pan over medium heat until soft.

2. Blend the flour into ½ cup of the chicken broth. Add to the onion mixture and stir over medium heat until thickened.

3. Transfer to the slow cooker and add the remaining broth to the onion mixture.

4. Cover and heat on a low setting for 2–3 hours.

5. An hour before serving, add the coconut milk to the slow cooker.

CURRY AND ZUCCHINI SOUP

If you or a neighbor has zucchini in the garden, use it in this soup. Fresh garden vegetables always provide great flavor.

Serves 6–8

INGREDIENTS:

3 zucchini

2 onions

4 cups Chicken Broth (this chapter)

1 tablespoon curry powder

1 cup cream

½ teaspoon salt

½ teaspoon pepper

1. Coarsely chop the zucchini and onions.

2. Combine the zucchini, onions, broth, and curry powder in the slow cooker.

3. Cover and heat on a low setting for 2–3 hours.

4. Half an hour before serving, transfer some of the zucchini and onions with a slotted spoon to a blender or food processor and purée with the cream, salt, and pepper; return the puréed material to the slow cooker to reheat.

PUMPKIN WILD RICE CHOWDER

You can substitute half-and-half for the heavy cream if you'd like. This hearty chowder is thick and full of flavor.

Serves 8

INGREDIENTS:

1 (16-ounce) package baby carrots

2 potatoes, peeled and cubed

1 cup wild rice, rinsed

2 tablespoons olive oil

1 pound beef sirloin tips

1 onion, chopped

4 cloves garlic, minced

1 (15-ounce) can solid pack pumpkin

2 cups Beef Broth (this chapter)

4 cups water

1 tablespoon curry powder

1 teaspoon salt

¼ teaspoon white pepper

½ cup heavy cream

1. Place carrots, potatoes, and wild rice in bottom of 4- or 5-quart slow cooker. In large skillet, heat olive oil over medium-high heat. Add beef; sauté for 2–3 minutes just until meat begins to turn brown; remove with slotted spoon and add to slow cooker. Add onion and garlic to skillet; cook and stir for 3 minutes, then add to slow cooker.

2. Add pumpkin and broth to skillet. Cook and stir until mixture blends and comes to a simmer. Pour into slow cooker; add water, curry powder, salt, and pepper and stir. Cover and cook on low for 8–9 hours, until beef is tender and wild rice is tender. Stir in heavy cream and cook for 20 minutes longer; serve.

Sirloin Tips

If you can't find sirloin tips (a beef sirloin steak that has been cut into cubes) you can cut it yourself. Trim the steak of excess fat and cut into 1" cubes, following the grain of the meat. Other cuts of beef will work as well; bottom round steak, sirloin tri-tip, chuck steak, or shoulder steak work well when cooked in the slow cooker.

WHITE BEAN AND BARLEY SOUP

Cool soup to room temperature before refrigerating or freezing in order to save energy.

Serves 8

INGREDIENTS:

2 (15-ounce) cans great northern beans, drained and rinsed

½ cup pearl barley

½ onion, diced

2 carrots, peeled and diced

2 cloves garlic, minced

¼ cup fresh parsley, chopped

2 sprigs fresh thyme

6 cups Vegetable Stock (this chapter)

1½ teaspoons salt

1. In a 4-quart slow cooker, add all ingredients; cover, and cook on low for 6–8 hours.

2. Remove the sprigs of thyme before serving.

CREAMY CHICKPEA SOUP

Beans can be puréed to make a creamy soup without the cream.

Serves 6

INGREDIENTS:

1 small onion, diced

2 cloves garlic, minced

2 (15-ounce) cans chickpeas, drained and rinsed

5 cups Vegetable Stock (this chapter)

1 teaspoon salt

½ teaspoon cumin

Juice of ½ lemon

1 tablespoon olive oil

¼ fresh parsley, chopped

1. In a 4-quart slow cooker, add all ingredients except for the lemon juice, olive oil, and parsley; cover, and cook over low heat for 4 hours.

2. Allow to cool slightly, then process the soup in a blender or using an immersion blender.

3. Return the soup to the slow cooker then add the lemon juice, olive oil, and parsley, and heat on low for an additional 30 minutes.

MUSHROOM BARLEY SOUP

Using three types of mushrooms in this soup adds a more robust flavor.

Serves 8

INGREDIENTS:

1 ounce dried porcini mushrooms

1 cup boiling water

1½ teaspoons butter margarine

5 ounces fresh shiitake mushrooms, sliced

4 ounces fresh button mushrooms, sliced

1 large onion, diced

1 clove garlic, minced

⅔ cup medium pearl barley

¼ teaspoon ground black pepper

½ teaspoon salt

6 cups Vegetable Stock (this chapter)

1. In a heat-safe bowl, place the dried porcini mushrooms; pour the boiling water over the mushrooms. Soak for 15 minutes.

2. Meanwhile, in a medium sauté pan, melt the butter or margarine. Sauté the fresh mushrooms, onion, and garlic until the onions are soft, about 3 minutes.

3. Drain the porcini mushrooms and discard the water.

4. In a 4-quart slow cooker, add all of the mushrooms, onion, garlic, barley, pepper, salt, and the stock. Stir, cover, and cook 6–8 hours on low.

PHO

This Vietnamese noodle soup is easy to make in the slow cooker. Try it instead of vegetable soup on a cold night.

Serves 6

INGREDIENTS:

1 tablespoon coriander seeds

1 tablespoon whole cloves

6 star anise

1 cinnamon stick

1 tablespoon fennel seed

1 tablespoon whole cardamom

4 knobs fresh ginger, sliced

1 onion, sliced

1 quart Vegetable Stock (this chapter)

1 teaspoon soy sauce

8 ounces Vietnamese rice noodles

1 cup shredded seitan

½ cup chopped cilantro

½ cup chopped Thai basil

2 cups mung bean sprouts

¼ cup sliced scallions

1. In a dry nonstick skillet, quickly heat the spices, ginger, and onion until the seeds start to pop, about 5 minutes. The onion and ginger should look slightly caramelized. Place them in a cheesecloth packet and tie it securely.

2. In a 4-quart slow cooker, place the cheesecloth packet. Add the stock, soy sauce, noodles, and seitan. Cover, and cook on low for 4 hours.

3. Remove the cheesecloth packet after cooking. Serve each bowl topped with cilantro, basil, sprouts, and scallions.

WILD RICE AND PORTOBELLO SOUP

Any variety of rice will work in this soup. It's fine to substitute white rice or brown rice if that's all you have on hand.

Serves 4

INGREDIENTS:

½ yellow onion, diced

2 small carrots, peeled and diced

2 ribs celery, sliced

1 cup chopped Portobello mushroom

½ cup uncooked wild rice

4 cups Vegetable Stock (this chapter)

1 bay leaf

1 sprig rosemary

1 teaspoon salt

½ teaspoon pepper

1. In a 4-quart slow cooker, add all ingredients. Cover and cook over low heat for 6 hours.

2. Remove the bay leaf and rosemary sprig before serving.

CELERY ROOT SOUP

Serve a bowl of this soup topped with green apple crisps.

Serves 6

INGREDIENTS:

2 tablespoons butter or vegan margarine

1 small leek (white and light green parts only), chopped

2 cloves garlic, minced

1 large celery root, peeled and cubed

2 medium russet potatoes, peeled and cubed

6 cups Vegetable Stock (this chapter)

1½ teaspoons salt

1 teaspoon pepper

1. In a large sauté pan over medium heat, melt the butter or margarine then add the leeks and sauté about 4 minutes. Add the garlic and sauté an additional 30 seconds.

2. In a 4-quart slow cooker, add the sautéed leeks and garlic, celery root, potatoes, stock, salt, and pepper. Cover and cook over low heat for 6–8 hours.

3. Let the soup cool slightly, then process in a blender or with an immersion blender until smooth.

Celery Root

Celery root, also known as celeriac, is not the root of the celery you know. It is similar in texture to a potato, and is cultivated for its root, not its leaves or stalk. It is grown in cool weather and is best in the fall, right after it has been pulled. The roots and crevices have to be trimmed away, so a 1-pound root will only yield about 2 cups after it is peeled and sliced or grated, something to keep in mind when buying for a recipe.

TOMATO BASIL SOUP

Fresh basil adds a different flavor than dried basil to dishes, and the fresh variety is more complementary to this soup.

Serves 5

INGREDIENTS:

2 tablespoons butter or margarine

½ onion, diced

2 cloves garlic, minced

1 (28-ounce) can whole peeled tomatoes

½ cup Vegetable Stock (this chapter)

1 bay leaf

1 teaspoon salt

1 teaspoon pepper

½ cup unsweetened soymilk

¼ cup sliced fresh basil

1. In a sauté pan over medium heat, melt the butter or margarine then sauté the onion and garlic for 3–4 minutes.

2. In a 4-quart slow cooker, add the onion and garlic, tomatoes, stock, bay leaf, salt, and pepper. Cover and cook over low heat for 4 hours.

3. Allow to cool slightly, then remove the bay leaf. Process the soup in a blender or immersion blender.

4. Return the soup to the slow cooker then add the soymilk and chopped basil, and heat on low for an additional 30 minutes.

RED LENTIL SOUP

Store-bought vegetable broth or stock typically contains much more sodium than the homemade variety, so adjust salt accordingly.

Serves 6

INGREDIENTS:

3 tablespoons olive oil

1 small onion, sliced

1½ teaspoons fresh ginger, peeled and minced

2 cloves garlic, minced

2 cups red lentils

6 cups Vegetable Stock (this chapter)

Juice of 1 lemon

½ teaspoon paprika

1 teaspoon cayenne pepper

1½ teaspoons salt

1. Rinse the lentils carefully and sort through the bunch to remove any dirt or debris.

2. In a sauté pan, heat the olive oil over medium heat then sauté the onion, ginger, and garlic for 2–3 minutes.

3. In a 4-quart slow cooker, add the sautéed vegetables and all remaining ingredients; cover, and cook on low for 6–8 hours. Add more salt, if necessary, to taste.

BEER-CHEESE SOUP

For the best results, use a pale ale beer in this recipe.

Serves 12

INGREDIENTS:

½ cup butter or margarine

½ white onion, diced

2 medium carrots, peeled and diced

2 ribs celery, diced

½ cup flour

3 cups Vegetable Stock (this chapter)

1 (12-ounce) beer

3 cups milk or unsweetened soymilk

3 cups Cheddar cheese or vegan Daiya Cheddar style shreds

1 teaspoon salt

1 teaspoon pepper

½ teaspoon dry ground mustard

1. In a sauté pan over medium heat, melt the butter or margarine then sauté the onion, carrots, and celery until just softened, about 5–7 minutes. Add the flour and stir to form a roux. Let cook for 2–3 minutes.

2. In a 4-quart slow cooker, add the cooked vegetables and roux then slowly pour in the stock and beer while whisking.

3. Add the milk, cheese, salt, pepper, and mustard. Cover and cook on low for 4 hours.

4. Let the soup cool slightly then blend until smooth, or you can skip this step and serve chunky.

Unsweetened Soymilk

Plain or original soymilk typically contains sugar and has a distinct flavor that will stand out in savory dishes. For these recipes, use plain unsweetened soymilk instead.

ZESTY PEANUT SOUP

This soup is one that you can make ahead because it tastes even better the next day. The rice cooks into the soup and acts as a thickener.

Serves 8

INGREDIENTS:

1 large sweet onion, peeled and diced

2 green onions, cleaned and diced

2 red bell peppers, seeded and diced

4 cloves garlic, peeled and minced

1 (28-ounce) can diced or crushed tomatoes

8 cups Vegetable Stock (this chapter)

¼ teaspoon freshly ground black pepper

½ teaspoon chili powder

½ cup brown rice

1 cup peanut butter

Salt

Optional: Sour cream

Optional: Roasted or dry-roasted peanuts, chopped

Optional: Hot sauce, to taste

1. Add the onions, bell peppers, garlic, tomatoes, stock, black pepper, chili powder, and rice to the slow cooker. Stir to combine. Cover and cook on low for 8 hours or until the onion is transparent and the red bell pepper is tender.

2. Stir in the peanut butter. Increase the heat to high, cover, and cook for 30 minutes or until heated through. Taste for seasoning; add salt and additional black pepper if needed.

3. To serve, ladle into soup bowls. If desired, add a dollop of sour cream and chopped peanuts to each serving. Have hot sauce available for those who wish to add it to their soup.

BACON CORN CHOWDER

This corn and potato chowder is given extra flavor with crunchy crumbled bacon.

Serves 4

INGREDIENTS:

4 slices bacon, diced

1 medium red onion, chopped

½ jalapeño chili, seeded and finely chopped

1 clove garlic, minced

2 tablespoons brown rice flour

½ teaspoon salt

¼ teaspoon pepper

2 (15-ounce) cans sweet corn kernels, drained, or 4 cups frozen sweet corn

3 red potatoes (about 1 pound), peeled and diced

4 cups Chicken Broth (this chapter)

2 cups half-and-half

1 cup chopped cherry tomatoes

3 tablespoons sliced fresh basil leaves

1. In a large pan, sauté bacon until crispy and browned. Remove bacon and set aside. Cook onion in bacon grease and sauté until translucent, about 3–5 minutes.

2. Whisk in jalapeño, garlic, flour, salt, and pepper and cook for 1 minute more until flour is toasted.

3. Grease a 4- or 6-quart slow cooker with nonstick cooking spray. Add onion mixture to the slow cooker. Add corn, potatoes, and broth. Stir ingredients together.

4. Cover and cook on high for 4 hours or on low for 8 hours.

5. One hour before serving stir in half-and-half. Add additional salt and pepper if desired. Serve chowder by ladling into large bowls and garnishing with bacon, chopped tomatoes, and fresh basil.

TUSCAN POTATO, KALE, AND SAUSAGE SOUP

An easy and delicious version of a popular soup at well-known Italian restaurant chain, this soup is so good you won't miss the breadsticks!

Serves 6

INGREDIENTS:

1 tablespoon olive oil

3 slices bacon, diced

1 pound Italian sausage, cut into bite-sized pieces

1 medium onion, chopped

2 cloves garlic, minced

3 tablespoons white wine

2 large russet potatoes, peeled and diced

4 cups Chicken Broth (this chapter)

¼ teaspoon red pepper flakes

½ teaspoon salt

½ teaspoon ground black pepper

2 cups fresh kale, chopped

1 cup heavy cream

1. In a large skillet heat olive oil and cook bacon and sausage until crisp and fat has been rendered, about 5 minutes. Remove bacon and sausage and add to a greased 4-quart slow cooker.

2. Sauté onion and garlic in the bacon fat until softened, 3–5 minutes.

3. Deglaze the pan with wine. Scrape the pan to remove all bits of vegetables and meat. Add all of the pan contents to the slow cooker.

4. Add potatoes, broth, pepper flakes, salt, and ground pepper. Cover and cook on high for 4 hours or on low for 8 hours, until potatoes are very tender.

5. An hour before serving stir in the kale and the cream. Continue to cook for 45 minutes to an hour until kale has softened and cream is warmed through. Be careful not to overcook at this point as the cream can curdle and separate if heated for too long.

Instead of Kale

If you aren't fond of kale, try adding 2 cups fresh baby spinach to the soup in the last hour of cooking.

SIMPLE GROUND TURKEY AND VEGETABLE SOUP

This soup is easy to throw together with pantry ingredients.

Serves 6

INGREDIENTS:

1 tablespoon olive oil

1 pound ground turkey

1 medium onion, diced

2 cloves garlic, minced

1 (16-ounce) package frozen mixed vegetables

4 cups Chicken Broth (this chapter)

½ teaspoon pepper

½ teaspoon salt

1. In a large skillet over medium heat, add olive oil and heat until sizzling. Cook ground turkey until browned about 5–6 minutes, stirring to break up the meat. Add meat to a greased 4-quart slow cooker. Sauté onion and garlic until softened, about 3–5 minutes. Add to the slow cooker.

2. Add remaining ingredients. Cover and cook on high for 4 hours or on low for 8 hours. Serve with crackers.

Pick Your Favorite

There are tons of different types of frozen vegetable mixes on the market today. One that works well with this soup is a mix of potatoes, carrots, celery, corn, and garden peas. However, if you don't like those vegetables, try a stir-fry mix or a Southwestern vegetables mix instead!

GREEK LEMON-CHICKEN SOUP

Lemon juice and egg yolks make this soup a lovely yellow color. It's a unique soup that's perfect for a spring luncheon.

Serves 4

INGREDIENTS:

4 cups Chicken Broth (this chapter)

¼ cup fresh lemon juice

¼ cup shredded carrots

¼ cup chopped onion

¼ cup chopped celery

⅛ teaspoon ground white pepper

2 tablespoons butter

2 tablespoons brown rice flour

4 egg yolks

½ cup cooked white rice

½ cup diced, cooked boneless chicken breast

8 slices lemon

1. In a greased 4-quart slow cooker combine the broth, lemon juice, carrots, onion, celery, and pepper. Cover and cook on high for 3–4 hours or on low for 6–8 hours.

2. One hour before serving, blend the butter and the flour together in a medium bowl with a fork. Remove 1 cup of hot broth from the slow cooker and whisk with the butter and flour. Add mixture back to the slow cooker.

3. In a small bowl, beat the egg yolks until light in color. Gradually add some of the hot soup to the egg yolks, stirring constantly. Return the egg mixture to the slow cooker.

4. Add the rice and cooked chicken. Cook on low for an additional hour. Ladle hot soup into bowls and garnish with lemon slices.

BARLEY AND BEAN SOUP WITH BEEF

You can substitute a 15-ounce rinsed and drained can of cannelini beans for the dried; if you do, you can add the tomatoes along with the other ingredients and omit the last hour of cooking time.

Serves 8

INGREDIENTS:

½ cup dried cannellini (white kidney) beans

2 pounds beef chuck

½ cup pearl barley, rinsed

2 cups fresh spinach

2 cloves garlic, peeled and minced

2 cups Beef Broth (this chapter)

2 cups water or Vegetable Stock (this chapter)

1 stalk celery, sliced

1 large onion, peeled and diced

1 cup baby carrots, sliced

1 parsnip, peeled and diced

1 turnip, peeled and diced

1 (15-ounce) can diced tomatoes

Salt and freshly ground black pepper, to taste

1. Rinse and drain the dried beans. Put in a bowl and add enough water to cover the beans by 2 inches. Cover and let soak for 8 hours or overnight. Drain the beans, rinse, and add to the slow cooker.

2. Trim off and discard any fat from the chuck roast and then cut it into bite-sized pieces; add to the slow cooker along with the rinsed pearl barley.

3. Remove the stems from the spinach; chop it and add to the slow cooker along with the garlic, broth, water or stock, celery, onion, carrots, parsnip, and turnip. Stir to combine. Cover and cook on low for 8 hours, or until the beans are cooked through.

4. Stir in the undrained diced tomatoes. Cover and cook for an additional hour. Taste for seasoning and add salt and pepper to taste.

BARBECUE BEEF AND BEAN SOUP

You can serve this soup as a main dish with a tossed salad and over or along with corn bread.

Serves 8

INGREDIENTS:

1 pound great northern beans, soaked

1 large onion, peeled and diced

⅛ teaspoon freshly ground black pepper

2 pounds beef short or Western ribs

6 cups water

¾ cup barbecue sauce

Salt and freshly ground black pepper, to taste

Optional: 1 tablespoon brown sugar

1. Soak the beans overnight and then precook them on the stovetop according to the instructions given in Slow Cooking Great Northern Beans (Chapter 23).

2. Once the beans are precooked, add them to the slow cooker. Stir in the onion and pepper. Add the beef ribs and pour in the water. Cover and cook on low for 8 hours or until the beans are cooked through.

3. Remove the short ribs and cut the meat from the bones. Stir the meat and barbecue sauce into the beans. Cover and cook on low for 1 hour. Taste for seasoning and add salt, pepper, and brown sugar if desired.

CHAPTER 20

STEWS

HOMESTYLE BEEF STEW

Your home will be filled with delicious aromas as this stew simmers all day in the slow cooker. Serve this stew over mashed potatoes for a hearty dinner.

Serves 6–8

INGREDIENTS:

2½ pounds beef stew meat, cubed

4 tablespoons flour

3 tablespoons olive oil

4 carrots

2 onions

2 beef bouillon cubes

4 cups water

½ cup red wine

2 tablespoons Worcestershire sauce

1 bay leaf

1. Dredge meat in flour. In skillet with olive oil, brown the beef on all sides, 7–10 minutes. Put beef in slow cooker.

2. Cut carrots into 1-inch pieces, and peel and quarter the onions. Add to the slow cooker.

3. Dissolve bouillon cubes in 4 cups boiling water. Add to slow cooker.

4. Add remaining ingredients, cover, and cook in slow cooker on low for 7–8 hours or until beef is fork tender.

Portion Control

Beef stew is a delicious meal to have on a cold wintry day, and with portion control freezing you can make it into a delicious lunch. Once stew has cooled, divide it up into lunch-sized portions and freeze in individual Tupperware containers. Defrost overnight in the refrigerator and you now have an easy meal you can heat up in the microwave in minutes.

CUBAN BEEF STEW

Serve Cuban Beef Stew over cooked rice or cooked rice and beans. Seeded and diced fresh jalapeño peppers can be substituted for the canned chilies.

Serves 6

INGREDIENTS:

2 pounds beef chuck roast

1 large onion, peeled and diced

2 cloves garlic, peeled and minced

1 red bell pepper, seeded and diced

1 green bell pepper, seeded and diced

4 strips bacon, chopped

1 (7-ounce) can green chilies, minced and drained

½ teaspoon dried thyme

½ teaspoon ground allspice

¼ teaspoon freshly grated nutmeg

1 cup Beef Broth (Chapter 19)

1 cup tomato juice

Salt, to taste

¾ teaspoon freshly ground pepper

3 large sweet potatoes

1. Trim the beef of any fat and cut into 1-inch cubes. Add it to the slow cooker along with all of the other ingredients except for the sweet potatoes. Stir to mix.

2. Peel and cut the sweet potatoes in half; add to the top of the other ingredients. Cover and cook on low for 8 hours or until the beef is tender.

Sweet Potato Choices

You can either serve a half slow-cooked sweet potato with each serving of the Cuban Beef Stew or, if you've added the sweet potato halves as instructed, cut them into cubes after they've cooked and carefully stir them into the stew. If you want sweet potato cubes that remain firm enough to stir into the stew without the risk of them falling apart, peel and dice the sweet potatoes and wait to stir them into the stew until the final 2 or 3 hours of the cooking time.

BRUNSWICK STEW

This stew is often made with rabbit. This Americanized version uses the easier to obtain and work with boneless, skinless pieces of chicken.

Serves 8

INGREDIENTS:

2 slices bacon, diced

3 small onions, peeled and thinly sliced

1 red bell pepper, seeded and diced

3 tablespoons all-purpose flour

1 teaspoon salt

½ teaspoon pepper

Pinch cayenne pepper

1 pound boneless, skinless chicken breast

1 pound boneless, skinless chicken thighs

1½–2 cups Chicken Broth (Chapter 19)

2 (15-ounce) cans diced tomatoes

½ teaspoon dried thyme, crushed

2 teaspoons dried parsley

1 tablespoon Worcestershire sauce

2 cups frozen lima beans, thawed

2 cups frozen whole-kernel corn, thawed

½ cup frozen sliced okra, thawed

1. Add the bacon, onion, and red bell pepper to the slow cooker; cover and cook on high for 30 minutes.

2. Put the flour, salt, pepper, and cayenne in a gallon-sized food-storage bag. Cut the chicken into bite-sized pieces, add to the bag, close the bag, and shake to coat the pieces with the seasoned flour.

3. Add the floured pieces to the slow cooker and stir them into the bacon, onions, and red bell pepper.

4. Stir in the broth, tomatoes, thyme, parsley, and Worcestershire sauce. Cover and cook on low for 6–8 hours.

5. Add the lima beans, corn, and okra; cover and cook on low for 1 hour or until the vegetables are heated through.

BEEF STEW WITH ROOT VEGETABLES AND RAISINS

The olives and raisins can either be stirred into the stew just before serving or you can have them at the table as condiments. Serve over or with hot biscuits.

Serves 8

INGREDIENTS:

1 tablespoon vegetable oil

1 tablespoon butter, melted

1 large onion, peeled and diced

1 stalk celery, finely diced

2 tablespoons all-purpose flour

Salt, to taste

¼ teaspoon freshly ground black pepper

1 (2-pound) beef chuck roast, cut into 1-inch cubes

1 (1-pound) bag baby carrots

2 large parsnips, peeled and diced

2 large Yukon gold or red potatoes, peeled and diced

2 (14½-ounce) cans diced tomatoes, undrained

2 cups Beef Broth (Chapter 19)

2 cloves garlic, peeled and minced

1 bay leaf

1 teaspoon dried thyme, crushed

½ cup almond- or pimento-stuffed green olives

⅓ cup golden raisins

1. Add the oil, butter, onion, and celery to the slow cooker. Cover and, stirring occasionally, cook on high for 30 minutes, or while you prepare the other ingredients.

2. Place the flour, salt, and pepper in a plastic bag and add the meat cubes; close and shake to coat the meat. Add half of the meat to the slow cooker, stirring it into the onion and celery.

3. Add the carrots, parsnips, potatoes, tomatoes, broth, garlic, bay leaf, and thyme to the cooker; stir to combine. Reduce the heat setting to low; cover and cook for 8 hours.

4. Remove and discard bay leaf. Serve warm.

BOUILLABAISSE

Serve this stew with garlic toast. For extra flavor, you can drizzle some extra-virgin olive oil over the top of each serving and then sprinkle on some minced fresh parsley.

Serves 8

INGREDIENTS:

2 tablespoons extra-virgin olive oil

1 large yellow onion, peeled and sliced

4 green onions, cleaned and sliced

1 clove garlic, peeled and minced

2 cups tomato juice or Chicken Broth (Chapter 19)

1 (14½-ounce) can diced tomatoes

1 cup Chardonnay or other dry white wine

2 cups water or Fish Stock (Chapter 19)

1 bay leaf

½ teaspoon freshly ground black pepper

1 teaspoon dried tarragon, crumbled

½ teaspoon thyme, crushed

1 tablespoon parsley, crushed

1 pound white fish (halibut, cod, snapper), cut into one-inch pieces

1 pound frozen cooked shrimp, thawed

2 (3.53-ounce) pouches of whole baby clams

1 (10-ounce) can boiled mussels, drained

1. Add the oil and onions to the slow cooker; cover and, stirring occasionally cook on high for 30 minutes or until the onion slices are transparent.

2. Stir in the garlic, tomato juice or broth, tomatoes, wine, water or stock, bay leaf, pepper, tarragon, thyme, and parsley. Cover, reduce the slow cooker heat to low, and cook for 4–8 hours.

3. Gently stir in the fish pieces; cover and cook on low for 15 minutes. Stir in the shrimp, clams, and mussels; cover and cook on low for 15 minutes or until the fish is opaque and cooked through and all ingredients are brought to temperature.

AFRICAN-INSPIRED CHICKEN STEW

Serve African Peanut and Chicken Stew with all of the optional condiments and it's an all-in-one meal and dessert.

Serves 6

INGREDIENTS:

8 chicken thighs

8 chicken legs

1 large yellow onion, peeled and sliced

½ teaspoon dried dill

2 bay leaves

4 cups water or Chicken Broth (Chapter 19)

½ cup peanut butter

3 tablespoons cornstarch

½ cup cold water

Salt and freshly ground pepper, to taste

Optional: 3–6 cups cooked long-grain rice

Optional: 5 bananas, peeled and cut lengthwise, then browned in butter

Optional: Unsweetened pineapple chunks

Optional: 4 ounces unsweetened coconut, toasted

½ cup roasted peanuts, chopped fine

1. Add the chicken pieces, onion, dill, bay leaves, and water or chicken broth to the slow cooker. Cover and cook on low for 4 hours, or until the chicken is cooked through. Remove the chicken from the pot and keep warm; discard the skin if desired. Remove and discard the bay leaves.

2. Add ½ cup of the hot liquid from the slow cooker to the peanut butter; mix well, and then pour the resulting peanut butter sauce into the pan. In a small bowl, mix the cornstarch and water together; remove any lumps. Whisk the cornstarch mixture into the broth in the pan, continuing to cook and stir until the broth thickens enough to coat the back of a spoon. (If you prefer a thicker sauce, mix additional cornstarch in cold water and repeat the process, cooking it long enough to cook out the raw cornstarch taste from the sauce.)

3. Taste the sauce for seasoning and add salt and pepper if needed.

4. For each serving, place a chicken thigh and chicken leg over some cooked rice. Ladle the thickened pan juices over the chicken and rice. If desired, top with fried bananas, pineapple, toasted coconut, and chopped peanuts.

Toasting Coconut

Preheat oven to 350°F. Spread the coconut out over a jellyroll pan. Place the pan on a shelf positioned in the center of the oven and, watching it carefully and stirring it every minute or two, bake the coconut for 6 minutes or until it's a very light golden brown.

SEAFOOD STEW

Serve the stew with warm garlic bread or topped with toasted garlic croutons.

Serves 8

INGREDIENTS:

2 tablespoons extra-virgin olive oil, plus more for serving

2 medium onions, peeled and diced

4 cloves garlic, peeled and minced

1 pound smoked sausage, sliced

½ teaspoon dried thyme

¼ teaspoon dried oregano, crushed

1 bay leaf

8 large Yukon gold potatoes, peeled and diced

8 cups Chicken Broth (Chapter 19)

1 pound kale, chopped

Optional: Hot water

2 pounds perch, cod, or bass fillets, skin and pin bones removed

2 (28-ounce) cans boiled baby clams, drained

Sea salt and freshly ground black pepper, to taste

Optional: ¼ cup fresh flat-leaf parsley, minced

1. Add the oil, onions, garlic, and sausage to the slow cooker; stir to coat the onions in the oil. Cover and, stirring occasionally, cook on high for 30 minutes or until the onion is transparent.

2. Add the thyme, oregano, bay leaf, and potatoes, stirring everything to mix the herbs and coat the potatoes in the oil.

3. Pour in the broth. Cover and cook on low for 4 hours.

4. Stir in the kale and fish. Add enough hot water to cover the fish if needed. Cover and continue to cook on low for 15 minutes.

5. Add the drained clams and cook on low for an additional 15 minutes or until the fish is cooked and the clams are brought to temperature. Taste for seasoning and add salt and pepper if needed. Garnish with chopped parsley if desired, and drizzle with extra-virgin olive oil.

Why Water Is Optional

The heat at which you cook a dish makes a difference in how much of the liquid will evaporate during the cooking process. Some vegetables in a dish also sometimes absorb more liquid than do others. If such evaporation or absorption occurs, the broth will become concentrated. Thus, water only reintroduces more liquid; it doesn't dilute the taste.

MARSALA BEEF STEW

This rich stew is good served over mashed potatoes, polenta, or cooked rice alongside a tossed salad. Top things off with some warm dinner rolls or whole-grain country bread.

Serves 6

INGREDIENTS:

2 tablespoons extra-virgin olive oil

1 tablespoon butter or Ghee (Chapter 16)

1 (2-pound) English-cut chuck roast, cut into bite-sized pieces

2 tablespoons all-purpose flour

1 small carrot, peeled and finely diced

1 celery stalk, finely diced

1 large yellow onion, peeled and diced

3 cloves garlic, peeled and minced

8 ounces mushrooms, cleaned and sliced

½ cup dry white wine

1 cup Marsala wine

½ teaspoon dried rosemary

½ teaspoon dried oregano

½ teaspoon dried basil

2 cups Beef Broth (Chapter 19)

2 cups water

Salt and freshly ground black pepper, to taste

1. Add the oil and butter or Ghee to a large nonstick skillet and bring it to temperature over medium-high heat.

2. Put the beef pieces and flour in a large plastic food-safe bag; close and toss to coat the meat in the flour. Add as many pieces of beef that will comfortably fit in the pan without crowding it and brown for 10 minutes or until the meat takes on a rich, dark outer color. Transfer the browned meat to the slow cooker.

3. Reduce the heat to medium and add the carrot and celery; sauté for 3–5 minutes, or until soft. Add the onion and sauté until the onion is transparent. Add the garlic and sauté for an additional 30 seconds. Stir in the mushrooms; sauté until tender. Transfer the sautéed vegetables and mushrooms to the slow cooker.

4. Add the remaining flour-coated beef to the slow cooker; stir to mix.

5. Add the wines to the skillet, and stir to pick up any browned bits sticking to the pan. Pour into the slow cooker. Add the rosemary, oregano, basil, broth, water, salt, and pepper to the slow cooker. Cover and cook on low for 6–8 hours or until the meat is tender. (You may need to allow the stew to cook uncovered for an hour or so to evaporate any extra liquid to thicken the sauce.) Taste for seasoning and add salt and pepper if needed. The taste of the stew will benefit if you allow it to rest, uncovered, off of the heat for a half hour, and then put the crock back in the slow cooker over low heat long enough to bring it back to temperature, but that step isn't necessary; you can serve it immediately if you prefer.

Contrary to Popular Opinion . . .

Searing meat does not seal in the juices. But it does intensify the flavor of a dish by adding another flavor dimension. Sautéing the vegetables and mushrooms adds flavor, too. The stew will still be good if you simply coat the meat in flour and add it to the slow cooker along with all of the other ingredients, but it's better if you take the time to do the searing and sautéing suggested in Step 1.

QUICK AND EASY STEW

A quick and easy way to thicken stew is to stir some leftover mashed potatoes into the broth.

Serves 8

INGREDIENTS:

1 (2-pound) chuck roast

1 (10½-ounce) can condensed French onion soup

1 (10¾-ounce) can condensed tomato soup

4 cups water

1½ (1-pound) bags frozen soup vegetables, thawed

Freshly ground black pepper, to taste

Optional: 2 tablespoons red wine or balsamic vinegar

1. Trim the fat from the roast and cut into bite-sized pieces. Add to the slow cooker along with the soups and water; stir to mix. Add the vegetables and pepper. Cover and cook on low for 8 hours or until the beef is tender and the vegetables are cooked through. Stir in vinegar (as a flavor-enhancer) if desired.

QUICK AND EASY STEW, VERSION 2

Unless you use low-sodium or salt-free soup, you probably won't need to add any salt to this stew.

Serves 8

INGREDIENTS:

1 (2-pound) chuck roast

1 (10¾-ounce) can condensed cream of celery soup

1 (10¾-ounce) can condensed cream of mushroom soup

1 (10½-ounce) can condensed French onion soup

2 cups water

1½ (1-pound) bags frozen soup vegetables, thawed

Freshly ground black pepper, to taste

1. Trim the fat from the roast and cut into bite-sized pieces. Add to the slow cooker along with the soups and water; stir to mix. Add the vegetables and pepper. Cover and cook on low for 8 hours or until the beef is tender and the vegetables are cooked through.

GREEN CHILI STEW

Serve this stew with a salad and over corn bread. It also works as an enchilada filling. One way to accommodate different tastes would be to use mild green chili peppers in the stew and have hot green salsa at the table.

Serves 6

INGREDIENTS:

1 stick butter, melted

¼ cup all-purpose flour

4 cups Chicken Broth (Chapter 19)

1 large yellow onion, peeled and diced

½ teaspoon dried oregano

½ tablespoon granulated garlic

1 tablespoon chili powder

1 (28-ounce) can heat-and-serve pork

3 (7-ounce) cans mild or hot green chilies, drained and chopped

Salt and freshly ground black pepper, to taste

Optional: Sour cream

1. Add the butter to the slow cooker and whisk in the flour, and then gradually whisk in the broth.

2. Stir in the onion, oregano, garlic, chili powder, pork, and canned chilies. Cover and cook on low for 6 hours. Stir well and taste for seasoning; add salt and pepper if needed. Add a dollop of sour cream over each serving if desired.

Other Options

Try substituting chicken for the pork, or use slow-cooked, pulled pork shoulder roast and part of its broth instead of the canned pork and some of the broth.

IRISH CODDLE

Serve this stew with Irish soda bread.

Serves 6

INGREDIENTS:

6 strips bacon

1½ pounds pork sausage

Salt and freshly ground black pepper, to taste

1 large yellow onion, peeled and diced

3 large potatoes, peeled and diced

3 large carrots, peeled and diced

1 cup beer, Chicken Broth (Chapter 19), hard cider, or water

1. Cut the bacon into 1-inch pieces and add to a large nonstick skillet along with the sausage. Cook the bacon and brown the sausage over medium-high heat for about 10 minutes, breaking apart the sausage as you do so. Add salt, pepper, and the onion; sauté the onion for 5 minutes or until it is transparent. Drain the meat and onion mixture of any excess fat; discard the fat.

2. Spread ⅓ of the meat-onion mixture over the bottom of the slow cooker. Add the potatoes in a layer, sprinkling them with salt and pepper if desired. Spoon another ⅓ of the meat-onion mixture over the potatoes. Top that with the carrots in a layer. Spread the remaining meat-onion mixture over the top of the carrots.

3. Pour in the beer, broth, hard cider, or water. Cover and cook on low for 6 hours or until the vegetables are tender. Stir to mix; taste for seasoning and adjust if necessary. Ladle into bowls to serve.

MOROCCAN CHICKEN STEW

You can substitute a cut-up, 3-pound whole chicken for the chicken thighs; if you do, remove as much of the skin as possible. When you season the dish, keep in mind that the olives and the preserved lemon will affect the saltiness.

Serves 4

INGREDIENTS:

8 small chicken thighs, skin removed

1 large yellow onion, peeled and diced

3 cloves garlic, peeled and minced

1 teaspoon ground ginger

½ teaspoon turmeric

¼ teaspoon cinnamon

Salt, to taste

½ teaspoon freshly ground black pepper

1 (15-ounce) can diced tomatoes

1 preserved lemon, rinsed and diced

1 teaspoon dried parsley

1 teaspoon dried coriander

1 (7½-ounce) jar pimento-stuffed olives, drained

2 cups cooked couscous or rice

1. Add the chicken, onion, garlic, ginger, turmeric, cinnamon, salt, and pepper to the slow cooker. Pour the tomatoes over the chicken and sprinkle the lemon over the tomatoes. Cover and cook on low for 6 hours or until chicken is tender.

2. Use a slotted spoon or tongs to remove the chicken from the slow cooker. Remove the meat from the bones; use two forks to shred it, and then return it to the slow cooker. Sprinkle the parsley, coriander, and olives over the top; cover and cook on low for additional 5 minutes. Serve warm over cooked couscous or rice.

Preserved Lemons

To make 5 preserved lemons, cut 5 lemons into partial quarters (leaving them attached at one end); rub kosher salt over the outside and cut sides of the lemons, and then pack them tightly in a sterilized 1-quart glass jar. Add 2 tablespoons kosher salt and enough lemon juice to cover the lemons. Seal and let set at room temperature for 14 days, inverting the jar once a day to mix. Store indefinitely in the refrigerator.

COUNTRY BEEF AND VEGETABLE STEW

Serve this country stew with French bread or biscuits and a tossed or steamed vegetable salad.

Serves 8

INGREDIENTS:

2 stalks celery, diced

1 (3-pound) boneless beef chuck roast

Salt and freshly ground black pepper, to taste

1 large onion, peeled and diced

2 cloves garlic, peeled and minced

2 cups Beef Broth (Chapter 19)

¼ cup red wine vinegar

1 tablespoon Worcestershire sauce

½ teaspoon dried thyme

1 teaspoon dried marjoram

4 large potatoes, scrubbed and diced

2 medium turnips, scrubbed and diced

1 (2-pound) bag baby carrots

1 (1-pound) bag frozen pearl onions, thawed

Optional: ¼ cup butter, softened

Optional: ¼ cup all-purpose flour

1. Add the celery, roast, salt, pepper, onion, garlic, broth, vinegar, Worcestershire sauce, thyme, marjoram, potatoes, turnips, carrots, and pearl onions to the slow cooker. Cover and cook on low for 8 hours or until the beef is tender and the vegetables are cooked through.

2. Optional: If you wish to thicken the pan juices, use a slotted spoon to transfer the meat and vegetables to a serving platter; cover and keep warm. Increase the temperature on the slow cooker to high. Skim and discard any fat from the pan juices. In a bowl, use a fork to blend together the butter and flour, and then whisk about a cup of the pan juices into the butter and flour. When the remaining pan juices begin to bubble around the edges, slowly whisk in the butter-flour mixture. Cook and stir for 10 minutes or until the mixture is thickened and the flour taste is cooked out of the sauce. Taste for seasoning and add salt and pepper if desired. Carefully stir the cooked vegetables into the thickened sauce. Cut the meat into bite-sized pieces and fold into the sauce and vegetables. Pour the thickened pan juices and vegetables into a tureen or serve directly from the slow cooker.

Steamed Vegetable Salad

Prepare a 12-ounce package of steam-in-the-bag frozen green beans according to package directions. When they're done, transfer them to a serving bowl and, before you've added the vegetables back into the thickened sauce in Step 2, mix some of the cooked potatoes, carrots, and pearl onions into the steamed beans. Dress the vegetables with red-wine vinaigrette. Salt and pepper to taste.

POT-AU-FEU

Pot-au-feu is French for "pot on the fire." When this Americanized adaptation of this French boiled dinner is made in a large slow cooker, you can add the potatoes so that they sit atop the meat and steam during the cooking process.

Serves 8

INGREDIENTS:

2 tablespoons butter

1 (1-pound) bag baby carrots

4 stalks celery, finely diced

2 large onions, peeled and sliced

2 cloves garlic, peeled

1 bouquet garni

1 (2-pound) boneless chuck, cut into 1-inch pieces

8 chicken thighs

1 pound Western-style pork ribs

Coarse sea salt and freshly ground black pepper, to taste

4 small turnips, peeled and quartered

1 medium rutabaga, peeled and cut into eighths

4 cups water

8 medium red or Yukon Gold potatoes

1. Add the butter to a large (6½-quart) slow cooker set on high heat. (You can make this dish in a 4-quart slow cooker, but you may need to omit the potatoes from the cooker and prepare them separately.) Finely dice 10 of the baby carrots and 2 of the onion slices. Add the diced carrots, celery, and onions to the slow cooker; cover and cook for 15 minutes.

2. In this order, add the garlic, bouquet garni, beef, chicken, and pork; sprinkle the salt and pepper over the meat and then layer in the onion slices, remaining carrots, turnips, and rutabaga.

3. Pour in the water. (If you're using a 4-quart slow cooker, you can add the water in stages throughout the cooking process. Start with about 2 cups of the water and check the cooker every 2 hours to see if you need to add more to prevent it from boiling dry.)

4. Arrange the potatoes on top of the rutabaga. Reduce the heat setting to low, cover, and cook for 8 hours.

5. For a casual supper, you can ladle servings directly from the crock. For a more formal dinner, use a slotted spoon to arrange the vegetables and potatoes around the outside of a large serving platter with the meats arranged in the center; ladle a generous amount of the broth over all. Strain the remaining broth; pour the strained broth into a gravy boat to have at the table.

6. Optional: Serve with toasted French bread rubbed with garlic and have coarse sea salt, cornichons, Dijon mustard, grated horseradish, pickled onions, sour cream, and whole-grain mustard at the table.

Bouquet Garni

For the Pot-au-feu recipe, create the bouquet garni by wrapping 2 bay leaves, 1 teaspoon dried thyme, 1 tablespoon dried parsley, 1 teaspoon black peppercorns, and 4 cloves in cheesecloth, or add them to a muslin spice bag.

PORK AND APPLE STEW

If you prefer a tart apple taste, you can substitute Granny Smith apples for the Golden Delicious. (You can also add more apples if you wish. Apples and pork were made for each other!)

Serves 8

INGREDIENTS:

1 (3-pound) boneless pork shoulder roast

Salt and freshly ground black pepper, to taste

1 large sweet onion, peeled and diced

2 Golden Delicious apples, peeled, cored, and diced

1 (2-pound) bag baby carrots

2 stalks celery, finely diced

2 cups apple juice or cider

Optional: ¼ cup dry vermouth

Optional: 2 tablespoons brandy

Optional: 2 tablespoons brown sugar

½ teaspoon dried thyme

¼ teaspoon ground allspice

¼ teaspoon dried sage

2 large sweet potatoes, peeled and quartered

1. Trim the roast of any fat; discard the fat and cut the roast into bite-sized pieces. Add the pork to the slow cooker along with the remaining ingredients in the order given. (You want to rest the sweet potato quarters on top of the mixture in the slow cooker.) Cover and cook on low for 6 hours or until the pork is cooked through and tender.

Herbs and Spice Test

If you're unsure about the herbs and spices suggested in a recipe, wait to add them until the end of the cooking time. Once the meat is cooked through, spoon out ¼ cup or so of the pan juices into a microwave-safe bowl. Add a pinch of each herb and spice (in proportion to how they're suggested in the recipe), microwave on high for 15–30 seconds, and then taste the broth to see if you like it. Season the dish accordingly.

PORTUGUESE BEEF STEW

Serve this stew over pieces of torn French bread. You'll want about an ounce of bread for each serving, or about 2 generous slices, depending on the circumference of the loaf.

Serves 8

INGREDIENTS:

2 tablespoons extra-virgin olive oil

3 pounds beef bottom round

Salt and freshly ground black pepper, to taste

1 large onion, peeled and diced

2 cloves garlic, peeled and minced

1 cup Zinfandel or other dry red wine

1 (6-ounce) can tomato paste

1 (28-ounce) can diced tomatoes

1 cup Beef Broth (Chapter 19)

1½ tablespoons pickling spices

1 bay leaf

2 teaspoons dried mint

1. Add the oil to the slow cooker. Trim the beef of any fat and cut it into bite-sized pieces. Add the meat to the cooker along with the salt, pepper, onion, and garlic. Stir to coat the meat and vegetables in the oil.

2. Add the wine, tomato paste, undrained tomatoes, and broth to a bowl or measuring cup. Stir to mix. Pour into the slow cooker. Add the pickling spices and bay leaf. Cover and cook on low for 7 hours or until the beef is cooked through and tender. Skim and discard any fat from the surface of the stew in the slow cooker. Remove and discard the bay leaf.

3. Stir in the dried mint; cover and continue to cook on low for 15 minutes to allow the mint to blend into the stew. (If you have fresh mint available, you can instead sprinkle about 1 teaspoon of minced fresh mint over each serving. Garnish each serving with a sprig of mint as well if desired.)

Handling Pickling Spices

When pickling spices are used in a dish, they're usually added to a muslin cooking bag or a tea ball or tied into a piece of cheesecloth. After the cooking time, they're pulled from the pot and discarded. For the Portuguese Beef Stew recipe, if you wish, you can simply stir them in with the other ingredients.

VEAL STEW

This recipe lets you stretch a small amount of expensive veal into lots of servings. This stew is good if each bowl is garnished with a dollop of drained yogurt or sour cream.

Serves 8

INGREDIENTS:

3 tablespoons all-purpose flour

½ teaspoon salt

¼ teaspoon freshly ground black pepper

1 pound boneless veal shoulder, cut into 1-inch cubes

2 tablespoons butter

1 medium yellow onion, peeled and sliced

2 small cloves garlic, peeled and minced

1 large green bell pepper, seeded and diced

1 medium eggplant, peeled and diced

1 medium zucchini, peeled and diced

1 cup leeks, white part only, well-rinsed and thinly sliced

2 small turnips, peeled and diced

1 cup celery root, peeled and diced

2 small parsnips, peeled and diced

2 large carrots, peeled and sliced

½ cup Beef Broth (Chapter 19)

½ cup dry red wine

2 teaspoons dried parsley

¼ teaspoon dried thyme

¼ teaspoon dried marjoram

1 tablespoon tomato paste

1 (15-ounce) can diced tomatoes

1 small head cabbage, cored and thinly sliced

1 (14½-ounce) can French-style green beans, drained

¼ cup seedless green grapes, cut in half

1. Add the flour, salt, and pepper to a large food-storage bag; shake to mix. Add the veal cubes and toss to coat in flour. Melt the butter in a large nonstick skillet over medium-high heat. Add the veal and brown for 5 minutes. Add the onions and sauté, stirring frequently, for 5 minutes or until the onions are transparent. Add the garlic and sauté for an additional 30 seconds. Transfer to the slow cooker.

2. Add the green bell pepper, eggplant, zucchini, leeks, turnips, celery root, parsnips, and carrots to the slow cooker. Stir to mix together with the meat and sautéed vegetables.

3. Add the broth, wine, parsley, thyme, marjoram, tomato paste, and diced tomatoes to a bowl or measuring cup; stir to mix, and then pour into the slow cooker. Add as much of the cabbage as will sit on top of the ingredients already in the slow cooker. Cover and begin to cook on low for up to 8 hours. As the cabbage wilts, add the rest, stirring it into the stew about halfway through the cooking time. An hour before the end of the cooking time, add the green beans and green grapes. The stew is done when the meat and all of the vegetables are cooked through and tender.

BRAZILIAN MEAT STEW

This goes well with fluffy white rice and a nice after-dinner coffee. You can substitute salt pork for the bacon.

Serves 8–10

INGREDIENTS:

3 slices bacon

2 onions

3 cloves garlic

1 pound beef

1 pound pork

1 pound spicy link sausage

4 cups cooked black beans with liquid

2 cups chopped tomatoes

1 cup water

1 tablespoon prepared mustard

½ teaspoon salt

½ teaspoon pepper

1. Dice and sauté the bacon in a pan over medium heat until crispy.

2. Finely chop the onions and garlic. Add the onions and garlic to the bacon and continue heating until the onions are soft.

3. Cut the beef, pork, and sausage into bite-sized pieces. Add the meat to the onion mixture and continue heating until the meat is browned. Transfer the meat-and-onion mixture to the slow cooker.

4. Mash 1 cup of the black beans and add both mashed and whole beans to the slow cooker. Add the tomatoes and the remaining ingredients to the slow cooker.

5. Cover and heat on a low setting for 3–4 hours.

BEEF AND GUINNESS STEW

This stew is filled with vegetables and is very flavorful. The small amounts of sugar and cocoa eliminate the bitterness occasionally found in similar stews without being detectable.

Serves 8

INGREDIENTS:

2 teaspoons canola oil

1 large onion, diced

2 parsnips, diced

2 carrots, diced

2 stalks celery, diced

3 cloves garlic, minced

2 russet potatoes, diced

2 tablespoons minced fresh rosemary

2 pounds lean top round roast, cut into 1" cubes

1 tablespoon dark brown sugar

¼ teaspoon salt

½ teaspoon freshly ground black pepper

1 tablespoon baking cocoa

1 cup water

½ cup Guinness extra stout

½ cup frozen peas

1. Heat the oil in a large skillet. Sauté the onion, parsnips, carrots, celery, garlic, potatoes, rosemary, and beef until the ingredients begin to soften and brown. Drain any excess fat.

2. Add to a 4-quart slow cooker. Sprinkle with sugar, salt, pepper, and cocoa. Pour in the water and Guinness. Stir. Cook for 8–9 hours on low.

3. Add the frozen peas. Cover and cook an additional ½ hour on high. Stir before serving.

Choosing Cuts of Beef

Leaner cuts like top round are excellent choices for slow cooking because the long cooking time tenderizes them. Look for cuts that have minimal marbling and trim off any excess fat before cooking. Searing and sautéing are good ways to cook off some external fat before adding the meat to the slow cooker. Drain any excess fat.

SEAFOOD AND CHICKEN GUMBO

Filé powder is made from ground, dried sassafras leaves; it helps flavor and thicken the gumbo. If you're using homemade chicken broth, you can skip Steps 1 and 2; simply omit the oil and add the bacon, chicken, onion, and celery to the slow cooker and proceed to Step 3.

Serves 4

INGREDIENTS:

1 tablespoon olive or vegetable oil

2 strips bacon, diced

4 chicken thighs, skin removed

1 large onion, peeled and diced

2 stalks celery, diced

½ cup aromatic brown rice

1 (15-ounce) can diced tomatoes

1 green bell pepper, seeded and diced

1 cup frozen okra, thawed

2 cups Chicken Broth (Chapter 19)

2 cups water

1 bay leaf

⅓ pound shrimp, peeled and deveined

⅓ pound scallops, quartered

⅓ pound cooked crabmeat

¼ teaspoon dried thyme

1 teaspoon dried parsley

2 teaspoons filé powder

Salt, to taste

1. Bring the oil to temperature in a nonstick skillet over medium-high heat. Add the bacon and chicken; fry the chicken for 3 minutes on each side. Use tongs to move the chicken to a plate.

2. Add the onion and celery to the skillet; sauté for 10 minutes or until the onion is lightly browned.

3. Add the rice to the slow cooker and spread it over the bottom of the crock. Place the chicken pieces over the rice. Pour in the sautéed onion and celery. Add the tomatoes, bell pepper, okra, broth, water, and bay leaf. Cover and cook on low for 6 hours.

4. Add the shrimp, scallops, crab, thyme, and parsley. Cover and cook on low for 15 minutes.

5. Turn off the heat to the slow cooker. Stir in the filé powder. Cover and let rest for 15 minutes or until the shrimp is pink and the scallops are opaque. Salt to taste. Ladle into bowls and serve immediately.

HERBED TILAPIA STEW

Any type of white fish fillets (such as haddock or cod) will also work in this recipe. Fish cooks very, very quickly even on the low setting in a slow cooker, so this is one recipe you will need to set a timer for.

Serves 6

INGREDIENTS:

2 pounds frozen boneless tilapia fillets

4 tablespoons butter

1 (14.5-ounce) can diced tomatoes, with juice

4 cloves garlic, minced

½ cup sliced green onions

2 teaspoons Thai fish sauce

2 tablespoons fresh thyme, chopped or 1 teaspoon dried thyme

1. Grease a 4-quart slow cooker with nonstick cooking spray. Place all ingredients in the slow cooker.

2. Cover and cook on high for 1½–2 hours or on low for 2½–3 hours. Watch the cooking time. If your fish fillets are very thin you may need to reduce the cooking time.

3. When fish is cooked through, fillets will easily separate and flake with a fork. Break the fish up into the tomatoes and cooking liquids. Serve stew over cooked rice or gluten-free pasta.

CHAPTER 21

CHILIS

RECIPE LIST

TEX-MEX CHILI

Serve this chili with warm flour tortillas or baked corn tortilla chips. It's good topped with a dollop of guacamole and sour cream.

Serves 6

INGREDIENTS:

1 pound turkey or chorizo sausage

Nonstick spray

1 medium onion, peeled and diced

1 (15-ounce) can Tex-Mex-style chili beans

1 (11-ounce) can whole kernel corn with peppers, drained

1 (6-ounce) package Spanish-style rice mix

6 cups water

1. Remove casings from the sausage, if present, and add to a nonstick skillet. Breaking apart the sausage as you do so, fry sausage and onions over medium-high heat for 8 minutes or until the sausage is no longer pink. Drain and discard any rendered fat. Treat the slow cooker with nonstick spray and add the browned sausage.

2. Stir in the undrained beans, corn, and seasoning packet from the rice. Pour in the water. Cover and cook on low for 6 hours.

3. Stir the rice mix into the contents of the slow cooker. Cover and cook on low for 1 hour.

TACO CHILI

Note that you don't drain any of the canned ingredients used in this recipe. You include the entire contents of each can.

Serves 8

INGREDIENTS:

3 pounds lean ground beef

1 (1.2-ounce) package taco seasoning mix

2 (15-ounce) cans chunky Mexican-style tomatoes

1 (15-ounce) can red kidney beans

1 (15-ounce) can whole kernel corn

1. Brown the ground beef in a large nonstick skillet over medium heat, breaking apart the meat as you do so. Remove and discard any fat rendered from the meat before transferring it to the slow cooker.

2. Stir in the taco seasoning mix, tomatoes, kidney beans, and corn. Cover and cook on low for 4–6 hours.

FIERY CHICKEN CHILI

For the hot and spicy lover! Serve with Corn Bread (Chapter 23).

Serves 8

INGREDIENTS:

1 pound ground chicken

3 cloves garlic, chopped

3 chipotle chiles in adobo

1 (15-ounce) can dark red kidney beans, drained and rinsed

1 (15-ounce) can black beans, drained and rinsed

1 teaspoon Worcestershire sauce

2 (15-ounce) cans diced tomatoes

1 (4-ounce) can diced green chiles

1 teaspoon ground cayenne pepper

1 teaspoon ground chipotle

1 onion, chopped

1 tablespoon habanero hot sauce

1 teaspoon paprika

1 teaspoon hot chili powder

1 teaspoon liquid smoke

1. Quickly sauté the ground chicken in a nonstick skillet until just cooked through. Drain all fat.

2. Place all ingredients in a 4-quart slow cooker. Stir. Cook on low for 8–10 hours.

What Is Liquid Smoke?

Liquid smoke is made by condensing smoke in water to form a fluid. It is found in a variety of flavors including hickory and mesquite and can be used to add the flavor of being slow cooked over a flame without actually having to grill.

LONE STAR STATE CHILI

Word has it that Texans prefer their chili without beans, but you can add a can or two of rinsed and drained kidney beans if you prefer it that way. Doing so will increase the number of servings to 10 or 12. Serve this dish with baked corn tortilla chips and a tossed salad with a sour cream dressing.

Serves 8

INGREDIENTS:

¼ pound bacon, diced

1 stalk celery, finely chopped

1 large carrot, peeled and finely chopped

1 (3-pound) chuck roast, cut into small cubes

2 large yellow onions, peeled and diced

6 cloves garlic, peeled and minced

6 jalapeño peppers, seeded and diced

Salt and freshly ground pepper, to taste

4 tablespoons chili powder

1 teaspoon Mexican oregano

1 teaspoon ground cumin

1 teaspoon brown sugar

1 (28-ounce) can diced tomatoes

1 cup Beef Broth (Chapter 19)

1. Add all of the ingredients to the slow cooker in the order given, and stir to combine. The liquid in your slow cooker should completely cover the meat and vegetables. If additional liquid is needed add crushed tomatoes, broth, or some water.

2. Cover and cook on low for 8 hours. Taste for seasoning, and add more chili powder if desired.

Hot Pepper Precautions

Wear gloves or sandwich bags over your hands when you clean and dice hot peppers. It's important to avoid having the peppers come into contact with any of your skin, or especially your eyes. As an added precaution, wash your hands (and under your fingernails) thoroughly with hot soapy water after you remove the gloves or sandwich bags.

SMOKY CHIPOTLE PORK CHILI

Chipotle peppers add a smoky, spicy flavor to this chili.

Serves 8

INGREDIENTS:

1 pound ground pork

30 ounces canned fire-roasted diced tomatoes

3 chipotle chiles in adobo, chopped

1 teaspoon liquid smoke

1 teaspoon chili powder

1 teaspoon ground chipotle

1 teaspoon hot paprika

1 teaspoon smoked paprika

30 ounces canned chili beans, drained and rinsed

1 medium onion, diced

3 cloves garlic, minced

1. Quickly sauté the pork in a nonstick skillet until just cooked through. Drain off any fat.

2. Place all ingredients in a 4-quart slow cooker. Stir. Cook on low for 8–10 hours.

What Are Chipotle Chiles in Adobo?

Chipotle peppers are smoke-dried jalapeños. They are then canned in a spiced onion, garlic, and tomato sauce. You can find them in the Mexican or ethnic foods section of most grocery stores.

SECRET INGREDIENT BEEF CHILI

The mango melts into the chili and adds a fruity depth of flavor.

Serves 8

INGREDIENTS:

1 pound 94% lean ground beef

30 ounces canned diced tomatoes

¼ cup cubed mango

1 teaspoon liquid smoke

1 teaspoon chili powder

1 teaspoon ground jalapeño

1 teaspoon hot chili powder

1 teaspoon smoked paprika

30 ounces canned kidney beans, drained
    and rinsed

1 medium onion, diced

3 cloves garlic, minced

1 teaspoon cumin

1. Quickly sauté the beef in a nonstick skillet until no longer pink. Drain off all fat and discard it.

2. Place the beef and all the remaining ingredients in a 4-quart slow cooker. Stir. Cook on low for 8–10 hours.

Why Use Canned Beans?

Canned beans are ready to eat directly out of the package, making them an excellent time saver. Dried beans need to be soaked or cooked before using. Properly cooked dried beans can be substituted for an equal amount of canned, but resist the temptation to use uncooked dried beans unless explicitly directed to in the recipe. They may not rehydrate properly.

ACORN SQUASH CHILI

Acorn squash keeps its shape in this chili, giving it a chunky texture.

Serves 8

INGREDIENTS:

2 cups cubed acorn squash

30 ounces canned petite diced tomatoes

2 stalks celery, diced

1 medium onion, diced

3 cloves garlic, minced

2 carrots, diced

1 teaspoon mesquite liquid smoke

2 teaspoons hot sauce

1 teaspoon chili powder

1 teaspoon paprika

1 teaspoon oregano

1 teaspoon smoked paprika

1 (15-ounce) can kidney beans, drained and rinsed

1 (15-ounce) can cannellini beans, drained and rinsed

1 cup fresh corn kernels

1. Place all of the ingredients except the corn in a 4-quart slow cooker. Cook for 8 hours on low.

2. Add the corn and stir. Cover and continue to cook on low for ½ hour. Stir before serving.

Cayenne Pepper versus Chili Powder

Contrary to popular belief, ground cayenne pepper and chili powder are not interchangeable. Ground cayenne is made from a dried cayenne pepper. Chili powder is a mixture of several different varieties of chiles.

THREE-BEAN CHILI

This meatless chili is quite hearty; even the most dedicated meat lover will love it!

Serves 8

INGREDIENTS:

1 teaspoon minced fresh jalapeño

2 (15-ounce) cans diced tomatoes

2 stalks celery, diced

1 medium onion, diced

3 cloves garlic, minced

2 carrots, diced

1 teaspoon ground cayenne pepper

1 teaspoon chili powder

1 teaspoon paprika

1 teaspoon cumin

2 teaspoons jalapeño hot sauce

1 (15-ounce) can black beans, drained and rinsed

1 (15-ounce) can kidney beans, drained and rinsed

1 (15-ounce) can cannellini beans, drained and rinsed

1 cup fresh corn kernels

1. Place all of the ingredients except the corn into a 4-quart slow cooker. Cook for 8 hours on low.

2. Add the corn and stir. Cover and continue to cook on low for ½ hour. Stir before serving.

Chili Pairings

Try chili topped with low-fat sour cream, diced avocado, diced onions, sharp Cheddar, or diced green onions. Serve over rice or crumbled tortilla chips. Stir leftovers into cooked whole-wheat pasta and sprinkle with cheese for an easy chili mac-n-cheese.

LEAN GREEN CHILI

Green chili gets its name from tomatillos and lots of green chiles.

Serves 8

INGREDIENTS:

2 (15-ounce) cans cannellini beans, drained and rinsed

1 teaspoon cumin

1 teaspoon ground jalapeño

1 jalapeño, minced

2 cloves garlic, minced

1 (4-ounce) can green chiles, drained

1 (28-ounce) can tomatillos, drained

1 medium onion, diced

1 tablespoon lime juice

1 teaspoon celery flakes

1 stalk celery, diced

2 cups diced cooked chicken breast

1. Place all of the ingredients except the chicken in a 4-quart slow cooker. Cook on low for 8 hours. Stir in the chicken, put the lid back on, and cook for an additional hour on low. Stir before serving.

Time-Saving Tip

Cube leftover cooked chicken or turkey breast and freeze in clearly marked 1- or 2-cup packages. Defrost overnight in the refrigerator before using. Cooked poultry should be added to a recipe during the last hour of cooking.

TURKEY-TOMATILLO CHILI

This is a great way to use up leftover turkey from Thanksgiving!

Serves 8

INGREDIENTS:

2 cups cubed tomatillos

1 green bell pepper, diced

1 onion, diced

1 teaspoon ground cayenne pepper

1 teaspoon cumin

1 teaspoon paprika

1 teaspoon chili powder

2 (15-ounce) cans chili beans, drained and rinsed

2 cups cubed cooked turkey breast

1. Place all ingredients except the turkey in a 4-quart slow cooker. Stir to mix the ingredients. Cook on low for 8 hours, and then stir in the turkey. Cook for an additional 30–60 minutes on high.

Tomatillo Tidbits

Tomatillos, like tomatoes, are a part of the nightshade family of vegetables. They look like small tomatoes covered in a papery husk. The husk should be removed before eating. Look for tomatillos that are unblemished, slightly heavy for their size, and solid to the touch. They are most commonly green but can also be purple or yellow.

CINCINNATI CHILI

This unusual regional favorite has a spicy sweet flavor that is wonderfully addictive! Serve over cooked spaghetti with any combination of the following toppings: kidney beans, diced raw onion, and shredded Cheddar.

Serves 8

INGREDIENTS:

1 pound 93% lean ground beef

15 ounces crushed tomato in juice

2 cloves garlic, minced

1 onion, diced

1 teaspoon cumin

1 teaspoon cocoa

2 teaspoons chili powder

½ teaspoon cloves

1 tablespoon apple cider vinegar

1 teaspoon allspice

½ teaspoon ground cayenne pepper

1 teaspoon cinnamon

1 tablespoon Worcestershire sauce

¼ teaspoon salt

1. In a nonstick skillet, quickly sauté the beef until it is no longer pink. Drain all fat and discard it.

2. Place all ingredients—including the beef—in a 4-quart slow cooker. Stir. Cook on low for 8–10 hours.

Sauté the Meat When Making Chili

Even though it is not aesthetically necessary to brown the meat when making chili, sautéing meat before adding it to the slow cooker allows you to drain off any extra fat. Not only is it healthier to cook with less fat, your chili will be unappetizingly greasy if there is too much fat present in the meat during cooking.

SPICY SAUSAGE CHILI

You can use hot or mild reduced-fat bulk sausage in this recipe.

Serves 8

INGREDIENTS:

1½ pounds spicy chicken sausage

2 teaspoons ground cayenne pepper

1 tablespoon ground chipotle

1 teaspoon hot paprika

1 teaspoon hot chili powder

1 (15-ounce) can cannellini beans, drained and rinsed

1 (15-ounce) can tomatoes with green chiles

1 (15-ounce) can hominy

1 teaspoon cumin

1. Brown the sausage in a nonstick skillet. Drain off all fat.

2. Add the sausage and remaining ingredients to a 4-quart slow cooker and stir to combine and break up the hominy as needed. Cook on low for 8–10 hours.

NO-BEAN CHILI

For a variation, try this with lean beef sirloin instead of pork.

Serves 6

INGREDIENTS:

1 tablespoon canola oil

1 pound boneless pork tenderloin, cubed

1 large onion, diced

3 poblano chiles, diced

2 cloves garlic, minced

1 teaspoon cumin

1 teaspoon dried oregano

1 cup Chicken Broth (Chapter 19)

1 (15-ounce) can crushed tomatoes

2 teaspoons ground cayenne pepper

1. In a large nonstick skillet, heat the oil. Add the pork, onion, chiles, and garlic. Sauté until the pork is no long visibly pink on any side. Drain off any fats or oils and discard them.

2. Pour the pork mixture into a 4-quart slow cooker. Add the remaining ingredients. Stir.

3. Cook on low for 8–9 hours.

Using Herbs

As a general rule, 1 tablespoon minced fresh herbs equals 1 teaspoon dried herbs. Fresh herbs can be frozen for future use. Discard dried herbs after 1 year.

CALIFORNIA CHILI

This chili was inspired by Gilroy, California, a town that is world-renowned for its garlic crop and annual garlic festival.

Serves 6

INGREDIENTS:

15 ounces hominy

15 ounces fire-roasted tomatoes with garlic

½ cup canned cannellini beans, drained and rinsed

1 teaspoon cumin

1 teaspoon ground jalapeño

2 Anaheim chiles, diced

6 cloves garlic, thinly sliced

1 medium onion, diced

1 stalk celery, diced

1 tablespoon lime juice

1 teaspoon chipotle chile powder

1 teaspoon California chile powder

2 cups diced cooked chicken breast

1. Place all of the ingredients except the chicken in a 4-quart slow cooker. Cook on low for 8 hours.

2. Stir in the chicken, cover the cooker again, and cook for an additional hour on low. Stir before serving.

SUMMER CHILI

This chili is full of summer vegetables. It is also great as a vegetarian chili; simply omit the chicken.

Serves 8

INGREDIENTS:

½ pound ground chicken

1 bulb fennel, diced

4 radishes, diced

2 stalks celery, diced, including leaves

2 carrots, cut into coin-sized pieces

1 medium onion, diced

1 shallot, diced

4 cloves garlic, sliced

1 habanero pepper, diced

1 (15-ounce) can cannellini beans, drained and rinsed

12 ounces tomato paste

½ teaspoon dried oregano

½ teaspoon black pepper

½ teaspoon crushed rosemary

½ teaspoon cayenne pepper

½ teaspoon ground chipotle

1 teaspoon chili powder

1 teaspoon tarragon

¼ teaspoon cumin

¼ teaspoon celery seed

2 zucchini, cubed

10 Campari tomatoes, quartered

1 cup corn kernels

1. Sauté the meat in a nonstick pan until just browned. Add to a 4-quart slow cooker along with the fennel, radishes, celery, carrots, onion, shallot, garlic, habanero, beans, tomato paste, and all spices. Stir.

2. Cook on low for 6–7 hours; then stir in the zucchini, tomatoes, and corn. Cook for an additional 30 minutes on high. Stir before serving.

MUSHROOM CHILI

Meaty Portobello mushrooms make this vegan chili very satisfying.

Serves 4

INGREDIENTS:

3 Portobello mushrooms, cubed

1 (15-ounce) can black beans, drained and rinsed

1 onion, diced

3 cloves garlic, sliced

2½ cups diced fresh tomatoes

1 chipotle pepper in adobo, minced

½ teaspoon jalapeño hot sauce

1 teaspoon cumin

½ teaspoon ground cayenne pepper

½ teaspoon freshly ground black pepper

¼ teaspoon salt

1. Place all ingredients into a 4-quart slow cooker. Stir. Cook on low for 8 hours.

SUPER-MILD CHILI

This is a chili for those people who like the idea of chili but who are not fond of spicy food.

Serves 6

INGREDIENTS:

1 pound ground turkey

2 (15-ounce) cans cannellini beans, drained and rinsed

2 (14-ounce) cans crushed tomatoes

1 teaspoon oregano

½ teaspoon cumin

1 teaspoon mild chili powder

1 bell pepper, diced

1 Vidalia onion, diced

2 cloves garlic, minced

1. Brown the turkey in a nonstick skillet. Drain if needed.

2. Add the turkey and all of the remaining ingredients to a 4-quart slow cooker. Stir. Cook on low for 7–8 hours. Stir before serving.

TEXAS FIREHOUSE CHILI

This no-bean chili is similar to dishes entered into firehouse chili cook-offs all over Texas.

Serves 4

INGREDIENTS:

1 pound cubed lean beef

2 tablespoons onion powder

1 tablespoon garlic powder

2 tablespoons Mexican-style chili powder

1 tablespoon paprika

½ teaspoon oregano

½ teaspoon freshly ground black pepper

½ teaspoon white pepper

½ teaspoon cayenne pepper

½ teaspoon chipotle pepper

8 ounces tomato sauce

1. Quickly brown the beef in a nonstick skillet. Drain off any excess grease.

2. Add the meat and all of the remaining ingredients to a 4-quart slow cooker. Cook on low up to 10 hours.

FILIPINO-INFLUENCED PORK CHILI

This chili, inspired by popular Filipino condiments and flavors, is a wonderful change from American-style chili.

Serves 8

INGREDIENTS:

1 pound pork loin, cubed

1½ cups crushed tomatoes

⅓ cup banana sauce

2 tablespoons lime juice

2 tablespoons cane vinegar

1 teaspoon ginger juice

1 teaspoon chili powder

½ teaspoon freshly ground black pepper

2 jarred pimentos, minced

1 onion, minced

3 unripe plantains, diced

2 tomatoes, cubed

1 large sweet potato, cubed

1. Sauté the cubed pork in a dry skillet for 5 minutes. Drain off any fat.

2. Add the pork and remaining ingredients to a 4-quart slow cooker. Stir. Cook on low for 8 hours. Stir before serving.

All about Banana Sauce

Banana sauce, also known as banana ketchup, is a popular condiment in the Philippines. Despite its similar appearance to tomato ketchup, it contains a mixture of bananas, sugar, vinegar, and spices rather than tomatoes. Banana sauce is found in Filipino-style spaghetti sauce and used on hot dogs, burgers, omelets, French fries, and fish.

ENCHILADA CHILI

Fresh cilantro should top each serving. If you're using freeze-dried cilantro, add a tablespoon to the slow cooker near the end of the cooking time and stir it into the chili.

Serves 8

INGREDIENTS:

2 pounds boneless beef chuck roast, cut into bite-sized pieces

1 (15-ounce) can pinto and/or red kidney beans, rinsed and drained

1 (15-ounce) can diced tomatoes, undrained

1 (10½-ounce) can condensed beef broth

1 (10-ounce) can enchilada sauce

1 large onion, peeled and chopped

2 cloves garlic, peeled and minced

1 cup water

4 tablespoons fine cornmeal or masa harina (corn flour)

2 tablespoons fresh cilantro, minced

1 cup (4 ounces) Queso Blanco or Monterey jack cheese, grated

1. Add the beef, beans, tomatoes, broth, enchilada sauce, onion, garlic, and water to the slow cooker. Cover and cook on low for 8 hours.

2. In a small bowl, whisk the cornmeal together with enough cold water to make a paste; stir some of the liquid from the slow cooker into the cornmeal paste and then whisk it into the chili. Cook and stir on high for 15–30 minutes or until chili is thickened and the raw cornmeal taste is cooked out of the chili.

3. Top each serving with minced cilantro and grated cheese.

Enchilada Chili Dip

To serve this chili as a dip, after Step 3, reduce the heat to low and stir in the cheese; continue to stir until cheese is melted. Reduce the heat setting to warm. Serve with baked corn tortilla chips. (According to your tastes, you may wish to increase the amount of cheese.)

TURKEY WHITE CHILI

This recipe creates a complete one-pot meal for two.

Serves 2

INGREDIENTS:

¼ cup drained canned hominy

¼ cup cooked or canned cannellini beans, drained and rinsed

¼ cup onions, diced

1 teaspoon lemon juice

½ teaspoon cumin

½ teaspoon paprika

½ teaspoon white pepper

2 ounces drained canned green peppers

½ cooked turkey breast, cubed

1. Place all ingredients except the turkey into a 2-quart slow cooker. Stir to mix the ingredients. Cook on low for 8 hours; stir in the turkey. Cook for an additional 30–60 minutes on high.

DUELING FLAVORS CHILI

This is a sweet and hot chili. The longer you cook it, the richer the flavor.

Serves 8–10

INGREDIENTS:

1 pound ground chuck

1 pound ground pork

2 large yellow onions, peeled and diced

6 cloves garlic, peeled and minced

1 teaspoon whole cumin seeds

2 tablespoons chili powder

¼ teaspoon oregano

1 (28-ounce) can diced tomatoes

¼ cup ketchup

¼ teaspoon cinnamon

¼ teaspoon ground cloves

2 tablespoons brown sugar

2 (15-ounce) cans kidney beans, rinsed and drained

1 (14-ounce) can lower-sodium beef broth

Optional: 1 tablespoon Worcestershire sauce

Water, if needed

Optional: Hot sauce to taste

Salt and freshly ground black pepper, to taste

1. Add the ground chuck, pork, onions, garlic, cumin seeds, chili powder, and oregano to a nonstick skillet; cook over medium heat until the beef and pork are browned and cooked through. Drain off any excess fat and discard. Transfer to the slow cooker.

2. Stir in the tomatoes, ketchup, cinnamon, cloves, brown sugar, kidney beans, beef broth, and Worcestershire sauce if using. Add enough water, if needed, to bring the liquid level to the top of the beans and meat. Cover and cook on low for 8 hours.

3. Taste for seasoning and add hot sauce, if desired, and salt and pepper if needed. You may also wish to add more brown sugar or chili powder, according to your taste.

CHAPTER 22

CASSEROLES

CHICKEN, BROCCOLI, AND RICE CASSEROLE

This is one of the few recipes cooked on high in this book. Using minute rice means the rice will be cooked correctly, and the shorter 4-hour cooking time makes this the perfect meal to put in the slow cooker to have ready for when you and the family get home from church or an afternoon at the kids' ball games.

Serves 8

INGREDIENTS:

Nonstick spray

2 (10¾-ounce) cans condensed cream of mushroom soup

1 (15-ounce) jar Cheez Whiz

½ cup mayonnaise

1 tablespoon lemon juice

2 soup cans hot water

½ cup milk

2 pounds skinless, boneless chicken breasts

1 (8-ounce) can whole water chestnuts, drained

2 (10-ounce) bags frozen broccoli florets, thawed

2 cups instant rice

1 medium onion, peeled and diced

2 stalks celery, diced

Optional: 1 (4-ounce) can sliced mushrooms, drained

Salt and freshly ground black pepper, to taste

Optional: Paprika

1 (4-ounce) bag blanched slivered almonds

1. Treat the slow cooker with nonstick spray. Add the mushroom soup, Cheez Whiz, mayonnaise, lemon juice, water, and milk; stir to combine.

2. Cut the chicken breasts into bite-sized pieces and chop the water chestnuts; stir into the soup mixture in the slow cooker along with the broccoli florets, rice, onion, celery, and sliced mushrooms if using. Cover and cook on high for 4 hours or until the rice is cooked through.

3. Taste the casserole for seasoning; stir in salt and pepper if needed. Sprinkle paprika over the casserole, if desired, and top with the almonds.

Disguise the Leftovers

Preheat oven to 350°F. Transfer the leftover Chicken, Broccoli, and Rice Casserole to a casserole dish treated with nonstick spray. Bake for 20 minutes while you pulse 2 slices of bread in the food processor until they're fine bread crumbs; mix together with 1 tablespoon melted butter. Top the casserole with the buttered bread crumbs and bake for 10 more minutes or until the casserole is heated through and the bread crumbs are golden brown.

HAM AND POTATO CASSEROLE

At 12 servings, this recipe obviously feeds a crowd, which makes it a great dish to take to a carry-in dinner.

Serves 12

INGREDIENTS:

Nonstick spray

1 cup sour cream

1 (10¾-ounce) can condensed cream of chicken soup

1 tablespoon dried minced onion

2 (16-ounce) bags frozen hash brown potatoes, thawed

2 cups (8 ounces) Cheddar cheese, grated

2 cups cooked ham, diced

1 (6-ounce) package herb-seasoned stuffing mix

¼ cup butter, melted

1. Treat the slow cooker with nonstick spray. Add the sour cream, soup, and dried onion to the slow cooker; mix well.

2. Stir in the hash brown potatoes, cheese, and ham.

3. In a bowl, toss the stuffing mix together with the melted butter. Evenly sprinkle over the hash brown potatoes mixture in the slow cooker. Cover and cook on low for 6 hours.

HAMBURGER-VEGETABLE CASSEROLE

When you taste this casserole for seasoning, you can stir in some dried herbs to add flavor. For example, oregano and red pepper flakes work well with tomato soup, or parsley and thyme go well with mushroom soup. Some Mrs. Dash Table Blend is almost always a good choice.

Serves 4

INGREDIENTS:

Nonstick spray

2 large potatoes, scrubbed and sliced

3 large carrots, peeled and thinly sliced

1 cup frozen baby peas, thawed

1 large onion, peeled and diced

2 stalks celery, sliced

1 pound lean ground beef, browned and drained

1 (15¾-ounce) can cream of tomato soup or cream of mushroom soup

1 soup can water

Salt and freshly ground black pepper, to taste

1. Treat the slow cooker with nonstick spray. Add the potatoes, carrots, peas, onion, celery, and cooked and drained ground beef in layers in the order given.

2. Mix the soup with the water and pour over the layers. Cover and cook on low for 8 hours. Stir and taste for seasoning; add salt and pepper if needed.

BEEF AND GREEN BEAN CASSEROLE

Serve this casserole with a tossed salad, steamed baby potatoes or rice, and warm dinner rolls.

Serves 6

INGREDIENTS:

1½ pounds round or sirloin steak

⅓ cup all-purpose flour

Salt, to taste

¼ teaspoon freshly ground black pepper

1 green bell pepper, seeded and sliced

1 (15-ounce) can diced tomatoes

3 tablespoons soy sauce

1 large onion, peeled and sliced

8 ounces fresh mushrooms, cleaned and sliced

1 (10-ounce) package frozen French-style green beans, thawed

1. Trim and discard any fat from the beef; cut the meat into short, thin strips.

2. Add the steak strips, flour, salt, and pepper to the slow cooker; stir to coat the steak in the seasoned flour.

3. Add the bell pepper, tomatoes, soy sauce, onion, mushrooms, and green beans. Stir to combine. Cover and cook on low 8 hours. Stir and taste for seasoning; add additional salt and pepper if needed.

PIZZA CASSEROLE

This casserole is easy to adjust according to your preferences. You can add ingredients like sliced green or black olives, roasted red peppers, and additional mushrooms. Likewise, you can add or substitute bacon or other meat toppings for what's called for in the recipe.

Serves 8

INGREDIENTS:

1½ pounds lean ground beef

½ pound ground sausage

1 large onion, peeled and diced

4 cloves garlic, peeled and minced

Nonstick spray

1 (10¾-ounce) can cream of mushroom soup

1 (26-ounce) jar pizza or pasta sauce

1 (16-ounce) box rigatoni, cooked

1 (4-ounce) package sliced pepperoni

8 ounces mushrooms, sliced

4 cups (1 pound) mozzarella cheese, grated

Salt and freshly ground black pepper, to taste

1. Add the ground beef, sausage, and onion to a nonstick skillet over medium-high heat. Sauté for 10 minutes, or until the meat is cooked through and the onion is transparent. Drain and discard any fat rendered from the meat. Stir in the garlic and sauté for 30 seconds. Treat the slow cooker with nonstick spray, and then transfer the cooked meat and onions to the slow cooker.

2. Add the soup and sauce to the slow cooker. Stir to mix into the meat. Fold in the cooked rigatoni, pepperoni, mushrooms, and cheese.

3. Cover and cook on low for 4 hours. Stir and taste for seasoning; add salt and pepper if needed.

TURKEY AND DRESSING CASSEROLE

If you want to add a vegetable to this casserole, stir in a can of creamed corn or a thawed box of frozen baby peas and pearl onions in sauce along with the gravy and cream.

Serves 4

INGREDIENTS:

Nonstick spray

2 cups leftover turkey

4 cups leftover stuffing

2 cups leftover gravy

2 tablespoons heavy cream

1. Treat the slow cooker with nonstick spray.

2. Cut the turkey and dressing into bite-sized pieces. Add to the slow cooker along with the gravy and cream. Stir to mix. Cover and cook on low for 3 hours, or until heated through.

Later, When the Family Will Appreciate It

You don't have to limit yourself to serving this casserole immediately after Thanksgiving. Freeze the leftovers called for in the recipe, and then later thaw them overnight in the refrigerator. Add them to the slow cooker and cook according to the instructions in Step 2.

PORK AND BEANS CASSEROLE

You can serve this casserole with mashed potatoes or steamed cabbage and corn bread. Grind a generous amount of black pepper over each serving.

Serves 8

INGREDIENTS:

4 strips bacon

1 (3-pound) pork roast

1 (10½-ounce) can condensed French onion soup

1 cup ketchup

¼ cup cider vinegar

3 tablespoons brown sugar

2 (15-ounce) cans pork and beans

Optional: Barbecue sauce, to taste

1. Cut the bacon into 1-inch pieces and add the bacon to the slow cooker. Cover and cook on high for 15 minutes, or until the bacon begins to render its fat. Add the pork roast, fat side down. Cover and cook for ½ hour. Turn the roast; cover and cook for another ½ hour.

2. Mix together the soup, ketchup, vinegar, and brown sugar. Pour over the meat. Reduce the slow cooker setting to low and cook covered for 6 hours or until meat pulls apart and registers 165°F in the center of the roast.

3. Lift the meat from the slow cooker crock and transfer it to a cutting board; shred the meat using two forks, removing and discarding any fat.

4. Skim and discard any fat from the top of the meat juices in the slow cooker, and then remove and discard all but 1 cup of those juices. Stir the shredded meat and pork and beans into the juices. Cover and cook on low for 2 hours. Taste for seasoning and add barbecue sauce to taste if desired.

Freshly Ground Black Pepper

Ground black pepper contains anticaking agents that can cause stomach upset for some people and can also change the flavor. In addition, whole peppercorns retain the succulent black pepper flavor, which tends to dissipate once the pepper is ground, which is why dishes always taste better when you grind the pepper yourself.

GROUND PORK AND EGGPLANT CASSEROLE

Serve this casserole with some toasted garlic bread and a tossed salad.

Serves 8

INGREDIENTS:

2 pounds lean ground pork

1 tablespoon peanut or olive oil

2 large yellow onions, peeled and diced

3 stalks celery, diced

1 green bell pepper, seeded and diced

6 cloves garlic, peeled and minced

4 medium eggplants, cut into ½-inch dice

⅛ teaspoon dried thyme, crushed

1 tablespoon freeze-dried parsley

3 tablespoons tomato paste

2 teaspoons Worcestershire sauce

Salt and freshly ground black pepper, to taste

1 large egg, beaten

Optional: Hot sauce, to taste

1. Add the ground pork, oil, onions, celery, and bell pepper to a large nonstick skillet over medium-high heat; sauté for 15 minutes or until the pork is cooked through, breaking it apart as it cooks. Remove and discard any fat rendered from the meat, and transfer the meat and sautéed vegetables to the slow cooker.

2. Add the garlic, eggplants, thyme, parsley, tomato paste, Worcestershire sauce, salt, pepper, and egg to the slow cooker. Stir to combine. Cover and cook on low for 8 hours, or until the eggplant is cooked through. Taste for seasoning and add additional salt and pepper, if needed, and hot sauce if desired.

SALISBURY STEAK CASSEROLE

To make this a complete meal, all you have to do is add a salad or coleslaw and some warm dinner rolls.

Serves 6

INGREDIENTS:

1 (10½-ounce) can condensed French onion soup

1½ pounds lean ground beef

½ cup dry bread crumbs

1 large egg

Salt and freshly ground pepper, to taste

Nonstick spray

1 (1-pound) bag frozen hash browns, thawed

1 (1-pound) bag frozen broccoli, green beans, onions, and peppers, thawed

¼ cup ketchup

¼ cup water

1 teaspoon Worcestershire sauce

½ teaspoon prepared mustard

1 tablespoon butter, softened

1 tablespoon all-purpose flour

2 tablespoons heavy cream

1. In a bowl, mix together half of the soup with the beef, bread crumbs, egg, salt, and pepper. Shape into 6 to 8 patties.

2. Add the patties to a nonstick skillet; brown on both sides over medium-high heat, and then pour off and discard any excess fat.

3. Treat the slow cooker with nonstick spray. Spread the hash browns over the bottom of the slow cooker. Top with the frozen vegetable mix. Arrange the browned meat patties over the vegetables.

4. In the soup can, mix the remaining soup together with the ketchup, water, Worcestershire sauce, and mustard. Add the butter and flour to a small bowl; mix into a paste and then whisk in the heavy cream. Add the flour mixture to the soup can and whisk to combine. Pour over the patties. Cover and cook on low for 8 hours.

SWEET POTATO CASSEROLE

This is a welcome side dish at almost any holiday buffet.

Serves 8

INGREDIENTS:

Nonstick spray

2 (29-ounce) cans sweet potatoes

⅓ cup plus 2 teaspoons butter, melted

2 tablespoons white sugar

2 tablespoons plus ⅓ cup brown sugar

1 tablespoon orange juice

2 large eggs, beaten

½ cup milk

⅓ cup chopped pecans

2 tablespoons all-purpose flour

1. Treat the slow cooker with nonstick spray.

2. Drain the sweet potatoes, add to a bowl, and mash them together with ⅓ cup of the butter, the white sugar, and 2 tablespoons of the brown sugar. Stir in the orange juice, eggs, and milk. Transfer the sweet potato mixture to the slow cooker.

3. Add the pecans, ⅓ cup of the brown sugar, the flour, and the remaining 2 tablespoons of butter to a bowl; use a fork to blend. Sprinkle over the sweet potatoes. Cover and cook on low for 6 hours.

RANCHO BEEF CASSEROLE

In this recipe, corn tortillas are used to thicken the casserole. Try this in other recipes to add a nice hint of corn flavor.

Serves 6–8

INGREDIENTS:

1 onion

3 cloves garlic

2 green peppers

2 pounds beef

1 teaspoon chili powder

2 tablespoons oil

1 pound tomatoes

2 cups water

2 bay leaves

1 teaspoon ground cloves

1 teaspoon oregano

½ teaspoon salt

½ teaspoon pepper

2 corn tortillas

1. Finely chop the onion and garlic. Chop the green peppers; cube the beef.

2. Sauté the onion, garlic, peppers, beef, and chili powder in oil in a pan over medium heat until the meat is browned. Transfer the meat mixture to the slow cooker.

3. Chop the tomatoes. Add the tomatoes, water, spices, salt, and pepper to the slow cooker.

4. Cover and heat on a low setting for 3–4 hours.

5. Half an hour before serving, crumble the tortillas and add to the slow cooker to thicken. Remove bay leaves before serving.

CHICKEN WHEAT-BERRY CASSEROLE

Wheat berries are the whole kernel of wheat and are nutritious and full of fiber. Plus they taste great!

Serves 8

INGREDIENTS:

1 cup wheat berries

1½ pounds boneless skinless chicken thighs

3 carrots, sliced

2 cups frozen corn

1 onion, chopped

3 cloves garlic, minced

2 cups Chicken Broth (Chapter 19)

1 teaspoon cumin

1 teaspoon salt

¼ teaspoon pepper

1 tablespoon cornstarch

¼ cup water

1. Rinse wheat berries and drain well. Cut chicken into 1½" pieces and combine with remaining ingredients, except for cornstarch and ¼ cup water, in a 4- to 5-quart slow cooker. Cover and cook on low for 8–9 hours or until wheat berries are tender and chicken is cooked.

2. In small bowl, combine cornstarch and water and blend well. Add to casserole in slow cooker, cover, and cook on high for 20–30 minutes until thickened, then stir again and serve.

Buying Grains in Bulk

One of the best places to buy grains and legumes in bulk is at a food co-op. These stores usually have a high turnover rate and their bulk products are quite fresh. These stores are also great places to find more unusual grains like the wheat berries used in this stew, along with grains like amaranth and quinoa.

CHORIZO AND POTATO CASSEROLE

If you don't have Mexican chorizo sausage available in your local grocery store, use mild breakfast sausage instead.

Serves 6

INGREDIENTS:

⅓ cup olive oil

1 small onion, diced

3 medium Yukon gold potatoes, peeled and cut into ½" cubes

8 ounces Mexican chorizo sausage, removed from casing

8 large eggs

Salt and freshly ground black pepper, to taste

1. In a heavy skillet, heat olive oil over medium heat until sizzling. Add onion and cook 3–5 minutes until soft.

2. Add potatoes and cook another 5–8 minutes until potatoes are fork tender. Using a large slotted spoon, remove potato mixture from skillet, place in a bowl, and set aside.

3. In the same skillet, brown chorizo over medium heat until cooked through.

4. Grease a 4-quart slow cooker. Layer the potato mixture with the cooked chorizo in the slow cooker.

5. In a large bowl mix together the eggs, salt, and pepper. Evenly pour over the layered ingredients.

6. Cook on high for 3–4 hours or on low for 6–8 hours until eggs are set. If necessary, add salt and pepper to taste, when serving.

REUBEN CASSEROLE

If you are a fan of the distinct tangy flavors of a Reuben sandwich, you will love this zesty, sauerkraut-filled casserole dish!

Serves 6

INGREDIENTS:

8 ounces corned beef, cut into ½" cubes

1 Granny Smith apple, peeled, cored, and chopped

1 (14-ounce) can sauerkraut, rinsed and drained

1¼ teaspoons caraway seeds

2 cups mashed potatoes

2 cups shredded Havarti or Swiss cheese, optional

Optional: ¼ cup Thousand Island dressing

1. Grease a 2½-quart or larger slow cooker. Add corned beef, apple, sauerkraut, and caraway seeds. Stir ingredients together.

2. Spoon mashed potatoes evenly over casserole ingredients. Cook on high for 3–4 hours or on low for 6–8 hours.

3. If desired, thirty minutes prior to serving, sprinkle cheese over mashed potatoes and cook until it is soft and melted. Drizzle a tablespoon of Thousand Island dressing over each serving.

APPLE AND SWEET POTATO CASSEROLE

This sweet side dish would be perfect for Thanksgiving or even as a dessert with a scoop of ice cream.

Serves 6

INGREDIENTS:

4 large sweet potatoes, peeled and sliced

1 (15-ounce) can apple pie filling

2 tablespoons butter, melted

¼ teaspoon salt

1. Grease a 4-quart slow cooker with nonstick cooking spray. Place sweet potatoes in the bottom of the slow cooker.

2. Add apple pie filling, butter, and salt. Cover and cook on high for 3–4 hours until sweet potatoes are fork tender.

Canned Shortcuts

Using apple pie filling in this recipe is an easy way to add apples, spices, and sugar without a lot of hassle. Apple pie filling is good not only with sweet potatoes, but also in oatmeal, in a cake, or as a topping for a cheesecake.

CABBAGE AND BEEF CASSEROLE

A lower-carbohydrate beefy casserole using cabbage and tomato sauce.

Serves 6

INGREDIENTS:

2 pounds ground beef

1 head cabbage, shredded

1 small onion, chopped

1 (16-ounce) can tomatoes

½ teaspoon garlic salt

¼ teaspoon ground thyme

¼ teaspoon red pepper flakes

½ teaspoon oregano

1 (8-ounce) can tomato sauce

1. In a large skillet brown the ground beef for about 5–6 minutes. Remove ground beef to a bowl and set aside. In same skillet sauté onion until softened, about 3–5 minutes.

2. In a greased 4- to 6-quart slow cooker, layer cabbage, onion, tomatoes, garlic salt, thyme, pepper flakes, oregano, and beef. Repeat layers, ending with beef. Pour tomato sauce over casserole.

3. Cook on low for 8 hours or on high for 4 hours.

SMOKED TURKEY SAUSAGE AND VEGETABLE CASSEROLE

Prepared Italian dressing adds great flavor to the vegetables in this simple casserole.

Serves 4

INGREDIENTS:

5 tablespoons bottled zesty Italian salad dressing

2 tablespoons Dijon mustard

2 medium potatoes, cut into ½-inch slices

2 medium onions, sliced

2 medium carrots, cut into ½-inch slices

2 cups green cabbage, chopped

1 ring (1 pound) fully cooked smoked turkey sausage, cut into 1-inch slices

1 (14.5-ounce) can petite-diced tomatoes with Italian seasonings

1. In small bowl whisk together dressing and mustard.

2. In a 4-quart slow cooker, arrange potato slices on the bottom. Drizzle with one-third of the dressing mixture. Lay onion slices evenly over potatoes and drizzle with one-third of the dressing mixture. Top with carrots and cabbage; drizzle with remaining dressing.

3. Arrange sausage slices on top of vegetables. Pour diced tomatoes over the casserole.

4. Cover and cook on low for 8 hours or on high for 4 hours.

Make Your Own Seasoned Tomatoes

Sometimes it can be hard to find canned petite-diced tomatoes with seasoning added to them. Instead you can use a can of plain petite-diced tomatoes and add 1 teaspoon Italian seasoning, ½ teaspoon of garlic powder, and ½ teaspoon of crushed basil.

SPICY BEANS AND RICE CASSEROLE

Using salsa instead of tomatoes and added spices makes this casserole super easy to put together. It's delicious topped with a dollop of sour cream.

Serves 8

INGREDIENTS:

1 (15-ounce) can whole kernel corn, drained

1 (15-ounce) can black beans, rinsed and drained

1 (10-ounce) can diced tomatoes with green chiles

1 cup brown rice, uncooked

2¼ cups Chicken Broth (Chapter 19) or water

1 cup salsa

1 cup Cheddar cheese, shredded

¼ cup chopped fresh cilantro

1. Grease a 4-quart slow cooker. Add corn, beans, tomatoes, rice, broth or water, and salsa. Cover and cook on high for 3 hours or on low for 6 hours.

2. Once rice has absorbed water and is fully cooked stir in Cheddar cheese. Cook an additional 20 minutes on high to melt cheese and serve. Garnish with cilantro.

Instead of Salsa

For an Italian/Tuscan flavor variation use cannellini beans instead of black beans, use your favorite marinara sauce or spaghetti sauce in place of the salsa, and garnish with freshly chopped parsley instead of cilantro.

MEDITERRANEAN CHICKEN CASSEROLE

Raisins may seem like an odd ingredient to add to a main dish, but they provide a slightly sweet flavor that beautifully complements the tomatoes and spices.

Serves 4

INGREDIENTS:

1 medium butternut squash, peeled and cut into 2" cubes

1 medium bell pepper, seeded and diced

1 (14.5-ounce) can diced tomatoes, undrained

4 boneless, skinless chicken breast halves, cut into bite-sized pieces

½ cup mild salsa

¼ cup raisins

¼ teaspoon ground cinnamon

¼ teaspoon ground cumin

2 cups cooked rice, for serving

¼ cup chopped fresh parsley

1. Add squash and bell pepper to the bottom of a greased 4-quart slow cooker. Mix tomatoes, chicken, salsa, raisins, cinnamon, and cumin together and pour on top of squash and peppers.

2. Cover and cook on low for 6 hours or on high for 3 hours until squash is fork tender.

3. Remove chicken and vegetables from slow cooker with slotted spoon. Serve over cooked rice. Ladle remaining sauce from slow cooker over the vegetables. Garnish with parsley.

HAM, SPINACH, AND RICE CASSEROLE

Use leftover ingredients to create a tasty main dish. This casserole is also ideal for a brunch or breakfast.

Serves 4

INGREDIENTS:

2 tablespoons butter

½ onion, chopped

2 tablespoons brown rice flour

1 cup Chicken Broth (Chapter 19)

½ teaspoon salt

½ teaspoon ground pepper

¼ teaspoon dried thyme

3 eggs, beaten

1 (10-ounce) package frozen spinach, defrosted and drained

1 cup cooked ham, chopped

1½ cups cooked rice

½ cup crushed Rice Chex cereal

1. In a small saucepan over medium heat, heat the butter. Whisk in onion and flour. Cook for 2–3 minutes to toast the flour.

2. Slowly whisk in the broth, salt, pepper, and thyme. Cook for 3–5 minutes until sauce has thickened, and set aside.

3. In a large bowl mix together the eggs, spinach, ham, and rice. Stir in the thickened broth. Pour into a greased 4-quart slow cooker. Top with crushed Rice Chex.

4. Cover and vent lid with a chopstick. Cook on high for 3 hours or on low for 6 hours, or until casserole is set.

THICK AND CREAMY CORN AND LIMA BEAN CASSEROLE

This makes a satisfying meal and can be made with chopped ham for added flavor and a serving of protein. Simply add 1–2 cups of chopped ham into the slow cooker with the ingredients in Step 2 and cook as directed.

Serves 4

INGREDIENTS:

2 tablespoons butter

½ sweet onion, finely chopped

½ cup minced celery

¼ cup minced roasted red pepper

½ cup Chicken Broth (Chapter 19)

1 (10-ounce) package frozen lima beans

1 (10-ounce) package frozen corn kernels

2 eggs, well beaten

1½ cups heavy cream or evaporated milk

1 teaspoon salt

1 teaspoon paprika

1 teaspoon ground black pepper

1 teaspoon ground coriander

½ teaspoon ground allspice

1 cup gluten-free bread crumbs

1. Melt butter in a large skillet. Sauté onion and celery until softened, about 3–5 minutes.

2. Grease a 4-quart slow cooker. Add sautéed onions and celery. Add remaining ingredients to slow cooker, except for bread crumbs. Stir together and sprinkle bread crumbs on top.

3. Cover and vent the lid with a chopstick. Cook on low for 6 hours or on high for 3 hours.

Better Than Canned

Stay away from canned creamed corn (as it contains wheat flour) and stick with fresh or frozen and make your own cream sauce. It's easy and gluten-free, and tastes so much better than the ones made with soups or mixes.

CORN TORTILLA CASSEROLE

Serve this casserole along with a tossed salad. Have some additional taco or enchilada sauce at the table along with an assortment of optional condiments, like chopped jalapeño peppers, diced green onions, sour cream, and guacamole.

Serves 8

INGREDIENTS:

2 tablespoons olive oil

2 pounds ground beef

1 small onion, peeled and diced

1 clove garlic, minced

1 envelope taco seasoning

½ teaspoon salt

½ teaspoon freshly ground pepper

1 (15-ounce) can diced tomatoes

1 (6-ounce) can tomato paste

2 cups refried beans

9 corn tortillas

2 cups enchilada sauce

2 cups (8 ounces) grated Cheddar cheese

1. In a large skillet, heat olive oil. Brown ground beef for approximately 5–6 minutes and set aside in a large bowl. In the same skillet sauté onions until softened, about 3–5 minutes. Add sautéed onions to ground beef.

2. Stir in the garlic, taco seasoning, salt, pepper, tomatoes, tomato paste, and refried beans into the ground beef and onions.

   Grease a 4-quart slow cooker with nonstick spray. Add ⅓ of the ground beef mixture to cover the bottom of the slow cooker insert. Layer 3 tortillas on top of the ground beef mixture and cover with ⅓ of the enchilada sauce, then ⅓ of the shredded cheese. Repeat layers. Cover and cook on low for 6–8 hours. Cut into 8 wedges and serve.

ZUCCHINI AND SAUSAGE CASSEROLE

Serve this casserole on a bed of mixed greens with a fruit salad on the side.

Serves 6

INGREDIENTS:

1 pound mild pork sausage

1¼ cups grated Parmesan cheese

½ teaspoon salt

½ teaspoon freshly ground pepper

2 teaspoons Greek seasoning or 1 teaspoon dried mint, ½ teaspoon dried oregano, and ½ teaspoon basil

2 eggs, beaten

1 cup whole milk

3 medium zucchini, sliced into ½" rounds

1 small onion, sliced

1. In a large skillet, brown ground sausage, drain the fat from the skillet, and set the sausage aside.

2. Grease a 4-quart slow cooker with nonstick spray. In a large bowl whisk together the Parmesan cheese, salt, pepper, and Greek seasoning. In another bowl whisk together the eggs and the milk.

   Place ⅓ of the zucchini over the bottom of the slow cooker. Add ⅓ of the sliced onions over the zucchini. Add ⅓ of the cooked sausage over the onions. Add ⅓ of the milk/egg mixture over the sausage. Lastly add ⅓ of the Parmesan cheese mixture over everything. Repeat layers two more times, ending with the last of the Parmesan cheese mixture.

3. Cover, vent lid with a chopstick, and cook on low for 6 hours or on high for 3 hours. Cut into squares to serve.

PART III
SIDES

CHAPTER 23

LEGUMES AND GRAINS

SLOW-COOKING GREAT NORTHERN BEANS

Presoaking beans removes the enzymes that make them difficult for some people to digest. Some claim that this method of soaking the beans is more effective at removing those enzymes than the quick-soaking method. The biggest advantage, however, is that the overnight soaking method results in beans that cook more evenly.

Yield varies according to the recipe

INGREDIENTS:

Great northern beans

Water

Salt and freshly ground black pepper, to taste

1. Rinse and drain the amount of beans called for in the recipe and then add them to a bowl or saucepan. Add enough water to cover the beans by 2 inches. Cover and let soak overnight or for 8 hours.

2. Drain the beans, then rinse and drain again. Add them to the slow cooker according to the recipe instructions unless the slow cooker recipe calls for tomatoes or sugar. Do not add salt to the slow cooker until the beans are cooked through.

3. If the recipe calls for tomatoes or sugar, speed up the slow-cooking process by cooking the beans together with enough water to cover the beans by 2 inches in a saucepan. Bring to a boil over high heat, and then reduce the heat and simmer the beans for 40 minutes to an hour or until they just begin to become tender. Drain, reserving the amount of cooking liquid to equal the amount of water called for in the slow cooker recipe, and add to the slow cooker. Continue to cook according to recipe instructions.

Cooking Beans Isn't an Exact Science

The amount of time it will take to cook (or slow-cook) beans depends on the size and variety of beans used and, due to the age of the beans and other factors, can even vary from bag to bag of the same variety of beans.

QUICK-SOAKING GREAT NORTHERN BEANS

This quick-soaking method will work with most beans, except for cannellini (white kidney beans), which will become mushy.

Yield varies according to the recipe

INGREDIENTS:

Great northern beans

Water

1. Rinse and drain the amount of beans called for in the recipe and then add them to a saucepan. Add enough water to cover the beans by 2 inches. Bring to a boil over high heat. Boil for 2 minutes. Remove the pan from the heat; cover and let sit for an hour.

2. Follow the instructions in Steps 2 and 3 in the Slow-Cooking Great Northern Beans recipe (this chapter).

FAT-FREE REFRIED BEANS

Some cooks like to mash the onion, jalapeño pepper, and garlic into the cooked beans; others prefer to discard them once the beans are cooked. (They've pretty much given up their flavors to the beans at this point anyhow.)

Serves 8

INGREDIENTS:

3 cups dried pinto beans

1 large onion, peeled and halved

½ fresh jalapeño pepper, seeded and chopped

6 cloves garlic, peeled and minced

Optional: ⅛ teaspoon ground cumin

9 cups water

Salt and freshly ground black pepper, to taste

1. Rinse and drain the amount of beans called for in the recipe and then add them to a bowl or saucepan. Add enough water to cover the beans by 2 inches. Cover and let soak overnight or for 8 hours. Drain the beans, then rinse and drain again.

2. Add the beans, onion, jalapeño, garlic, and cumin to the slow cooker. Pour in the water and stir to combine. Cover and, stirring occasionally and adding more water as needed, cook on high for 8 hours or until the beans are cooked through and tender. (If you have to add more than 1 cup of water during cooking, lower the temperature to low or simmer.)

3. Once the beans are cooked, strain them, reserving the liquid. Mash the beans with a potato masher, adding some of the reserved water as needed to attain desired consistency. Add salt and pepper to taste.

Reheating Fat-Free Refried Beans

Fat-Free Refried Beans can be reheated in the microwave or using any other traditional method that you use to warm up leftovers. However, if you want to add a touch of authentic flavor (and fat) to them, melt some lard in a nonstick skillet over medium heat, stir in the beans, and sauté until heated through.

MOCK ENCHILADAS

To make this a one-dish meal, serve this dish over shredded lettuce and topped with chopped green onion, a dollop of sour cream, and some guacamole.

Serves 8

INGREDIENTS:

2 pounds lean ground beef

1 large onion, peeled and diced

1 (4½-ounce) can chopped chilies

1 (12-ounce) jar mild enchilada sauce

1 (10½-ounce) can golden mushroom soup

1 (10½-ounce) can Cheddar cheese soup

1 (10½ ounce) can cream of mushroom soup

1 (10½-ounce) can cream of celery soup

2 cups refried beans

Plain corn tortilla chips, to taste

1. Add the ground beef and diced onion to a nonstick skillet over medium heat; brown the hamburger for 15 minutes, until cooked through, breaking it apart and stirring it into the onions as you do so. Drain and discard any fat that is rendered from the ground beef.

2. Add the cooked beef and onions to the slow cooker. Stir in the chilies, enchilada sauce, soups, and refried beans. Cover and cook on low for 6 hours.

3. Stir 8 ounces or more tortilla chips into the mixture in the slow cooker. Cover and cook on low for 15 minutes or until the tortilla chips are soft.

CRUSHED RED PEPPER BEEF AND PINTO BEANS

Serve this as a main dish along with a tossed salad and corn bread or as a side dish at your next cookout.

Serves 6

INGREDIENTS:

1 pound dried pinto beans

6 cups cold water

½ pound bacon, diced

1 pound beef chuck or sirloin steak

½ teaspoon dried red pepper flakes, crushed

1 large onion, peeled and diced

4 cloves garlic, peeled and minced

1 (6-ounce) can tomato paste

1½ tablespoons chili powder

Salt and freshly ground black pepper, to taste

1 teaspoon ground cumin

½ teaspoon dried marjoram or cilantro

1. Rinse and drain the dried beans. Put in a bowl and add enough water to cover the beans by 2 inches. Cover and let soak for 8 hours or overnight. Drain the beans, rinse, and add to the slow cooker along with the water.

2. Add bacon to a nonstick skillet over medium heat. Trim the steak of any fat, cut into bite-sized pieces, and add to the skillet along with the crushed red pepper flakes and onion; sauté for 15 minutes or until the onion is just beginning to brown. Stir in the garlic and sauté for 30 seconds. Stir the sautéed mixture into the beans and water in the slow cooker. Cover and cook on low for 8 hours.

3. Stir in the tomato paste, chili powder, salt, pepper, cumin, and marjoram or cilantro. Cover and cook on low for 2 hours or until the beans are cooked through. Taste for seasoning and adjust if necessary.

AMERICANIZED MOUSSAKA

This adaptation would probably make a Greek cuisine purist shudder, but it's a way to hide vegetables in a kid-friendly meal. With the addition of the optional Cheddar cheese it can also serve as a hummus-style party dip or spread, a baked potato topper, or even a warm salad dressing. As a bonus, it freezes well.

Serves 12

INGREDIENTS:

Meatless Moussaka (Chapter 14)

3 pounds lean ground beef, cooked and drained of fat

1 (8-ounce) package cream cheese

1 cup heavy cream

2 large eggs

Optional: 4 cups (1 pound) medium Cheddar cheese, grated

1. Prepare the Meatless Moussaka recipe according to the instructions in Chapter 14.

2. Stir in the cooked and drained ground beef. Cut the cream cheese into cubes and stir into the moussaka. Add the heavy cream and eggs to a bowl or measuring cup; whisk until the eggs are beaten into the cream and then stir into the moussaka. Cover and cook on low for an additional 1–2 hours.

3. If using the optional Cheddar cheese, gradually stir it into the mixture; cover and cook on low for 15 minutes or until the cheese is melted and can be completely stirred into the moussaka. If you won't be serving the moussaka immediately, reduce the heat on slow cooker to warm.

SAVORY RYE BERRIES

Whole grains of rye and wheat are called "berries," just as whole grains of corn are called "kernels."

Serves 6

INGREDIENTS:

1 onion

3 tablespoons butter

1 cup rye berries

2 cups water

1 teaspoon salt

1. Chop the onion; sauté in butter in a pan over medium heat until soft.

2. Put the rye, water, salt, and onion in the slow cooker.

3. Cover and heat on a low setting for 6–8 hours.

Beyond Rice

Move on from white rice. Take advantage of the power of slow cooking and start cooking unbroken grains, called "berries," which take longer to cook. Berries yield an entirely different taste, nutty and chewy. Try rye berries, wheat berries, or barley. Use 1 cup berries with 2 cups water, and cook for about 8 hours on low.

STEAMY POLENTA

You can vary this recipe by adding sweetness with raisins or fruit, or savory flavors such as mushrooms, cheese, or herbs.

Makes about 5 cups

INGREDIENTS:

3¾ cups Chicken Broth (Chapter 19)

1 teaspoon salt

¼ teaspoon black pepper

1¼ cups cornmeal

1 tablespoon butter

1. Heat broth, salt, and pepper to a boil in a saucepan over medium heat. Add the cornmeal while stirring.

2. Grease a baking dish using 1 tablespoon butter and place the dish on a trivet in the slow cooker. Transfer the cornmeal mixture to the baking dish.

3. Cover the dish with foil or a ceramic or glass lid and pour water around the base of the trivet. Cover and heat on a low setting for 2–3 hours.

CLASSIC POLENTA WITH HERBS AND PARMESAN

By using the slow cooker to make this creamy homemade polenta, you don't have to stand over the stove for nearly 2 hours stirring the pot.

Serves 6

INGREDIENTS:

7 cups water

2 tablespoons salt

2 cups yellow cornmeal

2–4 ounces unsalted butter

1 teaspoon dried basil

1 teaspoon dried parsley

1 teaspoon crushed rosemary

½ teaspoon freshly ground black pepper

½ cup freshly grated Parmesan cheese

1. Add all ingredients except cheese into a greased 4-quart slow cooker.

2. Whisk together thoroughly. Cover and cook on low for 6–7 hours or on high for 3–4 hours.

3. Thirty minutes prior to serving stir in Parmesan cheese.

HIGH-YIELD CLASSIC BROWN BREAD

This old-fashioned bread is dense and sweet. Slow cooking is the only way to bring out the rich, caramelized flavors of the grains.

Yields 3 loaves

INGREDIENTS:

1 pound rye flour

1 pound graham flour

2 pounds cornmeal

1 pound wheat flour

3 teaspoons baking powder

1 quart molasses

1½ quarts milk

2 teaspoons salt

2 cups water

1. Sift the flour, cornmeal, and baking powder together in a mixing bowl.

2. Mix the molasses, milk, and salt in a second mixing bowl. Add the milk mixture to the flour mixture to form a soft dough.

3. Grease and flour 3 loaf pans. Fill the pans one-half to three-quarters full; loosely cover each pan with foil or a glass or ceramic lid. Arrange the pans on a trivet or rack in the slow cooker, and pour 2 cups water around the base of the trivet.

4. Cover and heat on a high setting for 3–4 hours.

Shapely Sandwiches

Use cookie cutters to give your sandwiches fun and festive shapes. Cut the bread before adding sandwich toppings, or use the fun bread shapes in your breadbaskets. Also, use different types of bread for a colorful, as well as shapely effect.

BOSTON BROWN BREAD

This classic steamed bread goes perfectly with Boston baked beans or a hearty stew.

Serves 8

INGREDIENTS:

½ cup rye flour

½ cup stone-ground cornmeal

½ cup whole-wheat flour

½ teaspoon baking powder

¼ teaspoon fine salt

¼ teaspoon baking soda

½ cup dark molasses

½ cup buttermilk

1 large egg

Butter (for coating pan)

Boiling water

1. Add the rye flour, cornmeal, whole-wheat flour, baking powder, salt, and baking soda to a mixing bowl. Stir to combine.

2. Add the molasses, buttermilk, and egg to another mixing bowl or measuring cup. Whisk to mix and then pour into the flour mixture. Mix until a thick batter is formed.

3. Butter the inside of the container in which you'll be steaming the bread. Add enough batter to fill the container three-fourths full. Place the lid (see sidebar) over the container; center the container on the cooking insert inside the slow cooker.

4. Pour enough boiling water into the slow cooker to come up to about halfway up the container. Cover and cook on high for 2½ hours or until the bread springs back to the touch. (To test it, carefully remove the lid or foil and touch the top of the bread; if your finger leaves an indentation, place the cover back over the bread and continue to cook and test in ½ hour intervals.)

5. Remove the container from the water bath inside the slow cooker. Set on a cooling rack. When the bread is completely cooled, remove it from the container, slice, and serve.

Boston Brown Bread Steaming Container

You'll need a heatproof (stainless-steel or ceramic) bowl, pudding mold, 13-ounce coffee can, or other container that can sit on the cooking insert in the slow cooker and still have an inch of clearance between the top of the container and the lid of the slow cooker. Only fill the container three-fourths full. If the container doesn't have a lid, butter one side of a piece of foil large enough to fit over the entire top of the container and over the side far enough to press down to make a seal.

FAMILY DATE BREAD

Try this toasted with butter or honey. Or cream butter with honey and serve the mixture as a spread for the bread.

Yields 3 loaves

INGREDIENTS:

8 ounces dried dates

1½ cups water

4 tablespoons butter

2 cups sugar

½ teaspoon vanilla

1 egg

½ teaspoon salt

1 cup raisins

1 cup nuts

4 cups flour

2 teaspoons baking soda

4 teaspoons baking powder

1. Chop the dates. Boil the water and pour it over the dates; let stand.

2. Cream the butter and sugar. Add the vanilla, egg, and salt to the butter mixture. Add the cooled dates, and the water they're sitting in, to the egg mixture. Fold in the raisins and nuts.

3. Sift the flour, baking soda, and baking powder together in a bowl. Add the egg mixture to the flour mixture.

4. Grease and flour 3 loaf pans, or the equivalent. Fill the pans one-half to three-quarters full; loosely cover each pan with foil or a glass or ceramic lid. Arrange the pans on a trivet or rack in the slow cooker, and pour water around the base of the trivet.

5. Cover and heat on a high setting for 2–3 hours.

FRESH APPLE BREAD

You'll be amazed at the range of tastes different apple varieties take on after baking. Try this recipe with different types of apples for a change of flavor.

Yields 1 loaf

INGREDIENTS:

1 cup sugar

½ cup shortening

2 eggs

1½ teaspoons vanilla

1½ tablespoons buttermilk

½ teaspoon salt

1½ cups peeled and minced apples

1 cup pecans

2 cups flour

1 teaspoon baking soda

1 teaspoon cinnamon

3 tablespoons sugar

1. Cream the first cup of sugar with the shortening.

2. Beat the eggs. Add the eggs, vanilla, buttermilk, and salt to the creamed ingredients. Fold the minced apples and pecans into the liquid mixture.

3. Sift the flour and baking soda together. Add the liquid mixture to the sifted mixture.

4. Grease and flour 1 loaf pan, or the equivalent. Fill the baking dish one-half to three-quarters full. Sprinkle the batter with the cinnamon and sugar. Loosely cover with foil or a glass or ceramic lid to prevent condensation from falling in. Arrange the dish on a trivet or rack in the slow cooker, and pour water around the base of the trivet.

5. Cover and heat on a high setting for 2–3 hours.

Cheap Goods

Instead of a knife, use taut dental floss to slice cakes and breads. Just be sure you don't use flavored or heavily waxed floss. The great thing is, you don't even have to wash up afterward—just throw the used floss away!

CORN BREAD

Corn bread is the perfect accompaniment to chili or soup.

Serves 8

INGREDIENTS:

1½ cups stone-ground cornmeal

¾ cup all-purpose flour

1 cup fat-free evaporated milk

1 tablespoon sugar

¼ teaspoon salt

1 cup fresh corn kernels

3½ tablespoons canola oil

2 eggs

Nonstick cooking spray, as needed

1. In a medium bowl, whisk together all ingredients except the cooking spray. Spray a 4-quart round slow cooker with nonstick cooking spray.

2. Pour the batter into the slow cooker and cook on high for 2 hours. Slice the corn bread and lift out the slices.

A Bit about Corn Bread

Corn bread is a generic name for quick breads made with cornmeal. In the Northern states, corn bread is generally sweet and made with yellow cornmeal. In the South, corn bread is traditionally unsweetened and made with white cornmeal.

SLOW-COOKED PINTO BEANS

Pinto beans make a great side dish or vegetarian taco filling.

Serves 2

INGREDIENTS:

10 ounces canned pinto beans, drained and rinsed

1 small onion, diced

2 cloves garlic, minced

2 tablespoons diced fresh jalapeño

½ teaspoon hot Mexican-style chili powder

¼ teaspoon minced fresh thyme

¼ teaspoon ground cayenne pepper

¼ teaspoon habanero hot sauce

1. Add all ingredients to a 1½- to 2-quart slow cooker. Stir.

2. Cook on low for 8 hours.

QUINOA WITH CHORIZO

Try this as an alternative to rice.

Serves 2

INGREDIENTS:

¼ cup lean Spanish-style chorizo

¼ cup sliced onions

½ cup quinoa, rinsed

1 cup water

1. Sauté the chorizo and onions in a small nonstick saucepan until the onions are soft. Drain off any excess fat. Add to a 1½- to 2-quart slow cooker along with the quinoa and water. Cover and cook on low for 2 hours. Stir before serving.

Quinoa Basics

Although quinoa is treated like a grain, it is actually an edible seed. It is very high in protein and contains a balanced set of essential amino acids, making it a particularly complete source of protein. Quinoa is also high in fiber, iron, and magnesium.

BOURBON BAKED BEANS

Serve these at your next cookout or as a side dish for a ham or pork loin dinner.

Serves 8

INGREDIENTS:

4 strips bacon

1 large sweet onion, peeled and diced

3 (15-ounce) cans cannellini, great northern, or navy beans

2 ounces lean smoked ham, cubed

1 (15-ounce) can diced tomatoes

¼ cup maple syrup

3 tablespoons apple cider vinegar

4 cloves garlic, peeled and minced

2 tablespoons dry mustard

1½ teaspoons freshly ground black pepper

½ teaspoon ground ginger

¼ teaspoon dried red pepper flakes

2 tablespoons bourbon

Salt, to taste

1. Dice the bacon and add it to the slow cooker along with the onion. Cover and cook on high for 15 minutes; stir and cook for an additional 15 minutes or until the bacon is rendering its fat and the onion is getting soft.

2. Drain and rinse the beans. Add the beans to the slow cooker along with the remaining ingredients. Stir to mix. Reduce the setting on the slow cooker to low; cover and cook for 6 hours. Taste for seasoning and add additional salt if needed.

Try Adding More Tomatoes

This Bourbon Baked Beans recipe doesn't have as much tomato as some versions. If you prefer more tomato, you can add a 4-ounce can of tomato paste or some ketchup when you stir in all of the other ingredients.

RED BEANS AND RICE

You could also serve this as a hearty vegetarian main dish.

Serves 8

INGREDIENTS:

1 teaspoon canola oil

1 small onion, diced

3 cloves garlic, minced

1 stalk celery, diced

1 (15-ounce) can kidney beans, drained and rinsed

1 (15-ounce) can diced tomatoes

4 ounces canned green chiles

½ teaspoon dried oregano

½ teaspoon hot paprika

½ teaspoon cayenne pepper

½ teaspoon dried thyme

2 cups cooked long-grain rice

1. Heat the canola oil in a nonstick pan. Sauté the onions, garlic, and celery until the onions are soft, about 5 minutes.

2. Add the onion mixture, beans, tomatoes, chiles, and spices to a 1½- to 2-quart slow cooker. Cook on low for 6–8 hours. Remove the contents to a large bowl and stir in the rice.

TROPICAL BAKED BEANS

No one will guess the secret ingredient in these baked beans!

Serves 12

INGREDIENTS:

1 pound dried navy beans

Water, as needed

¼ cup cubed mango

1 large onion, diced

4 cloves garlic

½ cup chili sauce

½ cup water

1 tablespoon minced fresh ginger

1 tablespoon grainy mustard

1 teaspoon allspice

½ teaspoon cloves

½ teaspoon ground chipotle

½ teaspoon dried thyme

½ teaspoon freshly ground black pepper

1. The night before you want to make the baked beans, place the dried beans into a 4-quart slow cooker and cover with water. There should be at least 4" of water above the level of the beans. Soak overnight.

2. Drain the beans and return them to the slow cooker. Add the remaining ingredients. Stir to distribute all ingredients. Cook on low for 8–10 hours. Stir before serving.

CUBAN BLACK BEANS

Cuban-style black beans are traditionally served with rice.

Serves 4

INGREDIENTS:

½ teaspoon apple cider vinegar

¼ cup diced onion

1 (15-ounce) can black beans, drained and rinsed

2 cloves garlic, minced

1 jalapeño, minced

½ teaspoon oregano

¼ teaspoon cumin

1. Place all ingredients into a 2-quart slow cooker. Stir to distribute all the ingredients evenly.

2. Cook on low for 6–8 hours. Stir before serving.

CHAPTER 24

PASTA

PASTA AND BEAN SOUP

You can substitute a smoked turkey thigh for the ham hocks.

Serves 8

INGREDIENTS:

1 (1½-pound) pork shoulder roast

2 (15-ounce) cans cannellini or small white beans

2 smoked ham hocks

1 bay leaf

2 cloves garlic, peeled and minced

1 small yellow onion, peeled and diced

1 cup baby carrots, cut into thirds

¼ cup lovage or celery leaves, minced

1 (15-ounce) can diced tomatoes

Pinch dried red pepper flakes

¼ teaspoon dried oregano

Pinch dried rosemary

½ teaspoon dried basil

1 teaspoon dried parsley

½ teaspoon sugar

1 cup water

2 cups Chicken Broth (Chapter 19)

Salt and freshly ground black pepper, to taste

1 cup small pasta, like orzo or stars

1. Trim and discard any fat from the pork roast and cut the roast into bite-sized pieces. Add the pork and all of the other ingredients except for the pasta to the slow cooker. Cover and cook on low for 8 hours.

2. Remove the bay leaf and discard. Remove the ham hocks and set aside to cool enough to remove the meat from the bones. Use two forks to shred the ham and return it to the slow cooker.

3. Optional step: Remove several cups of the soup and purée in a blender or food processor. Return puréed beans to the pot. Return the soup to a simmer.

4. Cook the pasta according to package directions. Drain and add to the slow cooker. Stir to mix into the soup. Taste for seasoning and add additional salt and pepper if needed.

CHEESE-LOVER'S TORTELLINI

All it takes to make this dish a meal is a tossed salad and some garlic bread.

Serves 8

INGREDIENTS:

2 pounds lean ground beef

1 medium onion, peeled and diced

2 cloves garlic, peeled and minced

1 (26-ounce) jar pasta sauce

2 (15-ounce) cans diced tomatoes, drained

½ teaspoon sugar

1 (10-ounce) box frozen spinach, thawed

2 cups ricotta cheese

½ cup freshly grated Parmesan-Reggiano cheese

1 (1-pound) bag frozen cheese tortellini

Salt and freshly ground black pepper, to taste

1. Add the ground beef and onion to a nonstick skillet over medium-high heat; stir and fry for 8 minutes or until the onions are transparent and the meat is broken apart and no longer pink. Stir in the garlic and sauté for 30 seconds. Drain and discard any fat rendered from the meat.

2. Transfer to the slow cooker. Stir in the pasta sauce, drained tomatoes, and sugar. Cover and cook on low for 8 hours.

3. Skim any additional fat from the surface of the pasta sauce in the slow cooker and discard. Squeeze the thawed spinach to remove any excess moisture and stir it into the pasta sauce along with the ricotta and Parmesan-Reggiano cheeses. Cover and cook on low while you cook the pasta.

4. Cook the tortellini according to package directions. Drain and fold into the pasta sauce in the slow cooker. Taste for seasoning and add salt and pepper if needed. Serve directly from the slow cooker.

EASY MAC AND CHEESE

This is a popular dish for a carry-in supper or buffet.

Serves 8

INGREDIENTS:

Nonstick spray

2 cups milk

4 cups elbow macaroni

1 (2-pound) box Velveeta cheese

Salt and freshly ground black pepper, to taste

1. Treat the slow cooker with nonstick spray. Pour the milk into the slow cooker. To bring the milk to temperature, cover and cook on high while you cook the macaroni.

2. Cook the macaroni according to the package directions. Drain and add to the slow cooker. Stir into the milk. Reduce the temperature of the slow cooker to low.

3. Cut the cheese into small cubes. Stir into the macaroni and milk. Cover and cook on low for 1 hour. Stir. Add additional milk if needed.

4. Cover and cook on low for another hour, or until the cheese is completely melted and you can stir it into the macaroni. To serve, ladle the mac and cheese directly from the slow cooker. Add salt and pepper, if desired.

SLIMMED-DOWN MACARONI AND CHEESE

Although it is still a treat, this version of macaroni and cheese won't leave you feeling guilty. This method yields a very creamy dish that is easy to keep warm until everyone is ready for dinner.

Serves 6

INGREDIENTS:

1 teaspoon dry mustard

2 tablespoons cornstarch

¼ teaspoon freshly ground black pepper

2½ cups fat-free evaporated milk

1½ cups reduced-fat sharp Cheddar

8 ounces cooked macaroni

1. Spray a 4-quart slow cooker with nonstick cooking spray. In a small saucepan, heat the mustard, cornstarch, pepper, and evaporated milk until warmed through, whisking occasionally. Stir in the cheese.

2. Pour the macaroni into the slow cooker. Top with the cheese mixture and stir. Cover and cook on low for 1–2 hours or on high for 30 minutes.

MEXICAN-STYLE MACARONI AND CHEESE

Use mild or hot salsa, according to taste. Serve with a tossed salad and baked corn tortilla chips.

Serves 8

INGREDIENTS:

Nonstick spray

3 tablespoons butter

1 medium onion, peeled and diced

1 red bell pepper, seeded and diced

⅓ cup all-purpose flour

½ teaspoon salt

1 teaspoon dried cilantro, crushed

½ teaspoon ground cumin

3 cups milk

4 cups dried elbow macaroni

2 cups (8 ounces) Colby cheese, cubed

2 cups (8 ounces) Monterey jack cheese, grated

1 cup bottled salsa

⅔ cup halved pitted green and/or ripe olives

Salt and freshly ground black pepper, to taste

Optional: Chili powder, to taste

1. Add the butter, onion, and bell pepper to the slow cooker. Cover and cook on high for 30 minutes, or until the onion is transparent.

2. Stir in the flour, salt, cilantro, and cumin. Cook and stir for 3 minutes, adding a little of the milk, if necessary, to form a loose paste. Whisk in the milk. Cover and continue to cook on high while you cook the pasta.

3. Cook the macaroni according to package directions; drain.

4. Whisk the milk mixture in the slow cooker. Reduce heat to low. Stir in the drained macaroni, Colby cheese, Monterey jack cheese, salsa, and olives. Cover and cook on low for 2 hours or until cheese is melted and can be stirred into the sauce completely.

5. Taste for seasoning. Add salt and pepper, if needed, and chili powder, to taste, if desired. To serve, ladle from the slow cooker onto a dinner plate.

MUSHROOM CHICKEN

Serve this delicious chicken with spinach salad and garlic bread.

Serves 6

INGREDIENTS:

2 cups sliced fresh mushrooms

1 (15-ounce) can diced tomatoes with basil, garlic, and oregano

1 red bell pepper, seeded and diced

1 medium onion, peeled and thinly sliced

¼ cup dry red wine or Beef Broth (Chapter 19)

2 tablespoons quick-cooking tapioca

2 tablespoons balsamic vinegar

3 cloves garlic, peeled and minced

2½ pounds meaty chicken pieces (breasts, thighs, and/or drumsticks), skin removed

¼ teaspoon salt

¼ teaspoon paprika

¼ teaspoon freshly ground black pepper

1 (9-ounce) package fresh or frozen cheese tortellini or ravioli

Optional: Parmesan-Reggiano, grated

1. Add the mushrooms, undrained tomatoes, red pepper, onion, wine or broth, tapioca, balsamic vinegar, and garlic to the slow cooker. Stir to combine. Place the chicken pieces on top of the sauce. Sprinkle the salt, paprika, and black pepper over the chicken. Cover and cook on low for 8 hours.

2. Remove the chicken pieces and keep warm. (Or, if you prefer, once the chicken is cool enough to handle, remove the chicken from the bones; shred the chicken and discard the bones.)

3. Add the tortellini or ravioli to the sauce; cover and cook on high for 10–15 minutes or until the pasta is done. If using shredded chicken, stir it into the pasta and sauce. If using chicken pieces, arrange them on a serving platter and top with the pasta and sauce. Serve with additional grated cheese if desired.

Pasta and the Slow Cooker

While it's possible to cook fresh (or fresh refrigerated) pasta in the slow cooker, unless you can stay close enough to keep an eye on the slow cooker, don't attempt it. It only takes a few minutes and one more dirty pan to cook pasta according to the package directions. That's the foolproof way to fix it.

FREEZER TO THE PLATE CHICKEN PASTA SAUCE

Serve over your choice of cooked pasta along with a tossed salad and garlic bread. Have salt, a pepper grinder, and freshly grated Parmesan-Reggiano cheese at the table for those who want it.

Serves 4

INGREDIENTS:

1 (26-ounce) jar marinara sauce

8 frozen chicken tenders

1. Add the marinara sauce to the slow cooker. Add the chicken, pushing each piece down into the sauce. Cover and cook on low for 8 hours.

2. Use tongs or a slotted spoon to remove the chicken to a cutting board. Use two forks to shred the chicken. Return to the slow cooker and stir into the sauce.

TORTELLINI SOUP

Opening a few cans is the most labor involved in making this dish. The result tastes like you've been cooking all day.

Serves 6

INGREDIENTS:

1 tablespoon extra-virgin olive oil

1 small onion, peeled and finely diced

2 (14-ounce) cans chicken broth

1 (15-ounce) can stewed Italian tomatoes

1 (15-ounce) can chopped spinach, drained

1 (16-ounce) package fresh or frozen tortellini, your preferred flavor

Optional: Parmesan-Reggiano cheese

1. Add the oil and onion to the slow cooker. Stir to coat the onion in oil. Cover and cook on high for 30 minutes, or until the onions are transparent.

2. Stir in the broth, tomatoes, and spinach. Reduce the temperature of the slow cooker to low, cover, and cook for 4 hours.

3. Cook the tortellini according to package directions; drain and stir into the soup. Serve topped with grated cheese if desired.

TUXEDO SOUP

This soup, which gets its name from the bowtie pasta, is one that the kids will love. Serve it with a tossed salad and garlic bread.

Serves 8

INGREDIENTS:

1 pound lean ground beef

1 medium onion, peeled and diced

1 small green pepper, seeded and diced

1 stalk celery, diced

1 medium carrot, peeled and diced

4 cloves garlic, peeled and minced

2 (15-ounce) cans diced tomatoes, undrained

1 cup water

1 (26-ounce) jar spaghetti sauce

1 tablespoon sugar

½ teaspoon dried Italian seasoning, crushed

Dash dried red pepper flakes

1 cup bowtie pasta

Salt and freshly ground black pepper, to taste

Parmesan-Reggiano or mozzarella cheese, grated

Optional: Fresh flat-leaf parsley, minced

1. Add the ground beef, onion, green pepper, celery, and carrot to a nonstick skillet and, stirring frequently, sauté over medium-high heat for 8 minutes or until the vegetables are tender and the meat is no longer pink. Stir in the garlic and sauté for 30 seconds. Drain and discard any excess fat. Transfer to the slow cooker.

2. Stir in the undrained tomatoes, water, spaghetti sauce, sugar, Italian seasoning, and red pepper flakes. Cover and cook on low for 8 hours.

3. Cook the pasta according to package directions. Drain and stir into the slow cooker. Thin the soup with additional hot water if necessary. Taste for seasoning and add salt and pepper if desired. Ladle into soup bowls. Sprinkle cheese to taste over each serving. Garnish with parsley if using.

Extra Vegetables

Thanks to the spaghetti sauce, you can hide more vegetables in Tuxedo Soup and the kids won't even notice. For example, dice a few more carrots and stir them in with the other ingredients in Step 2.

CHAPTER 25

RICE

CLASSIC ITALIAN RISOTTO

Risotto should be very creamy on the outside, with just a bit of toothsome resistance on the inside of each grain of rice.

Serves 4

INGREDIENTS:

2 tablespoons butter

2 tablespoons olive oil

½ cup finely chopped sweet onion

2 stalks celery, finely chopped

¼ cup celery leaves, chopped

1½ cups arborio rice

1 teaspoon salt

5 cups Chicken Broth or Vegetable Stock (Chapter 19)

¼ cup chopped parsley

½ teaspoon freshly ground black pepper

⅔ cup freshly grated Parmesan cheese

1. Place the butter and oil in a heavy-bottomed pot, melt butter, and add the onion, celery, and celery leaves. Cook for 3–5 minutes, until vegetables are softened.

2. Add the rice and stir to coat with butter and oil. Stir in salt. Add rice and softened vegetables to a greased 4-quart slow cooker.

3. Add remaining ingredients, except cheese, to the slow cooker. Cover and cook on high for 3 hours or on low for 6 hours.

4. Twenty minutes before serving, stir in Parmesan cheese.

SHRIMP RISOTTO

Shrimp-Infused Broth will give this risotto a flavor boost. If you don't want to take the time to make it, substitute 1 cup of additional chicken broth and stir a pinch of crushed saffron threads directly into the slow cooker.

Serves 6

INGREDIENTS:

1 tablespoon olive oil

2 tablespoons butter, melted

2 medium white onions, peeled and diced

2 cups Arborio rice

½ cup dry white wine

1 cup Shrimp-Infused Broth (see sidebar)

5 cups Chicken Broth (Chapter 19)

1½ pounds shrimp, peeled and deveined

½ cup freshly grated Parmesan-Reggiano cheese

3 tablespoons fresh flat-leaf parsley, minced

Salt, to taste

1. Add the oil, butter, and onion to the slow cooker. Stir to coat the onions in the oil. Cover and cook on high for 30 minutes or until the onion is transparent.

2. Stir in the rice; continue to stir for several minutes or until the rice turns translucent. Add the broth. Cover and cook on high for 2½ hours or until the rice is cooked al dente.

3. Add the shrimp to the slow cooker, atop the risotto. Cover and cook on high for 20 minutes or until the shrimp is pink. Stir in the cheese and parsley. Taste for seasoning and add salt if needed. Serve immediately.

Shrimp-Infused Broth

Add 1 cup of chicken broth and the shrimp shells from 1½ pounds of shrimp to a saucepan. Bring to a boil over medium-high heat; reduce the heat and maintain a simmer for 15 minutes or until the shells are pink. Strain; crush a pinch of saffron threads and stir it into the broth.

PEPPER PORK AND RICE

This stew is good garnished with strips of green onion. (Only add the poblano and jalapeño peppers if you want a hot, spicy stew; otherwise, omit them entirely or substitute chopped green pepper.)

Serves 8

INGREDIENTS:

2 pounds boneless pork shoulder

1 tablespoon cooking oil

1 large onion, peeled and diced

Optional: 2 fresh poblano peppers, seeded and cut into 1-inch pieces

Optional: 1 fresh jalapeño pepper, seeded and chopped

4 cloves garlic, minced

1 2-inch cinnamon stick

2 cups converted rice

3 cups water

4 cups Chicken Broth (Chapter 19)

2 (15-ounce) cans diced tomatoes

1 tablespoon chili powder

1 teaspoon dried oregano, crushed

¼ teaspoon black pepper

Optional: ¼ cup snipped fresh cilantro or parsley

Optional: Salt, to taste

1. Trim and discard fat from the pork; cut the pork into 1-inch cubes.

2. Add the oil to the slow cooker and bring it to temperature over high.

3. Add the pork; cover and cook for 15 minutes. Stir the pork and brown for another 15 minutes. Drain off and discard any excess fat rendered from the meat.

4. Add the remaining ingredients (except for the cilantro or parsley); stir to combine. Reduce the slow cooker heat to low, cover, and cook for 8 hours or until the meat and rice are cooked through.

5. Discard cinnamon stick. Stir in additional broth if the stew is too thick and bring it to temperature. Stir in the cilantro or parsley if desired. Taste for seasoning and add salt if needed. Serve warm.

RICE AND VEGETABLES

This dish has all of the elements of a stuffed peppers and tomatoes recipe, but it saves you some time because instead of making a filling for the peppers and tomatoes, you instead prepare it in layers in the slow cooker.

Serves 8

INGREDIENTS:

1 cup long-grain rice

1 cup tomato juice

1 pound ground beef, browned and drained

½ pound ground lamb or pork, browned and drained

1 large yellow onion, peeled and diced

1 tablespoon dried parsley

¼ teaspoon salt

Freshly ground black pepper, to taste

1 teaspoon paprika

⅛ teaspoon ground allspice

Pinch ground cinnamon

1 teaspoon sugar

2 (15-ounce) cans diced tomatoes

4 green peppers, seeded and diced

1 cup Beef Broth (Chapter 19)

2 tablespoons lemon juice

Water or additional broth if needed

1. In a large mixing bowl, combine the rice, tomato juice, beef, lamb or pork, onion, parsley, salt, black pepper, paprika, allspice, cinnamon, and sugar. Set aside.

2. Add one can of the diced tomatoes to a 4-quart or larger slow cooker. Add half of the meat-rice mixture. Spread the diced green peppers over the top of the meat-rice mixture, then the top the peppers with the rest of the meat. Add the other can of diced tomatoes.

3. Pour in the broth and add the lemon juice. If needed, add additional water or broth to bring the liquid to almost the top of the solid ingredients. Cover and cook for 8 hours on low. Taste for seasoning and add additional salt and pepper if needed.

Soupy to Succulent

If too much liquid remains in the slow cooker, cook uncovered long enough to allow some of the liquid to evaporate.

OLD WORLD CABBAGE ROLLS

You won't use an entire head of cabbage in this recipe, but a large one gives you leaves large enough to make bigger cabbage rolls. If you prefer, substitute a small-to-medium head of cabbage and make more smaller rolls.

Serves 8

INGREDIENTS:

1 large head of cabbage

1 large egg

1 (8-ounce) can tomato sauce

½ cup brown rice

1 envelope onion soup mix

1 pound lean ground turkey

⅓ cup Parmesan-Reggiano cheese, grated

3 cups vegetable or tomato juice

1. Remove and discard the outer leaves of the cabbage. Peel off 8 large leaves. (Refrigerate the unused cabbage for another use.) Soften the cabbage leaves (see sidebar).

2. Add the egg, tomato sauce, uncooked rice, soup mix, ground turkey, and cheese to a bowl; mix well.

3. Spoon about ¼ cup of the meat mixture into the center of each cabbage leaf. Fold the ends of the leaf over the filling, and then roll the sides over the ends. Place seam side down in the slow cooker.

4. Pour the vegetable or tomato juice over the cabbage rolls. Cover and cook on low for 6 hours.

Softening Cabbage Leaves

To soften the cabbage leaves, one option is to layer them in a microwave-safe bowl and microwave on high for 2 minutes. The other alternative is to put them in a bowl, pour boiling water over the top of them and let them rest in the water for 2 minutes; use tongs to remove the cabbage leaves and pat them dry with paper towels or drain them on a clean, cotton cloth.

GREEK MEATBALLS

Serve this youvarlakia (Greek-style meatball) adaptation like a soup with some crusty bread. To complete the meal, add a salad tossed with a lemon juice and extra-virgin olive oil vinaigrette and topped with feta cheese.

Serves 8

INGREDIENTS:

1½ pounds lean ground beef

1 cup converted rice

1 small yellow onion, peeled and finely diced

3 cloves garlic, peeled and minced

2 teaspoons dried parsley

½ teaspoon oregano

1 teaspoon ground cumin

2 teaspoons dried mint

1 large egg

All-purpose flour

2 cups tomato juice or tomato-vegetable juice

2 tablespoons Greek extra-virgin olive oil

½ teaspoon ground cinnamon

1 tablespoon honey

4 cups water

Salt and freshly ground black pepper, to taste

1. Make the meatballs by mixing the ground beef together with the rice, onion, garlic, parsley, oregano, cumin, mint, and egg; shape into small meatballs and roll each one in flour.

2. Add the tomato or tomato-vegetable juice, olive oil, cinnamon, and honey to the slow cooker. Carefully add the meatballs. Pour in the water. (The water should take the liquid level up to where it completely covers the meatballs.)

3. Cover and cook on low for 6 hours or until the meatballs are cooked through. Taste for seasoning and add salt and pepper if needed.

BEANS AND RICE

You can add an additional boost to the flavor of this dish by substituting spicy tomato-vegetable juice for the broth or water.

Serves 6

INGREDIENTS:

Nonstick spray

1 tablespoon olive oil

1 cup converted long-grain rice

1 (15-ounce) can black beans, rinsed and drained

1 (15-ounce) can pinto beans, rinsed and drained

½ teaspoon salt

1 teaspoon Italian seasoning

½ tablespoon dried onion flakes

1 (15-ounce) can diced tomatoes

1¼ cups Vegetable Stock (Chapter 19) or water

1. Treat the slow cooker with nonstick spray. Add the oil and rice; stir to coat the rice in the oil.

2. Add the black beans, pinto beans, salt, Italian seasoning, onion flakes, tomatoes, and stock or water to the slow cooker. Stir to combine. Cover and cook on low for 6 hours or until the rice is tender.

SPANISH CHICKEN AND RICE

Have Spanish extra-virgin olive oil at the table for those who wish to drizzle a little over the rice. For more heat, sprinkle some additional dried red pepper flakes on top, too.

Serves 4

INGREDIENTS:

1 tablespoon olive or vegetable oil

4 chicken thighs

4 split chicken breasts

2 tablespoons lemon juice

4 ounces smoked ham, cubed

1 medium onion, peeled and diced

1 red bell pepper, seeded and diced

4 cloves garlic, peeled and minced

Nonstick spray

2½ cups water

1¾ cups Chicken Broth (Chapter 19)

1 teaspoon oregano

½ teaspoon salt

¼ teaspoon saffron threads, crushed

⅛ teaspoon dried red pepper flakes, crushed

2 cups converted long-grain rice

1. Bring the oil to temperature in a large nonstick skillet over medium-high heat. Put the chicken in the skillet skin side down and fry for 5 minutes or until the skin is browned. Transfer the chicken to a plate and sprinkle the lemon juice over the chicken.

2. Pour off and discard all but 2 tablespoons of the fat in the skillet. Reduce the heat under the skillet to medium. Add the ham, onion, and bell pepper; sauté for 5 minutes or until the onion is transparent. Stir in the garlic and sauté for 30 seconds.

3. Treat the slow cooker with nonstick spray. Pour the cooked ham and vegetables into the slow cooker. Add the water, broth, oregano, salt, saffron, red pepper flakes, and rice. Stir to combine.

4. Place the chicken thighs, skin side up, in the slow cooker and add the breast pieces on top of the thighs. Cover and cook on low for 6 hours or until the rice is tender and the chicken is cooked through. Place a split chicken breast and thigh on each serving plate. Stir and fluff the rice mixture and spoon it onto the plates.

Adding a Vegetable to Spanish Chicken and Rice

After you've removed the chicken from the slow cooker in Step 4, stir in 1 cup (or more) of thawed baby peas. Stir into the mixture remaining in the cooker when you fluff the rice. The heat from the rice should be sufficient to warm the peas so you can serve immediately.

WILD RICE WITH MIXED VEGETABLES

Wild rice cooks up perfectly in the slow cooker. Try it as a high-fiber alternative to white rice or potatoes.

Serves 8

INGREDIENTS:

2½ cups water

1 cup wild rice

3 cloves garlic, minced

1 medium onion, diced

1 carrot, diced

1 stalk celery, diced

1. Place all ingredients into a 4-quart slow cooker and stir. Cover and cook on low for 4 hours. After 4 hours, check to see if the kernels are open and tender. If not, put the lid back on, and continue to cook for an additional 15–30 minutes. Stir before serving.

Wild, Wild Rice

Wild rice is a bit of misnomer. It is actually a grass that grows in shallow water in North America. While it is often sold in mixes with white rice, it is also tasty all by itself.

SPANISH SAFFRON RICE

This fragrant dish goes well with grilled chicken or fish and looks very festive alongside shish kebabs. Use saffron threads instead of powder, if possible.

Serves 6–8

INGREDIENTS:

1 onion

4 stalks celery

2 tablespoons olive oil

3 tomatoes

1⅓ cups uncooked rice

4 cups water

2 teaspoons salt

¼ teaspoon cayenne pepper

1 green pepper

¼ pound Gruyère cheese

½ teaspoon saffron threads

1. Thinly slice the onion and celery. Sauté the onion and celery in oil in a pan over medium heat until soft. Transfer to the slow cooker.

2. Cube the tomatoes. Put the tomatoes, rice, water, salt, and cayenne pepper in the slow cooker.

3. Cover and heat on a low setting for 4–6 hours.

4. Mince the green pepper and grate the cheese. Half an hour before serving, stir in the green pepper, cheese, and saffron.

Serving Stations

Have you heard of multitasking? Try "multiserving" as well. Have slow cookers in three or four serving areas around your party zone, and guests will keep moving around to try all your creations. The more they move around, the more they will chat and enjoy each other.

CHINESE CONGEE (SIMPLE RICE PORRIDGE)

Congee is a very easy-to-digest rice porridge that's perfect for small children, those who are sick, or if you would simply enjoy a light meal.

Serves 8

INGREDIENTS:

¾ cup medium- or short-grain white rice

8 cups Chicken Broth (Chapter 19)

1 teaspoon ground ginger, or 2 tablespoons fresh ginger, peeled and grated

4–6 dried shiitake mushrooms, reconstituted, thinly sliced (or fresh baby bella mushrooms, thinly sliced)

½ teaspoon salt

½ teaspoon ground white pepper

1 cup cooked pork, diced

2 hard-boiled eggs, peeled and chopped

4 green onions, thinly sliced

⅛ teaspoon sesame oil

1. In a fine mesh colander wash rice and drain until the water runs clear.

2. Add rice, broth, ginger, mushrooms, salt, and white pepper to a 4- to 6-quart slow cooker. Cook on low for 12–16 hours or on high for 6–8 hours.

3. One hour prior to serving, add in the pork and chopped eggs.

4. To serve, ladle congee into bowls. Garnish with sliced green onions and a dash of sesame oil.

Congee or Jook

A simple rice porridge that's usually flavored with pork and/or eggs and sometimes with duck meat, this porridge is popular in many Asian countries and is called by a variety of names including congee or jook. The porridge is made of rice that has been cooked thoroughly until the grains have broken down into starches, creating a creamy and comforting soup.

CHAPTER 26

SIDE DISHES

GRANDMA'S GREEN BEANS

This recipe is easy to double if you need extra servings for a church social or buffet. Serve these green beans with meatloaf or any grilled meat.

Serves 6

INGREDIENTS:

1 (1-pound) bag frozen green beans, thawed

1 medium sweet onion, peeled and diced

6 medium red potatoes

1 teaspoon sugar

Salt and freshly ground black pepper, to taste

6 strips bacon

1. Add the green beans and onion to the slow cooker. Depending on your preference, you can either scrub and dice the potatoes or peel and dice them. Add the potatoes to the slow cooker along with the sugar, salt, and pepper.

2. Dice the bacon and add ⅔ of it to the slow cooker. Stir to mix well. Sprinkle the remaining bacon pieces over the top of the beans mixture. Cover and cook on low for 4 hours or until the potatoes are cooked through. Taste for seasoning and add additional salt and pepper if needed.

Fresh Green Beans

You can substitute a pound to a pound and a half fresh washed, trimmed, and cut green beans for the frozen. Increase the cooking time to 6 hours if you do.

FRESH ARTICHOKES

Preparing artichokes takes some work, but they're good served with an avocado salad and poached salmon.

Serves 4

INGREDIENTS:

2 large fresh artichokes

6 cups hot water

1 lemon

¼ cup butter, melted

Optional: ¼ teaspoon seasoned salt

1. Rinse the artichokes under cool running water. Use a sharp knife to slice about an inch off the top of each artichoke; cut off the stem near the base. Use kitchen shears to trim about ½ inch off the top of each leaf. Use the knife to cut each artichoke in half vertically. Use a spoon or melon baller to scoop out and discard the fuzzy center, or choke.

2. Place the artichoke halves in the slow cooker. Pour in the hot water. Cut 4 thin slices cut from the center of the lemon and add to the slow cooker; reserve the remaining lemon. Cover and cook on high for 4 hours or until the artichoke heart is tender when pierced with a knife. Use a slotted spoon to remove the artichoke halves from the slow cooker.

3. To prepare the butter sauce, add the melted butter to a bowl. Add the juice from the reserved portions of the lemon. Stir in seasoned salt if desired. Evenly drizzle over the artichoke halves. Serve immediately.

CREAMED CORN

This recipe is definitely not for somebody on a low-fat or low-carb diet. The cream cheese helps make the rich sauce for the corn. In fact, because of the cream cheese there will be enough sauce that if you need extra servings for a carry-in buffet, you can double the amount of corn you use and still have enough sauce.

Serves 12

INGREDIENTS:

4 cups frozen whole-kernel corn, thawed

1 (8-ounce) package cream cheese

½ cup butter

½ cup milk

1 tablespoon white sugar

Salt and freshly ground black pepper, to taste

1. Add the corn to the slow cooker. Cube the cream cheese and slice the butter; add them to the slow cooker along with the milk, sugar, salt, and pepper. Stir to combine.

2. Cover and cook on low for 4 hours. (After 2 hours, stir the corn mixture and watch carefully. Switch the slow cooker to the warm setting as soon as the cream sauce is thickened; keep warm until ready to serve. Otherwise, the corn can scorch and change flavor if the heat is left too high for too long.)

VINEGAR-BRAISED RED CABBAGE

This is a tart dish. Adding additional jelly or serving the cabbage with some additional butter melted on top can cut the tartness. Be sure to refrigerate any leftovers; the cabbage tastes better the next day and can be reheated and served warm or used cold as a pickle-replacement condiment on a sandwich.

Serves 8

INGREDIENTS:

1 medium head of red cabbage

4 tablespoons butter

1 tablespoon sugar

¼ teaspoon salt

⅓ cup water

⅓ cup white or white wine vinegar

1 small apple, peeled and grated

1 tablespoon red currant jelly, or to taste

1. Remove and discard the tough outer leaves of the cabbage. Cut the cabbage in half and remove the core; finely slice or shred the cabbage.

2. Add the shredded cabbage, butter, sugar, salt, water, vinegar, and apple to the slow cooker. Cover and cook on low for 6 hours or until the cabbage is cooked through.

3. Stir and taste for seasoning. Add additional salt and jelly if desired.

HOT GERMAN POTATO SALAD

Serve this with bratwurst sandwiches and chilled mugs of ice-cold beer.

Serves 6

INGREDIENTS:

6 baking potatoes

1 small red onion, peeled and diced

3 stalks celery, diced

1 small green bell pepper, seeded and diced

¼ cup apple cider vinegar

½ cup water

¼ cup light olive or vegetable oil, or bacon fat

2 tablespoons sugar

½ teaspoon celery seeds

¼ cup fresh flat-leaf parsley, minced

6 strips bacon, cooked until crisp, drained, and crumbled

Salt and freshly ground black pepper, to taste

1. Scrub the potatoes; slice them into ¼-inch slices and add to the slow cooker. Add the onion, celery, and bell pepper; stir to mix.

2. Add the vinegar, water, oil, sugar, and celery seeds to a bowl or measuring cup; whisk to mix and then pour into the slow cooker.

3. Cover and cook on low for 4 hours or until the potatoes are cooked through.

4. Stir in the parsley and crumbled bacon. Season with salt and pepper, to taste. Serve hot.

Another Option

You can omit the oil and bacon in the Hot German Potato Salad and instead add 8 ounces of diced smoked sausage in Step 1. The fat that renders from the sausage should be sufficient to offset the vinegar; however, if you think it's too tart when you taste the dish for seasoning, you can stir in a little vegetable oil when you add the salt and pepper.

SCALLOPED POTATOES

This recipe employs all sorts of labor-saving tricks. You use thawed frozen hash browns and therefore skip peeling and slicing the potatoes. You add soup, which lets you skip making a roux to thicken the sauce. You can even stir in a pound of diced ham if you want to turn it into a one-pot meal to serve along with a salad.

Serves 6

INGREDIENTS:

Nonstick spray

1½ (16-ounce) packages frozen hash brown potatoes, thawed

1 cup milk

½ cup sour cream

1 (10¾-ounce) can condensed cream of mushroom soup

1 cup (4 ounces) Cheddar cheese, grated

1 small green bell pepper, seeded and diced

½ cup butter, melted

1 small onion, peeled and diced

2 tablespoons pimentos, minced

⅛ teaspoon freshly ground black pepper

1 cup cheese cracker crumbs, divided

1. Treat the slow cooker with nonstick spray. Add the hash browns, milk, sour cream, soup, cheese, green pepper, butter, onion, pimento, black pepper, and ½ cup of the cracker crumbs. Stir to combine.

2. Top the mixture in the slow cooker with the remaining cracker crumbs.

3. Cover and cook on low for 7 hours or until the mixture is bubbly and the potatoes are cooked through. Serve ladled from the slow cooker.

STEWED SQUASH

Crisp and fresh, this is the perfect summer side dish to show off the season's bounty.

Serves 4

INGREDIENTS:

1 medium onion, cut into ¼" slices

3 cups sliced zucchini

1 tablespoon fresh dill

3 tablespoons lemon juice

¼ teaspoon salt

¼ teaspoon black pepper

¾ cup fresh corn kernels

1 teaspoon butter

1. Place the onions on the bottom of a 1½ to 2-quart slow cooker. Top with zucchini, dill, lemon juice, salt, and pepper. Cook on low for 3½ hours.

2. Add the corn and butter and stir. Cook for an additional 30 minutes on high.

ROSEMARY-GARLIC MASHED POTATOES

Slow-cooked mashed potatoes are the perfect side for busy holiday cooks. Not only does this dish leave a burner free for other cooking, there is no need to boil the potatoes before mashing them.

Serves 10

INGREDIENTS:

3 pounds red skin potatoes, quartered

4 cloves garlic, minced

¾ cup Chicken Broth (Chapter 19)

1 tablespoon fresh rosemary, minced

¼ cup 1% milk

1 tablespoon butter

⅓ cup reduced-fat sour cream

1. Place the potatoes in a 4-quart slow cooker. Add garlic, broth, and rosemary. Stir. Cover and cook on high until potatoes are tender, about 3–4 hours.

2. Pour in milk, butter, and sour cream. Mash with a potato masher.

LOADED MASHED POTATOES

This recipe is a healthier version of the popular restaurant side dish.

Serves 10

INGREDIENTS:

3 pounds small russet potatoes, peeled

4 cloves garlic, sliced

1 medium onion, diced

1 tablespoon bacon bits

¾ cup water

¼ cup skim milk

¼ cup diced green onions

2 tablespoons grated Parmesan

¼ cup fat-free sour cream

1. Place the potatoes, garlic, onion, and bacon bits in a 4-quart slow cooker. Add water. Stir. Cover and cook on high until potatoes are tender, about 3–4 hours.

2. Add the milk, green onions, Parmesan, and sour cream. Mash with a potato masher.

Using Dairy in the Slow Cooker

While evaporated milk is fine for long cooking times, cream, milk, and sour cream will curdle. Add them during the last part of the cooking time. Despite some advice, sweetened condensed milk cannot be used interchangeably with evaporated milk, cream, milk, or sour cream. It is very sweet and should never be used in savory dishes.

SIMPLE BAKED POTATOES

Here's a great way to keep your kitchen cool on a warm summer day. Serve these baked potatoes with grilled steaks or salmon.

Serves 4–6

INGREDIENTS:

4–6 medium-sized baking potatoes

1 tablespoon butter, per potato

¼ teaspoon salt, per potato

¼ teaspoon ground pepper, per potato

1. Wrap potatoes in aluminum foil and place in a 4-quart or larger slow cooker.

2. Cover and cook on high for 4 hours or on low for 8 hours until potatoes are fork tender.

3. When ready to serve, remove potatoes from cooker, remove foil, and cut potatoes in half. Add butter, salt, and pepper for each serving.

SALT-BAKED POTATOES

Despite an abundance of salt, these potatoes are not salty at all, just perfectly cooked and tender.

Serves 4

INGREDIENTS:

Kosher salt, as needed

4 medium-to-large russet potatoes

1. Pour about ½" of salt into the bottom of an oval 4-quart slow cooker. Place the potatoes in a single layer on top of the salt. Add more salt until the potatoes are completely covered. Cover and cook on high for 2 hours or until the potatoes are fork tender.

2. Crack the salt crust and remove the potatoes. Rub them with a towel to remove all of the salt before serving.

Picking Potatoes

Different potatoes are good in different recipes. Red skin potatoes are soft and creamy, perfect for potato salads or mashing with the skin left on. Russet potatoes are starchier and are well suited to baking or making French fries.

DILL CARROTS

The carrots in this side dish keep a firm texture even when fully cooked.

Serves 6

INGREDIENTS:

1 pound carrots, cut into coin-sized pieces

1 tablespoon minced fresh dill

½ teaspoon butter

3 tablespoons water

1. Place all ingredients in a 2-quart slow cooker. Stir. Cook on low 1½–2 hours or until the carrots are fork tender.

2. Stir before serving.

Dill Details

Dill is a delicate plant that has many culinary uses. The seeds are used as a spice, and fresh and dried dill, called dill weed, are used as herbs. Dill is an essential ingredient in dill pickles and gravlax, a type of cured salmon.

ROSEMARY-THYME GREEN BEANS

In this recipe, the slow cooker acts like a steamer, resulting in tender, crisp green beans.

Serves 4

INGREDIENTS:

1 pound green beans

1 tablespoon minced rosemary

1 teaspoon minced thyme

2 tablespoons lemon juice

2 tablespoons water

1. Place all ingredients into a 2-quart slow cooker. Stir to distribute the spices evenly.

2. Cook on low for 1½ hours or until the green beans are tender. Stir before serving.

LEMON-GARLIC GREEN BEANS

Lemon zest and sliced garlic add a fresh and bright flavor to these slow-cooked green beans.

Serves 4

INGREDIENTS:

1½ pounds fresh green beans, trimmed

3 tablespoons olive oil

3 large shallots, cut into thin wedges

6 cloves garlic, sliced

1 tablespoon grated lemon zest

½ teaspoon salt

½ teaspoon pepper

½ cup water

1. Place green beans in a greased 4-quart slow cooker. Add remaining ingredients over the top of the beans.

2. Cook on high for 4–6 hours, or on low for 8–10 hours. If you like your beans more crisp, check them on high after about 3½ hours or on low after about 6 hours. Fresh green beans are sturdy enough to withstand very long cooking temperatures without getting mushy.

POTATOES PAPRIKASH

This Hungarian classic is the perfect spicy side dish to serve with a roast.

Serves 8

INGREDIENTS:

1½ teaspoons olive oil

1 medium onion, halved and sliced

1 shallot, minced

4 cloves garlic, minced

½ teaspoon salt

½ teaspoon caraway seeds

¼ teaspoon freshly ground black pepper

1 teaspoon cayenne pepper

3 tablespoons paprika

2 pounds red skin potatoes, thinly sliced

2 cups Chicken Broth (Chapter 19) or Vegetable Stock (Chapter 19)

2 tablespoons tomato paste

½ cup reduced-fat sour cream

1. Heat the oil in a nonstick pan. Sauté the onion, shallot, and garlic 1–2 minutes or until they begin to soften. Add the salt, caraway seeds, pepper, cayenne, and paprika, and stir. Immediately remove from heat.

2. Add the onion mixture, potatoes, broth or stock, and tomato paste to a 4-quart slow cooker. Stir to coat the potatoes evenly. Cook on high for 2½ hours or until the potatoes are tender.

3. Turn off the heat and stir in the sour cream.

STEWED TOMATOES

For an Italian variation, add basil and Italian parsley.

Serves 6

INGREDIENTS:

28 ounces whole tomatoes in purée, cut up

1 tablespoon minced onion

1 stalk celery, diced

½ teaspoon oregano

½ teaspoon thyme

1. Place all ingredients into a 2-quart slow cooker. Stir. Cook on low up to 8 hours.

GINGERED SWEET POTATOES

For this festive recipe, look for candied ginger that is not coated in sugar; it's called uncrystallized ginger.

Serves 10

INGREDIENTS:

2½ pounds sweet potatoes

1 cup water

1 tablespoon grated fresh ginger

½ tablespoon minced uncrystallized candied ginger

½ tablespoon butter

1. Peel and quarter the sweet potatoes. Add them to a 4-quart slow cooker. Add the water, fresh ginger, and candied ginger. Stir.

2. Cook on high for 3–4 hours or until the potatoes are tender. Add the butter and mash. Serve immediately or turn them down to low to keep warm for up to 3 hours.

Sweet Potatoes or Yams?

Yams are not grown domestically, so the yams commonly found in supermarkets are actually varieties of sweet potato. True yams can be found in Asian or specialty stores and come in colors ranging from purple to yellow to white.

SWEET AND SOUR RED CABBAGE

Even those who don't like cabbage will enjoy this dish; the cabbage's texture becomes meltingly soft.

Serves 6

INGREDIENTS:

½ head red cabbage, shredded

1 medium onion, shredded

1½ tablespoons dark brown sugar

1 teaspoon butter

¼ cup water

½ cup apple cider vinegar

1 tablespoon white wine vinegar

½ teaspoon freshly ground black pepper

¼ teaspoon salt

⅛ teaspoon ground cloves

½ teaspoon thyme

1. Place all ingredients into a 4-quart slow cooker. Stir to distribute all ingredients evenly.

2. Cook on low for 4–6 hours or until the cabbage is very soft. Stir before serving.

MIXED SUMMER VEGETABLES

The vegetables in this dish end up with a texture that is very close to steamed.

Serves 4

INGREDIENTS:

1 medium onion, cut into ¼" slices

1½ cups sliced zucchini

1½ cups sliced yellow squash

1 tablespoon minced fresh thyme

¼ cup lemon juice

¼ teaspoon salt

¼ teaspoon black pepper

¾ cup fresh corn kernels

½ cup diced okra

1 teaspoon butter

1. Place the onions on the bottom of a 1½- to 2-quart slow cooker. Top with zucchini, yellow squash, thyme, lemon juice, salt, and pepper. Cook on low for 3½ hours.

2. Add the corn, okra, and butter, and stir. Cook for an additional 30 minutes on high.

MISO EGGPLANT

Miso Eggplant can be served hot or cold.

Serves 4

INGREDIENTS:

2 tablespoons water

¼ cup miso paste

1 1-pound eggplant, cubed

1. Place the water and miso into a 4-quart slow cooker. Stir to dissolve the miso. Add the eggplant and toss. Cook on high for 3 hours.

Not-So-Mysterious Miso

Miso paste might seem exotic, but it is available in most grocery stores in the refrigerated section. Miso is produced by fermenting rice, barley, or soybeans, and is then made into a savory paste. It is most commonly used in soup but can be used to braise vegetables or on grilled dishes.

STEWED OKRA

A Creole dish, this mixture of okra and tomatoes makes the most of seasonal ingredients.

Serves 4

INGREDIENTS:

2 large tomatoes, diced

1½ cups diced okra

1 small onion, diced

2 cloves garlic, minced

1 teaspoon hot sauce

1. Place all ingredients into a 2-quart slow cooker and stir. Cook on low for 2–3 hours. Stir before serving.

Serving Okra

Okra has a distinctive pentagonal shape and a thick stem that should be discarded. When cooked, it releases a slippery, gooey substance. This can be off-putting to some but is easily counteracted by pairing the okra with something acidic, like tomatoes.

CRIMINI MUSHROOM UN-STUFFING

"Stuffing" made in the slow cooker is moist and flavorful, the next best thing to being roasted with the bird.

Serves 18

INGREDIENTS:

1½ tablespoons butter

1 pound onions, diced

1 pound celery, diced

8 ounces crimini mushrooms, sliced

12 cups cubed bread

1 egg

1 quart Chicken Broth (Chapter 19)

½ tablespoon poultry seasoning

1 teaspoon marjoram

1 teaspoon dried sage

1 teaspoon dried parsley

1 teaspoon celery flakes

¼ teaspoon celery seeds

¼ teaspoon freshly ground black pepper

¼ teaspoon salt

1. Melt the butter in a large skillet. Sauté the onions, celery, and mushrooms until the onions are soft. Pour into a large bowl. Add the remaining ingredients and stir to combine.

2. Scoop into a 6-quart slow cooker, and cook on low for 6 hours.

ROASTED GARLIC

Roasted garlic is mellow enough to eat as-is, but it is also great in any recipe that would benefit from a mild garlic flavor.

Yields 4 heads garlic

INGREDIENTS:

½ tablespoon olive oil

4 heads garlic

1. Pour the oil onto the bottom of a 2-quart slow cooker. Place the garlic in a single layer on top.

2. Cook 4–6 hours on low or until the garlic is very soft and golden. To serve, simply squeeze the garlic out of the skin.

POACHED FIGS

Use these poached figs in any recipe that calls for cooked figs or eat as-is.

Serves 4

INGREDIENTS:

8 ounces fresh figs

1 cup water

1 vanilla bean, split

1 tablespoon sugar

1. Put all ingredients into a 2-quart slow cooker. Cook on low for 5 hours or until the figs are cooked through and starting to split.

2. Remove the figs from the poaching liquid and serve.

Shopping for Figs

Look for figs that are plump and soft but not squishy. The skin should not be split or oozing. Store figs in the refrigerator or in a cool dark cabinet until ready to use.

CORN ON THE COB

This is a great way to have hot corn on the cob without having to heat up the kitchen during the summer months. After cooking, turn the slow cooker to warm and let everyone help themselves!

Serves 6

INGREDIENTS:

6 ears corn, husks removed

½ teaspoon salt

Water, as needed

1. Place the corn in the bottom of an oval 4-quart slow cooker. Fill the insert with water until the water level is 1" below the top. Cover and cook for 5 hours on low or 2 on high.

CARAMELIZED ONIONS

Caramelized onions are a great addition to roasts, dips, and sandwiches.

Yields 1 quart

INGREDIENTS:

4 pounds Vidalia or other sweet onions

3 tablespoons butter

1 tablespoon balsamic vinegar

1. Peel and slice the onions in ¼" slices. Separate them into rings. Thinly slice the butter.

2. Place the onions into a 4-quart slow cooker. Scatter the butter slices over the top of the onions and drizzle with balsamic vinegar. At this point, the slow cooker may look full but the onions will quickly reduce. Cover and cook on low for 10 hours.

3. If after 10 hours the onions are wet, turn the slow cooker up to high and cook uncovered for an additional 30 minutes or until the liquid evaporates.

Storing Caramelized Onions

Store the onions in an airtight container. They will keep up to 2 weeks refrigerated or up to 6 months frozen. If frozen, defrost overnight in the refrigerator before using.

CARROT NUTMEG PUDDING

Carrots are often served as a savory side dish. In this recipe the carrots have just a little bit of sugar added to bring out their natural sweetness.

Serves 4

INGREDIENTS:

4 large carrots, grated

2 tablespoons butter

½ teaspoon salt

½ teaspoon nutmeg, freshly grated

2 tablespoons sugar

1 teaspoon vanilla

1 cup milk

3 eggs, beaten

1. Add carrots and butter to a large glass microwavable bowl. Cook on high for 3–4 minutes, until carrots are slightly softened.

2. Stir in remaining ingredients and pour into a greased 2½-quart slow cooker. Cook on high for 3 hours or on low for 6 hours. Serve hot or cold.

HARVARD BEETS

Beets are richly flavored, beautiful vegetables to serve at the dinner table. For those unaccustomed to the taste of beets, this sweet and sour recipe is a good place to start.

Serves 6

INGREDIENTS:

½ cup sugar

1 tablespoon cornstarch

¼ cup water

¼ cup white vinegar

¼ teaspoon ground cloves

2 (14-ounce) cans sliced or whole beets, drained (or 4 cups peeled and sliced fresh beets)

1. Grease a 2½-quart slow cooker with nonstick cooking spray.

2. Add sugar, cornstarch, water, vinegar, and cloves to slow cooker and whisk together. Add drained beets.

3. Cover and cook on high for 3 hours. Serve hot or cold.

Beets and Football

The origins of Harvard Beets is uncertain, but beets cooked in a sugar and vinegar solution have been eaten for hundreds of years in many different countries. The addition of cornstarch as a thickening agent is unique to America, though; specifically the northeastern states. One theory behind the name "Harvard Beets" is that the beets shared a similar color to Harvard's football team jerseys.

SWEET POTATO GRATIN WITH LEEKS AND ONIONS

The combination of sweet and savory makes this a fascinating, unique, and delicious dish.

Serves 6

INGREDIENTS:

2 leeks, white part only, rinsed and chopped

2 large sweet onions such as Vidalias, peeled and finely chopped

2 stalks celery with tops, finely chopped

4 tablespoons olive oil

4 sweet potatoes, peeled and sliced thinly

1 teaspoon dried thyme

1 teaspoon salt

½ teaspoon ground black pepper

3 cups 1% milk

1½ cups corn bread crumbs

2 tablespoons butter or margarine, cut in small pieces

1. In a skillet over medium heat add the leeks, onions, celery, and olive oil and sauté for 3–5 minutes, until softened.

2. Grease a 4-quart slow cooker with nonstick cooking spray.

3. Layer the sweet potato slices in the slow cooker with the sautéed vegetables. Sprinkle thyme, salt, and pepper on each layer as you go along. Finish with a layer of potatoes.

4. Add the milk until it meets the top layer of potatoes. Then add the corn bread crumbs. Dot with butter or margarine.

5. Cover and cook on high for 4 hours or on low for 8 hours, until the potatoes are fork tender. In the last hour of cooking, vent the lid of the slow cooker with a chopstick or wooden spoon handle to allow excess condensation to escape.

Instead of Corn Bread

Instead of corn bread, you can also use crushed corn tortillas as a topping.

SCALLOPED POTATOES WITH BACON

Scalloped potatoes is an ideal dish for the slow cooker. Potatoes cooked slowly over low heat are extremely tender and delicious.

Serves 8

INGREDIENTS:

2 tablespoons cornstarch

1 teaspoon salt

½ teaspoon pepper

2 cups milk

4 cups potatoes, thinly sliced (about 6–8 medium potatoes)

½ pound bacon, cooked and crumbled

3 tablespoons butter, cut in small pieces

½ cup Cheddar cheese, shredded

½ cup scallions, sliced

1. Grease a 4-quart slow cooker with nonstick cooking spray.

2. In a small bowl mix together the cornstarch, salt, pepper, and milk.

3. Place ⅓ of the potatoes in the bottom of the slow cooker. Pour ⅓ of the milk mixture over the potatoes. Sprinkle ⅓ of the bacon over the milk. Continue to layer ingredients, finishing with potato slices.

4. Dot butter over potatoes. Cover slow cooker and cook on low for 6–8 hours until potatoes are tender.

5. Thirty minutes prior to serving, sprinkle cheese and green onions on top of potatoes. Allow cheese to melt and then serve.

Make It Dairy-Free

For a recipe like this you can easily make it dairy-free by using coconut oil or olive oil in place of the butter, coconut milk or almond milk in place of the dairy milk, and Daiya (soy-free, gluten-free, and dairy-free cheese product) in place of the dairy cheese.

COLLARD GREENS

This is a Southern side dish staple that goes perfectly with barbecue chicken or ribs and Corn Bread (see Chapter 23).

Serves 8

INGREDIENTS:

1 meaty smoked ham hock, rinsed

1 large carrot, chopped

1 large onion, chopped

1 (1-pound) package fresh chopped collard greens, with tough stems removed

1 teaspoon garlic, minced

½ teaspoon crushed red pepper

¼ teaspoon black pepper

6 cups Chicken Broth (Chapter 19)

1 cup water

1. Place ham hock, carrot, and onion in a 6-quart slow cooker.

2. Add collard greens. Sprinkle greens with garlic, crushed red pepper, and black pepper.

3. Pour broth and water over collard greens.

4. Cover and cook on low for 8 hours. To serve, remove greens to a serving bowl. Remove meat from ham bone and discard fat and bones. Chop meat and add to greens. Ladle 1 to 2 cups broth over greens.

Make It Vegetarian

If you prefer, you can make these hearty greens without the ham hock. Simply leave the ham hock out of the recipe, use vegetable broth instead of chicken broth, and add 1 (15-ounce) can of diced tomatoes (or your favorite salsa) and a few tablespoons of olive oil. Cook as directed and serve with the vegetable broth ladled over each serving.

SIMPLE PEAS AND PEARL ONIONS

Garden peas have a naturally sweet flavor that pairs perfectly with pearl onions.

Serves 4

INGREDIENTS:

3 tablespoons butter

1½ cups pearl onions, skins removed

1 pound shelled peas, fresh or frozen

1 cup Chicken Broth (Chapter 19)

½ teaspoon black pepper

½ teaspoon salt

1 teaspoon sugar

1. In a small pan, melt butter and sauté onions until they become softened, about 3–5 minutes.

2. Add cooked onions, peas, broth, pepper, salt, and sugar to a greased 4-quart slow cooker.

3. Cover and cook on low for 6–8 hours or on high for 4 hours until peas are the desired texture.

Fresh Mint

Mint is an incredibly easy herb to grow in a home garden. It's drought tolerant and doesn't need much attention to thrive. Many different varieties of mint are available to grow such as lemon mint, pineapple mint, apple mint, and even chocolate mint! Adding 1–2 fresh chopped mint leaves to garden peas right before serving adds a fresh and bright flavor.

FINGERLING POTATOES WITH HERB VINAIGRETTE

Fingerling potatoes are small new potatoes. It's fun to use fingerling potatoes, because often they are small enough that they do not have to be chopped or diced. This dish is also delicious served cold as a potato salad.

Serves 4

INGREDIENTS:

2 pounds red or yellow fingerling potatoes, scrubbed

1 teaspoon salt

¼ cup lemon juice

⅓ cup extra-virgin olive oil

1 small shallot, minced (about 2 tablespoons)

1½ teaspoons minced fresh thyme leaves

1 tablespoon minced fresh basil leaves

1 tablespoon minced fresh oregano leaves

½ teaspoon Dijon mustard

1 teaspoon sugar

1. Place potatoes in a medium pot and cover with cold water. Bring to a boil and add salt to the water. Cook potatoes for 6–8 minutes until fork tender.

2. Drain potatoes and place in a greased 4-quart slow cooker.

3. In a small bowl whisk together lemon juice, olive oil, shallot, thyme, basil, oregano, mustard, and sugar. Drizzle vinaigrette over potatoes.

4. Cook on low for 4 hours or on high for 2 hours.

POTATO FRITTATA WITH CHEESE AND HERBS

Use both nonstick spray and butter in this recipe, or the starch in the potatoes will stick. You can experiment with different herbs and cheeses.

Serves 4

INGREDIENTS:

1 large Yukon gold potato, peeled

4 teaspoons butter, melted

6 eggs

½ cup grated Parmesan cheese

6 sage leaves, minced

½ teaspoon salt

½ teaspoon pepper

Fresh herbs, extra cheese, sour cream to garnish

1. Using a mandoline, slice the potato as thinly as possible. Grease a 4-quart slow cooker with melted butter and with a spritz of nonstick cooking spray and place the potatoes on the bottom in a thin layer.

2. In a medium bowl, beat the eggs well. Add the cheese, sage, salt, and pepper; stir to combine. Pour over the potatoes.

3. Cover and cook on high for 2 hours or on low for 4 hours.

4. Cut into squares and serve at once. Add chopped fresh herbs, additional shredded cheese, or sour cream to garnish.

An Untraditional Frittata

Usually frittatas are open omelets that are started in a heavy skillet on the stove and then finished by broiling in the oven. Using this slow cooker method you can put together the frittata the night before, then get up early, place it in the slow cooker, and 2 hours later breakfast is hot and ready!

COLCANNON

A traditional Irish potato and cabbage recipe, this side dish is an incredibly healthy way to include more vitamin-rich leafy green vegetables in your diet.

Serves 6

INGREDIENTS:

2½ pounds russet potatoes (about 4 large), peeled and cut into large chunks

1 teaspoon salt

6 tablespoons butter

3 cups chopped green cabbage (or kale, chard, or other leafy green)

1 cup whole milk

3 green onions, sliced

1. Add potatoes to a medium-sized pot on the stove. Cover with cold water and add salt. Bring to a boil. Cook potatoes until they are fork tender, about 10–15 minutes. Drain potatoes and add to a greased 4-quart slow cooker.

2. Add butter and chopped greens to slow cooker. Stir into potatoes.

3. Cover and cook on low for 4–5 hours or on high for 2½–3 hours.

4. An hour before serving, stir milk into the potatoes, and mash potatoes into the greens with a fork. Sprinkle with green onions.

A Frugal Main Dish

Colcannon is often eaten with boiled ham or Irish bacon and is a staple in some Irish homes. The greens used for the dish are normally kale or cabbage, depending on what's available seasonally. Both of these greens are extremely affordable healthy food sources and can also be stretched in soups and stews. An old Irish holiday tradition was to serve colcannon with small gold coins hidden in it.

BUTTERNUT SQUASH WITH WALNUTS AND VANILLA

Butternut squash has a very mild and slightly sweet flavor. Often people who don't like sweet potatoes enjoy this alternative side dish. Many grocery stores now sell butternut squash that has been peeled and precut into cubes, which can make meal preparation a breeze.

Serves 4

INGREDIENTS:

1 butternut squash (about 2 pounds), peeled, seeds removed, and cut into 1" cubes

½ cup water

½ cup brown sugar

1 cup walnuts, chopped

1 teaspoon cinnamon

4 tablespoons butter

2 teaspoons grated ginger

1 teaspoon vanilla

1. Grease a 4-quart slow cooker with nonstick cooking spray. Add cubed butternut squash and water to slow cooker.

2. In a small bowl mix together brown sugar, walnuts, cinnamon, butter, ginger, and vanilla. Sprinkle this brown sugar mixture evenly over butternut squash.

3. Cook on high for 4 hours or on low for 6–8 hours, or until butternut squash is fork tender.

SOUTHERN LIMA BEANS WITH HAM

Lima beans are a Southern favorite and can withstand extremely long cooking periods without being mushy. In this traditional recipe, lima beans are flavored with bite-sized pieces of ham and simmered in savory tomato-based sauce.

Serves 8

INGREDIENTS:

1 pound dry lima beans, soaked for 6–8 hours and rinsed with cold water

2 cups cooked ham, diced

1 sweet onion, chopped

1 teaspoon dry mustard

1 teaspoon salt

½ teaspoon freshly ground pepper

2 cups water

1 (15.5-ounce) can tomato sauce

1. Drain and rinse soaked lima beans. Add beans to a greased 4 to 6-quart slow cooker. Add all remaining ingredients. If needed add additional water to cover the beans by 1 inch.

2. Cook on high for 4 hours or on low for 8 hours. Serve over cooked rice or gluten-free pasta.

CANDIED BUTTERNUT SQUASH

Butternut squash has a delicious natural sweetness and is an excellent replacement for sweet potatoes. Also, you can now buy ready-cut and peeled butternut squash in many grocery stores (in the produce section), making this recipe incredibly easy to assemble.

Serves 4

INGREDIENTS:

4–5 cups butternut squash, peeled, seeded, and cubed

⅓ cup brown sugar

2 tablespoons molasses

1 tablespoon orange zest

½ teaspoon ground cinnamon

½ teaspoon ground cloves

1. Add all ingredients to a greased 4-quart slow cooker. Cook on high for 3–4 hours or on low for 6–8 hours, until squash is fork tender.

Butternut Squash Versus Sweet Potatoes

Wondering which might be better for you? Actually both are extremely healthy choices. Per cup, sweet potatoes have more fiber and protein than the squash, but one cup of butternut squash contains fewer calories, less overall carbohydrates, and the least amount of natural sugar. Both are high in vitamins A and C, and very low in sodium. In many recipes, they can be used interchangeably.

ROASTED WINTER VEGETABLES

This is a perfect side dish to roast chicken or roast beef. To make sure all the vegetables cook evenly, cut into small cubes that are similar in size. If you find the vegetables are becoming too dry, add in about ½ cup vegetable broth a little at a time until they are as moist as you would like them to be.

Serves 4

INGREDIENTS:

5–6 cups cubed root vegetables

2 tablespoons olive oil

½ teaspoon salt

1 teaspoon freshly ground pepper

1. Place cubed vegetables in a greased 4-quart slow cooker.

2. Drizzle with olive oil and sprinkle with salt and pepper.

3. Cover and cook on high for 3½–4 hours or on low for 7–8 hours, until vegetables are fork tender. Stir vegetables every hour or so to prevent them from overbrowning on the bottom.

Winter Root Vegetables

Use a variety of your favorite root vegetables such as carrots, turnips, sweet potatoes, white potatoes, parsnips, or onions. If using turnips, rutabagas, or sweet potatoes, make sure to peel the tough skin off before adding to the other vegetables.

PART IV

SOMETHING SWEET

CHAPTER 27

FABULOUS FRUITS

APPLESAUCE

You'll need about 4 pounds of apples for this size batch of applesauce, or enough to fill the slow cooker three-fourths full. The amount of sugar that you use will depend on the sweetness of the apples and your personal taste.

Yields about 4 cups

INGREDIENTS:

12 apples

½ to 1 cup pure cane sugar

Pinch salt

Optional: 1 tablespoon lemon juice

1. Wash, peel, core, and slice the apples. Add to the slow cooker. Cover and cook on low for 5 hours.

2. Stir in the sugar and salt. Use an immersion blender to purée the apples. Cover and cook on low for an additional 30 minutes or until the sugar is dissolved.

3. Optional: If the applesauce is too sweet, stir in the lemon juice to help balance the sweetness.

4. Serve warm as an accompaniment to pork chops or over pancakes. For leftovers, cool and store in the refrigerator for 2–3 days, or pour into appropriate covered containers and freeze for up to 3 months.

Spiced Applesauce

In Step 1, cook on low for 4 hours and then stir in 1 teaspoon ground cinnamon, ½ teaspoon ground cloves, ¼ teaspoon ground ginger, ¼ teaspoon allspice, and a pinch of freshly ground nutmeg. Cover and cook for another hour before proceeding to Step 2. Taste the applesauce after you've added the sugar and increase the amounts of spices if desired.

CINNAMON-SPICED APPLE BUTTER

The aroma that will fill the house while you make this apple butter is better than what you get from any plug-in air freshener. If you're using a less tart apple, add the brown sugar ¼ cup at a time until you reach desired sweetness. Apple butter and homemade biscuits or bread were made for each other.

Yields about 3 cups

INGREDIENTS:

8 large or 12 medium Granny Smith apples

½ cup apple cider or juice

¾ cup dark brown sugar

2 teaspoons ground cinnamon

½ teaspoon allspice

½ teaspoon ground cloves

Pinch salt

1. Wash, peel, core, and quarter the apples. Add to the slow cooker along with the cider or juice. Cover and cook on high for 4 hours.

2. Use an immersion blender to purée the apples. Stir in the brown sugar, cinnamon, allspice, cloves, and salt. Taste for seasoning and adjust if necessary.

3. Reduce the temperature of the slow cooker to low. Cook uncovered for 2 hours or until the apple butter is thick and dark. Store in the refrigerator for several weeks or freeze until needed.

Fruit Butter

You can substitute pears or peaches for half of the apples, or even throw in a few pitted prunes (dried plums), fresh peeled and pitted plums, or dried apricots if you wish. In Step 1, simply add your choice of fruit until the slow cooker is three-fourths full.

BAKED STUFFED APPLES

You can serve these baked apples as a warm dessert with some vanilla ice cream or along with some coffee cake for breakfast.

Serves 4

INGREDIENTS:

4 large tart baking apples

½ cup light brown sugar

Optional: 4 teaspoons orange zest, grated

1 teaspoon cinnamon

¼ cup golden seedless raisins

4 teaspoons frozen orange juice concentrate

4 teaspoons butter

½ cup apple cider or juice

1. Wash the apples and remove the core and the stem, but don't peel them.

2. Add the brown sugar, orange zest if using, and cinnamon to a small bowl; stir to mix.

3. Fill each apple with a tablespoon of raisins, a teaspoon of orange juice concentrate, and a generous tablespoon of the brown sugar mixture. Top the filling in each apple with a teaspoon of butter.

4. Pour the cider or juice into the slow cooker. Carefully place the apples upright in the slow cooker. Cover and cook on low for 5 hours or until the apples are cooked through and tender.

5. Use tongs and a spatula to remove the apples to dessert plates. Serve warm.

STEWED CINNAMON APPLES

These apples are wonderful with pork. The longer they are cooked, the softer they become.

Serves 4

INGREDIENTS:

1 teaspoon dark brown sugar

1 tablespoon ground cinnamon

2 tablespoons lemon juice

2 tablespoons water

4 crisp apples, cut into wedges

1. Place the sugar, cinnamon, lemon juice, and water into a 4-quart slow cooker. Stir until the sugar dissolves. Add the apples.

2. Cook on low for up to 8 hours. Stir before serving.

CHERRIES JUBILEE

You can substitute apple or peach pie filling for the cherry. (You can even sprinkle some chopped pecans or walnuts over the cake mix if you wish.) Serve warm directly from the slow cooker along with some ice cream, whipped cream, or whipped topping.

Serves 12

INGREDIENTS:

Nonstick spray

2 (21-ounce) cans cherry pie filling

1 (18-ounce) package yellow cake mix

½ cup melted butter

1. Treat the slow cooker with nonstick spray. Spread the pie filling over the bottom of the slow cooker. Sprinkle the dry cake mix over the cherries. Drizzle the melted butter over the cake mix.

2. Cover and cook on high for 2 hours or on low for 4 hours.

BANANA BREAD

Oat bran adds extra fiber to this recipe, making it a heart-healthier bread. The bananas impart a hearty enough flavor that few will notice the difference, but if the sweet taste of oat bran isn't to your liking, you can omit it and use 2 cups of flour instead.

Serves 8

INGREDIENTS:

1½ cups all-purpose flour

½ cup oat bran

¾ cup sugar

¾ cup baking soda

½ teaspoon salt

3 ripe bananas, mashed

6 tablespoons (¾ stick) butter, softened

2 large eggs, beaten

¼ cup plain yogurt

1 teaspoon vanilla

1¼ cups walnuts

Nonstick spray

1. Add the flour, oat bran, sugar, baking soda, and salt to a mixing bowl. Stir to mix.

2. Add the bananas, butter, eggs, yogurt, and vanilla to a food processor; pulse to cream together.

3. Add the walnuts and flour mixture to the food processor. Pulse to combine and chop the walnuts. Scrape down the sides of the container with a spatula and pulse until mixed.

4. Treat the slow cooker with nonstick spray. Add the batter to the slow cooker, using a spatula to spread it evenly across the bottom of the crock. Cover and cook on high for 3 hours, or until a toothpick inserted in the center of the bread comes out clean. Allow to cool uncovered before removing it from the slow cooker.

Spiced Banana Bread

For cinnamon-spiced banana bread, in Step 1 add a teaspoon of ground cinnamon; ¼ teaspoon each of ground cloves, ground ginger, and allspice; and the nutmeg to the flour.

CRANBERRY PEAR COMPOTE

You can serve this compote warm over pound cake or cooled with whipped cream. You can layer the chilled compote in parfait glasses with whipped cream and pieces of pound cake, broken fig-filled cookies, or graham cracker crumbs.

Serves 8

INGREDIENTS:

1 cup water

½ cup port or Madeira wine

½ cup sugar

6 allspice berries

4 cardamom pods, crushed

1 cup cranberries

4 large pears, cored, peeled, and sliced into quarters

1. Add the water, wine, sugar, allspice and cardamom to the slow cooker. Cover and cook on high for 30 minutes or until the liquid is bubbling around the edges. Stir to dissolve the sugar in the liquid.

2. Rinse and drain the cranberries. Remove and discard any stems or blemished cranberries. Stir into the liquid in the slow cooker. Cover and cook on high for 30 minutes or until the cranberries pop.

3. Wash, peel, core, and cut the pears into quarters. Stir into the other ingredients in the slow cooker. Cover and cook on low for 6 hours or on high for 3 hours.

4. Remove and discard the allspice berries and the cardamom pods. Serve warm from the slow cooker or allow to come to room temperature and pour into a covered container and refrigerate until chilled.

CRUSTLESS APPLE PIE

Adjust the cooking time depending on the type of apple you use. A softer golden delicious should be cooked through and soft in the recommended cooking times, but a crisper Granny Smith apple may take longer.

Serves 8

INGREDIENTS:

Nonstick spray

8 medium apples cored and sliced

3 tablespoons orange juice

3 tablespoons water

½ cup pecans, chopped

⅓ cup brown sugar

¼ cup butter, melted

½ teaspoon cinnamon

Optional: Whipped cream or topping

1. Treat the slow cooker with nonstick spray. Wash, core, and slice the apples and arrange them over the bottom of the slow cooker.

2. Add the orange juice and water to a small bowl or measuring cup; stir to mix. Evenly drizzle over the apples.

3. Add the pecans, brown sugar, butter, and cinnamon to a bowl. Mix well. Evenly crumble the pecan mixture over the apples. Cover and cook on high for 2 hours or on low for 4 hours. Serve warm or chilled topped with whipped cream or topping if desired.

PINEAPPLE UPSIDE-DOWN CAKE

Admittedly, it's a trick to invert this cake onto a serving plate. It's much easier to allow the cake to cool, cut it into 8 slices, and serve it from the crock of the slow cooker. Invert the slices as you put them on the dessert plate.

Serves 8

INGREDIENTS:

1 (18-ounce) box yellow or butter cake mix

Nonstick spray

¼ cup butter, melted

2 tablespoons brown sugar

1 (15-ounce) can crushed pineapple

Optional: Maraschino cherries

1. Prepare the cake mix according to the package directions.

2. Treat the bottom and sides of the slow cooker with nonstick spray. Pour the butter into the slow cooker, lifting and tilting the crock to evenly coat the bottom. Evenly sprinkle the brown sugar over the butter. Carefully spoon the crushed pineapple over the brown sugar, and then pour in any juice remaining in the can. If using, cut the maraschino cherries in half and arrange as many as you want cut side up over the pineapple.

3. Carefully pour (or ladle) the prepared cake batter over the mixture on the bottom of the slow cooker. Cover and cook on low for 4 hours or until a toothpick inserted into the cake comes out clean. If the cake is too moist on top, remove the cover and cook for another 15–30 minutes. Allow to cool and then serve.

BLACKBERRY JAM

This easy low-sugar jam does not need to be canned; it will keep up to a month in the refrigerator.

Serves 20

INGREDIENTS:

3 cups fresh blackberries

1¾ ounces low-sugar / no-sugar pectin

½ cup sugar

¾ cup water

1. Place all ingredients in a 2-quart slow cooker. Stir.

2. Cook on high, uncovered, for 5 hours. Pour into an airtight container.

3. Refrigerate overnight before using.

STRAWBERRY PANDOWDY

The pandowdy gets its name from the dowdy appearance that is achieved by breaking up the crust halfway through the cooking time to allow the juices to soak through.

Serves 4

INGREDIENTS:

4 cups whole strawberries, stems removed

½ teaspoon ground ginger

1½ tablespoons sugar

½ teaspoon cornstarch

¾ cup flour

3 tablespoons cold butter, cubed

3 tablespoons cold water

⅛ teaspoon salt

1. Place the strawberries, ginger, sugar, and cornstarch into a 2-quart slow cooker. Toss to distribute evenly.

2. Place the flour, butter, water, and salt into a food processor. Mix until a solid ball of dough forms. Roll it out on a clean surface until it is about ¼"–½" thick and will completely cover the fruit in the insert.

3. Drape the dough over the strawberries. Cover and cook on high for 40 minutes. Remove the lid. Using the tip of a knife, cut the dough into 2" squares without removing it from the slow cooker. Keep the lid off and continue to cook on high for an additional 40 minutes. Serve hot.

What's the Difference Between a Betty, a Cobbler, a Pandowdy, and a Slump?

A betty is a baked dish made by alternating layers of spiced, sugared fruit and buttered bread crumbs. A cobbler is a fruit stew in which biscuit dough is dropped onto the fruit before cooking. A pandowdy is a spoon pie with fruit on the bottom and a rolled pie crust on top that is broken up halfway through the cooking time. A Slump is a spoon pie as well that includes cooked fruit topped with biscuit dough.

SLOW-COOKED PINEAPPLE

Slow cooking makes pineapple meltingly tender. Serve as-is or with vanilla bean frozen yogurt.

Serves 8

INGREDIENTS:

1 whole pineapple, peeled

1 vanilla bean, split

3 tablespoons water or rum

1. Place all ingredients into a 4-quart oval slow cooker. Cook on low for 4 hours or until fork tender. Remove the vanilla bean before serving.

Cooking with Vanilla Beans

Vanilla beans have a natural "seam" that can easily be split to release the flavorful seeds inside. After using a vanilla bean, wash it and allow it to dry. Then place it in a container with a few cups of sugar for a few weeks to make vanilla sugar.

BERRY COBBLER

Try this with a mix of blackberries, raspberries, golden raspberries, and blueberries. If the berries are very tart, add an extra tablespoon of sugar.

Serves 8

INGREDIENTS:

4 cups mixed fresh berries

2½ tablespoons brown sugar

3 tablespoons minced fresh mint

1 cup flour

1½ tablespoons sugar

½ teaspoon ground ginger

1 egg

¼ cup fat-free evaporated milk

1½ tablespoons canola oil

1. Toss the berries, brown sugar, and mint. Set aside.

2. Whisk the dry ingredients in a medium bowl. Beat in the egg, evaporated milk, and oil until a thick dough forms.

3. Spray a 4-quart slow cooker with cooking spray. Spread the dough along the bottom, taking care to cover the entire bottom with no gaps. Add the berries in an even layer.

4. Cook on low for 2 hours.

Keep Your Berries Well

Berries are very fragile. For the best flavor, leave them out at room temperature rather than in the refrigerator. Avoid bruising berries by washing them directly before use. Buy local berries and eat them as soon as possible to avoid spoilage.

PEAR AND CRANBERRY CRUMBLE

Pears and cranberries make a sweet-tart base for this homey crumble.

Serves 6

INGREDIENTS:

3 Bosc pears, thinly sliced

¾ cup fresh cranberries

2 tablespoons light brown sugar

2 tablespoons melted unsalted butter

½ cup old-fashioned rolled oats

⅛ cup flour

½ teaspoon cinnamon

⅛ teaspoon nutmeg

½ tablespoon sugar

1. Spray a 2-quart slow cooker with nonstick spray. Add the pears, cranberries, and brown sugar. Stir. Cook for 3 hours on high.

2. In a small bowl, whisk the butter, oats, flour, cinnamon, nutmeg, and sugar. Sprinkle over the fruit and cook on high for 30 minutes. Remove the lid and cook an additional 10 minutes on high, uncovered.

Appealing Pears

Perhaps the most common variety of pear is the Bartlett. Sweet and juicy, it comes in both red and green variations. Bosc pears are uniformly brown and have a dull skin. Their denser texture makes them perfect for baking or slow cooking.

VANILLA POACHED PEARS

Slow poaching makes these pears meltingly tender and infuses them with a rich vanilla flavor.

Serves 4

INGREDIENTS:

4 Bosc pears, peeled

1 vanilla bean, split

2 tablespoons vanilla extract

2 cups water

1. Stand the pears up in a 4-quart oval slow cooker. Add the remaining ingredients. Cook on low for 2 hours or until the pears are tender. Discard all cooking liquid prior to serving.

SUMMER BERRY SLUMP

This is a fruit dessert served with fresh, steamed dumplings.

Serves 8

INGREDIENTS:

4 cups mixed fresh berries

1½ tablespoons sugar

1 teaspoon minced fresh ginger

1 cup flour

½ teaspoon ground ginger

1 egg

¼ cup fat-free evaporated milk

1½ tablespoons canola oil

1. Toss the berries, sugar, and fresh ginger together. Set aside.

2. Whisk the dry ingredients in a medium bowl. Beat in the egg, evaporated milk, and canola oil until a thick dough forms. Shape into 2" dumplings.

3. Spray a 4-quart slow cooker with cooking spray. Add the berries in an even layer. Drop in the dumplings.

4. Cook on low for 2 hours.

FRUIT CRISP

Serve with ice cream or with a dollop of whipped cream on top.

Serves 4

INGREDIENTS:

6 large peaches

¼ cup sugar

2 teaspoons ground cinnamon

Nonstick spray

¾ cup rolled oats

¼ cup all-purpose flour

½ cup brown sugar, packed

6 tablespoons butter

1 cup pecans

1. Wash and peel the peaches. Cut them in half, remove the pits, and slice the peaches. Toss together with the sugar and cinnamon.

2. Treat the slow cooker with nonstick spray. Arrange the peaches over the bottom of the slow cooker.

3. To make the topping, add the oats, flour, brown sugar, and butter to a food processor. Pulse until the topping is the consistency of coarse cornmeal. Add the pecans and pulse a couple of times to rough-chop the nuts and mix them into the topping.

4. Sprinkle the topping evenly over the fruit in the slow cooker. Cover and cook on high for 2 hours or until the peaches are tender and the topping is crisp. Serve warm or chilled.

Quicker and Easier Fruit Crisp

Fruit Crisp is a versatile dessert. You don't have to limit yourself to fresh fruit. If you need to throw together a dessert in a hurry, you can thaw some frozen peaches or open a can of any pie filling and use one of those instead.

AMISH APPLE BUTTER

Traditionally flavored with warm spices and sweetened with honey, this condiment is called a "butter" due to its thick consistency and soft texture. Since apple butter needs a long, unhurried cooking period to caramelize the fruit and deepen the flavors, the slow cooker is the most suitable modern cooking appliance to make it.

Yields 8 cups

INGREDIENTS:

10 cups (about 5 pounds) Gala apples, peeled, cored, and quartered

1 cup honey

3 tablespoons lemon juice or apple cider vinegar

1½ teaspoons ground cinnamon

½ teaspoon ground cloves

½ teaspoon allspice

1. Place apples in a greased 4-quart slow cooker.

2. Pour honey and lemon juice or vinegar over apples and add cinnamon, cloves, and allspice. Stir to coat apples.

3. Cover and cook on low for 14–16 hours (yes, 14–16 hours), until the apple butter is a deep, dark brown and is richly flavored.

4. Ladle into pint jars and store in the refrigerator for up to 6 weeks. You can also process and can the apple butter if you prefer.

Old-Fashioned Apple Butter Making

Apple butter used to be made in large copper pots while simmering over a hot fire all day long. It was often done by a church group, or a large family who could share the responsibility of stirring the pot throughout the long day to prevent it from burning. Once finished, the apple butter would be canned and sold to raise money for a good cause or shared among all who helped make it.

APPLE AND PEAR SPREAD

Make the most of in-season apples and pears in this easy alternative to apple or pear butter.

Yields 1 quart

INGREDIENTS:

4 Winesap apples, cored, sliced, and peeled

4 Bartlett pears, cored, sliced, and peeled

1 cup water or pear cider

¼ cup brown sugar

¼ cup sugar

¼ teaspoon ginger

¼ teaspoon cinnamon

¼ teaspoon nutmeg

¼ teaspoon allspice

1. Place all ingredients into a 4-quart slow cooker. Cook on low for 10–12 hours.

2. Uncover and cook on low for an additional 1–2 hours or until thick and most of the liquid has evaporated.

3. Allow to cool completely then pour into the food processor and purée. Pour into clean glass jars. Refrigerate up to 6 weeks.

Do-It-Yourself Brown Sugar

Brown sugar is simply white sugar that has been mixed with molasses. Make brown sugar by combining 1 cup granulated sugar with ¼ cup molasses. Store in an airtight container.

SWEET CITRUS CRANBERRY SAUCE

This combination of cranberries, brown sugar, orange and pineapple juice, simmered slowly during the day, will leave a wonderful aroma in your kitchen!

Serves 8

INGREDIENTS:

2 (12-ounce) packages fresh cranberries

Zest of 1 large orange

2 teaspoons cinnamon

1 cup pineapple juice

1 cup orange juice

1 cup brown sugar

1 cup sugar

1 cup water

1. Rinse cranberries through a strainer and toss out any bad ones. Pour cranberries into a greased 2½-quart slow cooker.

2. Zest the orange with a microplane grater or citrus zester. Sprinkle zest over cranberries. Add cinnamon, pineapple juice, orange juice, brown sugar, sugar, and water to the cranberries.

3. Cook on high for 4 hours or on low for 8 hours. In the last 2 hours of cooking vent slow cooker with a chopstick or spoon handle to allow excess moisture to escape the slow cooker.

4. Serve hot or cold. If serving hot, the sauce will be thinner than most cranberry sauces, but is delicious on ham or turkey. To serve cold, refrigerate 8 hours or overnight. The sauce will thicken after cooling.

FIGS IN COGNAC

These figs are sensational over ice cream. You can also serve them on plain white cake or ladyfingers.

Yields about 5 cups

INGREDIENTS:

2 pounds dried figs

3 cups water

2 cups sugar

1 cup cognac

1. Halve the figs with kitchen shears. Combine the figs, water, and sugar in the slow cooker.

2. Cover and heat on a low setting for 3–4 hours. Stir once after the first hour to distribute the sugar.

3. An hour before serving, add the cognac.

APRICOTS IN BRANDY

Try using a small round cookie cutter to cut your apricots for an attractive presentation.

Yields about 5 cups

INGREDIENTS:

2 pounds dried apricots

3 cups water

2 cups sugar

1 cup brandy

1. Halve the apricots with kitchen shears. Combine the apricots, water, and sugar in the slow cooker.

2. Cover and heat on a low setting for 3–4 hours. Stir once after the first hour to distribute the sugar.

3. An hour before serving, add the brandy.

Cutting Dried Fruit

Dip a clean pair of kitchen shears in hot water when cutting dried apricots, peaches, or other fruits. Chilling the fruit also helps, keeping them stiffer; the difference in temperature helps the blade cut more smoothly.

DRIED FRUIT COMPOTE

What dried fruits do you have available? Try substituting them in this recipe and see what combinations your guests like.

Yields about 6 cups

INGREDIENTS:

½ lemon

½ pound dried apricots

½ pound dried figs

½ pound prunes

½ pound dried pitted cherries

4 cups water

1½ cups sugar

⅔ cup bourbon

1 cup heavy cream

1. Thinly slice the lemon. Halve the apricots and figs with kitchen shears. Pierce the prunes with a fork so they don't burst.

2. Combine the lemon, dried fruits, water, and sugar in the slow cooker.

3. Cover and heat on a low setting for 3–4 hours.

4. An hour before serving, add the bourbon.

5. Whip the cream and provide as a garnish for individual servings.

HONEY RHUBARB SAUCE

This sweet sauce is delicious over virtually anything. Try it on cake, ice cream, or sweet bread.

Yields about 6–7 cups

INGREDIENTS:

4 pounds rhubarb

2 sticks cinnamon bark

1 cup sugar

½ cup honey

2 cups water

1. Cut the rhubarb in 2-inch pieces, discarding the leaves and the bases of the stalks. Leave the cinnamon sticks intact.

2. Combine the rhubarb, cinnamon, sugar, honey, and water in the slow cooker.

3. Cover and heat on a low setting for 3–4 hours.

STEAMY DRIED FRUIT

Use this fruit to dress up a simple bowl of vanilla ice cream or a piece of fluffy white cake.

Yields about 4 cups

INGREDIENTS:

½ lemon

1½ cups dried apricots

1½ cups dried apples

½ cup dried cherries

2 cups white grape juice

3 tablespoons honey

2 teaspoons ground anise seed

1 teaspoon ground cinnamon

1. Grate the rind of the lemon. Halve the apricots and apples.

2. Combine the rind, dried fruit, juice, honey, and spices in the slow cooker.

3. Cover and heat on a low setting for 3–4 hours.

Slow and Spicy

Extended cooking develops strong flavors from spices. When converting recipes, cut the amount of spices added in half until you have tested it once, especially if you are using fresh spices instead of dried ones.

BAKED PEACHES

Serve this simple fruit with fresh mint leaves as a bright garnish. Freeze any extras to use with future desserts.

Serves 12

INGREDIENTS:

12 fresh peaches

1 cup water

½ cup brown sugar

½ cup honey

1. Prick the peaches all over with fork tines. Slice the peaches into 8 sections. Cut through to the pits without releasing the slices from the pits.

2. Arrange in the slow cooker. Add the water, then sprinkle with the sugar and drizzle with the honey.

3. Cover and heat on a low setting for 3–4 hours.

VANILLA PLUMS

For a delicious twist, replace some of the water in this recipe with wine. The alcohol will burn off during cooking.

Serves 6–8

INGREDIENTS:

24 large ripe plums

1 cup water

1 cup white sugar

½ vanilla bean pod

1. Prick the plums all over with fork tines. Slice the plums into 8 sections. Cut through to the pits without releasing the slices from the pits.

2. Arrange the plums in the slow cooker. Add the water, then sprinkle with the sugar. Distribute segments of the vanilla bean pod in the liquid.

3. Cover and heat on a low setting for 3–4 hours.

Simple Can Be Good

A decadent serving of cake or ice cream slathered with dessert sauces is perfect—sometimes. Other times, like after filling meals, a small dish, a simple spoonful of spiced fruit, and a good dark coffee are all your guests will want after your dinner party.

PEACHES WITH BRANDY SAUCE

Peeling the peaches takes time, but it makes this dish much more decadent. Briefly dip the peaches in boiling water to aid the peeling.

Serves 6–8

INGREDIENTS:

8 peaches

1 cup sugar

4 sprigs fresh mint

½ cup water

1 cup brandy

1. Peel, quarter, and pit the peaches.

2. Arrange the peaches in the slow cooker. Sprinkle with the sugar and mint, then add the water.

3. Cover and heat on a low setting for 2–3 hours.

4. An hour before serving, add the brandy.

Fruit Emergency!

If you run out of fresh fruit, you can sometimes use dried fruit (plus a little extra liquid) in slow-cooker recipes. Don't be shy. Use those strange fruits or trail mixes buried in the back of your cupboard. You might find a winning combination.

ROSY CRANBERRY BANANAS

You can substitute dried apricots for cranberries, but in that case don't add the sugar.

Serves 10

INGREDIENTS:

2 cups fresh cranberries

10 bananas

1 cup sugar

½ cup water

1. Wash the cranberries; peel the bananas but leave them whole.

2. Arrange the bananas and cranberries in the slow cooker. Sprinkle with the sugar, then add the water.

3. Cover and heat on a low setting for 3–4 hours.

PEARS POACHED IN AMARETTO AND VANILLA

These pears will make it easy to eat your recommended five servings of fruit every day, especially if you eat them over ice cream.

Serves 12

INGREDIENTS:

12 ripe pears

½ lemon

1½ cups sugar

1 teaspoon vanilla extract

1 cup Amaretto

1 cup white wine

1. Core and halve the pears. Arrange the pears in the slow cooker.

2. Grate the peel of the lemon.

3. Sprinkle the pears with the grated peel, sugar, and vanilla. Add the Amaretto and wine.

4. Cover and heat on a low setting for 3–4 hours. Turn the pears twice.

SWEET RHUBARB BANANAS

This is delicious by itself or with a dish of ice cream. Also try serving it with small butter cookies for dipping.

Serves 10–12

INGREDIENTS:

8 stalks rhubarb

6 bananas

¼ cup water

1 cup sugar

¼ cup butter

¼ teaspoon salt

1. Cut the rhubarb into 2-inch pieces. Slice the bananas in half lengthwise.

2. Layer half of the rhubarb and half of the bananas in the slow cooker. Add the water, and sprinkle the fruit with half of the sugar. Add the rest of the rhubarb, bananas, and sugar, in that order. Dot the fruit with the butter and sprinkle with the salt.

3. Cover and heat on a low setting for 3–4 hours.

Using Overripe Bananas

Do you have some overripe bananas in the house? Peel and freeze them, mushy as they are. Use them later for cooking. The riper they are, the sweeter they will be, and cooking will make any bruising undetectable. Use them in compotes, breads, curries, and hot breakfast cereals.

SWEET CURRIED FRUIT

This is great hot or cold with desserts, or even with meats! Try some mixed into chicken salad or spooned over a slice of ham.

Serves 20

INGREDIENTS:

⅓ cup butter

¾ cup brown sugar

4 teaspoons curry powder

1 pound pears

1 pound peaches

1 pound apricots

2 pounds pineapple

1. Melt the butter in a saucepan over low heat. Add the brown sugar and curry powder, mixing well until blended.

2. Cut the fruit, fresh or canned, into bite-sized pieces and place in the slow cooker.

3. Spoon the curry mixture over the top of the fruit.

4. Cover and heat on a low setting for 3–4 hours.

TANGIERS ORANGE SAUCE

This is irresistible drizzled over slices of ham, or on ice cream, cakes, or sweet rolls. Also, try it on some otherwise bland vegetables, especially carrots.

Yields about 2½ cups

INGREDIENTS:

1¼ cups sugar

2 tablespoons cornstarch

1 teaspoon salt

1 teaspoon cinnamon

20 cloves

Zest of ¼ orange

2 cups orange juice

1 orange

1. Mix the sugar, cornstarch, salt, spices, and orange zest in the slow cooker.

2. Stir in the orange juice. Cover and heat on a low setting for 2–3 hours.

3. Stir occasionally.

4. Slice the whole orange in cross sections. Half an hour before serving, add the orange slices to the slow cooker.

CHAPTER 28

DESSERTS

CREAM CHEESE CAKE

Serve it as a shortcake topped with your favorite fresh or stewed fruit. It's also good topped with Butterscotch Caramel Sauce (this chapter) and is dense enough to dip into dessert fondue.

Serves 8

INGREDIENTS:

Nonstick spray

1 (8-ounce) package cream cheese, softened

1 stick butter, softened

1 (5.1-ounce) package instant vanilla pudding

3 large eggs

½ cup heavy cream

2 teaspoons vanilla

1 (18-ounce) package yellow or butter cake mix

1. Treat the slow cooker with nonstick spray. (Or if you want to remove the cake from the crock to cut it into layers, generously butter the inside and sides of the crock and dust the butter with some of the dry cake mix.)

2. Cream the cream cheese and butter together in a mixing bowl. Beat in the pudding, eggs, cream, and vanilla. Fold in the cake mix. (The resulting batter will be thick—like cookie dough.)

3. Drop the batter into the slow cooker and lightly pat it down so it's evenly distributed. Cover and cook on high for 3 hours or until a toothpick inserted in the center comes out clean. Serve warm by scooping it out of the slow cooker, or if you want to spoon fruit over the entire cake and cut it into wedges, let the cake cool, cut around the edges with a knife, and invert the cake onto a plate.

Freeze Leftovers

This cake works well as the cake portion for fruit, whipped cream, and chopped toasted nuts parfaits or in a trifle.

BREAD PUDDING

Serve this bread pudding by itself or top it with some warm Butterscotch Caramel Sauce (this chapter) and toasted chopped pecans or walnuts.

Serves 4

INGREDIENTS:

2 large eggs

2¼ cups milk

1 teaspoon vanilla

½ teaspoon cinnamon

¼ teaspoon salt

½ cup brown sugar

2 cups of 1-inch bread cubes

½ cup raisins or chopped dates

½ cup hot water

1. Add the eggs to a mixing bowl and beat lightly, and then whisk in the milk, vanilla, cinnamon, salt, and brown sugar. Fold in the bread cubes and raisins or dates.

2. Pour the bread pudding mix into a 1½-quart baking dish that will fit on the cooking rack inside the slow cooker.

3. Place the rack in slow cooker. Pour in the hot water. Set the baking dish on the cooking rack. Cover and cook on high for about 2 hours or until the eggs are set. Serve warm or cool.

BANANA COCONUT CAKE

You can substitute an equal amount of buttermilk for the cream and lemon juice.

Serves 8

INGREDIENTS:

1 stick butter

1 (8-ounce) package cream cheese, softened

1½ cups granulated white sugar

3 large eggs

½ cup heavy cream

1 tablespoon lemon juice

2 small ripe bananas, sliced

1⅓ cup all-purpose cake flour

1 teaspoon baking powder

¼ teaspoon salt

¾ teaspoon baking soda

½ cup unsweetened grated coconut

½ cup pecans, chopped

Nonstick spray

1. Add the butter, cream cheese, sugar, eggs, cream, lemon juice, and banana slices to a food processor. Process until well mixed.

2. Add the flour, baking powder, salt, and baking soda to a mixing bowl. Stir to mix. Scrape in the butter-banana mixture. Stir to combine. Fold in the coconut and pecans.

3. Line the bottom of the slow cooker with a round of parchment paper, coat the paper and the sides of the crock with nonstick spray, and pour in the batter. Cover and cook on low for 4 hours or until a toothpick inserted in the center comes out clean.

MOCHA CUSTARD

If you're impatient and indulgent, spoon this custard directly from the slow cooker and add even more calories by using the custard as hot sauce over ice cream. Otherwise, serve chilled according to the recipe instructions.

Serves 4

INGREDIENTS:

¼ cup instant espresso powder

2 tablespoons unsweetened cocoa powder

⅔ cup sugar

Pinch salt

4 cups half-and-half

6 large eggs

½ teaspoon pure vanilla or maple extract

Nonstick spray

Optional: Whipped cream

Optional: Additional cocoa powder

1. Add the espresso powder, cocoa powder, sugar, and salt to a blender or food processor. Pulse to mix and remove any lumps.

2. Add the half-and-half, eggs, and extract to the blender or food processor. Process until blended.

3. Treat the slow cooker with nonstick spray. Pour in the custard mixture. Cover and cook on low for 2½ hours, or until the edges of the custard begin to puff and a knife inserted in the center comes out clean.

4. Remove the crock from the slow cooker; place it on hot pads or a rack. Let the custard stand at room temperature for an hour or until cooled. Cover the top of the crock with plastic wrap or the slow cooker lid; refrigerate for 4 hours. Serve spooned into custard cups or your favorite dessert stemware. Top with a dollop of whipped cream dusted with cocoa powder if desired.

DATE PUDDING

This is a rich, decadent dessert that, when served with the quick sauce (see sidebar) or Butterscotch Caramel Sauce (this chapter), is in the tradition of an English sticky toffee pudding. You can double the number of servings if you layer the pudding in parfait glasses with sauce, chopped toasted pecans, and whipped cream.

Serves 8

INGREDIENTS:

2½ cups dates, pitted and snipped

1½ teaspoons baking soda

1⅔ cups boiling water

2 cups dark brown sugar, packed

½ cup butter, softened

3 large eggs

2 teaspoons vanilla

3½ cups all-purpose or cake flour

4 teaspoons baking powder

Pinch salt

Nonstick spray

1. Add the dates to a mixing bowl and toss them together with the baking soda. Pour the boiling water over the dates. Set aside.

2. Add the brown sugar and butter to a food processor. Process to cream them together, and then continue to process while you add the eggs and vanilla.

3. Use a spatula to scrape the brown sugar mixture into the bowl with the dates. Stir to mix.

4. Add the flour, baking powder, and salt to a bowl; stir to mix. Fold into the date and brown sugar mixture.

5. Treat the slow cooker with nonstick spray. Pour the batter into the slow cooker. Cover and cook on low for 4 hours or until the center of the pudding cake is set but it is still moist. Serve warm with your choice of sauce and a dollop of whipped cream if desired.

Quick Sauce

Add 1½ cups packed brown sugar, ½ cup butter, and 3 cups of heavy cream to a saucepan over medium heat. Stirring constantly, bring to a boil and then, while continuing to stir constantly, reduce the heat and maintain a simmer for 6 minutes.

ORANGE PUDDING CAKE

Creamsicle and Orange Julius fans will love this dessert. It also works well with lemon juice and lemon zest instead of the orange. The beaten egg whites act as the leavening; the pudding forms on the bottom as the cake cooks.

Serves 6

INGREDIENTS:

4 large eggs, separated

⅓ cup fresh orange juice

1 tablespoon orange zest, grated

3 tablespoons butter, softened

1½ cups milk

1 cup all-purpose or cake flour

1 cup sugar

Pinch salt

1. Add the egg yolks, orange juice, orange zest, and butter to a food processor; process for 30 seconds to cream the ingredients together. Continue to process while you slowly pour in the milk.

2. Add the flour, sugar, and salt to a mixing bowl. Stir to mix. Pour the egg yolk mixture into the bowl and combine it with the dry ingredients.

3. Add the egg whites to a separate chilled bowl; whip until stiff peaks form. Fold into the cake batter.

4. Pour into the slow cooker. Cover and cook on low for 2–2½ hours, or until the cake is set on top.

NOT YOUR GRANDMA'S CHOCOLATE CAKE

Serve this pudding cake warm with ice cream.

Serves 8

INGREDIENTS:

1 (21-ounce) package brownie mix

2 cups water

2 large eggs

¼ cup butter, melted

½ cup semisweet chocolate chips

Nonstick spray

1 cup sugar

¼ cup unsweetened cocoa powder

1. Add the brownie mix, ½ cup of the water, the eggs, and the melted butter to a bowl; stir to mix. Fold in the chocolate chips.

2. Treat the slow cooker with nonstick spray. Scrape the brownie mix batter into the slow cooker and spread evenly into the crock.

3. Add sugar and cocoa to a small bowl; stir to mix well. Add the remaining water to a saucepan over medium heat. Stir in the sugar-cocoa mixture. Bring to a boil and then pour over the brownie batter in the slow cooker. Cover and cook on high for 2–2½ hours.

Not Your Grandma's Banana Split

Serve the warm chocolate pudding cake over a banana sliced in half lengthwise. Add a scoop of strawberry ice cream; sweetened crushed pineapple; toasted, chopped peanuts, walnuts, cashews, pistachios, or pecans; and whipped cream. Top with a maraschino cherry.

LEMON SUGAR-CRUSTED CAKE

This cake is good with blueberry sauce, or you can add a cup of fresh blueberries to the batter before you cook it.

Serves 8

INGREDIENTS:

1 (18-ounce) lemon cake mix

4 large eggs

1 cup sour cream

¾ cup plus 1 tablespoon butter

1 cup milk

1 (3-ounce) package instant lemon pudding mix

3 drops lemon oil or ¼ teaspoon lemon extract

¼ cup sugar

1. Add the cake mix, eggs, sour cream, ¾ cup of the butter, milk, pudding mix, and lemon oil or extract to a mixing bowl. Stir by hand to mix.

2. Use the remaining butter to grease the bottom and halfway up the sides of the slow cooker. Pour the sugar into the slow cooker and turn the crock until the sugar is coating all of the butter.

3. Carefully spread the batter in the slow cooker. Cover and cook on low for 4 hours or until a toothpick inserted into the center of the cake comes out clean.

CARROT CAKE

Ice this cake with cream cheese frosting or glaze the cake while it's still warm (see sidebar).

Serves 8

INGREDIENTS:

1½ cups all-purpose flour

½ teaspoon baking soda

1 teaspoon baking powder

¼ teaspoon salt

¾ teaspoon cinnamon

¼ teaspoon ground cloves

⅛ teaspoon freshly grated nutmeg

2 large eggs

¾ cups sugar

⅓ cup butter

¼ cup water

1 cup carrots, grated

Optional: ½ cup walnuts, chopped

Nonstick spray

1. Add the flour, baking soda, baking powder, salt, cinnamon, cloves, and nutmeg to a mixing bowl; stir to combine.

2. Add the eggs, sugar, and butter to a food processor; process to cream together. Scrape into the flour mixture.

3. Pour in the water and add the grated carrots to the mixing bowl. Stir and fold to combine all ingredients. Fold in the nuts if using.

4. Treat the slow cooker with nonstick spray. Add the carrot cake batter and use a spatula to spread it evenly in the crock. Cover and cook on low for 2 hours or until cake is firm in the center.

Carrot Cake Glaze

Repeatedly pierce the top of the cake with a fork. Add ½ cup lemon, orange, or unsweetened pineapple juice; 1 teaspoon freshly grated lemon or orange zest; and 1½ cups of sifted powdered sugar to a microwave-safe measuring cup. Stir to combine. Microwave on high for 30 seconds. Stir and repeat until sugar is dissolved. Evenly pour over the cake.

BUTTERSCOTCH CARAMEL SAUCE

This recipe lets you eliminate the tedious step of cooking sugar until it caramelizes, which involves bringing it to 310°F or higher, depending on the amount of caramelization desired. By using brown sugar, you end up with a rich sauce with less work.

Yield: About 6 cups

INGREDIENTS:

½ cup (1 stick) butter

2 cups heavy cream

4 cups brown sugar

2 tablespoons fresh lemon juice

Pinch sea salt

1 tablespoon vanilla

1. Add the butter, cream, brown sugar, lemon juice, and salt to the slow cooker. Cover and cook on high for an hour or until the butter is melted and the cream begins to bubble around the edges of the crock. Uncover and stir.

2. Cover and cook on low for 2 hours, stirring occasionally. Uncover and cook on low for 1 more hour or until the mixture coats the back of the spoon or the sauce reaches its desired thickness. Stir in the vanilla.

Butterscotch Caramel Cake

Immediately after removing a yellow or white sheet cake from the oven, poke holes in the top of the cake with a fork. Generously ladle hot Butterscotch Caramel Sauce over the cake, allowing time for the caramel to soak into the cake before ladling on more.

HOT FUDGE FONDUE

Leftover hot fudge fondue can be stored in a covered container in the refrigerator for up to 3 weeks. Reheat to serve, whisking in additional cream if needed.

Yield: About 4 cups

INGREDIENTS:

2 sticks (1 cup) butter

1 cup heavy cream

½ cup light corn syrup

Pinch salt

1 pound (16 ounces) semisweet chocolate chips

1 tablespoon vanilla extract

1. Add the butter, cream, corn syrup, and salt to the slow cooker. Cover and cook on low for 1 hour. Uncover and stir with a silicone-coated whisk or heatproof spatula, cover, and cook for another hour. Uncover and stir or whisk until the sugar is completely dissolved.

2. Add the chocolate chips and vanilla. Stir or whisk until the chocolate is completely melted and incorporated into the fondue. Reduce the heat setting of the slow cooker to warm.

PEANUT BUTTER FONDUE

Leftover peanut butter fondue can be stored in a covered container in the refrigerator for up to 3 weeks. Alternatively, leftover fondue that has thickened can be poured into a buttered pan, allowed to cool, and then cut it into pieces of peanut butter fudge (that should be wrapped and stored in the refrigerator).

Serves 20

INGREDIENTS:

2 sticks (1 cup) butter

1 cup light corn syrup

2 (14-ounce) cans sweetened condensed milk

2 cups light brown sugar

Pinch salt

1 cup peanut butter

1. Add the butter, corn syrup, condensed milk, brown sugar, and salt to the slow cooker. Cover and cook on low for 1 hour. Uncover and stir with a silicone-coated whisk or heatproof spatula, cover, and cook for another hour. Uncover and stir or whisk until the sugar is completely dissolved.

2. Add the peanut butter. Cover and cook on low for 15 minutes to ½ hour to soften the peanut butter. Stir or whisk until the peanut butter is blended with the condensed milk mixture. Reduce the heat setting of the slow cooker to warm.

COCONUT RICE PUDDING

Evaporated milk gives this rice pudding an amazingly creamy texture without the fat of whole milk or cream.

Serves 8

INGREDIENTS:

¾ cup long-grain rice

3½ cups fat-free evaporated milk

⅔ cup sugar

⅓ cup unsweetened shredded coconut

½ teaspoon vanilla

¼ teaspoon salt

¼ teaspoon orange peel

1. Place all ingredients into a 4-quart slow cooker. Stir. Cook on low for 5 hours. Stir before serving.

Quick Tip

Rice pudding has a tendency to thicken as it cools. If you want a looser, creamier texture, stir in a bit of water to each bowl before serving. Reheat leftovers for optimum flavor and texture.

LIGHT AND CREAMY HOT FUDGE SAUCE

Try this over frozen yogurt or ice cream.

Yields 2 cups (about 30 servings)

INGREDIENTS:

12 ounces fat-free evaporated milk

10 ounces semisweet or bittersweet
  chocolate chips

1 teaspoon vanilla

½ teaspoon butter

⅛ teaspoon salt

1. Place all ingredients in a 1½- to 2-quart slow cooker. Cook on low, stirring occasionally for 2 hours. The sauce will thicken as it cools.

2. Refrigerate leftovers. Reheat in the slow cooker for 1 hour on high or on the stovetop until warmed through, about 10 minutes.

GREEN TEA TAPIOCA PUDDING

Tapioca pudding is simple in the slow cooker. There's no need to stir!

Serves 6

INGREDIENTS:

2 cups fat-free evaporated milk

¼ cup small pearl tapioca

1 teaspoon matcha or green tea powder

½ cup sugar

1 egg

1. Pour the evaporated milk, tapioca, matcha, and sugar into a 4-quart slow cooker. Whisk until the sugar dissolves. Cook for 1½ hours.

2. Stir in the egg. Cook an additional ½ hour on low. Serve warm.

Tapioca

Tapioca comes in several forms. Large pearl tapioca can be boiled to a chewy texture and served Taiwanese-style in cold drinks. Small pearl tapioca is better used in puddings and desserts. Tapioca starch is also used as a thickener in savory dishes.

CHALLAH BREAD PUDDING

This slimmed-down bread pudding is a wonderful way to use up leftover, even slightly stale, challah.

Serves 10

INGREDIENTS:

4 cups cubed challah

⅓ cup dried tart cherries or cranberries

2⅓ cups fat-free evaporated milk

2 eggs

⅓ cup dark brown sugar

1 teaspoon vanilla extract

1 teaspoon cinnamon

½ teaspoon ground ginger

¼ teaspoon nutmeg

1. Spray a 4-quart slow cooker with cooking spray. Add the bread cubes and dried fruit. Stir.

2. In a medium bowl, whisk the evaporated milk, eggs, brown sugar, vanilla, cinnamon, ginger, and nutmeg. Pour over the bread crumbs and dried fruit.

3. Cook for 5 hours on low or until the pudding no longer looks liquid.

Breaking Bread

It is important to cut the bread used for bread pudding into uniform 1"–2" cubes for maximum absorption and distribution of liquid. Slightly stale bread cuts easily and can be used in bread puddings or stuffing. Bread cubes can even be frozen for future use.

CHOCOLATE BREAD PUDDING

Fat-free evaporated milk gives this bread pudding a creamy texture, but it has several dozen fewer calories than heavy cream.

Serves 10

INGREDIENTS:

4 cups cubed Italian bread

2⅓ cups fat-free evaporated milk

2 eggs

⅓ cup light brown sugar

¼ cup cocoa

1 teaspoon vanilla extract

1. Spray a 4-quart slow cooker with cooking spray. Add the bread cubes.

2. In a medium bowl, whisk the evaporated milk, eggs, brown sugar, cocoa, and vanilla until the sugar and cocoa dissolve. Pour over the bread cubes.

3. Cook for 5 hours on low or until the pudding no longer looks liquid.

Suggested Bread Pudding Variations

Instead of white bread, use a mixture of white and whole wheat. Or add ½ cup coconut to the bread cubes. Or add ⅓ cup raisins or a mixture of dried fruit to the bread cubes. Or scrape a vanilla bean into the milk mixture for extra vanilla flavor.

CHEESECAKE

Making cheesecake in the slow cooker might sound odd, but it is actually the perfect appliance for the job. The constant low heat and moist environment keeps it from drying out or cracking, even when using low-fat ingredients.

Serves 8

INGREDIENTS:

¾ cup low-fat chocolate or cinnamon graham cracker crumbs

1½ tablespoons butter, melted

8 ounces reduced-fat sour cream, at room temperature

8 ounces reduced-fat cream cheese, at room temperature

⅔ cup sugar

1 egg, at room temperature

1 tablespoon vanilla paste or vanilla extract

1½ tablespoons flour

1 tablespoon lemon juice

1 tablespoon lemon zest

1. In a small bowl, mix together the graham cracker crumbs and butter. Press into the bottom and sides of a 6" springform pan.

2. In a large bowl, mix the sour cream, cream cheese, sugar, egg, vanilla, flour, lemon juice, and zest until completely smooth. Pour into the springform pan.

3. Pour 1" of water into the bottom of a 6-quart slow cooker. Place a trivet in the bottom of the slow cooker. Place the pan onto the trivet.

4. Cook on low for 2 hours. Turn off the slow cooker and let the cheesecake steam for 1 hour and 15 minutes with the lid on. Remove the cheesecake from the slow cooker. Refrigerate 6 hours or overnight before serving.

Homemade Graham Cracker Crumbs

There is no need to buy packaged graham cracker crumbs, it is easy to make them at home. Break graham crackers into medium-sized pieces. Place them into a food processor. Pulse until fine crumbs form. Store the crumbs in an airtight container.

APPLE BROWN BETTY

Apple Brown Betty is an American dessert that dates back to colonial times.

Serves 6

INGREDIENTS:

3½ cups cubed apples

1 tablespoon lemon juice

1 tablespoon sugar

½ teaspoon cinnamon

½ teaspoon ground ginger

¼ teaspoon nutmeg

¼ teaspoon allspice

1¾ cups bread cubes

1. Spray a 2-quart slow cooker with nonstick spray. Add the apples, lemon juice, sugar, and spices. Stir. Cook on high 2 hours.

2. Preheat oven to 250°F. Spread the bread cubes in a single layer on a baking sheet. Bake until browned, about 8 minutes.

3. Sprinkle the toasted bread cubes over the apples. Cook on high for 10 minutes prior to serving.

Lemon Juice

Lemon juice is a cook's best friend. It adds a bright note to most dishes. It is low in calories but high in vitamin C. It can even keep cut apples or pears from turning brown.

ORANGE-SCENTED CUSTARD

Orange blossom water is a common Middle Eastern ingredient that adds a fruity, floral note to this custard.

Serves 10

INGREDIENTS:

1 tablespoon orange blossom water, or ½ teaspoon orange extract

2 cups fat-free evaporated milk

5 eggs

⅓ cup sugar

1. Place all ingredients into a large bowl. Whisk until smooth. Pour into a 4-quart slow cooker. Cook on low for 8 hours, or until the center looks set and does not jiggle.

CHOCOLATE CRÈME BRÛLÉE

This elegant dessert can be cooking away all through dinner.

Serves 4

INGREDIENTS:

2 cups fat-free evaporated milk

2½ tablespoons cocoa

½ teaspoon vanilla extract

4 egg yolks

½ cup sugar

2 tablespoons brown sugar

1. In a small bowl, whisk the evaporated milk, cocoa, vanilla, egg yolks, and sugar until the sugar dissolves. Pour the mixture into a small pan and bring it to a boil. Remove the pan from the heat and allow the mixture to cool. Divide it among four 5- to 6-ounce broiler-safe ramekins.

2. Pour 1" of water into the bottom of an oval 6-quart slow cooker. Place the ramekins in the water. Cook on high for 3 hours or until the custard is set.

3. Sprinkle each Crème Brûlée with ½ tablespoon brown sugar. Place them under the broiler and broil until the sugar caramelizes.

Vanilla Extract Is Essential

When a recipe calls for vanilla, use real vanilla extract. Although real vanilla extract is more expensive than imitation, the flavor is far superior. Store vanilla extract in a cool, dark place to preserve the flavor.

CARAMEL POPCORN

The slow cooker provides an easy way to make caramel without a lot of hands-on time. If it is very thick, thin it out with a few tablespoons of water.

Serves 12

INGREDIENTS:

1½ cups light brown sugar

2 tablespoons butter, cubed

8 quarts air-popped popcorn

1. Place the sugar and butter into a 4-quart slow cooker. Cook for 1 hour on high, stirring occasionally, until caramel forms.

2. Drizzle over popcorn and toss. Serve immediately.

Popcorn Facts

Popcorn is an excellent source of fiber. It is a healthy choice for a snack, especially if it is popped in an air popper without any added fat. Drizzle with a small amount of caramel sauce for a sweet treat or sprinkle with Parmesan for a savory snack.

"BAKED" APPLES

Serve these lightly spiced apples as a simple dessert or a breakfast treat.

Serves 6

INGREDIENTS:

6 baking apples

½ cup water

1 cinnamon stick

1" knob peeled fresh ginger

1 vanilla bean

1. Place the apples in a simple layer on the bottom of a 4- or 6-quart slow cooker. Add the water, cinnamon stick, ginger, and vanilla bean. Cook on low for 6–8 hours or until the apples are tender and easily pierced with a fork.

2. Use a slotted spoon to remove the apples from the insert. Discard the cinnamon stick, ginger, vanilla bean, and water. Serve hot.

Baking with Apples

When baking or cooking, choose apples with firm flesh such as Granny Smith, Jonathan, McIntosh, Cortland, Pink Lady, Pippin, or Winesap. They will be able to hold up to low cooking times without turning to mush. Leaving the skin on adds fiber.

CHOCOLATE POTATO CAKE

Yes, you can convert those leftover mashed potatoes into something worth raiding the refrigerator for. Skip the gravy, though.

Yields 2 loaves

INGREDIENTS:

¾ cup butter

2¼ cups sugar

1 cup mashed potatoes

3 eggs

1¾ cups flour

2 teaspoons baking powder

1 teaspoon salt

½ teaspoon cream of tartar

½ teaspoon ground cloves

½ teaspoon ground nutmeg

1½ teaspoons ground cinnamon

½ cup milk

2 ounces unsweetened chocolate

1. Cream the butter and sugar in a mixing bowl; blend in the potatoes, then the eggs.

2. Sift the flour with the baking powder, salt, cream of tartar, and spices.

3. Add the dry mixture and the milk gradually to the potato mixture. Keep blending well. Grate the chocolate and add.

4. Fill 2 greased and floured loaf pans, or the equivalent, one-half to three-quarters full with the batter. Loosely cover each dish with foil or other lid. Place on a trivet or rack in the slow cooker, and pour water around the base of the trivet.

5. Cover and heat on a high setting for 2–3 hours.

Calling All Chocolate Lovers

Are you a chocolate fiend? Get some of your favorite chocolates and tuck them into the batter of your cake, pudding, or bread. The chocolates will melt and transform as your concoction cooks.

APPLE COCONUT CAKE

The coconut gives this cake a nice texture. This goes well with Tangiers Orange Sauce (Chapter 27).

Yields 2 loaves

INGREDIENTS:

4 cups apples, peeled, cored, and chopped

2 cups sugar

3 cups flour

2 teaspoons baking soda

1 teaspoon salt

1 cup vegetable oil

2 eggs

1 teaspoon vanilla

1 cup chopped nuts

1 cup shredded coconut

1. Mix the apples with the sugar and let stand until juice develops.

2. Sift together the dry ingredients and add to the apple mixture. Add the oil, eggs, vanilla, nuts, and coconut to this and mix well.

3. Fill 2 greased and floured loaf pans, or the equivalent, one-half to three-quarters full with the batter. Loosely cover each dish with foil or other lid. Place on a trivet or rack in the slow cooker, and pour water around the base of the trivet.

4. Cover and heat on a high setting for 2–3 hours.

Condensation Tip

When steaming cakes, breads, or puddings, use a small bit of foil to prop open the lid enough to let some steam escape. This will cut down on condensation on the lid, which could drop back down onto your baked goods.

CHOCOLATE POUND CAKE

Serve this cake with hot fudge sauce and vanilla ice cream. Add whipped cream and a cherry to make a pound cake sundae.

Yields 1 loaf

INGREDIENTS:

½ pound butter

½ cup shortening

2¾ cups sugar

5 eggs

1 tablespoon vanilla

3 cups flour

5 tablespoons cocoa powder

½ teaspoon baking powder

½ teaspoon salt

1 cup milk

1. Cream the butter, shortening, and sugar. Stir in the eggs and vanilla.

2. Sift the flour with the cocoa powder, baking powder, and salt.

3. Mix all the ingredients, alternating between adding the dry ingredients and the milk to the creamed mixture.

4. Fill 1 greased and floured loaf pan, or the equivalent, one-half to three-quarters full with the batter. Loosely cover with foil or other lid. Place on a trivet or rack in the slow cooker, and pour water around the base of the trivet.

5. Cover and heat on a high setting for 2–3 hours.

SAMANTHA'S BUBBLY CAKE

This is a fun cake to make with children. They'll enjoy pouring a can of soda pop into the mixing bowl.

Yields 2 loaves

INGREDIENTS:

½ cup butter

½ cup shortening

2 cups sugar

1 egg

1 teaspoon vanilla

1 teaspoon lemon juice

7 ounces lemon-lime soda pop

3 cups flour

1. Cream the butter, shortening, and sugar. Add the egg and mix well.

2. In a separate bowl, mix the vanilla, lemon juice, and soda pop.

3. Alternate adding the flour and liquid ingredients to the creamed mixture.

4. Fill 2 greased and floured loaf pans, or the equivalent, one-half to three-quarters full with the batter. Loosely cover each dish with foil or other lid. Place on a trivet or rack in the slow cooker, and pour water around the base of the trivet.

5. Cover and heat on a high setting for 2–3 hours.

Flour Power

Not all flours are alike. Cake flour is made from a variety of wheat that can be ground into smaller particles. All-purpose flour is made from a mixture of wheat varieties, adequate for cake but also suitable for bread.

AVOCADO CAKE

Top this cake with a dusting of powdered sugar. And don't tell your guests there's avocado in it until they've taken a bite.

Yields 2 loaves

INGREDIENTS:

¾ cup butter

2 cups sugar

3 eggs

2 avocados

2⅔ cups cake flour

¾ teaspoon cinnamon

¾ teaspoon allspice

¾ teaspoon salt

1½ teaspoons baking soda

¾ cup buttermilk

⅓ cup dates

¾ cup nuts

¾ cup white raisins

1. Cream the butter and sugar. Add the eggs and mix well. Dice and mix in the avocado.

2. Sift the flour, spices, and salt together. Dissolve the baking soda in the buttermilk.

3. Add the buttermilk and sifted ingredients to the creamed mixture, alternating between adding wet and dry. Mix well. Pit and chop the dates. Chop the nuts. Fold in the dates, nuts, and raisins.

4. Fill 2 greased and floured loaf pans, or the equivalent, one-half to three-quarters full with the batter. Loosely cover each dish with foil or other lid. Place on a trivet or rack in the slow cooker, and pour water around the base of the trivet.

5. Cover and heat on a high setting for 2–3 hours.

Stay Afloat

To keep fruits and nuts from sinking to the bottom of a cake, heat the chopped fruits and nuts for 5 minutes in a 250°F oven, then shake in a paper or plastic bag with flour before adding to your batter.

CINNAMON PEAR CAKE

Serve this cake warm. Use fresh sliced pears as a topping.

Yields 2 loaves

INGREDIENTS:

1½ cups vegetable oil

2 cups sugar

3 eggs

1 teaspoon vanilla

3 cups sifted flour

¾ teaspoon salt

1 teaspoon baking soda

1 teaspoon cinnamon

2 pears

1 cup pecans

1. Mix the oil, sugar, eggs, and vanilla.

2. Sift the flour, salt, baking soda, and cinnamon together. Add to the egg mixture.

3. Core and dice the pears; chop the pecans. Fold the pears and pecans into the batter.

4. Fill 2 greased and floured loaf pans, or the equivalent, one-half to three-quarters full with the batter. Loosely cover each dish with foil or other lid. Place on a trivet or rack in the slow cooker, and pour water around the base of the trivet.

5. Cover and heat on a high setting for 2–3 hours.

SPICY MOLASSES CAKE

This cake is delicious served warm with a cup of coffee and a scoop of vanilla ice cream on the side.

Yields 3 loaves

INGREDIENTS:

1 cup shortening

1 cup sugar

2 eggs

1 cup molasses

4½ cups flour

6 teaspoons baking powder

½ teaspoon baking soda

1 teaspoon salt

1 teaspoon allspice

1 teaspoon cinnamon

1 cup sour milk

1 cup raisins

1. Cream the shortening and sugar until fluffy. Add the eggs and mix well, then add the molasses and mix well.

2. Sift the flour with the baking powder, baking soda, salt, and spices. Alternately add the dry mixture and the milk to the creamed mixture. Fold in the raisins.

3. Fill 3 greased and floured loaf pans, or the equivalent, one-half to three-quarters full with the batter. Loosely cover each dish with foil or other lid. Place on a trivet or rack in the slow cooker, and pour water around the base of the trivet.

4. Cover and heat on a high setting for 2–3 hours.

Cutting the Cake

For nice, professional-looking slices, freeze cakes before cutting. As a bonus, cold cake is excellent with ice cream on a hot day. Or serve your cold cakes with a hot sauce, giving a nice contrast.

LEFTOVER CAKE PUDDING

Stockpile leftover cake in the freezer until you have enough.

Yields 1 loaf

INGREDIENTS:

3 cups cubed leftover cake

¼ pound raisins

3 eggs

¼ cup sugar

2 cups milk

¼ teaspoon nutmeg

½ teaspoon vanilla

1. Pile the cake cubes in a greased and floured loaf pan or the equivalent. Sprinkle with the raisins.

2. Beat the eggs; add the sugar, milk, nutmeg, and vanilla to the eggs. Pour the egg mixture over the cake pieces and raisins.

3. Loosely cover the dish with foil or other lid. Place on a trivet or rack in the slow cooker, and pour water around the base of the trivet.

4. Cover and heat on a high setting for 2–3 hours.

The Meaning of Pudding

In a slow cooker, pudding is different from the standard kind you find in a box. A "pudding" is traditionally a steamed sweet bread, like the well-known plum pudding, and is also a general term for a sweet that follows the evening meal.

LEMONY APPLE PUDDING

The combination of lemon rinds and mace gives this cake a nice zing. This is excellent with cinnamon-laced whipped cream or lemon sherbet.

Yields 2 loaves

INGREDIENTS:

1 cup butter

1 cup sugar

8 eggs

1 cup milk

3 cups flour

1 tablespoon baking powder

2 lemon rinds

4 apples

⅛ teaspoon mace

1. Cream the butter and sugar, then add the eggs and milk.

2. Sift the flour and baking powder together, then add to the liquid mixture.

3. Grate the rinds; peel, core, and dice the apples. Add the rinds, apples, and mace to the other ingredients.

4. Fill 2 greased and floured loaf pans, or the equivalent, one-half to three-quarters full with the batter. Loosely cover each dish with foil or other lid. Place on a trivet or rack in the slow cooker, and pour water around the base of the trivet.

5. Cover and heat on a high setting for 2–3 hours.

Whip It

You can freeze whipped cream. Make a big batch early, then spoon individual servings onto waxed paper and pop it into the freezer. When firm, move the frozen servings to a sealed container. Later, put each on a dessert, or a dessert drink, and it's ready to serve in minutes.

FLAMING PLUM PUDDING

Warm some brandy until it steams, heat the pudding, sprinkle with powdered sugar, drizzle with hot brandy, and light.

Yields 3 loaves

INGREDIENTS:

2 cups shortening

2 cups brown sugar

4 eggs

1 cup molasses

1 cup brandy

2 lemons

2 cups flour

½ teaspoon nutmeg

½ teaspoon ground ginger

½ teaspoon ground cloves

½ teaspoon cinnamon

½ pound orange peel

½ pound lemon peel

1 cup bread crumbs

1 pound currants

½ pound golden raisins

1. Cream the shortening and the sugar. Add the eggs, molasses, and brandy. Squeeze the lemons and add the lemon juice.

2. Sift the flour with the spices. Mince the orange and lemon peel. Mix the minced peel, crumbs, currants, and raisins together. Stir this into the dry ingredients.

3. Combine the ingredients, stirring the dry ingredients into the liquid mixture.

4. Fill 3 greased and floured loaf pans, or the equivalent, one-half to three-quarters full with the batter. Loosely cover each dish with foil or other lid. Place on a trivet or rack in the slow cooker, and pour water around the base of the trivet.

5. Cover and heat on a high setting for 2–3 hours.

EQUIPMENT SOURCES

Chicago Metallic Bakeware

- Chicago Metallic Professional and Professional Nonstick Bakeware
  www.chicagometallicbakeware.com

Cuisinart

Probably best known for their innovative food processors, Cuisinart also has a wide selection of countertop appliances and cookware:

- Cuisinart Brick Oven Toaster Oven with Rotisserie

- Cuisinart CleanWater Countertop Filtration System

- Cuisinart (countertop) Microwave Oven

- Cuisinart PowerPrep Plus 14-Cup Food Processor

- Cuisinart 4-quart and 6½-quart Programmable Slow Cookers
  www.cuisinart.com

General Electric

- Slow cookers
  www.gehousewares.com

Hamilton Beach

- Slow cookers
  www.hamiltonbeach.com

Kaiser Bakeware

- Baking sheets
  www.kaiserbakeware.com

Pleasant Hill Grain

A full-service distributor for a wide variety of helpful cooking appliances, which include:

- BAMIX Hand Mixer (immersion blender)

- Berkey Stainless Water Purifier System

- Nutrimill Grain Mill
  www.pleasanthillgrain.com

Reynolds Consumer Products Company

- Reynolds Slow Cooker Liners

- Reynolds Handi-Vac Vacuum Sealing System
  www.reynoldskitchens.com

Rival

- Slow cookers
  www.crock-pot.com

Taylor Precision Products LP

- Taylor Digital Oven Thermometer/Timer
  www.taylorusa.com

INDEX